The Jews of Modernity

THE JEWS
OF
MODERNITY

BY

Milton Himmelfarb

BASIC BOOKS, INC.

Publishers · New York

© 1973 by Basic Books, Inc.
Library of Congress Catalog Card Number: 72–89182
SBN 465–03674–0
Manufactured in the United States of America
DESIGNED BY VINCENT TORRE
73 74 75 76 77 10 9 8 7 6 5 4 3 2 1

For my mother,
and in memory
of my father

Preface

The dominant theme of the essays that follow, written between 1960 and 1971, is Jewish modernity. More exactly, the theme is the particular kind of modernity so long and so disproportionately favored by Jews, with its messianic politics and its devoutness about art and science; its grandeurs and servitudes; its temptations to self-righteousness and self-deception, whether among the bourgeois or among the intellectual; and its cumulative disillusionments and contradictions. For if modernity has been the honor of the Jew who can no longer be traditional, today a modern Jew must make an effort greater than that of his predecessor seventy years ago, who for his part had to make an effort greater than that of *his* predecessor a hundred and seventy years ago, to ignore the ever more obtrusive evidence that his modernity tends to consequences only equivocally honorable.

In discussing Jewish modernity I have also had to discuss the tradition and community against which it has defined itself. If my tone and argument are kinder to tradition than to modernity, that is because I am not especially traditional. In my debate with myself and with other modern Jews I consider that the needful thing is to question our own notions. I should like to think that if I were more traditional, it would be mostly the traditionalists' notions that I questioned.

Modernity tends to go with universalism, and modern Jews tend to look down upon Jewish particularism as parochial. For a long time now people have freely and proudly called themselves "Protestant" or "Quaker" or "Methodist," although originally those names were enemies' insults. Today "black" is joining that company. Among Jews, someday soon "parochial" may similarly go from pejorative to honorific. If that happens, it will be helped along by the spectacle of Jews who understand all the particularisms—black, Chicano, Welsh, Basque, Breton, "Palestinian"—except the Jewish. At this point in the twentieth century, a man from Mars might not readily think foolish or unworthy the proposition that if Jews do not bethink themselves of the Jews no one else is likely to. But then, a man from Mars would not be privy to the true inwardness of Jewish modernity.

Modern is not the same as contemporary or young: Spinoza was modern and my grandparents, *piae memoriae*, were not; nor are some people modern who are far younger than I. As for the young moderns, I refuse to concede that they are any more silly-clever than my generation, whether in our youth or in our middle age.

Noting that certain references and names recur here—Spinoza, the Mendelssohns, Heine, Durkheim, Berenson, Pasternak, the "Internationale," "My Country 'Tis of Thee"—I conclude that they must be insistent metaphors for me. If this book had been written differently the recurrences would have been fewer. In fact, they are fewer in something else I started. Wishing to encourage me to write a book about modern Jews and their choices, John Slawson, then Executive Vice President of the American Jewish Committee and now Emeritus, gave me a leave of absence. I wrote the book, and shelved it. More methodical than this, and more inclusive, it was also more monotone and languid. The essays here were written in response to sharper stimuli.

"Secular Society?" and "Those Catholic Schools" (the latter as "Jewish Sentiment") were published in *Daedalus* and *Commonweal*, respectively, and everything else in *Commentary*. I am grateful to their editors for permission to reprint. A few titles are new, and there are some minor changes in the text.

It is my pleasant obligation to thank Dr. Slawson and his successor, Bertram H. Gold; my sister Gertrude Himmelfarb and her husband Irving Kristol; and my colleagues and friends Lucy S. Dawidowicz, Marshall Sklare, Gerson D. Cohen, and Rose Grundstein. What I owe my wife Judith I cannot attempt to express.

M.H.

Contents

I

VISION, ILLUSION, DISILLUSION

II

OFF THE GRAPH

III

A PARENTHESIS ABOUT BIRTH, MARRIAGE, AND WORK

IV

JEWS WITH OTHERS

V

JEWS AND CHRISTIANS, JUDAISM
AND CHRISTIANITY

VI

NO MORE TRADITION'S CHAINS?

Contents

I

VISION, ILLUSION, DISILLUSION

.1.

Modern, Honorable, Masculine

We are modern, of course, but what does that mean? How long have we been modern? When did modern begin? In the schools modern history is generally understood to date from the years between 1450 and 1525—though Bury, of *The Idea of Progress*, a professor of modern history, did his specifically historical work on the later Roman Empire. It is not much of an objection to modernity beginning with the Renaissance and the Reformation that these entities may not be entities at all, that when one looks closely at them they seem to dissolve until almost nothing distinctively new is left. Granted that the scholars have long known about the twelfth-century renaissance and have long reminded us that there were reformations of various kinds centuries before the Reformation; whatever may be the microscopic view, when we step back there is a difference between Middle Ages and Renaissance, between Christianity before the Protestant Reformation and Christianity after. It is no disproof of the difference that students are examined on the medieval elements or survivals in Shakespeare. From 1450 to 1525 makes sense as the beginning of modernity. It was the time of Gutenberg, Copernicus, Machiavelli, Columbus, Luther. It was the time of the consolidation of nation-states as we know them, especially in Western Europe. It was the beginning of the ascendancy of Western power and Western thought in the affairs of the entire world.

So much for beginnings. The more modern modernity, our modernity, is somewhat younger. It came into being in the seventeenth century—"the century of genius"—with the end of the wars of religion. Nowadays historians say that the Thirty Years' War had to do more with dynastic and imperial ambitions than with religion, but to deny that it had anything to do with religion would be presumptuous. The denial would be equivalent to saying not only that we understand the seventeenth century better than it understood itself—which

3

may be so—but actually that we understand it completely and it understood itself not at all. The Thirty Years' War ended in religious stalemate, with a treaty establishing *cujus regio, ejus religio*: a victory of practical secularity if not yet theoretical secularism. Responsible statesmen and sober citizens put religion in a position from which they were determined not to let it escape, to destroy and ravage again. Not that religious persecution ended completely: when Louis XIV abrogated the century-old toleration of the Huguenots, he made them choose between oppression at home and exile. But in retrospect that was a kind of last gasp of a former state of affairs in the West, just as intellectually the Quarrel of the Ancients and Moderns was a last gasp of antimodernism.

Before modernity, to innovate in church or state was wrong on the face of it. In the Bible new things are good only when they are God's: "For behold, I create new heavens and a new earth, and the former things shall not be remembered" (Isaiah); "Behold, the days are coming, says the Lord, when I will make a new covenant with the house of Israel and the house of Judah" (Jeremiah); "A new heart I will give you, and a new spirit I will put within you" (Ezekiel). When the new things are men's, they are bad: "They sacrificed . . . to gods they had never known,/to new gods that had come in of late,/whom your fathers had never dreaded" (Deuteronomy). So reformers denied they were innovating. Whether in religion or in politics, they said and believed that they were only trying to restore pristine virtue and truth, cleansing it of later, newfangled, corrupt accretions.

It was the Royal Society, three hundred years old not long ago, that ratified the new respectability of newness. By charter the Royal Society was debarred from a concern with religion; even its papers were written in the new plain, unadorned style. Bacon was the Royal Society's grandfather, and the Society's mission was to cultivate Bacon's New Philosophy, science. Bacon had dared to draw attention to the newness of the things he said. He called his philosophy New, and his major work *Novum Organum*.

Today new is good, without question. Every detergent advertises itself as new and improved: "new" means "improved." President Kennedy could quote Lincoln in telling us that we must disenthrall ourselves from the past, which is to say, we must liberate ourselves from the bondage of the past. Pastness, nonmodernity, is bondage. Bacon had already said it: the idols he warned against included idols of the past.

Appropriately, therefore, the principles of modernity do not date from this year or last. One principle is expressed in the maximalist and yet normative slogan of Diderot: "Let us strangle the last king with the entrails of the last priest." Forcefully liberating ourselves from thralldom to the past, from mere tradition and from the guardians and beneficiaries of mere tradition, we shall come into our own. We shall be modern.

Diderot's predecessor was Spinoza, just as Spinoza honored Bacon as *his* predecessor. For our purpose it is less the Spinoza of the *Ethics* than of the *Tractatus theologico-politicus* who counts. That Spinoza is the first to speak explicitly for the secular, democratic state, in which the traditional religions will be subordinate to the state and to citizenship—a private matter, for landladies and others incapable of philosophy. The chief founder of modern biblical criticism, Spinoza undermines traditional religion. It is not easy for someone who has read the *Tractatus* to continue believing that the Bible is the literal, inerrant word of God.

This brings us to the Jews, because Spinoza was or had been a Jew. Spinoza is more than a father of modernity, he is the father of Jewish modernity. There are only two reasonable dates for the end of the Jewish Middle Ages and the beginning of Jewish modernity: Spinoza's, and Moses Mendelssohn's a century later. I prefer Spinoza's. My friend Charles Liebman has shown me a passage from Etienne Gilson's *The Philosopher and Theology* in which Gilson remembers three striking things about the Jewish philosophers at the Sorbonne in the early years of this century: that there were so many of them; that in fact they were not Jewish philosophers, but philosophers who were or had been Jews; and that each of them had two philosophies, his own and Spinoza's. Hume the Scot and Jefferson the American said, approximately, that an Enlightened man had two countries, his own and France. Spinoza is the modern Jew's second country.

Spinoza's secular state, in which the dominant principle is reason rather than tradition and the citizens' religions are irrelevant to the public life—that state is still our political ideal and passion. And Spinoza exemplified in his life the honor that has also been our ideal, if not always our actuality, insofar as we are modern. Having by reason proved to himself the unreasonableness of all traditional religion, Spinoza could not honorably be a Christian. He is the first man to have left the Jewish religious community without entering another—Christian, Moslem, or, in the ancient world, pagan.

If you wanted one theme around which to organize a modern Jewish history, honor could be that theme. Spinoza's immediate precursors in criticizing the Bible were Isaac de La Peyrère and Uriel da Costa—like him (or his parents), Marranos. La Peyrère, not a Jew by religion, dubiously a Christian, has an exalted vision of the Jews resuming the elect status that God conferred on them long ago. This depends on their becoming Christian—Jewish Christians or Christian Jews. The Jews he reminds, in language that can only be called ecstatic, of the happy future God has in store for them. With the Christians he pleads to make Christianity more reasonable by purging it of its unnecessarily numerous and onerous dogmas. How can Jews *honorably* embrace Christianity, he asks, when the burden of Christian dogma is even more grievous than the burden of the Torah?

Da Costa turns from Christianity to what he thinks is Judaism because the Christian dogma of a future life terrifies him. When he discovers that the real Judaism has that dogma too, he ceases to be a Jew. He is contemptuous of religious martyrdom: since the most precious thing is life, what folly to sacrifice it by stubborn adherence to one religion and stubborn refusal to pretend to adhere to another! Contemptuous of martyrdom—and, one might therefore think, of honor —da Costa regards it as a high honor to be martyred for the real truth, the truth that knows both Judaism and Christianity to be false.

Spinoza is no longer of the Jewish community. Why does he not make a career for himself as a professor of philosophy by becoming or seeming to become a Christian? Perhaps for reasons of prudence; as a nominal Christian he would be exposing himself to unpleasantness about heresy. But above all, it is honor that keeps him from the baptismal font. He will not pretend to believe what he does not believe.

Moses Mendelssohn, we are told by an early biographer, would have welcomed the society favored by his friend Lessing, the Spinozist —a society in which there were neither Christians nor Jews. This side of Lessing's society, Mendelssohn despised apostasy—"for reasons of honor." Mendelssohn's son, when he had his children and then himself baptized, did it for expediency (his word), the opposite of honor.

For expediency Solomon Maimon, the first modern East European Jew, was once prepared to be baptized, but for honor he refused to subscribe to a Christian confession of faith:

Maimon: The Jewish religion, in its articles of faith, comes nearer than Christianity to reason. But practically, the latter has an advantage. . . .

German parson: Don't you feel any inclination to the Christian religion apart from extrinsic considerations?

Maimon: I would be lying if I answered yes. . . .

Parson: You are too much of a philosopher to be able to become a Christian. Reason has taken the upper hand with you.

Maimon: Then I must remain what I am—a stiff-necked Jew. . . .

Mendelssohn's disciple, David Friedländer, thought of becoming a Christian, again for expediency, but he could not entirely forget honor, and honor required that he insist on a unitarian rather than a trinitarian confession of faith. That was not enough for the church. His children, giving even greater weight than he to expediency and even less to honor, became conventional Christians, or at least allowed themselves to be thought so.

Notoriously, Heinrich Heine was cynical about his baptism. He had contempt for the society that made baptism the price of ambition, and for himself and the many others who paid the dishonorable price. One of the others was his friend, Gans. In a letter Heine says:

. . . Gans is preaching Christianity and trying to convert the children of Israel. If he is doing it out of conviction, he is a fool; if out of hypocrisy, a knave. . . . I would much rather have heard Gans was stealing silver spoons. . . . If the law had allowed stealing silver spoons, I wouldn't have undergone baptism. . . .

Everyone knows that Heine called the baptismal certificate the ticket of admission to European culture. In a less well-known mot, he put the blame for his having become a Christian on Napoleon's geography teacher, who had failed to tell his pupil that in Moscow it is very cold in the winter.

Napoleon here is the embodiment of the French Revolution, which, if victorious throughout Europe, would have brought about the ideal society of Lessing and Spinoza. About a hundred and fifty years ago Richard Whately, a young man later to become an Anglican archbishop, wrote a brilliantly clever refutation-by-parody of Hume's kind of critique of the Bible, *Historical Doubts Relative to Napoleon Buonaparte*—a mock-critical analysis of a narrative, in biblical-sounding language, of the French Revolution and the Napoleonic wars. Names are reversed: France is Ecnarf, Louis is Sivol. Napoleon is Noelopan. Let us examine this Hebrew name No-el-opan, Whately's imaginary Humean critic says. It is not the name of an actual man, as so many foolishly suppose. Rather, the name person-

7

ifies a process. *No* must be from the root *nw'*, which means "reducing to nothingness." (In Ps. 33: 10 *heni'* is from that root: "He *maketh* the devices of the people *of none effect.*") *El* is "God." *Opan* (or *ophan*) is "wheel"—Ezekiel's "wheel within a wheel" is *ha-ofan be-tokh ha-ofan*—and by extension, "cycle," or "revolution." So *No-el-opan* can only mean "no-God-revolution": Godless Revolution. Heine was right.

As Gershom Scholem has shown, honor—of a sort—was the animating purpose of modern Jewish scholarship, the *Wissenschaft des Judentums*. Steinschneider wanted to give Judaism an honorable burial. The nineteenth century, the modern age, was the age of the death of all the positive-historical religions. Judaism, too, was dying. Like the others, it deserved to die. (He thought well of Ethical Culture, founded by modern Jews in America to be a meeting-ground, in honorable equality, for ex-Jews and ex-Christians.) Nevertheless, it was the part of honor for Jews to give an honorable burial to the religion, culture, and tradition with which they and their ancestors had been immemorially identified, and by which they had been molded. In the future, through the efforts of the scholars, let men know that in the olden times of positive-historical religions, Judaism had been no mean thing. In the meantime, as any undertaker would be, Steinschneider was upset whenever the corpse showed signs of life —revived Hebrew, Zionism, and the like. He was severe about such things. (He objected to having his work translated into Hebrew.)

It is said of the founder of modern Jewish scholarship, Zunz, that once someone introduced to him a young Russian Jew who was a Hebrew poet. "A Hebrew poet?" Zunz is supposed to have asked the young man. "When did you live?" Like the undertaker, the necrologist is displeased with signs of life in the deceased.

Many Jews who allowed themselves to be baptized, expedientially, had first to convince themselves or allow others to convince them that what they were doing was honorable. At the turn of the century Franz Brentano, an Austrian philosopher and former priest, was another who had concluded that the age of the positive-historical religions was at an end. He tried to get his disciples into positions of influence from which to propagate his philosophy, the destined successor to those religions—that is, he wanted his disciples to be professors, especially in German-speaking universities. But many of his disciples were Jews, and those universities allowed few Jews to be professors of philosophy. Husserl was not the only one of Brentano's students persuaded by their master to be baptized. The argument was that it was their duty to do so—in other words, that it was the course of honor to do so—because scruples about baptism were unworthy of a philosopher. No more should a philosopher hesitate to change his formal religious affiliation, Brentano told them, than to change his clothes for a formal occasion. To Hugo Bergmann he once wrote that there was nothing morally wrong—or, as we may put it, dishonorable —about talented young Jews giving lip service to what they disbelieved. (Whatever philosophical reputation Brentano still has rests on what he published about truth.)

For other modern Jews, honor required that they formally remain Jews or that they proclaim themselves as without a formal religion, *konfessionslos*. Both honor and interest required that they should try to change the state or society in which it made a substantial political and social difference whether one was a Jew or a Christian. Temperament and circumstances determined whether they would work for that change in conventional or in revolutionary ways.

Closely related to the theme of honor is that of masculinity. Politically this expresses itself in the will to be a subject, not object, of history, active not passive. The ideal of masculinity was influential in the outlook and the political striving of nationalists and revolutionaries. (Nationalism was one way of being revolutionary.) The factor common to all Jewish modernity, hostility to traditional religion, was present with the Zionists and other Jewish nationalists, too; but in addition they thought the Jews needed autonomy or sovereignty, either as a substitute for the Spinozaic state or as a necessary condition for it. They differed from the older Jewish modernists in insisting upon a Jewish state, or Jewish autonomy. They agreed with them in insisting that that state, like any state, should be secular.

In Chaim Weizmann's autobiography we can see how close to the surface modernity could be even with traditional Jews. He says that his old-fashioned mother agreed neither with him that Zionism was "the solution to the Jewish problem" nor with his brother Samuel that a Russian revolution was the solution. She refused to take sides. Whoever is right, she said, it will be good for us. If Chaim is right we will have a country of our own, and if Samuel is right we will be able to live like human beings in Russia.

Here, too, the origins go back to Spinoza. Besides being the father of the secular, democratic state, he is also the first man to have set forth, if not the desirability, then at least the possibility of a secular Jewish state. What he says about this in the *Tractatus* has been known to get blurred in translation, so before it gets blurred here we may as well look at the exact words: ". . . *nisi fundamenta suae religionis eorum animos effeminarent, absolute crederem, eos aliquando, data occasione, ut sunt res humanae mutabiles, suum imperium iterum erecturos.*" ". . . since human affairs are changeable, if the foundations of their [the Jews'] religion did not make their characters feminine I would be convinced that, with an opportunity, someday they will re-establish their state." Not only is Spinoza talking of secular Jewish state-building, he also is saying that establishing a state depends upon overcoming femininity, and that the Jews' religion effeminates them. No wonder Mr. Ben Gurion has called for lifting the excommunication the Jewish community of Amsterdam imposed on Spinoza.

(Some years ago a scholar suggested that the Amsterdam Jews excommunicated Spinoza because they were afraid of irritating the Gentiles and endangering their tolerated status by a failure to dissociate themselves from a notorious unbeliever. I think that is far-fetched. How else could the Jews of that time have dealt with a Jew who denied the God and the Torah of Judaism? There may be something, too, in the suggestion that the Amsterdam Sephardim, reverent about their ancestors' martyrdom and the continuing martyrdom of their Marrano relatives in the Iberian peninsula, could not forgive Spinoza's scoffing at the Judaism for the sake of which the martyrs gave their lives at the stake.)

To Spinoza and modern Jews since, what have masculine and feminine meant? To have a masculine character is to resist, to fight, to be active; to have a feminine character is to submit, to be resigned, to be passive. Masculine is brave, feminine is at best only obstinate. Masculine is modern, feminine is old-fashioned or traditional.

In our century, after the Kishinev pogroms it was the new Jewish Socialist Bund and the new Labor Zionists who organized self-defense units, acquired arms, and shot back; and it was the old-fashioned Jews whom Bialik (and others) raged against for their passivity. More recently, especially in Israel there has been insistent questioning whether the European Jews who died in Hitler's crematoria were not again showing that old feminine passivity. Nor is this frame of mind political only. Both Freud—if I remember correctly—and Babel saw their fathers as not standing up to Gentile ruffians; and both were affected, in intimate attitude and general outlook. The gifted Otto Weininger, that textbook case of Jewish self-hate, killed himself out of loathing for what he took to be the femininity of the people into which he had been born.

Was Spinoza justified in saying that the religion of the Jews made them feminine? No. He carefully blamed the very basis—*"fundamenta"*—of Judaism; for him Judaism was feminizing not accidentally or circumstantially but inherently and necessarily. Yet R. Akiba, who certainly knew the basis of Judaism, had supported Bar Kokhba's entirely masculine rebellion against Rome, and had paid for that support with martyrdom. Again, Spinoza was a close student of Maimonides, and Maimonides—if only to calm the feverish messianic yearnings of his time—had selected from the complex rabbinical tradition that alternative which defines the Days of the Messiah as differing from ours in only one respect: that then we shall no longer be enslaved by foreign kingdoms. Maimonides wants the Jews to be interested in political realities, not eschatological fantasies. Spinoza must have known he was wrong. Spinozas are different from us. They do not make the innocent, ignorant mistakes we make.

Let us pause here for a moment. The deliberately prosaic character of the Maimonidean view is representative of much else in Judaism that Christian theology has traditionally decried as carnality—fleshliness—and contrasted to an infinitely superior Christian spirituality. Over the centuries many have gone over from Judaism to Christianity, in all honor and sincerity, because they have accepted the Christian valuation. I have heard Professor Yosef Yerushalmi read a fine paper about two Marrano brothers, Spinoza's contemporaries, who fled the Spanish royal court to return to full Judaism. The younger became a zealous follower of the false messiah Shabbethai Zevi, but the elder refused. Shabbethai Zevi cannot be the Messiah, he reasoned. These are not the Days of the Messiah, we are still enslaved to the foreign kingdoms. If we abandon that touchstone, why do you and I reject the Christian claim that Jesus was the Messiah? To this the younger brother gave an enraged answer, which showed how Christian doctrine had influenced even an anti-Christian Marrano: his brother's literalism—"the letter killeth"—and inability to see the messianic, spiritual grandeur that was all about them proved the mere carnality of conventional Judaism.

Let me risk being accused of what I have heard called Jewish triumphalism. Things are changing. The old spirituality is being devalued—by Christians. The things that count now are carnal, fleshly: racial equality, justice to the poor, peace. I have heard Protestant and

Catholic theologians agree that this reversal is a wholesome return to a Jewish-biblical union of flesh and spirit. I have even heard them argue that "Incarnation" is from the same root as "carnal."

To return to Spinoza—if he was deliberately wrong about the passivity of Judaism, he was not completely wrong. Besides knowing what Maimonides had affirmed, Spinoza knew what Maimonides had passed over—including not only statements of feminine doctrine, which can be offset by masculine statements, but also the ritualization of feminine doctrine. Here is our holiday of Hanukkah, instituted to celebrate an earlier, more successful rebellion than Bar Kokhba's. For the Sabbath of Hanukkah the Rabbis could have chosen a Prophetical reading about a victory over the enemies of Israel and its God, or else about reconsecrating a defiled Temple, or even about a miraculously prolonged supply of oil. Instead they chose Zechariah 2:14–4:7 (though it is also the Prophetical lesson after some priestly chapters, 8-12, in Numbers): " . . . Then he showed me Joshua the high priest standing before the angel of the Lord. . . . And the angel of the Lord enjoined Joshua: Thus says the Lord of hosts: If you will walk in my ways and keep my charge, then you shall rule my house and have charge of my courts. . . . This is the word of the Lord to Zerubbabel: Not by might, nor by power, but by my spirit, says the Lord of hosts. . . . "

The Hasmoneans recapture and reconsecrate the Temple, and into the celebration of that glory the Rabbis insert propaganda against the Hasmoneans' right to be high priests. Manly might and Jewish power triumph, and the Rabbis make us read a text from a powerless time, which rationalizes powerlessness as if it were good in itself. The Jews win independence, and the Rabbis implicitly prefer foreign rule: Zerubbabel was an agent of the Persian crown.

No more than Spinoza does can modern Jews approve those Rabbis. We are glad he was wrong in equating their influence on the tradition with the very basis of the tradition. For us, manly honor is the truth. It is our truth. It makes sense of what we are, or what we want to be.

But there is another, adversary truth, and though two truths are hard to entertain at the same time, especially when we like one and dislike the other, let us make the effort. It will be easier if we think of the conflict between those truths in the history of India, rather than the history of the Jews. In the last century Tocqueville protested against the common notion that the Hindus were cowards. We think so, he said, because the many Hindus allowed the few Europeans in

India first to conquer and then to rule them. But in the Hindus' recurrent famines they will die of hunger before violating the laws of their religion and eating beef. Is that cowardice?

A preoccupation with manly honor can decline into the grotesque. I am fond of those jokes about the Jewish duelist ("Don't wait for me if I'm late, shoot anyway"); but I think the duel—as fact, as impulse, and as ideal—is a neglected element in modern Jewish history. In the future Jewish state of Herzl's vision the duel was to be an institution. With the opera house, with the state itself, it would mark off the new, worldly, modern, erect Jew from the old, narrow traditional, cringing one. In Horthy's Budapest, Jews fought duels against antisemites who had impugned their honor as Jews, or Jewish honor. In Vienna the members of the antisemitic fraternities at the university, denying that Jews were *satisfaktionsfähig*, would not duel with them; so Arthur Koestler and the others in the Zionist fraternity brawled with the antisemites in defense of Jewish honor and rights.

So far, so good (except for Herzl). But what about Ferdinand Lassalle? He was a socialist—the leader of German socialism—yet he was killed in a "feudal," silly duel. Honor and courage were important to him. As a boy he had dreamt of putting himself "at the head of the Jews, weapon in hand, to win them national independence."

And last, poor Jack Ruby. Uneducated and befuddled and disreputable, he was no less a modern Jew than the educated and rational and respectable. In his words, he shot Oswald to show that Jews have guts.

I began by saying that we are modern, "of course." But are we still modern? Are we not coming to the end of modernity? Are we not becoming postmodern, as some have long been insisting?

If I ask these questions, it is not because—like most people?—I am tempted to exaggerate the newness of the times. In these matters my own temptation has been to doubt newness since the *Commentary* symposium of the young Jewish intellectuals in April 1961. The most remarkable thing about it was what Norman Podhoretz noted in his introduction: how surprisingly little change there had been since the symposium of an earlier generation of Jewish intellectuals in the *Contemporary Jewish Record*, in 1944. The world had changed, America had changed, American Jews had changed—at least by the accepted standards of economics, sociology, and demography—but Jewish intellectuals had changed almost not at all. Is it likely that a change which failed to come about between 1944 and 1961—or, if we think

13

of Western Jews generally, between earlier than 1800 and 1961—
should have come about between 1961 and now?

There is much evidence that the modern world may indeed be
moving toward something postmodern; except that the Jews, on the
whole, remain conservatively attached to the old modernity of
Spinoza. In this conservative attachment Jewish intellectuals differ
little from nonintellectuals. At least in this they are all Jews together.
All are more comfortable with modernity than with anything else.

Of the many things Romanticism was, one was an argument with
modernity. Romanticism tends to make people respectful of religion,
if not religious. Irreligious, even a Max Weber was not combative
about religion in the classical modern manner. He said only, with the
hint of a sigh, that he was religiously unmusical. For the eighteenth-
century Enlightenment, *Gothic* was a term of abuse—the barbarian
Goths had disappeared long before the later Middle Ages, when that
style was invented—and Joan of Arc was the subject of bawdy jokes.
Romanticism has taught us to think well of Gothic, of Joan, and of
the religion and culture that produced them. Moderns who have been
affected by Romanticism find it easy to think that while Christianity
may not be true, at least one must say this for it, that it has had a
powerful effect on culture and personality. Many Jews have gone
over to Christianity because of that Romantic way of thinking,
learned from teachers who were Romantic Christians.

Spinoza and the Enlighteners drew a clear distinction between
society and state as the realm of the secular, on the one hand, and
religion as a private matter, on the other. Romanticism was to discover that culture and national histories, not private but social, are
entangled with religion—particularly Christianity in its various forms,
or the memories and continuing influences of Christianity. In Poland
and France, Marxist philosophers and literary scholars (including
Jews) seem more attracted to seventeenth-century Christianity than
to seventeenth-century irreligion.

The effect on Jews is best seen in art history, or rather in the history
of art historians. A high proportion of the most significant art historians have been German Jews. As modern Jews they hold to
Spinoza's primary ideals, as Germans they are especially influenced
by Romanticism. This produces an unlikely or paradoxical state of
affairs: modern Jews who are authorities on medieval and Renaissance Christian iconography. The paradox is compounded by the fact
that the Jewish tradition—which made their ancestors who *they* were

and which, though less directly and visibly, prolongs its influence into their own lives—is unimpressed by the aesthetic. Matthew Arnold knew what he was doing when he contrasted Hellenism and Hebraism; and Hebraism itself was aware of the contrast. Judah Ha-levi says, "Let not Greek thought [*ḥokhmat yewanit*] seduce you, for it bears no fruit, but only flowers."

Art historians invest emotion, intellect, and career in something not immediately or unquestionably natural for people who are simultaneously non-Christians, irreligious, and Jews. The seriousness with which they have to take Romanticism—otherwise why be art historians?—is at odds with Spinozist purity.

It is not new that the substitute religions deriving from the Enlightenment are dead, but some people who should know it do not seem to. In a university journal a professor of English publishes a lecture to the effect that the humanities humanize. Can he be serious? Does he still believe in the religion of culture? Arnold hoped that culture would make people humane, and we know that it does not. Lovers of Goethe and Beethoven ran Hitler's death machine. Apparently Nietzsche was right, after all: God having died, other deaths must follow.

If that defender of the culture-faith does not want to let uncultured reality in, he might at least listen to colleagues like Lionel Trilling and George Steiner. In the 1920s when clergymen preached sermons about the grounding of humane behavior in religion. Mencken's boys would laugh. When professors of classics preached about the grounding of humane letters (and mental acuteness) in the study of Latin and Greek, undergraduates would make remarks about old fogeys afraid for their jobs. Who will now say what needs to be said of professorial sermons about the grounding of humane feeling in literature and art?

Not only do consumers or connoisseurs of culture fail to be made humane (or human) by the humanities, the very producers fail. The two greatest English-language poets of this century were Yeats and Eliot, reactionaries who at times were something worse; the oldest great living poet in English is Pound, the virulent antisemite who broadcasted in wartime for Mussolini; and Genet, whom Sartre has canonized as a saint, is not exactly a spokesman for humanism.

Right-minded people know that society hounds the artist. Yet if Genet had been only a criminal who loved his profession and not also an artist, they would not have let him out of jail. If Pound were not an artist but a carpenter or merchant or veterinarian, first they would not have let him take asylum in an asylum, and then they would not have let him out.

Of all the religions prolific of cant, the religion of art and culture is most prolific. The hounded artist is a minor piece of culture-cant, life-enhancing art a major one. I think it was Berenson who taught us the syllogism: what is life-enhancing is good; art is life-enhancing; therefore, art is good. And contrariwise: if it is not life-enhancing, it is not art. Curiously, the Nazi death chiefs were most rapacious about precisely those works of art that Berenson held to be life-enhancing. Nor could he even give its plain meaning to "life": he was gloomily proud of not having children. *Fin de race*, end of the biological line, he said of himself.

The enhancement of life; creativity. "Create" is a biblical word, the first verb in the Bible. In the Bible *bara'* ("create") can have only God as its subject, only God creates. From the first verse in Genesis, in which He creates the heavens and the earth, "create" is a signal that something emphatic is being said about His self-definition in act and word. Its greatest frequency is in Deutero-Isaiah, especially Isaiah 45. "I form light and create darkness,/I make peace *and create evil*" (Isaiah 45:7). This is so bold that it had to be softened for liturgical use: in the first obligatory blessing of our morning prayers, immediately after *Barekhu*, we say, "Thou formest light and createst darkness, Thou makest peace *and createst all things.*" And Isaiah 45:18: "For thus says the Lord who created the heavens/(he is God),/who formed the earth and made it/(he established it;/he did not create it a chaos,/he formed it to be inhabited):/'I am the Lord, and there is no other.'"

Even in English, until well into modernity the various forms of "create" are apt to have a numinous feeling about them. "Creative" in an unambiguously human sense is not much more than a hundred years old. "Creativity" is more recent still. It is a coinage of modern culture-religion, for which man is creator, especially man as artist. As we would expect, the Oxford English Dictionary gives as the first recorded use a statement about Shakespeare's "poetic creativity." I have not found "creative art/arts" in OED, so I take this phrase to be a twentieth-century invention. Modern culture-religion made claims that even Hellenism did not make: for classical antiquity art is not creative but mimetic—imitative. A religious mood accompanied the modern contemplation of art, a ritual of pilgrimage and solemnity prevailed, and men hoped for salvation.

But the religion of creativity, frail to begin with, has become funny. First every other college catalogue in America listed courses in creative writing—an art-sanctimonious name for helping students to learn how to write fiction or poetry. Afterward "creative man" was taken over as a technical term by the personnel directors of advertising agencies, on a par with "account executive." And now the inspirational literature of commerce hymns creative salesmanship.

A few years back I read a neofeminist's approving review of another neofeminist's book. The reviewer said she agreed with the author that for a woman, a career is more creative than being a mother. That puzzled me: without having given much thought to it, I had assumed that about the closest the human race can get to creation is a woman bearing a child, nurturing him, and caring for him. A little later I was looking through the racks in a drugstore and came across a specimen of a common subliterary genre—books for adolescent girls about a young heroine with an interesting/creative job/career. The title of the book was *Priscilla White, TV Secretary.* Then I understood. How can being a mother compare in creativity with being a TV secretary?

Political Messianism was modernity's other substitute religion. Its obsoleteness is not news: *The God That Failed,* about the Revolution, preceded by ten years or so *The Death of God,* about traditional religion. (Each was addressed to the worshippers of the particular deity whose failure or demise it announced.) Yet a book wins such prizes and acclaim that one would think the last fifty years had never happened. At the end of Malamud's *The Fixer,* the hero Yakov speaks the author's moral or conclusion: "What is it Spinoza says?" (Always Spinoza.) "If the state acts in ways that are abhorrent to human nature it's the lesser evil to destroy it. Death to the anti-Semites! Long live revolution! Long live liberty!"

Whose revolution is Malamud thinking of, Kerensky's or Lenin's? Lenin's: a few pages before, Yakov daydreams that he kills the Tsar. The historical reality behind Malamud's novel was the Tsar's Beilis trial. Have we forgotten that just before Stalin died, he was about to stage a trial that would have been far more abhorrent to human nature? Under Stalin the Jewish doctors—so they were universally referred to—would not have been set free, as the Jew Beilis was under the Tsar; and their conviction would have touched off a repression of Russian Jews worse than all the others they had had to suffer in those last Black Years of Stalin's life. Our ancestors would have seen the finger of God in Stalin's death at just that time, and would have celebrated a new Purim of thanksgiving.

Tsarism was abhorrent; and that revolution of Yakov's brought into being something more abhorrent still. "Death to the anti-Semites?" Antisemites are still in power in Russia. Stalin's daughter Svetlana Alliluyeva, asked about Judaism and Jews in the Soviet Union, answers that while she knows little about Judaism, she can testify as an eyewitness that Jews are discriminated against. Aside from Arabs, only Soviet representatives say antisemitic things in the UN.

So the proclamation of revolutionary enthusiasms from before World War I is not serious. Neither is much of the political rhetoric of the intelligentsia, with its apocalyptic shrillness. These only confirm again Marx's second most famous saying: when history repeats itself, it can re-enact tragedy as farce.

Classical modernity is in decay. When Marx said religion is the opiate of the people—his most famous saying—both Marxists and religious people considered that to be a serious criticism, if true. Both agreed that opium was bad. Both agreed that life was real, life was earnest, life was purposeful. (The Yiddish word is *takhlis*.) Today, we are told, opium—in the broad sense: LSD, marijuana—is religion for the avant-garde. Timothy Leary, Allen Ginsberg, and Norman Brown are for "opium"—the thing itself and the symbol of inwardness and sensuality. These men are not irreligious. The new young have been known to say: Freud was a fink. If Freud—because too repressive—why not Marx? Marx and Freud: in that *Commentary* symposium these great ancestors were invoked repeatedly, in the same breath with *their* ancestor, Spinoza.

This is not to say that Leary, Ginsberg, and Brown provide much comfort for upholders of the traditional religions. The new religiousness seems to be some kind of syncretistic paganism—syncretism is the polite word for mishmash—and the traditional religions will have to take its measure. But that paganism is not what Peter Gay had in mind with his *Enlightenment: The Rise of Modern Paganism*. Gay meant atheism. For him, modern paganism is atheist. Then postmodern paganism is postatheist; hippies can sound like Fundamentalist evangelists.

Even the political young take religion more seriously than their elders did. A generation ago, who on the Left would have hoped for more from the churches than from labor? Who would have depended on marching or picketing nuns to be there when the going got rough? The change is hard for middle-aged moderns to accept. George Lichtheim, reviewing works blaming the Pope for what he did and failed to do in World War II, is impatient. What is the point of criticizing? he asks. Who does not know better than to expect anything of an elderly gentleman and the large, complex organization he administers? Just so. The very criticism of the young shows they expect something, and the expectation shows respect. Maybe that is because the popes of secularist modernity have not done all that well, either.

No author would dare to contrive something so pat: in the fiftieth-anniversary year of the Bolshevik Revolution, Alliluyeva leaves Russia and says she believes in God and human decency, not in the dogmas of atheism and conflict she was brought up on. Voznesensky, the most highly regarded of the younger Soviet poets, says: "What is bad is when man, hypnotized by technology, becomes a technological object himself. . . . Theoretically, everything a man can do can be programmed into a machine and the machine will do it—everything except this: man's capacity for religion and poetry." Dialogues are held between Christians and Marxists—that is to say, between Christians and a combination of intellectuals and apparatchiks from Communist countries and mass Communist parties; and in the dialogue the Communists are less sure of their own rightness and the religious people's wrongness than ever before. The Communist party of Great Britain issues a manifesto calling for a multiparty political system, with legitimacy for parties opposed to socialism; insisting on the freedom of religion, and granting that religion can have progressive and beneficial as well as reactionary and evil effects.

Another thing Alliluyeva has said is that although she is generally rather than specifically religious, because she is Russian she has had herself baptized into the Russian Orthodox church. The multiple irony of it: Alliluyeva, with her father and her training; religion after fifty years of unrelenting, official, monopolistic, persecuting, deriding, cajoling, "scientific" atheism; and not just religion, but the Russian Orthodox church.

Is it only because I'm an ignorant outsider, a prejudiced son of Russian Jews, that I am amazed? The Russian Orthodox church! Of all the churches in Europe, the Russian Orthodox has always seemed—only to Jews?—the lowest. It is the church of the Beilis trial, and Rasputin. It excommunicated Tolstoy. In the first ten or fifteen years of this century a few intellectually and morally superior men chose to identify themselves with it, but on the whole it is the church that an outsider would have thought least able to win the affection or even the nominal allegiance of intellectuals brought up on fifty years of official Dialectical Materialism and 150 years of Russian literature.

The memoirs of prerevolutionary Russia tell of the contempt students used to have for the *gymnasium* teachers of religion. Now the objects of that contempt are the university lecturers in Dialectical Materialism—Diamat for short. (I understand that Russian students give to the Diamat lectures the old name of the course in religion—God's Law.) Now all kinds of people are Russian Orthodox or pro-Russian Orthodox. Some years ago a Soviet newspaper printed a complaint from a worker: he was under pressure from the other workers in his plant to have his children baptized in church. "You're Russian," they would tell him, "and Russians are Russian Orthodox." When the poet Akhmatova died, honored by the younger generation, her funeral was Russian Orthodox. Stalin's cultural executioner, Zhdanov, had reviled her in good Stalinist fashion: a sign of her degeneracy, he said, was that one of her favorite haunts was the chapel. But she was of the pre-Revolutionary generation. Among the intellectuals born or educated since the Revolution and pro-Russian Orthodox are Solzhenitsyn and Sinyavsky.

Yet that is not the end of the irony—and, for Jews, the pain. The poet Pasternak, a good and brave man, the son of modern Jews, became Russian Orthodox in the Soviet Union—that is to say, after the Revolution. Or if he did not become officially Russian Orthodox then, if—for the record is unclear—he was baptized earlier, his nominal Russian Orthodoxy became actual precisely in the days of the Godless Revolution. Of Josef Brodsky, the young man sentenced to a killing term in the North for daring to write poetry without an official poet's license, one hears that he has a Russian Orthodox cross over his cot. Is that because he, too, is now Russian Orthodox, or is it because a cross is the only religious symbol this Jew can find? One also hears that some of the best young scientists in the Soviet Union are turning to Russian Orthodoxy, and that among these, in turn, are Jews.

Is that where Jewish honor has led? Surely that is not what modern Jews intended when they yearned for the creation of a state that would be neither Christian nor Jewish; surely what they wanted was a new Napoleon, who, subordinating every religion, would not exact baptism as the price of a Jew's ambition and desire for equality; and surely the Soviet Union is the state that has done most to subordinate religion, and actually to repress it. In that state, to find not Spinoza's landlady but so many of the morally and intellectually best people religious or proreligious is a shock. To find their religion or proreligion expressing itself in the form not merely of Christianity or pro-Christianity, but actually of Russian Orthodoxy or pro-Russian Orthodoxy, is doubly a shock. How much more of a shock must it be to find that some of those best Russian Orthodox people are Jews? O Cunning of Reason!

In Israel the so-called Oriental immigrants have taken the dominant Ashkenazim as models for how to be modern and up to date. One thing they learn quickly is that modern Israelis are not religious, that to be religious is the best way not to be modern. I heard the following story from a professor at the Hebrew University, a German Jew who, influenced by Buber and Franz Rosenzweig, went up to Palestine in the 1920s as a *ba'al teshuvah,* a returner to Judaism from coldness and Jewish ignorance.

Military service integrates the Israeli population—as they say, it makes one nation out of many tribes. During military service this man's son became a noncommissioned officer, and with his new stripes he was assigned one day to a new unit and barracks, where he was both senior and the only Ashkenazi. The next morning he put on his *tefillin* and prayed. The other soldiers stared, and a few began to cry. Later he discovered the reason. Here was their noncom, an Ashkenazi of the Ashkenazim, praying—and with *tefillin.* They had been deceived. All the sacrifice of habit and feeling and belief they had thought necessary was unnecessary. It was possible both to be *moderni* and to put on *tefillin.*

But at least Chaim Weizmann was right, and his brother Samuel wrong, in one crucial respect. In Chaim's Israel a Jew going from modernity to religion—either going back to it or advancing to it on a higher turn of the spiral—is rather more likely to go to Judaism and *tefillin* than to Christianity and the three-barred crucifix.

Most of what I know about da Costa and La Peyrère, and much of what I know about Spinoza, I owe to Leo Strauss's *Spinoza's Critique of Religion*—a book all the more impressive because the author was a young man when he wrote it, in Weimar Germany. (I have also learned much from the chapter on the *Tractatus* in his *Persecution and the Art of Writing.*) In 1965 Schocken published the English translation of *Spinoza's Critique,* together with a new preface by Professor Strauss. Above all the preface is a personal document, about the author as a young German Jew who has to come to grips with Spinoza. Before him Hermann Cohen and Rosenzweig also have had to come to grips with Spinoza; more than Jews who are thinkers, these are Jewish thinkers. Strauss is not the disciple of either. He is his own man and thinks his own thoughts, phrasing them with greater or lesser transparency, greater or lesser opaqueness, as he sees fit. In the new translation of his book about Spinoza's critique of religion he keeps the old dedication: "to the memory of Franz Rosenzweig."

—July 1967

.2.

Secular Society?

The situation of modern Jews has remained basically unchanged, both in their relation to Judaism and in their relation to the societies and cultures of the West, with its mixture of Christianity and secularism: secularized Christianity and Christian-related secularism. Although the kinds of change that come under the heads of demography, economics, acculturation, and the like are not unimportant, the situation of the Jews today has a continuity that starts from a revolutionary discontinuity at the time of Moses Mendelssohn in the eighteenth century, or even of Spinoza in the seventeenth.

Jews, insofar as they have been modern, have wished to be of, as well as in, their societies. They have made progress in this direction, simultaneously or preliminarily moving away from the older Jewish desire and fact of being in but not of their societies;[1] but they have met obstacles. In general, these have been obstacles deposited by the history that secularism was supposed to neutralize or nullify. The various societies, together with their traditions and memories, are still Christian—at least as far as the Jews are concerned. However secular these societies have been from one perspective, they have not been secular in the sense of being neutral between Christianity and Judaism, Christians and Jews.

At the beginning of Jewish modernity, Moses Mendelssohn, its representative figure, was caught up in an experience neatly paradigmatic for all modern Jews since his time. Mendelssohn wished to live in Berlin—the city, the center of Enlightenment and culture. Since

Jews needed special permission to live there, he asked a friend to intercede for him with Frederick the Great. The Marquis d'Argens, a French intellectual who was what we would call today a cultural adviser to Frederick, wrote his Francophile (and Judaeophobe) master a letter that is a fine example of eighteenth-century *esprit*:

> An intellectual [*philosophe*] who is a bad Catholic begs an intellectual who is a bad Protestant to grant the privilege [of residence in Berlin] to an intellectual who is a bad Jew. There is too much *philosophie* in all this for reason not to be on the side of the request.[2]

Now Mendelssohn was not really so bad a Jew as that, but to be allowed—grudgingly—to live in Berlin, he had to be thought a bad Jew. This, then, was the first lesson that modern Jews learned: If you want to be admitted to the delights and excitements of modern culture, do not be a good Jew. The second lesson was that the only people who were willing to let you live in Berlin were the bad Christians; good Christians would not have you whether you were a good Jew or a bad one. The third lesson, which was learned later than the first two, was that while Jews had to be bad to live in Berlin, Christians could be good or bad as they chose.

But the chief lesson was that reason was the modern Jew's ally; from this it was only a small step to a reverence for Reason. Christians had less reason to revere Reason, since they could live in Berlin without it. Enthusiasm for modernity and secularism was, therefore, unevenly distributed between Jews and Christians.

Especially in Europe, it has been easy, intellectually and emotionally, for Jews to situate themselves in relation to the "good" Christians—the Constantinians, the upholders of the Christian state and the alliance between Throne and Altar. These have been the enemy, from long before the French Revolution to Vatican II, from the Catholic south to the Lutheran north, from Anglican England to Orthodox Russia.[3]

Liberal Christians are harder to place. Some liberal Christian thought has turned out to be harsh toward Jews and Judaism.[4] The society many liberal Christians have seen as secular, either gladly or sadly, is less secular and more Christian from a Jewish perspective. Even those who call themselves secularist rather than Christian tend to have different standards from Jews for judging a culture's secularism and religious neutrality. Two tests of this proposition are the place of Christmas in American life and the question of religious influence in the public schools.

For a Jew, no matter how secular, Christmas must be more problematic than it is for a Christian (or ex-Christian) of equal secularity. Despite all the efforts, frequently by Jews, to show that Christmas is no longer Christian (and never was),[5] even Jews removed from Jewish tradition find themselves obliged to engage in casuistries: a tree in the parlor but no wreath on the door or windows, "Season's Greetings" rather than "Merry Christmas"—the list is long and wryly comical. The great-granddaughter of a Forty-eighter from Germany recalls that when she was a little girl, she asked her mother why their Christmas tree had no star on top and was told that only Christian Christmas trees had a star.

On the more serious matter of religious influence in the public school—prayers, Bible reading, and the like—the Supreme Court has been saying no. To no one's surprise, most of the ensuing expressions of protest and annoyance have come from the Constantinians, but two have come from an unexpected quarter, liberal Harvard. Both the Dean of the Law School and the James Bryant Conant Professor of Education, Emeritus, think that the Court is wrong.

Dean Griswold:

Is it not clear as a matter of historical fact that this was a Christian nation? . . . Are the Mayflower Compact, Anne Hutchinson, Cotton Mather, Jonathan Edwards, William Penn, and many others no part of our history? It is true that we . . . developed a tolerance in matters of religion. . . . But this was not a purely humanistic type of thought. Nor did it deny the importance and significance of religion.

. . . The First Amendment forbade Congress to pass any law "respecting an establishment of religion or prohibiting the free exercise thereof." These are great provisions, of great sweep and basic importance. But to say that they require that all trace of religion be kept out of any sort of public activity is sheer invention. Our history is full of these traces. . . . God is referred to in our national anthem, and in "America," and many others of what may be called our national songs. Must all of these things be rigorously extirpated in order to satisfy a constitutional absolutism? What about Sunday? What about Christmas? Must we deny our whole heritage, our culture, the things of spirit and soul which have sustained us in the past and helped to bind us together in times of good and bad?[6]

Professor Ulich:

The serious opponents [of the Supreme Court's decisions] . . . are aroused by . . . the threat of an unhistorical disruption of national customs and symbols, which today probably have a more patriotic and aesthetic appeal than a deeply felt religious one. But there are even more profound, though sometimes unconscious, reasons for the anxiety of many. . . . The Jewish people would not have survived the long years of persecution without faithful adherence to their rituals, festivals, and prayers. May then the loss of the Christian past not jeopardize the future of *this* nation, just as the desertion from the covenant would have jeopardized the survival of the Jews? Nations, as well as men, though living by bread, do not live by bread alone.[7]

Ulich is right: the decisions and the protests against them have been about symbol, not substance. A Jewish parent can testify that whether or not Christmas is evident in the schools, it is thoroughly evident on television and on Main Street, and these have more effect on children than what formally takes place in school.

Griswold mentions Sunday. As it happens, the Supreme Court has ruled on Sunday in a matter of substance for Jews, or at least for some Jews. The ruling is that a Jew in Massachusetts who does not do business on his Sabbath, Saturday, may not make up for it by doing business on Sunday—though the Massachusetts law refers to Sunday as the Lord's Day, and though a lower court ruled that the state was discriminating against the Jewish merchant on religious grounds.[8]

We may soon have a Sabbath question in the schools. If it is decided that education in the last third of the twentieth century needs six days a week, the sixth day will be Saturday, of course, not Sunday. In the Third French Republic, anticlerical and even irreligious children attended the state schools on the Jewish Sabbath, not the Christian one. They still do in the Fifth Republic.[9]

While the secular society in the lands that used to be Christendom is neutral in matters of religion, it is more neutral against Judaism than against Christianity. The French distinguish between the legal country and the real country. In the legal country religious neutrality is imperfect, and in the real country much more imperfect. In every Western nation Christianity is too inseparable from the national culture for religious neutrality to be truly possible.[10]

Nor does this obtain only in lands where the Revolution paused at the bourgeois stage. It obtains also where the Revolution is or calls itself Marxist. Although all religions are equally bad in Russia, one is worse—Judaism.[11] But 1917's failure to "solve the Jewish problem" is much more recent than 1789's. It was long possible for Jews to believe that only the bourgeois character of the society in which they lived kept them from being truly of it. This belief led many to yearn, with a

25

secularist-messianic fervor, for a socialist transformation of man and society.[12] Now socialist revolutions have come, but for Jews the transformation has not come. Henceforth, faith in socialism as the solution must increasingly be recognized as contrary to experience and reason, if not to Reason.

From this point of view, even a socialist revolution does not go far enough. What is needed is a cultural revolution, or more accurately, a linguistic one. If national languages persist, so will national cultures, and so will the Christianity or the Christian influence—or symbolism, or vocabulary—that is so deeply imbedded in Western culture. How can one understand and appreciate Dante, Shakespeare, Donne, Milton, Racine, Pascal, Hegel, Kierkegaard, Dostoevski, Tolstoi, Hawthorne, or Eliot, if one does not understand and appreciate Christianity?

Since *The Psychopathology of Everyday Life*, we have known that it is in trivialities we reveal ourselves. Let us consider some of these trivialities. In English *crusade* is an O.K. word; *Pharisee* or *pharisaic* is a bad word. But *crusade* is O.K. only from the traditional point of view of Western European Christianity, not necessarily from the point of view of modern scholarship and certainly not from the point of view of Slavs, Greeks, Armenians, Moslems, and Jews. For the Jews the Crusades meant massacres in Europe and Palestine. The First Crusade was more or less the beginning of the Jews' systematic degradation and persecution in England, France, and Germany. Centuries after the Christian Roman Empire had made Jewish proselytism among Christians a capital crime, Jews continued to proselytize. It was the Crusades that effectively terrorized the Jews into passivity.[13]

As for *Pharisee* and *pharisaic*, the meaning given to these words is a triumph of Christian (New Testament) propaganda. Yet even secularized Jews, and even secularized Jews who have a somewhat positive attitude toward Jewish tradition and culture, do not hesitate to use these words in preference to *self-righteous* or *hypocritical*, just as they use *crusade* in its honorific sense. Their being unaware of what they are doing would only prove the inherently anti-Jewish force of the culture and its language; their awareness would prove it all the more. They are trying to show—themselves as well as others—that they are not parochial Jews, that they hold truth to be more important than Jewish sensibilities. So they equate truth with the Christian propaganda that is now ineradicably a part of our secular culture.[14] Western culture prefers Christian to Jewish parochialism—or rather, it takes for granted that Christian parochialism is universalism.

26

Logically, the best way to solve this problem would be to abolish it. Do the languages of the West transmit old Christian memories and habits? Replace them by a new, universal language, a linguistic (and cultural) *tabula rasa*. Zamenhof, the inventor of Esperanto, was a Jew, and his vision included an element of barely modified Jewish messianism.[15] But in no foreseeable future, whether its emblematic date is 1789 or 1917, are we likely to find Esperanto substituted for English or French or German or Italian or Russian or Spanish; nor, despite the rise of Asia and Africa, are we likely to find the nations and continents that were once Christendom—and Islam, too, for that matter—shorn of all power and influence. Cultures linked to Christianity or Islam cannot be as indifferently neutral in these things as, say, Buddhist cultures.

Even under the sign of Marxism, half a century after the Russian Revolution, some of the noblest and most impressive figures in the lands of the new, socialist cultures are Christian or near-Christian— by deliberate, almost provocative choice: Pasternak, Solzhenitsyn, Sinyavsky, Mihajlo Mihajlov.

From the beginning of Jewish modernity, Jews have had three choices: to be Jews, to be Christians, to be secularists. Many have decided that they cannot conscientiously be Jews because they cannot believe what Judaism requires them to believe: that there is a God, the Creator who revealed himself as Lawgiver to the patriarchs and prophets, that he wishes the children of Israel to preserve themselves in faithful and loving obedience to him, and that all men will yet join them in acknowledging and worshipping him. If a Jew cannot believe this, however freely he interprets it, shall he choose to be a Christian or shall he choose to be a secularist?

If a Jew cannot conscientiously believe in Judaism because he holds it to be unreasonable, then all the more can he not believe in Christianity. If he finds the dogmas of Judaism offensive to Reason, he must find the dogmas of Christianity more so, if only because there are more of them. The dogmas of Judaism are preserved in Christianity, at most with a change of tense (for example, that the Law revealed to the patriarchs and prophets was once binding but no longer is). To these dogmas Christianity adds others, Christological and ecclesiological.

But if not conscientiously, then expedientially, a Jew devoted to Reason can become a Christian. A nineteenth-century biographer tells us that Moses Mendelssohn "despised apostasy as dishonorable, but would gladly have joined his friend Lessing in a society where there were neither Jews nor Christians."[16] Then the years pass. Impatience grows, and with impatience comes a feeling that honor is a costly luxury. So Moses Mendelssohn's son Abraham decides to do the expedient thing, as he later told *his* son Felix:

My father . . . did not want to be a Christian. . . . As long as it was permitted by the [Napoleonic] government under which we lived, I reared you without religion in any form. I wanted you to profess whatever your convictions might favor or, if you prefer, whatever expediency might dictate. But it was not so to be. . . . Naturally, when you consider the scant value I placed on any form in particular, I felt no urge to choose the form known as Judaism. . . . Therefore I reared you as Christians, Christianity . . . being the . . . form . . . most accepted by the majority of civilized people. Eventually I myself adopted Christianity, because I felt it my duty to do for myself that which I recognized as best for you.[17]

Or, as Heinrich Heine said, "the baptismal certificate is the ticket of admission to European culture."[18] A later nineteenth-century oral tradition has it that the Russian scholar Daniel Chwolson said he had been baptized out of conviction—the conviction that it was better to be a professor in St. Petersburg than a wretch teaching the rudiments of Hebrew reading in a mud-sunk village in Lithuania. A similar conviction inspired Bernard Berenson to be (or call himself) an Episcopalian in Boston and a Catholic in Florence.[19] Today prudential baptisms are apt to be of a somewhat different character. In France the atheist daughter of Russian Jewish parents has her children baptized as Catholics at birth so that they will not be the prey of a new Nazism.[20]

But, of course, the preferred alternative is secularism, the vision of Lessing and Moses Mendelssohn. Only now, two hundred years later, we ought to see in retrospect what Mendelssohn could not see in prospect—that the secularism of the West is not quite neither Christian nor Jewish equally. Especially does it not have equal effects on the children and grandchildren of the ex-Jew and the ex-Christian.

Suppose that the children or grandchildren, in their turn, rebel against *their* fathers and grandfathers; suppose that they become disillusioned with the religion of Reason and turn to one of the traditional religions. Which will that be? Given the culture they have absorbed not only in the mind but also through the pores, the result is not in doubt. The religion-minded children or grandchildren become Christians.[21] Bergson, a Catholic in spirit, would have been one in fact if it had not been for his honor, which would not allow him formally to abandon the Jews when they were under attack by Hitler.[22] Franz Rosenzweig, perhaps the greatest modern Jewish theologian, was almost baptized; his cousins Hans and Rudolf Ehrenberg were baptized.[23] Edith Stein became a nun.[24] Boris Pasternak became a Tolstoian Russian Orthodox Christian—under the Soviets.[25]

Notably, these conversions were to the particular forms of Christianity dominant in the respective countries: Catholicism in France, Lutheranism and Catholicism in Germany, Eastern Orthodoxy in Russia.[26] Expediential conversions could be to the dominant form of Christianity—Chwolson to Russian Orthodoxy; Disraeli, as a boy and upon his father's initiative, to Anglicanism. But in the Romanoff and Hapsburg empires they tended to be to a minority sect, Protestantism. This was the case in Russia for the family of Vladimir Medem, who was to be an early leader of the Jewish Socialist Bund,[27] and for the banker and economist Ivan Bloch;[28] in Austria it was almost the case for Freud.[29] A calculation in these conversions to Protestantism in Central and Eastern Europe seems to have been that Protestantism was not "really" so Christian as Catholicism or Eastern Orthodoxy, and therefore that one was somehow less of an apostate (to Judaism? to the Jews? to Reason?) if one became a Protestant.[30]

Because Bergson was culturally so French, Pasternak and Frank so Russian, and Rosenzweig's cousins so German, they became sincerely Catholic, Russian Orthodox, and Lutheran.[31] In Western Europe Jews did not become Eastern Orthodox Christians. In Russia they did not become Anglicans. This tendency in Jewish conversions does not strengthen the anti-Constantinian argument that Christianity loses by involvement in culture.

These people could become sincere Christians because they had been brought up in the religion of Reason. Few even wished, like Rosenzweig, to "enter Christianity, as did its founders, as a Jew, not as a 'pagan.' "[32] There is no comparable record of sincere conversions to Christianity among those really brought up as Jews.

A Jew who is brought up without religion and who remains without religious feeling may nevertheless marry someone who has such feeling. Statistically, the odds are that that person will be a Christian, not a Jew, and that their children will then be Christians. The religious *potential* of our society is Christian. If a secularist Jew, or his child or grandchild, is to be within reach of a Jewish potential—in the second and especially the third generation—he must actively will it, he must make a decision. To be within reach of the Christian potential needs no decision, no act of will.

In the modern Jewish experience Unitarianism has been perceived as a kind of secularist-Christian hybrid, with the secularist element dominant. But this is a Jewish perception, perhaps even a willful (though unwitting) self-deception. For Jews, at least, Unitarianism has been a way station on the road toward a more traditional kind of Christianity.[33] Since American Unitarianism has not grown much,[34] we must infer that those who enter are more or less offset by those who leave. Few leave for Judaism. President Taft was a Unitarian, his son the Senator was an Episcopalian.

Ethical Culture was founded in 1876 by Felix Adler, an American. The son of a rabbi, Adler had been studying in Germany to become a rabbi himself when he decided that "right living could stand on its own ground, and was . . . far more important than belief or unbelief about the matters which Judaism and Christianity both deemed essential."[35] From the beginning the movement has attracted many ex-Jews, but it has not realized its ambition of attracting many ex-Christians. For some of the people associated with it, it has served as a kind of passageway from Judaism to Christianity, allowing the passage to extend over two or three generations and obviating the dramatic and traumatic act of formal conversion by baptism. How conscious all this has been we cannot say; but even if not fully conscious, it may still not be unintended. Since Ethical Culture is an alternative to theistic religion, it would be dishonorable for an Ethical Culturist to abandon Jewish for Christian theism; but if it just happened that one's children or grandchildren were raised as Christians by their non-Ethical Culture parent, should one be a religious fanatic and object?

For two hundred years secularist Jews have tried to evade admitting to themselves that they know what this process is. As experience accumulates with the years, the evasion becomes increasingly difficult. The choice for Jews has not really been whether to be a Jew or a Christian or a secularist. It has been whether to be a Jew or a Christian. Other things being equal, secularism has been, for Jews, a propaedeutic to Christianity.

But Jews know that whatever else they may or may not be, they are not Christians. A growing realization that they have only the two choices rather than three—and the realization may be less than fully conscious or articulate with most—may account in part for the rise in Jewish affiliation, and perhaps sentiment, in the past generation.

Perhaps nothing need be said here about Zionism and Israel,[36] but two other questions must be touched on, if not answered: America as specifically American, and the autonomy of the future with respect to the past.

Whatever may be the present state of the old cultural and historical controversy over American uniqueness—or, as Marxists used to call it, exceptionalism—America is rather special in the Jewish experience.[37] Unlike Europe, America has had no premodern past—no Middle Ages, no feudalism, no union of Throne and Altar. Unlike such multinational states as the Hapsburg empire, ethnically diverse America is a unitary nation; but unlike most unitary nations, it has been religiously pluralist from its earliest days, when the pluralism was Protestant. In America the civic equality of the Jews was never an issue and never had to be legislated, at least nationally. A corollary of the triumph of the American Revolution, so obvious it did not have to be put into words, was that Jews were citizens like all other (white) men. By contrast, the French Revolution is to some degree still, as it once was, the rift that separates France; and the well-being and safety of the French Jews have varied with the fortunes of the French Revolution. As for Germany—

The Jewish folk expression "It's hard to be a Jew" means not only that it is hard to fulfill God's commands as he wishes them to be fulfilled, but also that minority existence is painful. In America today it is less hard to be a Jew, in the second sense, than ever before, anywhere else.

Specifically, therefore, America is different; but the specific difference is enacted within what is generically common to a West that used to be Christendom. The West has become secular—but not all that secular. From the perspective of Jewish experience and of contemporary Jewish reality, the Western secular society is Christian as well as secular—and that includes America.

What of the future? Granted that everything said here has been so and is so, it will not necessarily continue to be so. The future may not be completely independent of the past, but neither is it completely dependent. It has its own realm of autonomy and newness—in a word, of futurity.

Yet, though the openness and newness of the future have been asserted in the past, too, each successive, realized future has been less new than it was expected to be when it was still a future future. All may yet change, and we may be standing at the edge of a newness that will truly be new; but the probabilities are that the past will not give up its old habit of putting its mark on the future.

—Winter 1967

NOTES

1. Before the last partition of Poland in the eighteenth century, there was official talk of emancipating the Jews, whereupon Jewish communal leadership collected money to send representatives to Warsaw to "forestall the danger so that, God forbid, no new reforms be introduced": cited by Salo W. Baron, *A Social and Religious History of the Jews*, 3 vols. (New York, 1937), Vol. 2, p. 243.

2. Cited by Karl Thieme in "Une Enquête: L'Enseignement chrétien concernant les Juifs," *Evidences*, No. 87 (Paris, January–February 1961), p. 5.

3. Those who believed that the state was or should be Christian also had to believe that Jews could not or should not be equal citizens with Christians. Cecil Roth, *A History of the Jews in England*, 3d ed. (Oxford, 1964), p. 249: "As late as 1818 it was possible to maintain in the courts Lord Coke's doctrine that the Jews were in law perpetual enemies, 'for between them, as with the devils, whose subjects they are, and the Christian there can be no peace.'" Yet for the Jews England was a far more tranquil and tolerant land than most.

In the last quarter of the nineteenth century, in Catholic France and Austria and in Protestant Prussia, "Christian" in the name of a political movement or party usually meant "antisemitic." In 1896 the French Dominican Hippolyte Gayraud, for whom "a convinced Christian is by nature a practicing antisemite," urged a convention of the Christian Democrats to have faith that "Christian life itself spreads an effective antisemitism," though "some repressive laws are needed too": Robert F. Byrnes, *Antisemitism in Modern France* (New Brunswick, 1950), pp. 208–209, 215. In our time another French Dominican, a liberal, states the contrary proposition as self-evident; but even in a UNESCO pamphlet he feels he has to justify the record of repressive laws: Yves Congar, *The Catholic Church and the Race Question* (Paris, 1953), pp. 53–54: "As regards religion and respect for the human person and the primary natural rights, the Catholic protest against anti-Semitism is definite, united and absolute; it is equally so in the matter of anti-Jewish discrimination based on racism. As regards the political and sociological aspects of the question, the Catholic attitude is qualified. For example, in pre-1939 Hungary the Catholic bishops, as members of Parliament, accepted the *numerus clausus* laid down for the admission of Jews to certain professions and schools. Here the bishops were acting as national leaders in a country where the Jewish minority (5.3 per cent of the population) had a practical monopoly in a number of spheres (press, theatre, etc.) or at least had a higher proportion of posts than its numbers warranted, even taking its cultural level into account."

The Chief Procurator of the Holy Synod of the Russian Orthodox Church, K. P. Pobedonostsev, was credited with predicting happily that as a result of the policy he was advocating about the Jews, "a third of them would be converted, a third would emigrate, while the rest would die of hunger": Alexander Kornilov, *Modern Russian History* (New York, 1924), p. 284.

In that innocent age before genocide, the Constantinian attitude toward the Jews was generally in consonance with Arthur Hugh Clough's "Latest Decalogue": "Thou shalt not kill; but need'st not strive/Officiously to keep alive."

4. Franklin H. Littell, "The Protestant Church and Totalitarianism (Germany 1933–1945)," in *Totalitarianism*, ed. Carl J. Friedrich (Cambridge, Mass., 1954), pp. 108–119; Uriel Tal, "Liberal Protestantism and the Jews in the Second Reich, 1870–

1914," *Jewish Social Studies* 26 (1964), 23–41; Milton Himmelfarb, "Some Attitudes Toward Jews," *Commentary*, May 1963, pp. 425–428.

5. For instance, Joseph L. Blau, "On the Celebration of Christmas," *Columbia University Rapport: A Newsletter of the Graduate Faculties*, Christmas 1964–New Year 1965, pp. 3–6.

6. Erwin N. Griswold, "Absolute Is in the Dark. . . ," *Utah Law Review* 8 (1963), 173–174.

7. Robert Ulich, "The Educational Issue," in Paul A. Freund and Robert Ulich, *Religion and the Public Schools* (Cambridge, Mass., 1965), p. 40.

8. *Gallagher* v. *Crown Kosher Market*, 366 U. S. 627 (1961): "It would seem that the objectionable language [Lord's Day] is merely a relic." See Milton Himmelfarb, "Festivals and Judges," *Commentary*, January 1963, pp. 67–70.

9. The Ecole Normale Supérieure, the nursery of the French intellectual elite, trains *lycée* professors. It has traditionally been republican, anticlerical, secularist, anti-anti-semitic—in short, it affirms the French Revolution: H. Stuart Hughes, *Consciousness and Society* (New York: Vintage Edition, 1961), pp. 55–57, 347–348. Its student body, which has long included secularist Jews, has in the past generation come to include practicing Catholics as well. Yet Arnold Mandel reports (*American Jewish Year Book* 66 [1965], p. 369): "In May [1964] . . . a sensation was produced by the refusal of the Ecole Normale Supérieure to permit the candidacy of a Jewish student who was a Sabbath observer. . . . The examinations [were] on Saturday . . . as French university examinations often were. He asked their postponement on the basis of the freedom of worship guaranteed by the French constitution. The [Ecole Normale Supérieure] replied that Sabbath observance was incompatible with the duties of a civil servant as well as of a student . . . [and that] the young man should give up the idea of attending the Ecole Normale and becoming a teacher. . . . The young man was finally able to take the examinations, which had been postponed to another date, and to enter the Ecole Normale."

10. A presidential address to the American Historical Association, melancholy over the state of history and the historians, notes that "many of the younger practitioners of our craft, and those who are still apprentices, are products of lower-middle-class or foreign origins, and their emotions frequently get in the way of historical reconstructions. They find themselves in a very real sense outsiders to our past and feel themselves shut out. This is certainly not their fault, but it is true": Carl Bridenbaugh, "The Great Mutation," *American Historical Review* 68 (1963), 322–323.

On America's openness in academic and intellectual life, contrasted to Germany's restrictiveness, see Milton Himmelfarb, "Jewish Sentiment," in *Federal Aid and Catholic Schools*, ed. Daniel Callahan (Baltimore, 1964), pp. 90–91; on Durkheim and Marc Bloch in a culture that has Joan of Arc as a central figure, *idem*, "Two Cheers for Hedonism," *Commentary*, April 1965, pp. 64–65.

11. Out of many possible references, Walter Kolarz, *Religion in the Soviet Union* (New York, 1961), especially pp. 388–389, and Thurston N. Davis and Eugene K. Culhane, "Religion in the Soviet Union," *America*, February 19, 1966, p. 259. For the testimony of an American philosopher, Lewis S. Feuer, "Jews in the Soviet Union," *New Republic*, November 30, 1963, pp. 11–12: of an American scientist, David W. Weiss, "Plight of the Jews in the Soviet Union," *Dissent*, July–August 1966, pp. 447–464.

12. Lucy S. Dawidowicz and Leon J. Goldstein, *Politics in a Pluralist Democracy* (New York, 1963), pp. 76–90; R. V. Burks, *Dynamics of Communism in Eastern Europe* (Princeton, 1961), pp. 163–165; Annie Kriegel, "Léon Blum vu par les communistes," *Preuves*, No. 182 (Paris, April 1966), pp. 44–46; J. L. Talmon, "The Jewish Intellectual in Politics," *Midstream*, January 1966, p. 10: "Their fatherland was the Revolution which had no frontiers; their country was mankind or the proletariat. . . .

What other people had even remotely experienced universalist Messianism with the same intensity? . . . One of Rosa Luxemburg's letters from prison to a Jewish friend [says]: 'Why do you pester me with your Jewish sorrow? There is no room in my heart for the Jewish troubles.' And she goes on to speak most eloquently of the suffering of the Chinese coolies and of the Bantus in South Africa. Twenty-five years later, after the Germans had occupied it, there was not a single Jew left alive in Rosa's native Zamosc, which was also the home-town of I. L. Peretz [the great Yiddish writer]."

13. Bernhard Blumenkranz, *Juifs et chrétiens dans le monde occidental, 430–1096* (Paris and The Hague, 1960), pp. xivff., 159–212, 382–385.

14. Some Christian scholars have long since written major works about Pharisaism (or classical rabbinic Judaism) that try to penetrate behind the propaganda—for example, H. Travers Herford, *The Pharisees* (New York, 1924), and George Foot Moore, *Judaism in the First Centuries of the Christian Era*, 3 vols. (Cambridge, Mass., 1927–1930); but only parochial Jews and Christian specialists seem to know about them.

15. For his proposed new religion of humanity, Hillelism, see Marjorie Boulton, *Zamenhof* (London, 1960), pp. 96–105. Zamenhof's father "had abandoned the observance of Judaism and wished to see Jews assimilated into the Gentile community" (p. 1).

16. S. L. Steinheim, *Moses Mendelssohn und seine Schule* (Hamburg, 1840), pp. 27–28, cited by Isaac E. Barzilay, "Moses Mendelssohn. . . ," *Jewish Quarterly Review* 52 (1961), 92.

17. Cited by Eric Werner, *Mendelssohn: A New Image of the Composer and His Age* (New York, 1963), p. 37.

18. Hugo Bieber (ed.), *Heinrich Heine: Jüdisches Manifest* (New York, 1946), p. 265. Heine also said: "My becoming a Christian is the fault of . . . Napoleon, who really didn't have to go to Russia, or of his teacher . . . of geography, who didn't tell him that in Moscow it's very cold in the winter" (p. 263). Napoleon is the personification of the French Revolution, the friend of secularism and the enemy of religion; if the Revolution had been victorious in Germany, there would have been no need for Heine to be baptized. Cf. Abraham Mendelssohn's statement that as long as the German city he lived in had been under Napoleonic rule, "I reared you without religion in any form," *supra*.

19. Michael Fixler, "Bernard Berenson of Butremanz," *Commentary*, August 1963, pp. 135–143.

20. Robert Pietri, "L'Antisémitisme: A voix haute, à voix basse," *L'Arche*, No. 109 (Paris, March 1966), pp. 20–21.

21. Ernest Renan's grandson was Ernest Psichari. Teilhard de Chardin was a collateral descendant of Voltaire.

22. John M. Oesterreicher, *Walls Are Crumbling: Seven Jewish Philosophers Discover Christ* (New York, 1952), p. 43. All seven were born into Mendelssohnian-secularist families. For Simone Weil, see *nn.* 26 and 31.

23. They had in common a great-grandfather whose pride was that, in the approving words of Leopold Zunz, the founder of modern Jewish scholarship (*Wissenschaft des Judentums*), he had taken "a talmudic academy in which a few general disciplines were tolerated" and made it into an "institution in which Talmud was tolerated, and finally a high school without Talmud instruction." At the time of the Revolution of 1848, he urged the Jews to delete from the Passover Haggadah the passage that says, "Though now we are slaves, next year may we be free men": Nahum Glatzer, *Franz Rosenzweig: His Life and Thought* (Philadelphia, 1963), p. xf.

24. Oesterreicher, p. 331, and see *n.* 26.

25. His parents were Mendelssohnian-secularist. For Russian Orthodox influencies and symbols in *Dr. Zhivago*, see Edmund Wilson, *The Bit between My Teeth* (New York, 1965), pp. 427–430, 441–445, 447–472.

26. Another convert to Russian Orthodox Christianity was the philosopher and theologian Simeon L. Frank. When his posthumous *Reality and Man* (London, 1965) was reviewed in the *Times Literary Supplement* (August 5, 1965, p. 683), the reviewer noted that Frank's "mother's father was a practicing . . . Jew"; he went on to associate Simone Weil and Edith Stein with Frank: "And strangely the three . . . are all of Jewish birth. . . ." It would be more exact to say "Mendelssohnian-secularist Jewish birth." See also Nicolas Zernov, *Russian Religious Renaissance of the Twentieth Century* (London, 1963), especially pp. 158–159ff. For Simone Weil, see Leslie A. Fiedler, "Simone Weil: A Prophet out of Israel," *Commentary*, January 1951, p. 43: "Neither she nor her parents nor two of her grandparents had ever seen the inside of a *shul* [synagogue]"; Martin Buber, "The Silent Question: About Henri Bergson and Simone Weil," *Judaism*, April 1952, pp. 99–109; Hans Meyerhoff, "Contra Simone Weil," *Commentary*, September 1957, pp. 240–249.

27. Vladimir Medem, "Youth of a Bundist," *Commentary*, November 1950, pp. 477–485: "Oddly enough, all [the members of Medem's family] became Lutherans, as did most [Russian] Jews who joined the Christian church. I believe it was because conversion to Protestantism involved less ceremonial and fewer technical difficulties [?] than Orthodoxy. . . . Only I . . . belonged to the . . . Orthodox church" (p. 479).

28. N[ahum] Sokolow, "The Late M. Jean de Bloch," *Jewish Chronicle* (London), 24 January 1902, p. 11: ". . . his biography? The old story 'that is ever new.' His father was . . . intellectually inclined. . . . He . . . went to St. Petersburg. . . . Having gone over to Calvinism, he developed a capacity for commerce and finance which . . . brought him fortune and influence."

29. Ernest Jones, *Life and Work of Sigmund Freud*, 3 vols. (New York, 1953–1957), Vol. 1, p. 167: ". . . Freud thought of joining the Protestant 'Confession' so as to be able to marry without having the complicated Jewish ceremonies [?] he hated so much." Jones was a psychoanalyst. Did he really believe that that was the cause of Freud's thinking of baptism?

30. In the Hapsburg empire in the late nineteenth and early twentieth centuries, the philosopher Franz Brentano persuaded a number of Jewish disciples—including Husserl—to be baptized in order to be eligible for professorships of philosophy, and thus to be able to discharge their moral duty by spreading his philosophical truth in an age when all the positive-historical religions had become outmoded: Samuel Hugo Bergmann, "Emil Utitz: The Tragic Course of a Jewish Scholar" (Hebrew), *Molad*, Nos. 113–114 (Tel Aviv, December 1957), especially pp. 626–627. Brentano, who had been a Catholic priest, "advised his Jewish disciples to affiliate themselves with Protestantism, which he called, half-jestingly and half-respectfully, 'the religion of the irreligious' " (p. 626). Few could resist the argument that it was their moral duty to do the expedient thing, and that a philosopher had no right to attach more importance to changing his official religious designation than to changing his clothes for an official occasion.

Brentano once wrote Bergmann: "For the more gifted of the members of your people there is no moral prohibition against giving lip service to what they do not believe in their hearts": Hugo Bergmann (ed.), "Briefe Franz Brentanos an Hugo Bergmann," *Philosophy and Phenomenological Research* 7 (1946), 103. A 1966 addition to the International Library of Philosophy was Bretano's *The True and the Evident*, a translation of *Wahrheit und Evidenz*. Evidently his philosophical truth permitted or rather required creedal falsehood.

All this must have been in the air for a long time, because not even the figure of changing clothes was new. Much earlier Heine had said of his own baptism: ". . . for me none of the positive religions was superior to any other; I could wear their uniforms out of courtesy—like the Russian Tsar, for example, who, when he does the King of Prussia the honor of attending a review of the troops in Potsdam, dresses as a Prussian

35

guards officer": (Bieber [ed.], *Heinrich Heine*, p. 258). Earlier still, Abraham Mendelssohn had spoken of the Jewish and Christian "forms," *supra*.

31. Simone Weil said that her tradition was "Christian, French, and Greek": Fiedler, "Simone Weil," p. 43.

32. Glatzer, p. xvii.

33. In 1799 a disciple of Mendelssohn's, David Friedländer, anonymously proposed to a Berlin clergyman that the Jews would become Christians if allowed to subscribe to a unitarian rather than a trinitarian credo: Simon Dubnow, *Weltgeschichte des jüdischen Volkes*, 10 vols. (Berlin, 1928–1929), Vol. 8, pp. 202–207.

34. "The first half of the twentieth century for both the Universalists and the Unitarians was from a statistical point of view a time of relative stagnation or decline": Edwin Scott Gaustad, *Historical Atlas of Religion in America* (New York, 1962), p. 128.

35. Henry Neumann, *Spokesmen for Ethical Religion* (Boston, 1951), pp. 3–4. There is a curious lack of objective inquiry into the social history of Ethical Culture.

36. For the "defensive" and the "messianic" elements in Zionist thought, see Arthur Hertzberg (ed.), *The Zionist Idea* (Garden City, N.Y., 1959), especially pp. 29f. See also Isaiah Berlin, "Jewish Slavery and Emancipation," *Forum for the Problems of Zionism, World Jewry and the State of Israel*, No. 1 (Jerusalem, December 1953), pp. 52–68, and Arthur Koestler, *Promise and Fulfilment* (London, 1949), pp. 332–335.

37. The best short statement is Ben Halpern, *The American Jew* (New York, 1956).

.3.

Two Cheers for Hedonism

Four men made the revolution that has transformed the world in the past century: Darwin, Marx, Freud, and Einstein. Two of them, Freud and Einstein, were Jews. (Some friends and many enemies have called Marx a Jew, too, but he disagreed.) How could the Jews, a tiny minority, account for half of the most significant names in the intellectual history of modernity? For it is not mere chance, as we might suspect when dealing with a small number. The Nobel Prize winners are of the second rank in the universe of those four, but they are in the same universe; and while Jews have not been half of all Nobel Prize winners, their share has been strikingly disproportionate.

A persuasive explanation was offered by Thorstein Veblen, in an essay in 1919 on the "Intellectual Pre-eminence of Jews in Modern Europe": the modern Jewish intellectual was alienated—bilaterally, so to speak. Enlightenment had made the Jewish tradition impossible for him, and the Jewish community too confining; but Gentile society was in no hurry to receive him, and with his unillusioned eyes he saw through its conventions more readily than the Gentile intellectual, who had grown up in them.

It is not a bad theory, but it needs to be heated up a few degrees from the low temperature where, as often, Veblen cooled it. His Jewish intellectual wore the mask of a skeptical, objective watcher, but the mask concealed a passionate seer. An exile as much by election as by compulsion, we are told, the Jewish intellectual liked his endless journey; but I agree with those who think that he had had a revelation of journey's end just beyond the horizon, in an edenic recompense for the years of exclusion and in the final abolition of all alienation and division, between men and within men. In short, the Jewish intellectual, as a pure type, was a more ardent believer than his grandfather in the imminent coming of the Messiah. The grand-father had believed so long, had said so often in his prayers, "And though he tarry, yet will I await him," that the waiting had slowly grown less expectant. (He had also inherited institutional defenses against being gulled by impostors.) The grandfather trusted in Messiah, son of David, to redeem him and creation. The grandson trusted even more hotly in Enlightenment, or Science, or History, or Revolution.

For Lewis S. Feuer, who has a chapter on the "Scientific Revolution among the Jews" in his *Scientific Intellectual: The Psychological and Sociological Origins of Modern Science*; Veblen's answer of alienation to the question about intellectual preeminence is wrong— though Veblen is a side issue for him, together with the Jews. Formally the book is a polemic against two accounts of the rise of modern science: the first, originating with Max Weber, which links science, like capitalism, to ascetic Protestantism; and the second, as put forth in Arthur Koestler's *Sleepwalkers*, which roots the thinking of the founders of modern science in ancient, nonscientific systems, like those of Plato or the Pythagoreans, and in nonrational influences of a Freudian character.

Feuer will have none of this. As he sees it, science—together with all other good things—is the fruit of a hedonist-libertarian spirit, and the great enemy of science is the spirit at the opposite pole, masochist asceticism. Medieval Christianity, with its cult of the Virgin and its horror of the body and sexuality, was death to science, as to all clear thinking and healthy feeling. Since Calvinism was only slightly less masochistic-ascetic, it should not be allowed to take the credit for begetting or nurturing science. An instrumental or utilitarian asceticism, on the other hand, could be a rational preparation for libertarian hedonism: for example (it is Feuer's example), the American pioneers' decision to undergo present hardship in the hope of future ease and prosperity.

His strategy here is a little complicated. He has to narrow the distance between hedonism and asceticism, if only because his scientists were not all that hedonistic: Freud's motto was *travailler comme une bête*, "work like a horse." Enter abstinence, to connect moderate hedonism and instrumental asceticism. But abstinence, to anyone so learned in social science as Professor Feuer, ought to suggest Manchester, not the Northwest Territory. The abstinence of the capitalist, his willingness to abstain from consuming all his income this year in exchange for a dividend or interest next year, is his great moral justification in classical economics. Feuer would not want to accept that. Besides, once you start talking about capitalism, Max Weber is back, and the battle of the Protestant ethic—which is by now a weariness of the flesh, anyway—has to be fought all over again. So while Feuer has to bring in abstinence, he wants it to remind us of log cabins, not of dark, satanic mills.

There remains the problem of Confucian China, hedonistic and unscientific. This he solves by calling China's hedonism authoritarian and placing it below instrumental asceticism.

Formally, intellectually, that is what the book is about, but emotionally—and there is a powerful emotion at work in it—it reads like a rallying cry to the defense of something precious and fragile about to be crushed by brutish enemies. The emotion seems excessive. Can Professor Feuer believe that science is in danger? He says that the superiority of French to English scientists in prestige and pay during Napoleon's years was cause and proof of science's vigor in France and decline in England. By those standards, science and scientists have never had it so good. We have been told repeatedly that 90 percent of all the scientists who ever lived are living and working today.

Or has Feuer noted a contraction of the hedonistic libertarian spirit and a boom in masochistic asceticism? There is a lot more hedonistic libertarianism around than there ever was.

Feuer's anxiety for science is not so much that it is being crushed as that it is being betrayed. Classically, science was an enterprise that rejoiced, enlarged, and liberated the men who engaged in it, but it has become bureaucratized, and those who do science are increasingly technicians by outlook rather than whole, free men. Science was supposed to bring us healing and ease, and now threatens us with death and destruction with the consent of most scientists and by the actual will of some. The philosophy of classical modern science was life-affirming and optimistic, but science and its practitioners today tend to be pessimistic. Something, Feuer is saying, has gone dreadfully wrong. His book is a call to science and scientists to return to the old, true ways of the New Philosophy.

We can agree with Feuer that something has gone dreadfully wrong without agreeing about causes or cure. The New Philosophy may have been everything Feuer says it was, but science has to be *wertfrei* (Weber), devoid of all values that are not generated from within science itself, however much those values may have fostered its birth and growth. I am not sure I fully believe that, but I am sure that Feuer must, with his firmly antitraditional and antitranscendental position. And what does it mean to say that science should be optimistic and life-affirming? Feuer himself has been a significant critic of the policy that commands Soviet social science—though he doubts that such a thing exists—literature, and philosophy to celebrate "the singing tomorrows" (if we may transpose French Communist cant to Russia). Huygens wrote Descartes about someone who expected science to put an end to "this vexatious custom of dying," and Feuer cites the hope to show the glad confidence of that dawn when it was bliss to be alive. But what has that to do with science? It is messianism. Behind all prophecies of the death of death stands Isaiah: "He will swallow up death for ever;/And the Lord God will wipe away tears from off all faces. . . ."

André Malraux it was, if I am not mistaken, who said that he stopped being a socialist when it suddenly occurred to him that socialism would not end auto accidents or unrequited love. Evidently he had become one in the first place because he assumed it would. The canonical writings may not have promised that in so many words, but they *are* resolutely optimistic about the life of man on earth. When Marx (or Engels?) was asked how he could reconcile his vision of an endless glorious future for mankind with the conclusion of science—scientific, not messianic science—that the sun would inevitably burn out and our solar system die, he evasively answered that it was too far in the future for us to worry. Are we to reproach science for its unoptimistic finding that the sun is not immortal, let alone human beings? Is science unfaithful to itself when, faithful to its own method, it reaches unoptimistic conclusions? That is what Feuer almost seems to imply—while making an exception for the pessimist Freud, whom he honors.

Science is being bureaucratized—Weber would not have been surprised—and has become the handmaiden of war. With science so big, how can it escape bureaucratization? Feuer certainly does not want science small, since for him its wide diffusion is an index of a society's intellectual, moral, and emotional vigor. As for war, just as Randolph Bourne said that war is the health of the state (and condemned the state), so there is a body of scholarship to show that war has been the health of science. Feuer is pleased about the contributions of French scientists to Napoleon's war effort. In principle, what difference is there between the scientists Feuer likes, who worked on cannon and gunpowder for Napoleon, and the scientists he dislikes, who worked on the Bomb?

It cannot be the betrayal of science and scientists that makes Feuer so uneasy, because he must know that there is no more of it now than there always has been. (About the earlier scientists he is indulgent, even when they stole from each other: hedonistic-libertarian boys will be boys.) I think that what makes him uneasy is something he finds harder to admit than the supposed delinquency of contemporary science. What makes him uneasy is the crisis of hedonistic libertarianism itself. Hedonistic libertarianism is not being overwhelmed from without, it just does not seem to be working out very well.

Ours is a sensate culture, Pitirim Sorokin said. We are fun worshippers, as everyone knows, avid for novelty, impatient with tradition. Put them all together, they spell hedonistic-libertarian. And if the culture in general is h.-l. in a mindless sort of way, the intellectual community and the academy are almost universally h.-l. in full consciousness, by choice and philosophy—one might say by ideology. Now it happens that there is a copious literature about the intellectuals and the academy. Does this literature show us the larger, freer, more autonomous, more joyful men and women of the h.-l. promise? Hardly. For the characters in this literature—and, one must assume, for the people in the world from which it is drawn—hedonistic libertarianism may be a philosophy, but more than that it is a condition they cannot help. It is their absurd, their given. Feuer tells us that acedia, a pronounced listlessness, was the prevailing emotional illness of the Christian Middle Ages, bred by their masochistic asceticism. If that is so, why all the acedia—not under that name, of course—in the literature about the h.-l. crowd?

Revenons à nos Juifs. Feuer has difficulties with the Jews. When he is talking of medieval Christian masochistic asceticism, he praises

Judaism as healthy and moderately hedonistic. Yet when he turns to the Enlightenment, he holds it to be a revolt against "the masochist asceticism of ghetto Judaism." Feuer saves himself from the contradiction by saying that this was not inherent in Judaism but had developed "in response to external pressures":

Spinoza, precursor-rebel against ghetto Jewry and the spokesman for the coming age of the scientific intellectuals, voiced the criticism of the hedonist-libertarian ethic against ghetto masochistic asceticism. "The foundations of their religion," Spinoza wrote, may have "emasculated their minds," but not to such an extent, he hoped, as to preclude their national renaissance. *"Effeminare"* ("to make feminine") was the vivid word Spinoza used to characterize the masochism of the ghetto.

"Masochism of the ghetto" is Feuer, not Spinoza. Spinoza does not say the ghetto emasculated the Jews' character (or minds), he says "the foundations of their religion" did that. But the Jews—not Hebrews or Israelites, Jews—had had the same religion when they rose three times between 66 and 132 and threatened mighty Rome; including, in 115–117, the Diaspora Jews of Egypt, Cyrene, and Cyprus. Spinoza, the son of Marranos who had fled to Holland and the relative of others still in the Iberian peninsula, must have known that if the Jews were dejected and subdued, it was not their religion that had made them so, but persecution.

That being so in the nineteenth as well as the seventeenth century, why, without further discussion, does Feuer approve of the tendency in the Jewish Enlightenment which led to repudiation of Judaism entirely? If Judaism was intrinsically healthy, why not simply have tried to restore its health? Why visit the sins of the "ghetto" upon Judaism?

When he is denying that Sir Isaac Newton was a Calvinist, or even a trinitarian, he shows him to have been instead a follower of Maimonides. The Maimonidean-Jewish philosophy, according to Feuer, was favorable to science, while Calvinism was not. Then why is he so pleased with all those yeshivah students who went overnight from Talmud to atheism?

. . . there was among the Jewish scientists the phenomenon which we can call the "vigor of skipped stages" . . . Orthodox [Jewish] religion was hopelessly more intellectually irrelevant than the various Protestant compromises. The Jewish scientists usually became freethinkers and agnostics; they did not pause in a metaphysical stage.

Poor, pre-Comtean, unscientific Isaac Newton, to have paused in a metaphysical stage! If Maimonides was good enough for Newton, how can Feuer say that "Orthodox religion was hopelessly . . . intellectually irrelevant"? To be sure, the Judaism of Ashkenaz subordinated the philosophical to the rabbinical Maimonides. But again, that was a historically conditioned circumstance, which in principle could have been corrected, and then those new scientists—or, more broadly, the new Enlightened—might have been Jewish and scientific, as Newton had been Christian and scientific. That the possibility did not even suggest itself to most of them (or to Feuer); that so few thought of creating Jewish compromises which would be as reasonably adequate as "the various Protestant compromises"—this must mean something. They were not engaged in an intellectual movement as such, and not in an emotional turn from asceticism to hedonism, but in a new messianism. Its hymn, more eschatological than political, was to be the "Internationale": *"C'est la lutte finale"* ("it is the final struggle") and *"du passé faisons table rase"* ("let us wipe clean the slate of the past").

Spinoza's contemporary, Shabbethai Zevi, called himself a messiah and ended by leading his followers into apostasy. What happened, later, to the messianists of Enlightenment and science? Some of them, tired of waiting for the latter days, apostatized, too. The Reason that had led them to reject Judaism was flexible enough to allow them to embrace Christianity—though a less accommodating Reason might have been expected to find Christianity, which to all the dogmas of Judaism adds many peculiarly its own, the more unreasonable.

The paradigm of all this is the history of the Mendelssohn family. Of Moses Mendelssohn, second only to Spinoza in pathfinding for Jewish modernity, his biographer Steinheim wrote that he "despised apostasy as dishonorable, though he would gladly have joined his friend Lessing in a society where there were neither Jews nor Christians." His son Abraham was less stubborn about honor, perhaps because he lived to be disillusioned by the Revolution's ebb. To maintain a posture of honor long after Lessing's society had failed to arrive—that was too great a strain. So Abraham made the decision that he justified to *his* son, Felix the composer, in this fashion:

. . . my father . . . did not want to be a Christian . . . as long as it was permitted by the [Napoleonic] government [of occupation] under which we lived, I reared you without religion in any form. I wanted you to profess whatever your convictions might favor or, if you prefer, whatever expediency might dictate. But it was not so to be. . . . Naturally, when you consider the scant value I placed on any form in particular, I felt no urge to choose the form known as Judaism. . . . Therefore I reared you as Christians, Christianity being the . . . form . . . most accepted by the majority of civilized people. Eventually, I myself adopted Christianity, because I felt it my duty to do for myself that which I recognized as best for you. . . .

Feuer is gentle and understanding with the *meshummadim*:

. . . the enlightenment in Germany was followed quickly by the conversion of many middle-class Jewish families to Christianity. . . . [The mathematician] Leopold Kronecker—liberal in his youth, later successful in business, a cynical realist in politics—embraced Christianity in his last years. . . .

The large number of converts . . . , among the German groups especially, testified to an increasing identification with German liberal culture.

What he means, or should mean, is that they grew cynical about honor and about the dream of an imminent day of judgment when the *infâme* would be *écrasé*. He should not confuse the Christianity they entered with liberalism. It was German Lutheranism. And Kronecker did not need to be converted to do mathematics—at sixty the bulk of his work was behind him—he needed it to be a professor. Yet he is offered to us, this man whose vanity and ambition were so paltry that he longed only to be called *Herr Professor*, as an exemplar of hedonistic-libertarian virtue! Spinoza had refused both invitations, to become a Christian and to become a professor. (When the *meshummad* Heinrich Heine was on his mattress-grave, he was asked how he felt. He answered, "All *meshummadim* should feel how I do.")

The German apostates did not even have the excuse of some of the Russians, that through baptism they could help the Jews—like the banker and economist Ivan Bloch and the scholar Daniel Chwolson, especially Chwolson. He is said to have been asked, after his conversion, why he had done it, and to have answered that he had done it from conviction. "Conviction?"—"Yes, I was convinced that it was better to be a professor in St. Petersburg than a *melammed* [an infants' teacher] in Eyshishok." Chwolson's help to the Jews included scholarship about the crucifixion and a refutation of the blood libel.

Yet, granted that it was a fine thing to be a professor in St. Petersburg, was it the finest? A German contemporary of Chwolson's, Seligmann Baer, lived out his days as, precisely, a *melammed*, though he was a leading authority on the Masorah and though his *Seder 'Avodat Yisrael* remains the best critical edition of the Jewish prayer book we have. Chwolson and Baer were born in 1819 and 1824, respectively. Arnold Ehrlich, born in 1848, is still cited for his sensitive notes on biblical Hebrew. Having immigrated to the United States, Ehrlich, too, was a *melammed*—after graduating from an earlier job, rolling barrels. The scholars Baer and Ehrlich have stood up better than Chwolson and, though I know nothing of mathematics and incomparables should not be compared, probably not worse than Kronecker. The men Baer and Ehrlich earn our admiration as Chwolson and especially Kronecker cannot.

Why, then, does Feuer burden himself with a Kronecker? Here we return, finally, to Veblen. The conversions, the "identification with German liberal culture," are to refute alienation, which has a nasty, ascetic ring to it. Identification is the opposite of alienation, and those nineteenth-century Jews, with or without conversion, were identified (he says). He forgets that he has earlier complimented Einstein—invoking also Newton, Freud, and Darwin—for *not* seeking identification:

I [Einstein] have never belonged wholeheartedly to any country or state, to my circle of friends, or even to my own family. . . . I do not regret being cut off from the understanding and sympathy of other men. . . . I am compensated for it in being rendered independent of the customs, opinions, and prejudices of others. . . .

Feuer quotes Cecil Roth:

It was unnecessary for the Italian Jews, as it was for some of their coreligionists beyond the Alps, to become assimilated to the ruling culture. . . . Their Italianità was already so complete that the period of transition was reduced to almost nothing. . . .

Then he says this about Emile Durkheim:

Durkheim, the scion of a rabbinical family, was the first to teach sociology in France. . . . [In the 1920s Friedrich Gundolf—born Gundelfinger—a friend of Stefan George's, was curious to know what sociology was all about, so he attended a sociological congress in Berlin. Afterward he said, "Now I know what sociology is. Sociology is a Jewish sect."] Yet [Durkheim,] this student of "anomie," of alienation, was himself a person who experienced a fullness of identification with French life. . . . Despite the anti-Semitism of the Dreyfus years, "he was a soulful French patriot." . . . In his words, *"La Patrie, la Révolution française, Jeanne d'Arc . . . are sacred to us, and we will allow no one to touch them."*

For one who acknowledges his intellectual debt to Marx and Freud, Feuer is surprisingly ready to take things at their face value.

Two Cheers for Hedonism

The Italianità of the Italian Jews and the Frenchness of a Jew like Durkheim (or the great historian Marc Bloch, who was also to speak of reverent love for both the French Revolution and Joan of Arc as the indispensable element in really being French) were complete— to a point. What that point was we can infer from Durkheim and Bloch's recognition of Joan of Arc. The gentile Voltaire had been far less respectful of Joan than these two Jews, but between his time and theirs it had been firmly decided that no true Frenchman could approve the Enlightenment's ribald skepticism about her.

Later another French sociologist, the Protestant André Siegfried (no friend of the Jews), was to call the village *curé* part of the domestic furniture of France. You could be clerical or anticlerical, that had nothing to do with whether the *curé* belonged to you. What you could not be was Protestant. So that a Protestant, when he was honest with himself, felt like an outsider. And yet the Protestants have deep roots in France and can recall glorious victories and defeats almost as glorious. When one of *their* elite left, it was not for a professor's chair. It was for a king's throne.

All the more must a Jew have felt like an outsider. He could associate himself easily enough with the French Revolution; but St. Joan? Charles VII, whom she caused to be consecrated in Rheims Cathedral—where all French kings were consecrated, in honor of St. Remigius, bishop of Rheims, who baptized Clovis—was the ancestor of Their Most Christian Majesties and the descendant of St. Louis, who burned the Talmud, and Philip the Fair, who banished the Jews. After all, Durkheim was a rabbi's son. How could he not feel alienated, for instance, during the bad years of the *affaire?* Dreyfus wanted to identify, too. He, too, was a patriot (or jingo), of whom they said that if he had not been Dreyfus, he would have been anti-Dreyfusard. With those people, even in more quiet times it was a matter of so-near-and-yet-so-far, and perhaps that is the hardest alienation. Either they were at war with themselves for not being able to relate simply to Joan of Arc, or at war with her for standing between them and the identification they could never fully claim.

Across the Rhine *la patrie* was *das Vaterland,* and the German Jews of their outlook matched them in asserting an identification that was more wish than reality. Otherwise there is no accounting for the things that some allowed themselves to say: e.g., Ludwig Geiger, whose father, Abraham, was a far more distinguished rabbi and scholar than Durkheim's. When a German Jewish relief committee was collecting money for the victims of pogroms in Russia, Ludwig raged. How dared they send all that money out of Germany? Could they find no German fellow-nationals who needed help?

Feuer does not mention Bernard Berenson, whose beautiful vulgarity can teach us much. The Italianità of the Italian Jews, the Frenchness of Durkheim and Bloch? Berenson knew that in Boston he had to be an Episcopalian and in Florence a Catholic. From Italy he once wrote his future wife:

[The art historian Gustavo Frizzoni] is a trifle obtuse and I hope you won't think I am too intolerant, but I am sure it is due to his being a Protestant. I simply can't tell you how indecent it seems to me for an Italian to be a Protestant.

In John Milton's eyes the Italian Protestants had been slaughtered saints; in Berenson's, they were indecent, "a branch that has been hacked off from its parent trunk." Italian Protestants evidently reminded him of the Jews. What right had they to persist, and by their persistence reproach him for his life? Berenson was as good a hedonist-libertarian as Kronecker. Not for them minority stubbornness. If *dis victrix placuit causa, victa Catoni,* then Cato was not merely a fool for refusing to favor the winner, he was downright immoral.

Durkheim was born in 1858, the philosophers Henri Bergson and Edmund Husserl—who do not figure in Feuer's book—in 1859. The German Jew Husserl, h.-l. and irreligious, became a Lutheran because, like Kronecker, he wanted to be a professor—though Hermann Cohen could be a philosopher and a professor and a very good Jew, and though in any case it is unnecessary to be a professor to do philosophy. (Husserl is said to have later regretted his conversion.) The French Jew Bergson, greatly attracted to Catholicism, refused baptism because he would not turn his back on his people in their danger. (He was attracted to Catholicism, a Jew likes to assume, because his was an *anima naturaliter religiosa* and the religion that French culture presented to him was Catholicism. The Judaism that he knew, the Judaism of his milieu, was respectable and quite, quite dead. It was from a similar Judaism, in Germany, that Franz Rosenzweig almost went over to Lutheranism, for religious and not careerist reasons.) I do not know who is the better philosopher of the two, Bergson or Husserl, but I know whom we cannot help regarding as the better man. Does hedonistic libertarianism nevertheless prefer Husserl? So much the worse for it.

—*April 1965*

.4.

Reason Thunders in Her Crater

An exercise in hymnology may tell us something about ourselves.

Two hundred years ago, when an English Jew heard "God Save the King" he must have thought it entirely natural for such a song to be sung. A straightforward piece of tribal patriotism, it expresses a simple desire—that *we* shall defeat *them*. There is nothing highfalutin about it, no pretense that we, or "our gracious king," should win because we are better or wiser or more deserving.

Today such sentiments may be less respectable, but they are none the weaker. When the Mets were making their drive for first place in the Eastern Division of the National League, and then for the pennant, and at last for the Series, my family and my neighbors were not indifferent. We hoped, we feared, we desponded, we rejoiced. We did not pretend that the Mets were purer than the other teams, nobler, more liberal, more the instrument of History. It was enough for us that they were *our* team. To judge by the accounts of rioting over soccer games in all three worlds—capitalist, socialist, and Third—the simple, reflexive we-emotion of "God Save the King" is still distributed pretty widely.

Of course, two hundred years ago that English Jew could not really feel himself to be included in the "we" of the anthem. The king was the chief of a clan, an extended family, but the Jew was not of that family. Neither the others nor he thought he was. To be part of the family you had to be a Christian, or better, a Protestant. A Jew was a guest. There were bad gentiles and good gentiles. The English were good. They were better hosts than almost anyone else.

Perhaps, that Jew may have thought, part of their goodness was to be explained by the debt of their culture and religion to his.

"God save the king," itself, is from Psalm 20:10(9) (in the Septuagint-Vulgate tradition; the King James Version, following the received Hebrew text, punctuates differently): "Lord, save the king. . . ."

47

"O Lord our God, arise,/Scatter his enemies" is from Numbers 10:35, which we sing when we remove the Torah scroll from the Ark: "Rise up, O Lord, and let thine enemies be scattered." (Didn't Montgomery, a bishop's son, use this in one of his orders of the day?)

The charming "Confound their politics,/Frustrate their knavish tricks" is from Psalm 33:10: "The Lord bringeth the counsel of the heathen to nought,/He maketh the devices of the people of none effect." (Revised Standard Version: ". . . he frustrates the plans of the peoples.")

"Thy choicest gifts in store,/On him be pleased to pour" may be a recollection of I Kings 3:12,13 (God's answer to Solomon's prayer): ". . . lo, I have given thee a wise and understanding heart. . . . And I have also given thee . . . both riches and honour. . . ."

"Long may he reign" need not be from the Bible, but a Bible-reading people knew it could find "Long live the king" there. And on the principle that divinity doth hedge a king, what the Bible says of God the anthem can say of the king (as with scattering his/Thine enemies). "Long may he reign," therefore, may reflect Psalm 146:10, or Exodus 15:18: "The Lord shall reign for ever (and ever)."

A Jew who prays with any frequency will know nearly all these verses by heart.

The premodern quality of "God Save the King" is best seen in "May he defend our laws." To defend the laws was to preserve them unchanged. For premodern people, change and novelty are evil.

Is there a useful lesson here for moderns? If, as the Mets have taught us, the we-emotion underlying "God Save the King" has not disappeared, perhaps the emotion for which change and novelty are evil has not disappeared, either. Politicians or concerned citizens who keep urging people to vote for this candidate or support that program because he or it will effect change may be less persuasive than they think, or than they could be. In the last century a British royal duke, retiring after nearly forty years as commander in chief, addressed his fellow officers somewhat as follows: "My lords and gentlemen, in my lifetime I have seen many changes in the Army. Many changes. But I can say this, that every change has come at the right time. And the right time for a change is when it can't be helped." The duke was not speaking for the people. His interests and theirs differed, and differ. But his ducal mind may be closer than better-endowed and better-educated minds to the mind of the people.

These days why do politicians and concerned citizens say "change"? Why not say "progress"? No doubt "progress" has for years had an embarrassingly quaint ring about it to intellectual ears, and even the people seem more skeptical about it than before. Yet "progress" still sounds better than "change": I know of a Progress Laundry and even a Progressive Cigar Store and Luncheonette; and Progresso foods and condiments do well in the supermarkets. Can it be that those who campaign on a platform of change, when they could be four-square for progress, want to lose? Does winning scare them?

Political modernity comes in with the American and French Revolutions. Here the ancestral, the hereditary, the ascriptive are put aside. Instead, universal reason and universal ideals are appealed to: in "My Country, 'Tis of Thee" liberty, freedom, freedom's holy light —which, like Emile Durkheim's sacred French Revolution and *amour sacré de la Patrie*, sounds not quite so desacralized as modernity is supposed to be—and in the "Marseillaise" *liberté, liberté chérie*.

For modern Jews this was promising. (By definition, modern Jews were those who had become tired of being outsiders, even though comfortable or tolerated.) In the name of universal reason and ideals, all would be active and equal citizens alike, and Jews would come in from the cold. Actually, to be universally rational and idealistic you may have to abolish all distinctions between Christian and Jew. Has the French Revolution adopted a Declaration of the Rights of Man and Citizen? Then maybe there should no longer be Christian and Jew at all, only men who are citizens.

But the very anthems of the American and French Revolutions, "My Country 'Tis of Thee" and the "Marseillaise," already hint at what history is yet to unveil: universal reason and universal ideals are all very well, but they do not put an end to family feeling. The anthems are not squeamish about family words or images—land where my fathers died, our fathers' God (many Jewish prayers are to "our God and our fathers' God"), *Patrie, parricides*. If you speak of fathers, I cannot forget that while officially I may be in, my fathers were out. And what is this about God? God belongs in "God Save the King." What is He doing in a song for moderns? For moderns, universal reason and ideals should be enough. Look forward not backward. (If only those others, who are or used to be Christians, were as modern and forward-looking as we, who used to be Jews!)

One may say that those Americans fudged their revolution from the beginning: after all, the very oath of office their Constitution prescribes for their President—to "defend the Constitution"—recalls the "defend our laws" of the premodern "God Save the King." It should not be surprising, therefore, that the Americans also had the bad taste or inconsistency to put God into their national anthem. Decidedly, better things are to be expected of the French. If so, what is one to make of the "Marseillaise"? In their revolutionary hymn why should the French, of all people, invoke *grand Dieu*?

With fathers and *Dieu* the bourgeois American and French Revolutions took back what they gave with freedom and *liberté*. The revolution that would let the out be truly in was still to be consummated. With that revolution, everyone would forget about ancestors. The past would disappear.

That is the promise or the vision of the hymn that celebrates the revolution which will complete all that is incomplete. In the "Internationale" one sings, *"Du passé faisons table rase,"* let us erase the past. Thus is Reason obeyed, thus will Reason exercise her full and rightful dominion.

There is nothing cool about Reason. The "Internationale" invokes *la raison* rather more passionately than "My Country 'Tis of Thee" invokes "our fathers' God" or the "Marseillaise" *grand Dieu*. The singers of the "Internationale" worship (or worshipped) *la raison* more passionately than the singers of the other anthems worship their conventional, fathers' God. The "Internationale" is the hymn of political Jehovah's Witnesses, for whom eschatology is the news of the day: *"C'est la lutte finale . . . demain . . ."*—final [!] struggle, tomorrow.

The most vigorous image is of Reason in action: *"La raison tonne en son cratère, c'est l'éruption de la fin,"* Reason is thundering in her crater, the end is bursting forth. Reason reveals herself thunderously, volcanically.

Where else have we been told of a thunderous, volcanic Revelation?

. . . there were thunders and lightnings and a thick cloud upon the mountain . . . , so that all the people who were in the camp trembled. . . . And Mount Sinai was all in smoke, because the Lord had come down upon it in fire; . . . and the whole mountain quaked greatly. And as the sound of the trumpet grew louder and louder, Moses spoke, and God answered him in thunder. . . . And God spoke all these words, saying: "I am the Lord your God, who brought you out of the land of Egypt, the house of bondage. You shall have no other gods besides Me. . . . for I the Lord your God am a jealous [*or* impassioned] God. . . ."

In "God Save the King" the biblical echo needs no explanation. But the "Internationale" expressly denies God: "*Il n'est pas de . . . Dieu. . . .*" No matter. In secular messianism, substantive dominates adjective.

Even for those who wish to abolish memory, the memory of Sinai persists, the repressed returns. A jealous (or impassioned) deity thunders from his volcano. People believe in that deity less because they heed universal Reason, as they may have supposed, than because, trembling at the foot of a volcano quaking and flaming and thundering, they have had a particular revelation.

By now, to be sure, for some the belief has become more conventional, less passionate. Reason is *their* fathers' god.

—*January* 1970

.5.

A Pole in Denmark

The influence of wrong texts and interpretations: Magna Carta. Now we are taught that in its time Magna Carta was a defense of feudal powers and privileges against necessary central government, but the Englishmen who overthrew Stuart absolutism appealed in good conscience to the precedent of the Great Charter of liberty under law. Or Shakespeare: for the authorities, the last time I looked, Hamlet's too, too solid flesh was too, too sullied. And so with that verse in Job, "Though He slay me, yet will I trust in Him." Bible scholars now prefer "let Him slay me, I will not quail" (reading *lo'* "not" with the *kethibh* rather than *lo* "to him" with the *qere* and transposing *'yhl* to *'hyl*).

Job affirms God's justice. At a burial a mourner recites the *zidduq ha-din*, the justification of the Judgment, beginning with Deuteronomy 32:4: "The Rock, His doing is perfect;/Indeed, all His ways are justice." When the mourner goes home he must not *lern*: learning Torah—which of course is not only Pentateuch, and not only Bible, but also the whole corpus of Rabbinical literature—is a delight (Ps. 119:70: "I delight in Thy Torah") and therefore forbidden to him,

51

together with less recondite delights. But there is a way out. Since it would be too cruel to withhold Torah from a Jew altogether, a distinction is made between studying Torah, which remains forbidden, and merely reading in the Bible. That is permitted, provided the reading is appropriately somber: Job, for instance. Job, after rejecting conventional theodicy, ends by affirming a divine justice invisible to human eyes.

"Though He slay me, yet will I trust in Him" has always been understood to teach the faithfulness unto death. It has taught that lesson even to Juliusz Katz-Suchy. Banished by the Communist government of Poland as a Zionist—i.e., as a Jew—Katz-Suchy is now lecturing at a Danish university. In Warsaw he was a professor of international relations. Earlier he had been Polish representative at the United Nations, where he was the consummate Stalinist. Then the order against Stalinism was passed down, and he dutifully became a liberal: what's in a name? What he could not become was a non-Jew, though the only thing Jewish about him was what he thought to be an irrelevant genealogical datum.

In Denmark Katz-Suchy has told a reporter that the anti-Jewish campaign in Poland, of which he is one of many victims, is used to "exploit presumed [!] anti-Semitism among Poles," but that "the presumption is an error. . . . " According to Freud, it is not when an intelligent man says an intelligent thing that he most reveals himself: what else should he say? He most reveals himself when he says a silly thing. A UN representative and university professor may be expected to have an I.Q. above rather than below 100. Yet not only does Katz-Suchy speak of presumed Polish antisemitism, he also says: "I am still a Pole and Poland will always be my country"; and, "Even if some of my ideas have let me down. I still believe in socialism. . . ."

For Katz-Suchy, socialism—that heavenly word, Mesopotamia—must mean Marxism. (Surely it cannot mean what Harold Wilson represents.) Among other things, Marxism means atheism. Marxist atheism is more than the theoretical negation of God. It is also the insistence on men's practical duty to negate God if they are to be men not babies, active not passive, autonomous not heteronomous, rational not irrational. If we are looking for theodicy, usually we do not go to a Marxist. Nevertheless, theodicy is the Marxist Katz-Suchy's matter and manner. Let us put the two affirmations side by side:

A Pole in Denmark

<table>
<tr><td>JOB</td><td>KATZ-SUCHY</td></tr>
<tr><td colspan="2" align="center">*concessive clause*</td></tr>
<tr><td>Though He slay me . . .</td><td>Even if some of my ideas have let me down . . .</td></tr>
<tr><td colspan="2" align="center">*apodosis*</td></tr>
<tr><td>. . . yet will I trust in Him. . . .</td><td>. . . I still believe in socialism. . . .</td></tr>
</table>

The structure is the same—with some slight literary superiority in Job—and so is the thought: above all, "trust in Him"="believe in socialism." And not the least of the irony is that Katz-Suchy's confession of faith corresponds not to the modern but to the traditional reading of that verse. The Marxist reveals himself as a pious, submissive believer—far more submissive, far less Promethean, than Job himself. (Marx was a Promethean.) Traditionalists and moderns agree that Job's verse ends, " . . . but I will argue my ways to His face." Katz-Suchy's sentence ends, " . . . the future is socialism."

How do you reason with a man who, in despite of all the evidence, wills himself to believe? Not the capitalist countries and, aside from the Arab states, not even the all but fascist ones are expelling and persecuting Jews. Some people deny that the Soviet Union and Poland are really socialist, but we have not heard Katz-Suchy deny it. A country that this socialist accepts as socialist persecutes and banishes him, and others like him, on racial grounds alone—for under his socialism, "Zionist" again means what "non-Aryan" meant under Nazism. One may almost say that the willfulness of Katz-Suchy's belief is Christian. It was from a Church Father and not a Rabbi that our stock of quotations received *credo quia absurdum*, "because it is absurd, I believe." Jewish believers have tried to be more reasonable than that. The Rabbis know of a foolish piety, and do not like it.

As for Katz-Suchy's pledge of allegiance—"I am still a Pole and Poland will always be my country"—two jokes are current:

1. The five thousand Jews remaining in Poland have stood firm against successive opportunities, inducements, and pressures to emigrate. They are as Polish as Katz-Suchy, if that were possible, and as little Jewish. If tomorrow the borders of Poland were opened wide, all 32 million Poles would run—except those five thousand.

When Hitler came to power, Erich-Maria Remarque was one of the few German writers neither of the Left nor non-Aryan to go into exile. The Nazi Ministry of Culture cared not a whit about the non-

53

Aryans nor about Aryans like Heinrich and even Thomas Mann, distinguished though they were. Because the culture bureaucrats did care about Remarque, whose self-exile they thought damaging to the reputation of the New Germany, they sent an emissary to persuade him to return. The emissary warned Remarque that away from the German landscape—the literal, physical landscape and the figurative one of German speech and habit—a German, especially a German writer, must be homeless. "That would bring tears to my eyes," Remarque is said to have answered, "if I were a Jew."

2. Someone much like Katz-Suchy went to Israel. In Israel he would be a Polish Communist. In Poland he would be a dirty Jew.

—*April 1970*

. 6 .

Power to the People

Typically, Black Panthers and other black nationalists, or asserters of *négritude*, are not impressed by advice from Jews offered as success-story lessons from Jewish history—for example, the advantages of mutual aid. When our advice is not greeted with the respect or gratitude we know it deserves, we are hurt. Like the Gilbert and Sullivan character, we complain: "And yet everybody says I'm such a disagreeable man!/And I can't think why!" Maybe they would listen if we spoke of Jewish mistakes and failures.

"Power to the people!" the Panthers cry. If the slogan is meant to be taken literally, they are asking for trouble. An American referendum, the voice of the people, will be antiblack. Those least unfriendly to black men and women are not the people but the Constitution, the courts, the elites. Imagine the power of the American people not hedged about by the Constitution and all the rest, and imagine no impediments to a nationwide referendum about deporting blacks to Africa. A bettor might hesitate to offer even money on its defeat.

Since the Panthers know that as well as anyone, their slogan is not to be taken literally. The "people" of the slogan must be like the "people" in "people's democracy," a small fraction of the people.

Power to the People

"Power to the people" means power for those who rule over the people to keep power from the people.

Why should revolutionaries want a government that keeps power from the people? Reword the question: why should they want "socialism"? Socialism is the remedy for a disease, capitalism. The ravages of capitalism are exploitation, poverty, inequality. Transparently opposed to the needs of the people, capitalism preserves itself by dividing the people, inciting national, religious, and racial hatreds. Only socialism will cure exploitation, poverty, and inequality, and only socialism has an interest not in cultivating but in uprooting national, religious, and racial hatreds. At the start, the wisest, most trustworthy part of the people see to it that the rest of the people shall not have power to indulge the depraved tastes they were seduced into by the capitalists in the bad old days; but soon, soon the masses, now temporarily being coerced toward virtue, will no longer need coercion. Made into new men by socialism, they will not be tempted by archaic vices. They will be immune both to selfish individualism and to national, religious, and racial hatred. Then they will be given their power. Soon, soon. In the meanwhile, to hasten the reign of virtue, the wise and trustworthy are busy in the jails and execution cellars.

What more piteous than a vigorous theory done in by an insensate fact? As Mr. Katz-Suchy's experience testifies, if not his words, the people in the people's democracies are so bossed around by "the people," so enraged by haughtiness and yammer and mess and cruelty, that they solace themselves by turning upon old enemies. Jews become doubly hateful, because conspicuous in the service of "the people." And "the people" do not mind if the masses blow off steam so harmlessly. After all, "the people" calculate—Stalin taught them—we can spare those Jews; they have served their purpose; you don't have to be Jewish to like being in the secret police, we can find replacements. If the masses do not themselves think of their old sport, we can give them a signal.

If "power to the people" ever happens in America, most Americans will hate more intensely than ever. To invert an expression of the civil-rights days, "there will be too many black faces": too many associated with intolerable reminders of "socialism" and "power to the people," too many—it is inevitable—beneath the helmets of "the people's" police (Volkspolizei). What better bone for the rulers of the American people's democracy to throw the masses, what better distraction, than to put the blame for everything on the blacks, to

55

encourage a hatred of them that hardly needs encouragement, and finally to kick them out—but not all at once, because as whipping boys they are too valuable to let go of completely?

That is a Jewish lesson that Katz-Suchy and the five thousand teach.

Say this for the Panthers: it is not easy to picture one of *them* hounded out by "the people" he had served, telling a Brazilian or Indonesian reporter, "I am still an American and America will always be my country"; or saying that the purpose of the antiblack campaign in "socialist" America was to exploit presumed racism among American whites, and that the presumption was an error.

—April 1970

.7.

The Topless Tower of Babylon

When the whole world had the same language and the same words . . . men said to one another, . . . "Come, let us build ourselves a city, and a tower with its top in the heavens, and make a name for ourselves; or we shall be scattered all over the world." But when the Lord had come down to see, . . . He thought, "Well, it is because they are one people, all with the same language, that they have begun to accomplish this, and now nothing they decide to do will be out of their reach. We had better go down and confuse their language there, so that they will no longer be able to understand one another's speech." Then the Lord scattered them all over the world, and they stopped building the city. That is why it was named Babel—because the Lord had made a babble there of the whole world's language. . . .

This myth is as compelling as the earlier one in Genesis, of Eden and the expulsion from the Garden. The myth of Eden explains why we are unhappy. Knowledge and thought, sundering us from the animal life of instinct, have given us shame and guilt. Knowledge and thought have made us mortal: it is because we know we are going to die that we are mortal. We have subjugated nature, only to be haunted by that dream, or anamnesis—the dawn-age water hole at which a man drinks, an animal crouching side by side with the other animals. He does not know he is going to die, does not cast the

56

shadow of death over his life, does not torment himself with reproach and judgment. What happiness to be an animal! Still greater happiness it would be to know and think and yet to be animal. In the Garden that was not yet impossible, but God has cast us out of the Garden. Or else a fatal weakness in us has led us to body forth from our self-alienation, in order to perfect our unhappiness, a God or gods.

But even granted that that water hole and the Garden are no longer for us, why should the City and the tower with its top in the heavens not be for us? Why have we not built on earth a Heavenly City? The Bible itself blurts out the answer. It is religion's fault: God was jealously fearful of what men could achieve undistracted and undivided. (Or was it the gods who were jealously fearful? In those Genesis verses the Lord comes down and scatters, in the singular; but "we" are exhorted to go down and confuse, with plural verbs. Those could be plurals of majesty, but equally they could be literal.)

If religion used to divide, today we are rather less religious than we used to be. What else, by dividing us, still keeps us from building the City? Again the myth instructs us. Speaking one language we would be undivided, and undivided we could build. The multitude of religions may do less harm than it used to, in a more credulous time, but the multitude of languages is as bad as ever. It is appropriate that Zamenhof, the Jew who thought of Esperanto as the one, unifying language, should also have thought of Hillelism as the one, unifying religion.

More than anyone else, a modern Jew would yearn for the end of religious difference. In the past, religious difference had caused persecution of the Jews; and even now, even in the most tolerant countries, even if you were only ambiguously a Jew, it caused you some discomfort. You could not really approve what your forerunner Heine had done, half-heartedly—the cynical baptism, the second-best of pretending to acquiesce in an official incorporation of your small tribe into a larger. You wanted more than an equivocal exemption from paying your tax for difference, you wanted the honorable transcendence of difference. With Zamenhof, Hillelism; in the United States, Ethical Culture.

As to language, if Zamenhof had been alive he would have predicted that a General de Gaulle would do battle against *le franglais* and the expansion of English. Zamenhof was not only a modern Jew, he was also a modern Polish Jew (the son of a *maskil*, an Enlightener). He lived amid Polish, Russian, German, Lithuanian, Ukrain-

57

ian, Yiddish, Hebrew; and he could not believe that one would yield peacefully to another. He could more easily believe that all would yield to something else entirely. For Poles, Esperanto might mean the defeat of Polish, but at least it would not mean the victory of Russian. Poles would be less ready to speak Russian, or Russians to speak Polish, than both to speak Esperanto—just as Jews would be less ready to become Christians, or Christians to become Jews, than both to become Hillelists, or Ethical Culturists. Universalism is the peace with honor that ends the wars of particularisms.

There is a similar argument for socialism. Is not war the ultimate, most inhuman division of men from men? Capitalism means war. Socialism means internationalism: the socialist hymn is the "Internationale." It was to Jews above all that the internationalist promise of the socialist revolution appealed. Jews were conspicuous in the opposition to Stalin and his Socialism in One Country.

As a boy I would sometimes glimpse, out of the corner of an eye, certain people who though Yiddish-speaking or -accented were unlike my parents or that other kind of middle-aged Jew I was aware of, the member of the Workmen's Circle. These odd people were vaguely bohemian, as well as vegetarian and unconventionally socialist, or anarchist. (Not many were Communists, I think. I do not associate them with the newspaper *Freiheit*.) They also had a way of letting you know they were Esperantists. In short, if I thought of it at all I thought Esperanto went with anarchist vegetarianism, or vegetarian anarchism. After I had begun to reflect on such things, it appeared to me that logically some Communists, too, ought to have been Esperantists. And since what can be will be, the missing link has turned up.

Juliusz Katz-Suchy is the refugee in Denmark who once was the ambassador of "socialist" Poland to the United Nations and then to India. The American Hebrew-language weekly *Ha-do'ar* has published an open letter to him from a classmate in the University of Lwow in the early 1930s. Do you remember, the classmate asks Katz-Suchy, our professor of economics, author of the plan for a cold, economic pogrom against Polish Jewry? Do you remember how the Polish and Ukrainian students used to beat Jews, in or out of the university? Do you remember the segregated benches they made us occupy? In the Jewish students' association I was president of the Zionists. Do you remember how I used to deliver an oration in Hebrew at our annual assemblies? Because you Communists objected to Zionism and to the "dead and reactionary" Hebrew language, your spokesman used to deliver a counter-oration—in Esperanto, the language of brotherhood and the friendship of peoples.

In Denmark Katz-Suchy has insisted that he is a Pole and that Poland is his country. More recently, attending a scholarly conference in Jerusalem, he has insisted on his family's centuries of settlement in Poland and on the loveliness of his birthplace. Whatever happened to his Esperanto and internationalism?

Esperanto was necessary for Katz-Suchy at a certain time. The Zionists and Hebraists challenged him and his friends with this: "We are Jews. What are you?" Speaking in Esperanto and invoking the Revolution that would build the Heavenly City, Katz-Suchy (or anyone else like him) could answer: "Your question belongs to the dead past, with its petty and murderous division of men into tribes and dialects and superstitions. You ask what I am, and you think that if I don't want to say, a Jew, I will have to say, a Pole; and then you will laugh. How foolish I must be, you will think, to imagine that the centuries of Jewish settlement in Poland have made Poles of Jews! For the real Poles a Pole is a Catholic, or just possibly a lapsed Catholic, whose grandparents spoke Polish not Yiddish and prayed in Latin not Hebrew. So I answer you in Esperanto, and the medium is the message. I belong to no tribe, the dead have no claim on me. I define myself by the future not the past. I am of those who are building the City of one mankind, with one language."

At the time Katz-Suchy may have thought he meant what he was saying, because only later would a Jew's laughable claim to being a Pole become less obviously or less permissibly laughable. Then, the Revolution having been imposed, he was in and Esperanto lost its charms. Esperanto-universalism, which had been thought a destination, proved to have been only a way station—or a decompression chamber. The *function* of Esperanto-universalism had been to allow Katz-Suchy and his friends to pass from their own particularity, which they despised, to another, which they valued; and to conceal from themselves what they were doing. The concealment was necessary if they were to avert the self-contempt that Heine's shuffle to the baptismal font had cost him.

In Katz-Suchy's triumph he did not know that the dialectic of Revolution had yet a further turn to make. In his defeat he knows. Now the new Poles are denying his claim to the quality of Pole as effectively as the old Poles denied it—more effectively, in fact, because the old ones did not expel him, and told fewer lies about him. They did not call him a Zionist, they called him a Communist. (In Israel, Katz-Suchy has recalled that until the age of fourteen he belonged to a youth group of Ha-shomer Ha-za'ir, the left-socialist Zionists. Pirqe Avot teaches that this world is like a *prozdor*, a vestibule, to the next. Between the two wars some Polish Jews used to say that Ha-shomer Ha-za'ir was like a *prozdor* to the Communist party.) And now it is too late for Katz-Suchy to resume the game of Esperanto.

Like the Polish Jews' Esperanto, the American Jews' Ethical Culture served as a way station, or a decompression chamber. Like the Esperantist, the Ethical Culturist was challenged, at least implicitly, by the Jews who remained Jews. They asked him: "We are Jews. What are you?" To which he gave this reply: "You think I must be either a Jew or a Christian. Why? A Jew is a man who can believe what the congregation affirms when the scroll is elevated: 'This is the Torah that Moses set before the children of Israel [Deuteronomy 4:44]—at the Lord's command, by Moses [Numbers 9:23].' I cannot believe that, modern biblical scholarship does not let me believe it. Neither can I believe what Christians affirm, like the divinity of Jesus. Anyway, look to the future not to the past, to deeds not creeds. How do I define myself? I am of those who, of Jewish birth but unable conscientiously to be Jews, and associating in honorable equality with those of Christian birth but unable conscientiously to be Christians, devote themselves to the improvement and unification of mankind."

So much for the ideology. The function was to prevent or mitigate, for some Jews in their passage from the Jewish community to a Christian denomination of high social status, Heine's trauma. There is an American. As was said of King David, he is full of years, riches, and honor. His parents (generation A) were Jews. Him (generation B) they brought up in Ethical Culture. He married an Episcopalian lady. Why should he not? His children (generation C) and grandchildren (generations D, E, and so on) are likewise Episcopalian. Why should they not be? One can only admire the smoothness and easy conscience of the whole thing. Neither A nor B had to do or say anything spectacular or shocking, like baptism or a Christian confession of faith. Unlike Heine, they need not reproach themselves or see merit in others' reproaches. It has been a baptism prolonged and attenuated over two or even three generations, and at the end C, D, and E are more secure, are on a more exalted plane, than mere Jews can be. Some people are lucky. They can take the cash without having to let the credit go.

The Topless Tower of Babylon

The question asked of the student Katz-Suchy, Jew or Pole?, is a variant of the older, more encompassing question, Jew or Christian? That is an infuriating question. Why should intelligent people accept the limitations set by limited people? You ask me to choose one or two. Can you count no higher? What makes you so sure your two are exhaustive, or immutable? What makes you so sure your two are not about to be subsumed by something greater than either, which, consummating both, will make both obsolete?

The most unforgivable thing limited people can do to the intelligent is to be more right than they. Denial and evasion of the narrow, stupid *either/or* go back to the French Revolution; but narrow and stupid as the *either/or* may be, it has stood the test of a long reality, while the denials and evasions should be an embarrassment to all. Katz-Suchy's experience lengthens the long reality. In Israel, when a *Ma'ariv* reporter pressed him to define himself now, he answered, at last ("quietly"), "I am a Jewish refugee from Poland sojourning in Denmark."

After the initial Danish publicity about Katz-Suchy, a dispatch was sent to the New York *Times* about others like him, but less well-known. Parts of it are prime:

Some [of the Polish Jews in Denmark] have become Catholic or Lutheran. Some younger [Jewish] Poles are firmly anti-Israel, reflecting the Warsaw regime's denunciation of Israel as imperialistic. Some . . . are strongly nationalistic [Poles] and some were members of the Polish Communist party. . . .

Rabbi Melchior [of Copenhagen] said that many of the Polish Jews told him that they had been subjected to humiliation and harassment before they left. But the refugees have a curious way of talking about it.

A university professor from Warsaw told friends here that he was discharged in 1968 and that he took a job as a milkman to support his wife and two children. He found this impossible and thus he came to Denmark last year for, as he expressed it, "financial reasons." . . .

[An] architectural student . . . expressed it this way: "My father is a lawyer and . . . my sister . . . was a doctor at a hospital. . . . There was a general uncertainty everywhere. I felt there was no future. It was very much a strain.

"I suppose we left for moral reasons," he said.

It pays to be smart. Who else but a professor, lawyer, doctor, or architectual student could have come up with those reasons for being in Denmark? The reporter's "a curious way of talking" shows he is puzzled. If he were a Jew he would not be puzzled. He would be used to such smartness.

Financial reasons, moral reasons.

Q: Doctor, I'm from the *Times*. Why are you in the street, and wearing pajamas?

A: Well, the room was getting hot, with all that fire spreading. I suppose I jumped for comfort reasons.

Q: Professor, will you tell the viewers, please, why you aren't in your laboratory?

A: Well, after the explosion there was glass in the air and chemicals were beginning to mix—that sort of thing. I suppose you can say I left the lab for health reasons.

The Rabbis tell us that not Yom Kippur alone but every day is judgment day. For modern Jews every day is Election Day. For modern Jews there are only two parties, the Jews and the Christians. You have to vote for one or the other. There is no such thing as not voting. If you refuse to vote, you vote Christian. If you write-in a third or fourth or twelfth party—Esperanto, Hillelism, the unity of mankind, socialist internationalism, the republic of learning—you vote Christian. If you try to jam the voting machine, you vote Christian. For a Jew, everything but voting Jewish is voting Christian. To vote Christian you don't have to pull the Christian lever, to vote Jewish you have to pull the Jewish lever.

It is unfair. Citizens of the world, whose parents or grandparents just happen to have been Jews, find themselves compelled to make up their minds whether they want their own grandchildren to be Jews or Christians. The local color of "Christian" is secondary. Berenson when Bostonian was Episcopalian, when Florentine Catholic. Those refugees know that in Poland one is Catholic and in Denmark Lutheran.

What will smart people do now, seeing they cannot evade or deny the *either/or*? They will do as they have always done. They will evade or deny it.

—December 1970

II

OFF THE GRAPH

.8.

Like Everyone Else, Only More So?

The ancients knew it and we learn it afresh every day: no opinion is so absurd as not to be professed by some learned man. A favorite and long-lived absurd opinion of many who are learned and many who are intellectual (they are not entirely the same), especially if they are Jews, is about the Jews. In a current formulation, by a Jewish professor–social scientist–intellectual–radical, M. M. Tumin, it is this:

> . . . it would indeed be radical in American politics if there were an identifiable Jewish vote . . . [which] stood for a morally radical position on the political spectrum. And it would be a beautiful challenge to America. . . . [But] what do Jews stand for in America? For a normal distribution of political opinions along the same spectrum and in the same proportions as non-Jews. . . .
>
> The American Jewish community seems to be living on the rapidly shrinking psychic income from the capital investment of Jews of the last two thousand years—or the last thirty years. What can it mean, in all honesty, for the average Jew in America to claim . . . a heritage and tradition of social justice, of respect for knowledge and learning, of concern for culture? He appears today to care for these things no more than anyone else around him.

Here is an important sociological generalization. It would be all true if it were not, transparently, all false.

First, as to the assertion that we "stand for . . . a normal distribution of political opinion . . . in the same proportions as non-Jews": if you tried, you could not say anything more unreal. In 1948 *Public Opinion Quarterly* published a graph of attitudes toward guaranteed economic security. It was an ascending line from predominant hostility in denominations with a low proportion of manual workers, like

65

the Congregationalists, to predominant support in denominations with a high proportion of manual workers, like the Baptists and Catholics. Seven major American denominations were represented by points on that line. One was not: the Jews, as low in manual workers as the Congregationalists, were as high in support for guaranteed security as Catholics and Baptists. When seven successive points are on a graph line and an eighth is completely off the line, the thing represented by that point must differ materially from the things represented by all the other points.

If a similar graph were to be drawn today, for voting, the Jewish point would still be off the line. In November 1964 we voted about 90 percent against Goldwater—more than any other white group, whether defined by income, region, religion, or ethnic character, and possibly as much as the Negroes. In Memphis a defeated Republican candidate for the House of Representatives annoyed the Jews by his bewilderment about them: "I had hoped against hope that the Jewish group would see things my way. I am a businessman. They are businessmen. Apparently I didn't succeed. I am amazed that I couldn't. If ever there was a group that should be conservative, they should."

Earlier in 1964, in a Democratic Presidential primary, the Jews of Baltimore and the rest of Maryland voted against Governor Wallace of Alabama more than any other group of whites, and almost as much as the Negroes. In 1960, at each level of income, proportionately many more Jews voted for Kennedy (or against Nixon) than anyone else—including the Catholics, with their special reason for wanting to see Kennedy elected. In 1952 and 1956, and again during the Democratic convention in 1960, Jews were more enthusiastically for Stevenson than any other body of Americans. Tumin's "last thirty years" must mean the era of Franklin D. Roosevelt. We have not changed, in any essential way, from what we were then. Whose political worship is oriented to Roosevelt's shrine but the Jews'?

Second, as to a living tradition of social justice: in the thirties, as we know, Jews made up half of the membership of the radical movements. (Let us not inquire too closely into the beauty of some aspects of *that* "beautiful challenge," which as late as 1948 drew so many Jewish dupes to the other Wallace—who later realized he himself had been a dupe—that Truman lost New York to Dewey.) In the *Commentary* symposium of 1961 a young man not long out of college reported scornfully that *only* half of the campus radicals in his time had been Jews. In 1964 half or more of the white young men and women who went down to Mississippi to work with the Negroes and risk their lives were Jews. Most of them feel superior to the Jewish solid-citizen community, but are they so totally different from the community as they would like to believe? Proportionately, more rabbis have gone South, and have been jailed or beaten, than any other white clergymen. The Jews of Baltimore are solid citizens, and we have seen how they voted about Governor Wallace. The Jews of Kansas City and Detroit, in referenda on open housing (to benefit Negroes), have voted for it in a huge disproportion to other whites. In California two-thirds of all the votes were *for* an anti-Negro constitutional amendment on housing; but two-thirds of the Jewish votes were *against* it.

In the 1961 symposium one writer said that he had always been for Negro equality, because members of one minority naturally sympathize with other minorities. The year 1964 was a good one for testing his proposition that minorities naturally sympathize with each other. That must be why commentators singled out Polish backlash and Italian backlash within the general category of white backlash. (Yet objectively the others have as much of a stake in a liberal society as the Jews. A country ruled by Wallaces could not be a happy place for Slavs and Mediterraneans.) These differences between the Jewish and the other minorities just possibly could mean that when the Jewish minority behaves well, it does so less because it is a minority than because it is Jewish.

If we think of social justice to the poor, no others nearly so prosperous as the Jews, on the average, so ardently favor a welfare state. That is as much so now as in 1948, the year of the graph. If we think of social justice as including civil liberties, the polls consistently found a much higher proportion of Jews than others opposed to Senator McCarthy, and more strongly opposed. And does anyone imagine that the membership and financial support of, say, the American Civil Liberties Union are proportionately Jewish and no more?

Third, as to respect for knowledge and learning: let the colleges and universities testify. At a time when America has broken every precedent the world has ever known by sending so high a proportion of its young people to college, the American Jewish community is sending even more. Or are we to understand that few young Jews are studying for advanced degrees? That would be news in the graduate schools. Or is the professor asserting that Jews have been turning their backs on teaching in the universities? The mind, as Mr. Wodehouse might say, boggles.

Finally, as to a deficient concern for culture: who, us? A few years ago someone in the publishing business estimated that something like a fifth or a quarter of the buyers of books in the United States were Jews. In his *Culture Consumers*, Alvin Toffler is struck by the share of Jews among those who go to concerts, theaters, and museums, support orchestras, and buy works of art. What appears in print only confirms what everyone knows by direct observation. That is the way things are, and it is the way they used to be in Berlin and Vienna, Budapest and Prague. When the bourgeoisie stopped saying daily prayers, Hegel noted, it started reading daily newspapers. When the Jews of those cities became modern, they put a piano in the parlor and the collected works of Goethe, Lessing, and Schiller in the bookcase; and many, especially the women, went so far as to play the pianos and read the books. In America today, where you find culture consumption there you will not find Jews lacking.

As I was reading Tumin's jeremiad against the backsliding of the children of Israel, I had a feeling of *déjà lu*: Jeremiah, of course, and the other prophets; and of course the Jewish preachers in every generation, as Marshall Sklare suggests, who were convinced that there had been a sad decline in piety and learning from the days of their grandparents. (A distinguished historian, Jacob Katz of Jerusalem, has discussed the difficulty of using sermons as data for social reality.) But then it came to me. Tumin was raising the standard of the Jewish thirties, and the Jews of the thirties had been judged in a 1944 symposium in *Commentary*'s predecessor, the *Contemporary Jewish Record*. Alfred Kazin, Lionel Trilling, and Clement Greenberg, among others, took part. Tumin might have been quoting them.

Kazin: " . . . timidity . . . parochialism . . . dreary middle-class chauvinism. . . . "

Trilling: " . . . provincial and parochial. . . . no sustenance to . . . the artist or intellectual. . . . "

Greenberg: " . . . suffocatingly middle-class. . . . No people on earth are more correct, more staid, more provincial, more commonplace. . . . "

(There was yet another symposium, in 1951, to discuss Morris Freedman's anticipation of Tumin—an accusation that the Jewish student was not what he had been in the former, great times. In the meanwhile, the woman who never let you forget her son the doctor was being overtaken and surpassed by the woman who was quick to remind you of her son the assistant professor.)

Tumin is no more alone now than the symposiasts of 1944 were then. In 1964 a sociologist issued a preposterous report alleging that the Jews studied by his graduate students were more prejudiced than others. The students had done the rating of prejudice. Probably most of them were Jews, and it would be no surprise if they were so eager to see the Jews as no better than the rest that they rated them as worse than the rest. Similarly, in a work that appeared some years ago on the sociology of a Jewish community, the Jewish authors adduce the Jewish country club as proof that the Jews are as bad as the others. A few pages later the authors note that an applicant for membership had better have a record of substantial contributions to Jewish philanthropies. Is that bad? For the authors, it shows that the Jews vie with each other in splashy expenditure.

Anyone who looks at country clubs must note real differences between Jewish and gentile clubs, which ought to be particularly notable to sociologists. Since the sociologists in question are Jews, it is left to *Sports Illustrated* to instruct us:

> Discrimination aside, Jewish country clubs generally differ from their Christian counterparts in a couple of ways. For one, the Jewish clubs put greater emphasis on charity; a prospective member is expected to be philanthropic (one club in the New York area requires that an applicant must have given $10,000 to United Jewish Appeal). For another, members of Jewish clubs habitually eat more and drink less than do Christian club members. It is possible to pick out the Jewish clubs from the clubs surveyed in Horwath and Horwath's annual anonymous study simply by checking the food and beverage expenditures of the average member. In one Jewish club, for instance, the average member spent $455 on food and only $134 on drink. At a comparable Christian club the average member spent $275 for food and $240 for drinks.

I have never been, am not, and do not expect ever to be a member of any country club; and I am mindful of what a symposiast said in 1944 about American Jews being "self-indulgent" (that would go with eating more than gentiles) "and self-admiring" (for drinking less, I suppose, and exacting large sums for philanthropy). The point of all this is that on the evidence that has been amassed, even about country clubs, no objective sociologist could deny Jewish difference.

Radicals and intellectuals may not know it, but they have enthusiastic allies in pretending that the Jews are like everyone else, only more so. Most Jews, at one time or another, believe it and say it, but those who say it loudest and most often are the kind one would suppose to be at the furthest remove from the radical intelligentsia. Tumin says that we stand for "a normal distribution of political opinions . . . in the same proportions as non-Jews." For its part, the

American Council for Judaism is reported in the New York *Times* as having said, after the 1964 election, that "although [Republican] Senator Keating [of New York] had 'made the strongest appeal in history [?] to Jewish voters, as Jews,' he had made only small gains among Jewish voters." Small gains? In Jewish districts Keating's Democratic opponent, Robert Kennedy, did more than 15 percent worse than his brother, the President, had done in 1960. He did not do so poorly in other districts. The radicals and intellectuals, on the one hand, and the American Council for Judaism types, on the other, are united in insisting that in those things where we are in fact significantly different the Jews are like-everyone-else-only-more-so.

Why should ACJ and the radicals agree with each other in rejecting the plain evidence of their senses? For ACJ the answer is simple. They do not want the Jews to be different, and particularly do they not want the Jews to look different. Only Jewish invisibility could make them comfortable, and they try by incantation to persuade themselves—even they must know they are not persuading others—that the Jews are an optical illusion.

For the radicals and intellectuals, suitably, the answer is less simple. As the independent repetition of the words must demonstrate, they detest provincialism and parochialism. Particularisms are obstacles in the way of the Messianic Age, secular style. The Jewish community, or Jewish society, is particular and also—so they say— provincial and parochial. But they are upset because something is clearly wrong in this chain of observation, reasoning, and profession of faith. If they were not upset, so many intelligent people would not be saying so many foolish things.

You have to deny the special propensity of Jews, because they are Jews, for the very values you cherish. Otherwise you would have to ask yourself, more insistently than you would like, how attached you yourself would be to those values if you had not been born to Jewish parents. That sort of thing could shake a faith blended of cosmopolitanism and individualism. Individualism is my shy conviction that when all is said and done, I have, unassisted, achieved my present moral and intellectual grandeur because in the inmost core of my self, I am—no two ways about it—morally and intellectually pretty grand. In a bourgeois this appears as the myth of the self-made man. "For he says: 'By the strength of my hand I have done it, and by my wisdom, for I have understanding. . . .' "

Worse still, you might have to recognize that if you truly want people who care for social justice, respect knowledge and learning, and are concerned about culture—why, the hard fact is that such people are more likely to be found among the Jews than anywhere else. Since that has also been the hard fact in so many other places for so long, a good breeding ground for those desirable propensities might be the Jewish community, that distressingly particular and parochial thing. The Jewish community, though obviously quite awful, must equally obviously be less awful than practically anything else. Instead of your values requiring a dissolution of the Jewish community, may they not rather need a Jewish community to assure that an important base of support for them will continue to exist?

But to go on with such thinking could lead to all kinds of reactionary conclusions, possibly even of a personal character. There is a way out. All you have to say is what your predecessors said—that while the Jewish community may have been all right somewhat earlier, the contemporary Jewish community has practically nothing in common with it; and to say that, all you have to do is to prefer fable to fact.

Postscript

Engineers know that Murphy's Law is inexorable: what can go wrong will go wrong. Soldiers have Moltke's Law: what can be misunderstood will be misunderstood. The more general law is in itself neither pessimistic nor optimistic: what can be will be. Its unceasing operation was again revealed to me after I had finished the part about the unexpected agreement of the radical intellectuals and their opposites, the American Council for Judaism. A colleague showed me some ACJ publications, and there it was, almost as explicitly as if it had been written to make my point. What can be will be.

ACJ was shocked because Rabbi Joachim Prinz had declared from his pulpit before Election Day: "A Jewish vote for Goldwater is a vote for Jewish suicide." It impeached Rabbi Prinz for three sins: violating the political neutrality of the pulpit; unpatriotically suggesting—ACJ is nothing if not patriotic—that the United States was threatened by something fascist; and encouraging Jewish self-ghettoization.

On Goldwater and a fascist threat, Tumin must be closer to Rabbi Prinz than to ACJ. Yet ACJ's *Education in Judaism* admired

Tumin's article: "provocative" and "well worth reading." Why so? Because he said: "No one has a right to self-ghettoization." Blessed word! For its sake much is forgiven and an embrace is offered.

Politics, as someone said when a candidate went back to living with his wife, makes strange bedfellows.

The Case of Senator Keating

There must have been something about Kenneth Keating that caused the Jews of New York State to give him a far greater share of their votes (though not a majority) than they normally give a Republican. In looking for that cause, the first thing we can rule out is conservative trends. For the Jews who backed Keating, he was more, not less liberal than Robert Kennedy. Even if they were prepared to admit that the two were equally liberal, they thought a vote for Keating would serve liberalism better.

The most compelling urgency of all was to defeat Goldwater crushingly, conspicuously, exemplarily. Keating had made an honorable, acceptably liberal record for himself. He won sympathies by firmly dissociating himself from Goldwater and by so earning the hatred of the Goldwater enthusiasts that the rightist Conservative party ran a candidate and directed most of its propaganda against him. In voting for such a man, his Jewish supporters reasoned, they would be rewarding someone who deserved it and at the same time helping to discredit right-wing fanaticism. Especially if he won, but even if he did not lose badly—while Goldwater was losing very badly indeed, they hoped—the Republican party thenceforth might see the advantage of nominating people like him, and America might be blessed for a long time to come with the happy necessity of choosing between liberals called Democrats and liberals called Republicans.

Since his election to the Senate in 1958, Keating had been cultivating the Jews. He had made himself heard repeatedly in favor of Israel and against Soviet antisemitism, and he had seen to it that his person and his words came to the attention of people whose names were on the mailing lists of Jewish organizations. During the campaign he could not be accused of neglecting this means of recalling to the Jews who he was and what he stood for. Neither could Kennedy. Of course, both worked just as hard at doing the same sort of thing with the Italians, the Negroes, the Puerto Ricans, and all the rest.

To determine how much this helped Keating with the Jews, or how much it ever helps any other candidate who does it, is extraordinarily hard. The better-informed the politician, the better he knows that you have to approach us with something else than simple pro-Jewish oratory. What we want is a broadly liberal program and tone, with a subtle, barely audible Jewish undertone—of recognizable Jews on the speaker's platform and recognizable Jewish names on the lettterhead or in the advertisements. The Jews I heard praising Keating did not mention his specifically pro-Jewish stands, but presented the "unparochial" argument I have been summarizing. If anything, they were probably a little embarrassed by the Jewish note that was sounded. (Naturally, there are Jewish voters who respond to political appeals couched in explicitly Jewish language. It is a question of proportions. More than others we have, or want to think we have, a broad view of political questions.)

But perhaps the subtleties are subtler than that. Some who spoke the language of unparochial liberalism on behalf of Keating—and meant it—may have secretly wanted, too, to show their approval of his specifically pro-Jewish deeds and intentions. Either they were uneasy about it within themselves or they feared that even to mention it would get them lectured at by the other Jewish liberals they were talking with—who themselves may have had the same feelings, and therefore did not say anything aloud, either.

Possibly, also, some would have been more dissatisfied with the absence of an explicitly pro-Jewish appeal than they were embarrassed by its presence. If a groupy appeal is made to everyone else, if it is normal American practice, what could be the meaning of not making one to the Jews? Are we abnormal? Are we so taken for granted that a candidate can believe that only for us need he not bestir himself? If a big part of politics is the competition of interests, and if in many things the general interest is defined as a kind of moment of the forces of particular interests, why exclude ours? Jewish abnegation would not abolish self-interest, it would only injure Jewish self-interest; and by remaining quiet while everyone else was shouting, we would be allowing the final consensus to be worse (from our point of view, at least) than if we, or our representatives, had spoken up, too.

This kind of thinking should not prevail at the expense of liberalism, but neither is it to be disdained. It has intrinsic worth. And let those who dislike it for extrinsic reasons, out of an anxiety about what the gentiles will say, remember that what is natural rarely puzzles or alarms, and nothing is more natural than the ties of like people with each other. One knows where one is with that. It is familiar, limited, of the same order as all the other ties of all the other families of mankind. More than a century ago it was an American, a naval officer leading his squadron without authorization to the rescue of a British flotilla in China, who said that blood is thicker than water.

An apparent lack of such natural impulses, a devotion to what seems to others only abstract, general, ideological—that is what puzzles and alarms. There is something almost uncanny about it, making for discomfort in the beholder. If that Republican candidate had had it explained to him that the Jewish businessmen of Memphis were voting as they did because they saw in the Goldwater movement a threat to themselves as Jews, as well as a threat to liberal values, even he might have understood. Neither he nor anyone else can understand claptrap—a denial of anything specifically Jewish about how all those individual businessmen, who *happened* to be Jews, also happened to vote differently from the gentile businessmen.

—January 1965

. 9 .

The Jewish Vote

With a Catholic candidate for the presidency, the so-called Jewish vote was bound to attract the scrutiny of reporters and the attention of politicians.

The statistics of group voting or opinion are unambiguous. A hundred workers, chosen at random, will vote and answer pollsters quite differently from a hundred farmers, chosen at random. Similarly with college graduates and grade-school graduates, Southerners and Northerners, Catholics and Protestants, Congregationalists and Baptists. In the 1950s Gallup reported that 24 percent of the Catholics, 31 percent of the Protestants, and 65 percent of the Jews disapproved intensely of McCarthy. (The percentages for intense approval were 21, 12, and 5.) There is nothing surprising about such differences. A man's circumstances, associations, and traditions affect his values and even his perception of reality.

The ambiguity in the discussion of group voting lay elsewhere, in the possible implication that the groups had more or less the same kind of political organization—that since organized labor urged the support of candidates and parties, and since Negro organizations and newspapers assessed issues and personalities in terms of Negro interests, Protestants and Catholics and Jews must be doing the same. That is not so.

In any event, people tend to exaggerate the effect of recommendations from headquarters. When John L. Lewis failed to deliver the miners' vote to Willkie it became clear that it was not he who had delivered their vote to Roosevelt four years earlier, and official labor's war against Robert A. Taft did not keep him from getting more than enough workers' votes for easy re-election to the Senate in 1950. As for the Jews, they have no political headquarters and they do not take orders.

A good deal is known about the political attitudes and behavior of American Jews. Practically, there are two kinds of liberalism, one relating to such matters as civil liberties and international affairs and the other to minimum wages and social security. The first kind finds most of its support among the college-educated and the prosperous, and the second kind in the working class. American Jews, uniquely, are liberal in both senses. To understand why, we would have to understand the whole of modern Jewish history. This Jewish liberalism exists everywhere, not only in the United States; in England the Jewish Tory has always been the exception, and it was in France that the Jewish political stance received its classic formulation: *Juif, donc libéral.*

Almost by definition, when the members of any group show such consistency in their political behavior and outlook, a powerful self-interest must be present. Yet an obvious Jewish self-interest is ordinarily hard to find, in the sense, for example, that Negroes have an obvious political self-interest. Certainly a candidate or a party judged to be anti-Israel could not expect to win the support of most Jews. Still, Israel is not really primary, as we can see from the tendency of Jews to assume that political figures they like must be pro-Israel—rather than liking them because they are pro-Israel. In his last years Roosevelt was, if not decisively pro-Arab, at least not strongly for the Palestine policy that most Jews wanted. Nevertheless, to this day most Jews take it for granted that FDR was a firm friend in Palestinian affairs.

Nor can Jewish candidates expect to find as much automatic support from their fellow Jews as candidates in practically any other comparable group can from their fellows. If the Jews of New York had been determined to see a Jewish mayor, there would long since have been one. In general, Jews will vote for a candidate because he is a Jew only when other things are equal—reputation, party affiliation, and the like—or when they feel they have been slighted politically.

Most Jews, therefore, take liberalism as such to be their self-interest, though I doubt that they think of themselves consciously as Jews when they think of politics. There is no point in being self-gratulatory about this. It is an old tradition, and it has had its fatuous episodes.

—December 1960

. 10 .

Universalist Elite

Arthur Goren, examining the Socialist campaigns for Congressman in the Lower East Side of New York early in the century, explains why Morris Hillquit, a Russian Jew and a leading figure in American and even international socialism, was not elected to Congress in 1906 and 1908, while Meyer London, the later Socialist nominee, a man without much prestige beyond the East Side, was elected three times between 1914 and 1920. As a national figure Hillquit could not accommodate himself to the demands of the East Side. For many Socialists, Hillquit lost—honorably—because the East Side refused to prefer the general goals of the American Socialist party to its own special interests. Those Socialists felt better about Hillquit's defeat than about London's victory; Louis Boudin, writing in their newspaper, was unhappy about the "racial and subracial prejudices of voters. . . . The Russian Jews were appealed to because Comrade London was also a Russian Jew."

The Socialist party was against immigration, agreeing with the American Federation of Labor that the bosses were using immigrants to lower wages and fight the unions. For their part, the Jews of the East Side understood only that to stop immigration would mean to close the gate of the Russian prison on their families. Hillquit, though in his campaigns he tried to make distinctions, was identified with the Socialists' anti-immigration plank, while London was able to dissociate himself from that plank because his record on the East Side

76

made it impossible for his enemies to persuade the people that he lacked sympathy with them.

The East Siders were also worried about their reputation and their security. General Bingham, the police commissioner of New York, had said that half the criminals in the city were Russian Jews, and Julia Richman, an East Side school superintendent for whom a high school was later named, wanted to deport immigrants who violated the pushcart ordinance. In Hillquit's speeches the East Side was painted as a repulsive example of the suffering and the social disintegration caused by capitalism. For the East Siders, that made him the Socialist Bingham. They also remembered, if only because his opponents kept reminding them, that he had changed his name (from Hilkowitz) and that his opposition to nationalist prejudice was so pure that he had refused to take part in their giant parade of protest against the Russian pogroms in 1905, organized by Judah Magnes. The voters agreed with the anti-Hillquit press that if he were elected, the Jews of the United States, and particularly those of the East Side, would have no representative or protector in Congress.

The man who defeated Hillquit was Henry M. Goldfogle, a Tammany Congressman. Goldfogle denounced Russian pogroms and Russian discrimination against Jewish holders of American passports. More generally, he let the East Siders see that they had a representative and defender.

They knew what they were doing when they chose Goldfogle over Hillquit and Tammany over Hillquit's socialism. Tammany was corrupt, but it respected people's needs. (There is a remarkable similarity here between the Socialists and the Progressive Republicans of Richard Hofstadter's *Age of Reform*.) The Socialists were against immigration because organized labor was against it, while their stated reason was that they were struggling for a world in which the disappearance of capitalism would make mass migration unnecessary. When in the 1920s the old free immigration was outlawed, that was mostly a victory for the Ku Klux Klan spirit abroad in the land (not least in the Brahmin class), but labor and the Socialists had done their part. The Jews, fighting to keep immigration going because their families needed it, were also fighting for a right and generous principle. More than fifty years later those Socialists remain less attractive than the Tammany voters they called parochial and given to nationalist prejudice.

After finishing Goren's paper, I read "Eichmann and Jewish Identity," by Paul Jacobs. This records the discomfort aroused in him by his five-week attendance at Eichmann's trial in Jerusalem and the questions it made him ask himself.

Why did the radicals disregard or play down Nazism's persecution and murder of the Jews? Why was it so important for them to insist that Nazism was merely capitalism *in extremis*? (In 1940 a splinter from a Trotskyite splinter produced a pamphlet which demonstrated, marxicologically, that the Battle of Britain, then being waged over burning London, was a put-up job by the London and Berlin branches of world capitalism to fool the proletariat.)

Ordinary Jews were anti-Nazi because they understood that Hitler was out to murder Jews, and they understood that such a man and such a system must be bad for everybody. Then and later, they did what they could for the Nazis' victims. They were the children of the East Side Tammany voters. The radical intellectuals were the children, in the spirit, of the Hillquit Socialists. The parochials' self-interest and the awareness it bred had more worth and truth than the pretensions of the elite.

—*September 1961*

.**11**.

Still Liberal

For the attention of the linguistic philosophers, a problem having to do with the ethics of words: There is an organization—a department of the civil service, the army, a school, a corporation—in which supervisors periodically submit reports on the people under them. Suppose that in large part this consists of checking one of three ratings on a form: outstanding, satisfactory, unsatisfactory. That is the *de jure* situation. But suppose also that *de facto*, by long custom, anyone whose work is not clearly unsatisfactory is marked outstanding, with "satisfactory" commonly understood to mean "unsatisfactory" (as "literally" has come to mean "figuratively": I was literally petrified with fear). Careers depend on the reports.

If a supervisor, disliking a subordinate, grades as satisfactory what he would otherwise call outstanding, he cannot justify himself by an appeal to the dictionary's definitions. It is unethical to apply dictionary definitions exceptionally and maliciously. But what if the supervisor is not malicious or partial? What if he believes that the prevailing custom prevents truly superior work from being recognized and rewarded, and that the *de jure* system should be restored? In his report he is telling the truth and striking a blow for efficiency. At the same time, his subordinates are going to be penalized merely because they have had the bad fortune to come under his authority, not someone else's. Is he right or wrong?

All kinds of difficulties can arise from the different meanings words have in different situations and for different people. One should tell the truth, but which truth? The truth people want to hear or the truth they ought to hear? A truthful man can make what seem to be two contradictory speeches on Vietnam, one to American Legionnaires and the other to campus radicals, leading the first to call him unpatriotic and the second an apologist for war criminals. Of course his speeches will not really be contradictory. They will only emphasize different things, different aspects of the truth, according to his estimate of each audience and of his responsibility for shaking up convention and prejudice. His problem is easy. All he needs is a thick skin.

The hard problem arises when the audience is diverse and opaque. What should one say, and how say it, to a mixed audience of Legionnaires and radicals—and perhaps also of people who aren't sure they know where Vietnam is, or even whether they're interested? That is hard enough. The speaker need not complicate it by allowing one moral obligation, concern, to make him forget another, the obligation to know what he is talking about.

When Jews spoke a language of their own, they could criticize and admonish each other without worrying about giving ammunition to enemies. They could repeat acerbities like the one attributed to the Gaon R. Elijah, who had impressed upon the notables of Jewish Vilna that they were not to ask him to a meeting of the community council unless they were considering a new ordinance. Once, they asked him, he attended, and he complained. The chairman was hurt. As the Gaon must have observed, he said, they were in fact considering a new ordinance—to forbid beggars approaching householders directly. "You call that new?" the Gaon asked, rising to leave. "They had that ordinance in Sodom and Gomorrah." Or Jews could relish what Shemariah Levin was to say, more frivolously and secularly, in our parents' time: *dos yidishe folk iz a kleyn folk, ober a paskudne,* the Jews are a small people, but a repulsive one.

Now it is notorious that if you want to gather incriminating evidence about nations or religions, you will find they have done much of your work for you. Most of the documentation of British and French imperialism was published in London and Paris, and most of the basic criticism of American policy is made in the U.S.A. If you want to read informed, hard words about Protestantism, read Protestants, and about Catholicism, read Catholics. In one sense, Jewish criticism of Jews is the same sort of thing, and Jews have no peculiar right to be outraged by it. But only in one sense. The enemies of Englishmen, Frenchmen, Protestants, and Catholics have not often been intent upon murdering them.

This does not mean that Jews should avoid criticizing themselves except in languages that others do not understand. There are no such languages any more, and besides, translations of Jewish self-critical literature go back a long time. After the rise of Christianity, some of the Rabbis thought the Septuagint a disaster, but the early Christians who cited the Prophets to prove the inveterate wickedness of the Jews did not have to use a Greek (or Aramaic) translation. They were Jews themselves, and read Isaiah and Jeremiah in Hebrew. Still, a Jew is tempted to believe that the standards of truth and uprightness, which should apply to all speech, by anyone about anything, should apply above all to the speech of Jews about Jews.

Let us not exaggerate. At this time and in this place, the chief damage done by wrong speech about us, especially when it is by us, may only be that it misleads us. It also makes necessary periodic demonstrations that what everyone—or everyone who is anyone— says is so, is not so. Without the tiresome error there would be no need of the tiresome correction.

These days the error is to complain that the Jews of America are becoming selfishly conservative, above all in how they think and act about Negroes. The most recent complaint is over an alleged Jewish defection from liberalism in the 1966 voting on a civilian review board for the police in New York City.

The total vote for the review board was only about one in three. The white vote was less, one in four or five. The Irish and Italian votes were between one in six and one in eight. Of the Jews, it appears that half voted for the board. In tabular form:

Italians	13-17%
Irish	13-17
Jews	50
All Whites	20-25

These figures do not show Jews behaving like selfish conservatives, they show them behaving with a striking readiness to favor liberal ideology over interest and need. If not for ideology, Jews would have been as opposed as anyone else to the board.

The ostensible issue was police brutality, specifically brutality against Negroes (and Puerto Ricans). The experts kept saying that whether the review board won or lost, actual police brutality would hardly be affected one way or the other, but no one listened. For some it was a battle of liberalism, tolerance, and humanity against reaction, bigotry, and cruelty; for others, of hard-pressed policemen against unfriendly outsiders and innovators; for others still, of law and order against crime, riot, and anarchy. Whatever the civilian review board was supposed to be, for the citizenry it was a Rorschach inkblot.

Knowing something about the Jews of New York—how they earn their livings, where they live, what they hope for and what they are fearful of—we can eliminate any great concern of Jews for cops as cops: conditions of work, pay, prestige, hurt feelings, and the like. The Irish have a concern. There can be few Irish families in New York without at least a cousin on the force, and the image of the police is Irish. Few Jews have cousins who are cops, and the question of image does not arise.

Neither does the question of cruelty arise in any direct or personal way. Nearly all Jews in New York are the sort of people the police do not trouble, whom they deal with correctly when the need to deal with them arises at all. Most Jews are in the middle class, whether the lower or upper middle class. By now they are part of the old stock of New York City. Even of those Jews who do not speak English well, most are elderly, and no policeman need feel threatened or annoyed by them. The serious complaint that Jews are likely to have about the police is that there are not enough of them to do the job of keeping the peace.

Most New Yorkers think there is more violence to be feared now, more crime and disorder, than ever before in their lifetime. Whether or not this is objectively true, what is socially perceived to be a fact becomes a social fact. Routinely, New Yorkers pick up the newspaper and read that a druggist or a jeweler or a cab driver has been shot in a holdup, or a tenant stabbed in an apartment-house elevator. For Jews, especially, this is threatening, because while few Jewish cousins are policemen, many are druggists, jewelers, cab drivers, and apartment-house tenants. A Jew who reads such news cannot help thinking, They're killing people like me, they're killing people like us. The brutality that makes a personal impression on Jews is not the brutality of policemen but the brutality of criminals.

If the opponents of the civilian review board included numbers of unsavory people uttering unsavory slogans, the advocates of the board included unprepossessing people who said things not calculated to reassure friends of law and order—things like the scrawls on the façades of buildings: "No police state"; "Stop scum cops." (Or "slum cops"? The capital letters can be read either way.)

We would expect Jews to dislike the thought of downgrading the police, and therefore of downgrading law and order. We find instead that the Jews—addicts of law and order, not themselves victims of police brutality, with no first-hand knowledge of police brutality, whose families or friends have not personally complained of police brutality—gave half of their vote to the review board. Voting for the review board was the liberal thing to do. For elderly Jews the ideology is weaker and the fear and the need stronger; and in fact, most of the elderly voted against the board.

Almost to a man, the Italians voted against. But not only in 1966 and not only in New York have the Italians shown themselves antagonistic to the demands of Negroes, or what they take to be the demands of Negroes. They have been doing it for years, all over the country.

For Jews this is saddening, because most Jews like Italians. If there has not been actual friendship between the Jews and Italians in America, there has been peaceful coexistence, all the more to be prized because we cannot always say as much about our relations with the Irish or Poles. For many of us it is still hard to forget that a Jewish boy walking home from his public school past an Irish or a Polish Catholic parochial school used to be in danger of a beating. We were not so afraid of Italians, if only because there were no Italian parochial schools. From the Italian side, too, as well as from the Jewish, there seems to have been a feeling of closeness. A social scientist of Italian parentage once told me that when he was a boy in New York, he always thought of Jews and Italians as belonging together, as differing together from the real Americans, the Irish. The

Irish were the real Americans because they had the important American and Americanizing jobs: they were the teachers, the principals, the police, the politicians. (For the Italians, they were also the bishops.) And the Irish were the real Americans, too, because they were the only ones we actually knew who came from families in which English was the language that had always been spoken at home.

Probably what Jews feel about the Italians derives from more than American circumstances alone. When there was a collision between Italian and Scandinavian steamships, I thought first, of course, of the loss of life. My second thought, spontaneous and prerational, was to hope that the fault was not the Italians'. As between the Nordics and the Mediterraneans, I was pro-Mediterranean. When I realized what I was thinking, I was amused and a little embarrassed. Then I remembered that Freud had said something like that about himself. When he was in school in Vienna and studying ancient history, for his teachers and classmates the Romans were the good guys in the Carthaginian wars, while for him the Semitic Carthaginians and their general Hannibal were the good guys. On the other hand, in the wars between Rome and the early Germans, as at the Teutoburger Wald where Arminius/Hermann defeated Varus, Freud's gentile teachers and classmates were for the Germans and against the Romans, while he was for the civilized Mediterraneans against the barbarian Teutons of the dark Northern forests.

So I am pro-Italian, and sorry about many Italians' unsympathetic attitude toward Negroes and their just demands. But because I am pro-Italian, I cannot assume that the Italians are only being wicked. I have to seek a reason that in some measure will mitigate their fault. In seeking that reason, perhaps I will discover something that will help me when I come to think of public policy generally.

We say that every man has a right to live where he wishes (and where he can afford to pay the rent). If you said that to Italians they could scarcely disagree, because as an abstract proposition it is hard to deny. What we do not see is that for Italians, where a man and his wife live is not an individualistic matter. It is a matter of neighborhood, of community—above all, of the extended family.

Few Jewish couples live within walking distance of parents, and almost none within walking distance of grandparents. Many Italians, having grown up near grandparents, uncles, aunts, and cousins, stay in the same neighborhood when they get married, and bring up their own children there. The neighborhood is their village, their family demesne. They do not object to the other fellow having a desirable place to live in. They just do not want him, by moving in, to make their neighborhood less of a home for them. Italians are not guiltless of racism, but racism is not their only reason for objecting to Negroes moving in. Italian family people and non-Italian white single people have been getting on each other's nerves for years in Greenwich Village. No question of racism there.

That is to say, residential integration or residential racial balance, as an ideal deriving more or less directly from the idea of liberal individualism, means little to Italians. When they object to what they consider to be an attack upon the family coziness of their neighborhoods, from their own point of view they are not being selfish or heartless, they are only trying to protect themselves. The call for a civilian review board they interpreted as the latest in a whole series of programs and decisions and policies that they think has done too little for them and too much for the newcomers, Negro or Puerto Rican.

Italians have no great love for Puerto Ricans, but not for the obvious reasons. Like Italians, most Puerto Ricans are Catholic—not very Catholic, to be sure, but then, neither are Italians, especially the older, immigrant men; both Puerto Ricans and Italians have a kind of anticlerical, folk Catholicism. The Caribbean Puerto Ricans are in their way quite Mediterranean. They even speak a language which, though an Italian cannot understand it when it is spoken, he could nevertheless understand reasonably well if he had to read it. Yet in East Harlem Italians have long been resisting Puerto Rican intrusions.

Concessions never made to Italians are being made to Puerto Ricans. The school system and the police are making special efforts to be nice to Puerto Ricans: Spanish is a kind of second language in some public schools, and policemen are urged to learn Spanish so that they can understand Puerto Ricans and make themselves understood to them. If not jealous, an Italian can be resentful. He resents the rules of the game being changed now, after he has had to live with their rigors. When the children of Italian immigrants were going to school in New York, it was sink or swim. If they did not learn English on their own, they failed in school. Nobody then told teachers to learn Italian, so that they could guide children from Italian-speaking homes into the mainstream of American education; or policemen, so that they could understand Italians and make themselves understood by them.

Still Liberal

With jobs, too, the rules of the game have been changed. When the Italians came to this country, the job market and the trades were ethnic. The good jobs belonged to others—in New York to the Irish and Germans—and the Italians did the unskilled labor. Slowly, in the course of years, some industries and trades became theirs, and finally an Italian could bequeath to his son preferential access to a job paying good wages. (Most Italians are not yet able to bequeath to their children the most useful thing of all, the diploma of a good college.)

Now ethnic monopolies and favoritisms have become illegal. Now an Italian father may not put his son at the head of the line for entry into a trade, though the father has been in it for many years and though it is Italian. Now able to benefit from them, Italians find that the old rules have been abolished—to the unfair advantage, as they see it, of Negroes and other newcomers unwilling to pay the price of similar waiting. And it is not only the newcomers who offend. For Italians, there seems to be a conspiracy between the Negroes at the bottom of the ladder and the educated and liberal at the top of the ladder to take away what Italians have worked so hard to earn.

The Italians are wrong. The rules of the game have had to be changed because the game itself and its conditions have changed. The economy is not what it used to be. The new job market, the new importance of education, the specific disabilities of Negroes and Puerto Ricans, changes in the general conception of justice and what justice requires—these make the new legislation and new outlook necessary and just. But the necessity and justice do not remove the Italians' sense of grievance, unfairness, being encroached upon. They can demonstrate against civil-rights demonstrations and vote against civilian review boards all the more easily because, unlike Jews, the Italians have no strong tradition of liberal ideology.

Not only for Italians does the very principle of order seem to be endangered. Any society that is not a tyranny rests on order and liberty, but when it thinks there is a clash between the two it will sacrifice liberty to order: not McKinley or Harding suspended *habeas corpus*, Lincoln did.

Jews are not becoming illiberal. In California they voted for Brown, not for Reagan. In Georgia they voted for Arnall, not for Maddox or Callaway. In Arkansas they voted for Winthrop Rockefeller, not for Jim Johnson. In New York many voted for the other Rockefeller, but who will maintain that the clearly liberal thing was to vote for O'Connor? The Jews of New York State contributed not at all to the

85

Conservative party's capture of the third line on the ballot from the Liberals. If even these persistently liberal people gave only half of their votes to the civilian review board, we must ask whether the board—or better, whether the agitation for the board—was a Good Thing or a Bad Thing.

The contest over the civilian review board in New York can teach us two things. (That we need to be taught shows we have been unwilling to learn what we should have known all along.) The first is that to call something liberal and to have it advocated by indisputably liberal people does not mean that the electorate will want it —even elements of the electorate who normally can be counted upon for loyal service in the liberal army. The second is that we must respect people's anxieties about symbols of order and try to allay people's fears that order is being overthrown.

Take the cash and let the credit go: let us leave the symbols of order undisturbed and unthreatened, concerning ourselves with the substance of liberty and justice. The fight about the civilian review board was a fight about symbols. We did not understand sufficiently that for many the board was a symbol of disorder.

Take the cash and let the credit go: let us leave the symbols of order undisturbed and unthreatened, concerning ourselves with the substance of liberty and justice. The fight about the civilian review board was a fight about symbols. We did not understand sufficiently that for many the board was a symbol of disorder.

Television, with all its immediacy, showed us police brutality in Selma, Alabama. In the North it shows us something unintended by the people who shout police brutality. In New York there was a demonstration against the building unions for refusing to admit Negroes to their membership, and picketing stopped the construction of a public project. On television we saw and heard not brutality by the police but psychological brutality *against* the police, accompanied by cries that the police were being brutal. The mode of demonstrating was illegal, blocking traffic, and it could not be permitted to continue for long. Repeatedly the picketers were asked to get off the streets and not to compel the police to arrest them. The picketers refused. That was their moral if not their legal right, since they were prepared to pay the price of imprisonment or a fine for their defiance. But then they also refused to walk into the police wagon. Husky men went limp and made the police carry them.

How great an act of provocation that was, I realized when I found myself admiring the police for their ability to resist the temptation that anyone in their place would have felt—to hit out at those people who were making things so needlessly hard for them. The police resisted the temptation because they had discipline, and no doubt their knowledge that the television cameras were trained on them helped, too. Yet, when the police started carrying those husky men to the wagons, the other picketers raised a cry of police brutality. They were making it harder to believe any future accusations of police brutality. One might almost say they were preparing the way for an election in which the average white voter would find it easy to dismiss the accusations as so much malevolent nonsense.

Television has shown us the picketing of Girard College. Cecil Moore of the Philadelphia NAACP, haranguing his followers, recalled newsreels of sinister harangues in Rome and Nuremberg thirty years ago, though Moore is neither Mussolini nor Hitler, and could not be even if he wished to be. With such scenes on television, you do not have to be a racist to be upset. You only have to be committed to the Negro cause with less than all your emotions and energy, which is to say, you only have to be practically any white man or woman.

Since what was at work here was not exclusively a matter of race— though it was in great measure a matter of race—the antics of the New Left from Berkeley, California, to Cambridge, Massachusetts, did not help very much, either. It was not so much the decision of most of the New Leftists in California to vote neither for Brown nor for Reagan. It was not even the decision of some to vote for Reagan, though I could find that disquieting if I were so minded. In the so-called Third Period in Communist history, the Communists' name for a Social Democrat was Social Fascist, and their attitude toward the imminent victory of Hitler was "after Hitler, our turn"—with the death of liberalism, the revolution will triumph; so let's hasten the death. The lapidary expression of this logic goes: worse is better. (It seems to have been more or less contemporary with a similar phrasing of Bauhaus aesthetic doctrine: less is more.) The New Left in California has helped to turn people to Reagan by threatening their sense of order and by making them feel they are besieged on both sides, from below by the Negro poor, as in Watts, and from above by the highly educated.

On the other side of the continent, the day before the 1966 election some Harvard students almost manhandled the Secretary of Defense. The McNamara affair must have confirmed people in their suspicious fear of Harvard students, or of Harvard generally, or of everything that Harvard symbolizes. Many New Yorkers must have felt that in voting against a civilian review board they would be voting against rioters in Harvard as well as in Harlem. Those students in Cambridge did a fine job of propaganda for the Right in New York. The sugar daddies of the Right would have paid well for it, and they got it for nothing.

A painful irony in all this is that the Negroes themselves, and the Puerto Ricans, and the poor generally did not want the antipolice symbolism. At least as much as the middle class, the poor want police protection. In polls among the poor, their anxiety about police brutality ranks well below their anxiety about crime and drug addiction and too few police on the streets. In the middle class only the sociologists know, but among the poor everyone knows that crime hurts the poor more than anyone else.

Who, then, is opposed to the police—not brutal police, but the police as such? Those mural inscriptions yield a clue. "Stop scum [or slum] cops" could be anyone's, but "no police state" is educated, ideological. It means "no police." At a guess, it is the sort of thing that would be written by a young radical from an educated, upper-middle-class family—the inner circle of conscientious and enlightened liberalism. The educated and prosperous are generally more optimistic about human nature than the uneducated and poor. Optimistic about human nature, some—especially their avant-garde—can think the police unnecessary. And besides looking down on the police function, they tend to look down on policemen. Authoritarian personalities, they say; lower-middle-class rigidity. The snobbish bias is evident. They do not use such categories against lawyers (orality) or surgeons (sublimated sadism)—though a century or two ago, before the surgeon had reached his present eminence, they would not have let him forget that etymologically he was only a manual laborer.

The poor are more pessimistic and—who knows?—more realistic. Subjected to unpleasantness and danger, they do not look down on the police function; low in social status, they do not look down upon the policeman.

In deciding how to vote, many Negroes and Puerto Ricans suffered uncomfortable cross-pressures. On the one hand, they did not want their votes to be interpreted as an antipolice gesture. On the other, the issue had become racial: not all the opponents of the board were white racists, but all the white racists were opponents of the board. In the event, most Negroes and Puerto Ricans voted for the civilian review board, with varying degrees of enthusiasm.

The choice was unnecessary in the first place. It was the strategists, the leaders, who made the mistake of choosing this fight on this terrain, with humiliating defeat for the liberals, for liberalism, and for a chance to accomplish something substantive. Naturally, the leaders blame everyone else. Some even blame the Jews—their most dependable troops. After the East German Communist party suppressed the workers' uprising in 1953, Brecht said that the masses had forfeited the confidence of the government. The mass of Jews seem to have forfeited the confidence of the liberal leadership.

There are two kinds of politics: substantive or instrumental, and symbolic or expressive. The first has to do with getting something done, the equivalent of cash in the bank; the second with the gratification of emotions. Since liberty and order can conflict with each other, in a given case to decide for liberty may mean to decide for a diminution of order. It will be hard to win the voters' approval for such a decision, and impossible if you also make them needlessly anxious. Why go out of your way to frighten people who are already frightened enough by the erosion of order?

Once, there was a football coach in a college that denied him the usual latitude and resources, but whose alumni demanded occasional victories. Asked how he managed, he answered that his policy was to keep the alumni surly but not mutinous.

The insolence of office weighs heavily on the poor. They have a tale to tell about the police, but also about welfare departments, clinics, housing authorities, schools. If liberals had proposed measures to protect citizens against bureaucrats, everyone would have cheered. Instead, they singled out the police; and the white voters mutinied.

—*April 1967*

. 12 .

Crisis

It is easy to praise the Athenians to Athenians: thus Plato. If easy, then unnecessary; but if necessary, then perhaps not easy? For some years, after each Presidential or midterm election I have found it necessary to praise the Jews to Jews. By praise I mean defend. The defense has been against the accusation, undeterred by mere fact, that

American Jews have become selfishly conservative, or downright reactionary.

Since those who make this mistake should know better, they must want to make it. Yet, on the improbable assumption that they are honestly mistaken, maybe they ought to be told about statistics, helped to become "numerate."

I remember a high-school math teacher who used to say, "They always understand when I put it in dollars." Instead of talking about money, let us talk about baseball. In 1968 the leading hitter in the American League had a batting average of .300 (to be exact, .301). Batters with an average of .200 were common, and poor. The difference in kind between the one best batter and the crowd of poor batters, what was it in degree? That a player has a .300 average means that in every ten official times at bat, he gets a hit three times and fails to get a hit seven times. That a player has a .200 average means that in every ten times at bat, he gets a hit twice and fails to get a hit eight times. The player with seven failures out of ten was the leading hitter in his league, and those with eight failures out of ten were the poor hitters. The small difference was not small.

Now from baseball to politics—the voting in the 1968 Presidential election (Nixon 43.4 per cent, Humphrey 43.0 per cent, Wallace 13.6 per cent).

In descending order of support for Nixon there were three sets of voters.

Pro-Nixon:

	NIXON	HUMPHREY	WALLACE
High-income (National Broadcasting Co.)	63%	29%	5% [?]
Professional and business (Gallup)	56	34	10
College-educated (G)	54	37	9
Protestant (G)	49	35	16
White (G)	47	38	15
White-collar (G)	47	41	12
Middle-income (NBC)	44	43	13

Moderately pro-Humphrey:

	NIXON	HUMPHREY	WALLACE
Blue-collar (G)	35%	50%	15%
Catholic (G)	33	59	8
Trade-union (NBC)	29	61	10
Slav (NBC)	24	65	11

90

And strongly pro-Humphrey, anti-Wallace:

	NIXON	HUMPHREY	WALLACE
Mexican (West Coast; NBC)	17%	81%	2%
Puerto Rican (East Coast; NBC)	16	81	3
Nonwhite (G)	12	85	3
Negro (NBC)	5	94	1

How may the Jews be expected to have voted? Well, in which of the three sets do we belong? Bogue's *Population of the United States* (1959) gives this socioeconomic information about us:

Two religious groups stand out above all others as well-educated: . . . Jewish and . . . Episcopal. . . .
. . . being in the upper income brackets is closely related to . . . Episcopal or Jewish religion. . . .

Socioeconomically, therefore, the Jews ought to be toward the top of the pro-Nixon set. But on the one hand, we know that Jews have voted left of their bank accounts. On the other hand, everyone had a scary anecdote—what a certain Jewish taxi driver had said, or a shop-keeper, or even a teacher—which led him to predict that this time Jews were going to make a sharp right turn. Hedging our bets, we may expect Jews to have voted midway between the old habits and what seemed to be the new mood: with the moderately pro-Humphrey voters. We would be wrong if we did. Jews voted like the Mexicans of the West and the Puerto Ricans of the East—the poor, the racial minorities.

	NIXON	HUMPHREY	WALLACE
Jews (NBC)	17%	81%	2%

Even the Negroes could hardly have voted less for Wallace.

Before we leave statistics, let us learn from Gallup about the sturdy independents, and about crabbed age and idealistic youth. Watch the Wallace column:

	NIXON	HUMPHREY	WALLACE
Independents	44%	31%	25%
Under 30	38	47	15
30–49	41	44	15
50 and older	47	41	12

Was the choice between Humphrey and Nixon a choice between Tweedledum and Tweedledee? The American people did not think so. In 1968 they voted as they almost always do, most of the prosperous for the Republican and most of the poor for the Democrat. The Jews continue to be unique among American voters.

The old Soviet joke goes: "If everything is so good, Comrade, why is everything so bad?" For us it is no joke. If we are so good, or anyway less bad than others, why are things becoming so bad for us?

Sure that Left is better than Right, liberal better than conservative, radical better than reactionary, we are attacked from our own side. George Wallace said nothing antisemitic (whatever he may have thought). It is black nationalists who compete with each other in variety and intensity of antisemitic language; and I. F. Stone, of the Old Left but acceptable to the New, puts the current line in these words: "The Jews owe the underprivileged a duty of patience, charity, and compassion. It will not hurt us Jews to swallow a few insults from overwrought blacks." (That "us Jews" is lovely.) He does not tell us when, at what point on the dialectical spiral, it became improper for socialists to remember that antisemitism is the socialism of fools.

Some years ago I was a guest at a conference of historians and sociologists who had met to consider the public-opinion polls, which showed high antisemitism from the 1930s till after World War II and then an uninterrupted decline. The scholars agreed that the polls reflected reality. A new stage had been reached in the evolution of American society—education, detachment from old communities and traditions, scientific or cerebral ways of making a living—where antisemitism had just about disappeared. Not that it had been replaced by philosemitism; the best way to describe the new situation was to call it asemitism. Whether someone was a Jew was of no importance, it made no impression one way or the other, no emotion attached to it.

I was one of a skeptical minority. We had no data, we only doubted that something so old and deep and widespread could disappear so quickly. We said—not to prove our point, because it was no proof at all, but to show how we felt—that in the McCarthyite years some of us used to wonder about what we called the mystery of the missing antisemitism: though Senator Joe McCarthy was a rightist demagogue, he had not merely abstained from engaging in antisemitism, he had gone out of his way to show he was not engaging in it (as with the low-comedy team of Cohn and Schine). To which a scholar

we all respect said the skeptics must have a vested interest in antisemitism. We were too accustomed to reckoning with antisemitism, it
had too important a place in our understanding of history, for us to
recognize easily that it had passed on.

I wish he had been right and we, with our old, parochially Jewish
belief in antisemitism's power to endure, had been wrong. But even
the less parochial need not altogether deny antisemitism's endur-
ance. Toward the end of his life Isaac Deutscher said:

An unrepentant Marxist, an atheist, an internationalist . . . I come
unexpectedly close to the fears of an Orthodox Jew and a Zionist. I do
not believe that antisemitism is a spent force. I fear that we may be living
in a fools' paradise in our Western welfare state. The trustful feeling of
freedom from antisemitism may well be one more illusion, a particularly
Jewish one, engendered by our "affluent society."

It is the direction from which antisemitism comes at us now that
perplexes and wounds us. We know that there has been leftist antisemitism from the beginning of the time when it makes sense at all
to speak of Left and Right, say about two hundred years ago. But
there has been much more antisemitism on the Right. In our minds
we transformed that into a rightist monopoly on antisemitism; or
rather, into an identity of Right and antisemitism. Having gradually
acknowledged the antisemitism of Stalin, Khrushchev, their successors in Russia, and their vassals in Poland (and other countries that
call themselves socialist), we are still unprepared for antisemitism on
the American Left.

We had taken it for granted not only that all reasonable and just
men would not do or say antisemitic things, but also that they would
repudiate those who said or did antisemitic things. Anyway, why
antisemitism? Why pick on the Jews? What other white group voted
so pro-Negro; or, if that is too strong, so little anti-Negro? In Milwau-
kee, in Chicago, in Buffalo, in Boston, in Newark, in New York,
Negroes have learned in unmistakable, physical ways how Poles,
Italians, Irish oppose Negro demands. It is not Jews who throw
stones, use fists, light fires, and go to the polls against Negroes. Yet in
the black rhetoric the Negro seems to have only two external enemies
in the United States, whites generally and Jews specifically. Jews—
but not Italians, or Poles, or Irish. (Or WASPs. Look at those Wallace votes again.)

What is it they say we are doing to Negroes? Genocide, emascula-
tion, rape. Black Panther types say that; and also black teachers, professors, intellectuals, community leaders—in print, on the radio, on

93

television, and at hearings of the New York City Board of Education. The executive director of the Interreligious Foundation for Community Organization says that Jews engage in economic rape of the Negro slums; but in Cincinnati a CORE leader turned storekeeper is angry when his customers complain that he overcharges them. You ought to realize, he says, that a merchant's prices have to cover his costs, and costs are high in the slums: insurance rates, losses by pilferage, and so on. We are repeatedly told that the black community resents Jewish storekeepers and teachers leaving every night, taking their persons and their gains with them. The black director of a Harlem bank does not live in Harlem, and the black $30,000-a-year administrator of those schools in Brooklyn lives neither in Brownsville nor in Bedford-Stuyvesant.

When someone at a public hearing of the New York City Board of Education testifies for less decentralization of the school system than the board has proposed, and less community control, the board members respond. We must move forward, one of them answers, the crisis we are in does not allow us to stand pat. When antisemitic harangues are made at those hearings, or antisemitic leaflets distributed, the same board members are silent. Challenged, they explain that of course they do not agree, but by the First Amendment everyone is free to say what he wishes.

Zionism and Israel are held to be the enemies of black people everywhere. Is the president of the teachers' union a Jew? Then call him a Zionist and warn him he will not be allowed to perpetrate in Harlem the genocide that the Israelis are supposed to be perpetrating in the Middle East. Before the election my son, a student in junior high school, asked the Democratic organization in our town how he could help. He was given literature and sent to the low-income, mostly Negro housing project—but cautioned not to hand out the leaflet of the Democratic candidate for Senator that boasted how much the candidate had done for Israel. Moslem Arabs are systematically murdering black people—in Sudan—and Israel is supposed to be the enemy of blacks. In 1967 social scientists from ten colleges and universities in and near Chicago asked people whether they agreed or disagreed with a number of statements, including one that Jews are more sympathetic than other whites to Negroes. More than 60 percent of the Negro respondents agreed; and there is no reason to suppose Chicago is exceptional. But how can that withstand the activists insisting that the Jews are the black man's enemies?

If that is not bad enough, the quota system is being introduced.

Or reintroduced—only this time not, as in the universities and professional schools of the 1920s, to keep those pushy Jews (greasy grinds) from dispossessing the gentlemen, but to do justice to Negroes. Negroes are about 11 percent of the population of the United States. At Brown University the administration agrees that future entering classes will have 11 percent of Negroes. At Radcliffe care is taken to avoid mentioning a percentage, but the number the administration announces for future entering classes turns out to equal something like 11 percent. (At Brown and Radcliffe they refuse to call the quota a quota; thereby, of course, preventing it from being one.) In Philadelphia Negroes are about a third, so a demand is made that the medical schools in Philadelphia put aside a third of the places in their entering classes for Negro students. That has not, or not yet, been conceded.

Quotas send a shiver down Jewish backs. They announce bad times. In the Soviet Union Khrushchev said enough "native cadres" had been developed for education, government, and the economy, so the Jewish share had to go down. For a semifeudal country the *numerus clausus*—"closed number"; quota—has been explained as follows (in a UNESCO pamphlet) by a liberal Catholic priest:

As regards religion and respect for the human person and the primary natural rights, the Catholic protest against anti-Semitism is definite, united, and absolute; it is equally so in the matter of anti-Jewish discrimination based on racism. As regards the political and sociological aspects of the question, the Catholic attitude is qualified. For example, in pre-1939 Hungary, the Catholic bishops, as members of Parliament, accepted the *numerus clausus* laid down for the admission of Jews to certain professions and schools. Here the bishops were acting as national leaders in a country where the Jewish minority (5.3 per cent of the population) had a practical monopoly in a number of spheres (press, theatre, etc.) or at least had a higher proportion of posts than its numbers warranted, even taking its cultural level into account.

The French Revolution was as much about meritocracy as about liberty, equality, and fraternity. Of all the revolutionary slogans, "careers open to talents" spoke most directly to the heart of the ambitious young man from the provinces, and Napoleon would have been less revolutionary if the *ancien régime* had not decided to be strict about noble birth for army officers. The objection to the principle of noble birth is that while the sons of the people are eager to make their way by talent and work, you aristos—*vous vous êtes donné la peine de naître*, you have taken the trouble to get born.

To hear some people talk these days, one would think that the merit principle is a Jewish conspiracy. The last thing those who made the French Revolution had in mind was to benefit the Jews. In the British civil service Scots seemed particularly successful, but apparently that did not lead to accusations of unfairness or to notions of a Scottish conspiracy. Yet here and now, somehow, suddenly, it is hard to find anyone who will defend the anonymous examination. If Jews do disproportionately well in these meritocratical contests, the reasoning goes, then the whole thing is unfair, a Jewish conspiracy in effect if not in original intention.

Today school principals and college students, tomorrow professors. If the municipal colleges in New York must have students ethnically representative of the city's population—though for at least seventy years most of the students at City College have been Jews, sometimes disliked as radical but seldom as ethnically unrepresentative—why should they not have faculties that are ethnically representative? If the students of Radcliffe and Brown, why not professors? Why not the students and professors of MIT?

Intellectuals (mostly writers, editors, and publishers) who are Jews—or rather, who had Jewish parents—are disgusted by teachers and principals who do not step aside in favor of ethnically more representative competitors. But the same principle can apply to intellectuals. Who knows? Under the aspect of eternity, quotas may be just. It is only that such justice has invariably hurt Jews. If Father Congar can argue that in Hungary the Jewish minority was only 5.3 per cent, how long will it be before someone argues that in the United States the Jewish minority is less than 3 per cent?

Now that we find ourselves so unexpectedly in trouble, we have no allies. We are not even our own allies, necessarily. Depend upon it, Dr. Johnson said, when a man is to be hanged in a fortnight, it concentrates his mind wonderfully. Our minds it seems rather to distract than to concentrate. Many of us approve or at least *understand* the trouble we are in; Jews are a large part of those white, liberal audiences that pay for the delight of hearing black actors or activists fleer and menace whites, liberals, and Jews. In the New York *Times* a Jew reviews a black intellectual's antisemitic book, notes the antisemitism, is silent about the intellectual poverty, and concludes that the book is "vigorously written . . . fiercely and honestly argued . . . a mind-plowing experience of the first order." For its part, the Jewish-label civil-liberties outfit is busy protecting us against—against a

Christmas stamp with the archangel Gabriel from Jan van Eyck's "Annunciation," and a lottery ticket with a menorah and Shield of David. (The lottery ticket's Santa Claus is pronounced kosher.)

Nobody wants to hear any more about the teachers' strike in New York City, but one thing still needs to be said. The teachers, criticized for this strategy and that tactic, would have been criticized no matter what they did, short of giving in. While Herman B. Ferguson was appealing his conviction for conspiracy to murder Roy Wilkins and Whitney Young, "the community"—the local governing board—tried to appoint him as principal of a Brownsville school. When that fell through, the board's chief educational officer put him on the payroll as a consultant. Mr. Ferguson is the author of an article on black pedagogy, according to which the education of black children should be organized around the gun. (In mathematics, for example, they could calculate trajectories.) Suppose the teachers' union had done something that corresponded even remotely to "the community's" appointments of Mr. Ferguson. The outcries would not yet have ceased; but in the eyes of radicals and most liberals the Ferguson appointments did not detract from "the community's" cause. The teachers were wrong to begin with. Justice, justice—as in that exemplary instruction to the jury:

> And when, amid the plaintiff's shrieks,
> The ruffianly defendant speaks
>   Upon the other side,
> What he may say you needn't mind.
> From bias free, of every kind,
>   This trial must be tried.

I mention the appointments of Ferguson, who adores the gun, rather than the cult of Malcolm X, who was an antisemite, because it is pointless to keep amassing evidence that antisemitism is no longer unacceptable. The thing hardly anyone remarked on when the black students occupied that building at Brandeis—even parochial Jews, so accepted has it all become—is the new name under which those students organized themselves: Malcolm X University. (The pacific Mr. Ferguson was the Freedom and Peace candidate for Senator from New York.)

So our allies are not going to come from the Left, whether liberal or radical—even though, or perhaps precisely because, so many of the liberals and radicals are Jews. They will not come from the Wallace or Birch Right. They will not come from the ethnics. Why should

Poles or Italians bestir themselves for the Jews? In national elections they and the Jews were in the New Deal coalition, but otherwise they and the Jews are usually at odds. In voting on money for the public schools, the Jews are for, they are against. On aid to parochial schools and on smut control, they are for, the Jews are against. The Jews go to college, they do not. They hunt, the Jews do not.

Perhaps our allies are to be found in the Establishment—the Establishment which may be called enlightened, if not actually liberal? So far as the enlightened Establishment has thought about the matter at all, it has decided against the Jews.

Imagine yourself part of that amorphous entity, the Establishment. Would you not reason as follows? The big domestic problem is the problem of the Negroes, who have been moving in large numbers from the rural South to the cities of the North. They come from the South poor, uneducated, unskilled, remembering oppression, hating and fearing their oppressors. In the North, where they need not fear so much, they can express their hatred. For understandable reasons they, or rather their children, direct that hatred more against the Northern whites with whom they now come into contact—policemen, store-keepers, teachers—than against the deputy sheriffs back home. What is more, these people are lower-class migrants. White or black, native or foreign, lower-class migrant families break up, their delinquency and crime increase.

For these newcomers to settle down (the reasoning continues), their elite must first be given a stake in the system. The last threat to the system came in the 1930s, with the unions. Tom Girdler of Republic Steel, a kind of fundamentalist of capitalism, fought the unions as hard as he could, and lost. It was lucky he lost, because the system has benefited from their victory. In return for union recognition and satisfactory wages, American industry enjoys labor discipline, the more effective because imposed by labor itself. Cheap at the price.

Who (the Establishment asks itself) can impose discipline on the black newcomers, especially in the schools? Not whites. Blacks are in no mood for that. Besides, white teachers are no longer tough or authoritarian enough. By their education, and maybe by their temperament, tough authoritarianism is foreign to them. It is not foreign to blacks. When the black elite of Newark wanted to cool a disturbance, they sent their people into the streets to knock a few heads together—their language—and the cooling was accomplished. If whites had tried to knock those heads together there would have been racial warfare, and the civil libertarians would have yelled. There was no civil libertarian yelling about blacks doing it.

Some part of the black elite want good jobs. They want to be principals, school administrators, welfare directors. Others want their turn at honest graft—real-estate transactions and building contracts— or at bribes, kickbacks, and theft. These are the traditional spoils of office. The earlier migrants have had their chance at the spoils, and now the time has come for the blacks. How give them their turn? By decentralization and community control.

For us, the Establishment, an extra dividend of decentralization and community control is that it can be cheap: the mayor of New York City, the hero of "the community" and its friends, reduced the school budget, with hardly anyone to pay attention, in the heat of the fight between union and "community." Another dividend is that we will be able to cut labor down to size. Labor has been strong and fairly popular, if only because it represents so many of the people. For us, it is too big for its breeches, and everyone will think we are cutting from and for the Left rather than from and for the Right. A third dividend is that we may be able to detach the blacks from the New Deal coalition. We want the New Deal coalition weakened, because it has kept us from exercising in the cities and in the nation the power none is better fitted than we to exercise.

Everything has a price (the argument goes on). What is the price of this? The weakening or destruction of the merit principle. Is the price too high? Especially in the schools, not really. The meritocratic machine produces people who may know subject matter well enough and may even know "how to teach"—whatever that may be—but it does not produce what we know to be most needful: people who can impose discipline, whose appointment will win them over while yielding their fellow-Negroes those symbolic gratifications that are so sweet to receive and so cheap to bestow.

Who will be hurt most? Jews. Well, fair is fair, and as between blacks and Jews we have no reason to reproach ourselves when we give preference to the blacks. It is not as though the Jews were suffering. They have done pretty well for themselves, and they have no right to complain if they are now asked to move over and make room for someone else. Anyway, the particular Jews in question here are a bit strident and given to hysteria. If they are no longer quite lower-middle-class, they still show the signs. And what can they do? Blacks can cause trouble, real trouble. Jews only talk. It would be nice if dislocating the Jews were not the price to be paid; but a price must be paid, and this is both the easiest and fairest.

Quotas in the universities? (The reasoning is coming to the end.) That is only another way of asking about the merit system, and merit is not now the most needful thing. Lord Melbourne said he liked the Order of the Garter because "there is no damned merit in it." We got along well enough when there was damned little merit in the universities. How long is it since students in our best colleges got their gentlemen's C's, and went on to run the country? Besides being a political necessity, admitting those black students there will give a voice and glory to people who would otherwise go to their graves as mute inglorious Miltons and Cromwells. Professors? The world did not come to an end when our colleges chose teachers, too, without much finicky regard to merit. The country, the system, depends on having a large number of people with reasonable competence, not on invariably selecting or promoting the man with the highest decimal in his test score. Besides, it is funny when the Jews get all solemn about individual merit. They must think so many of them do so well in college-entrance and civil-service tests because each of them is some kind of genius, biologically. Would they be able to show all that merit in those tests if they had not been born of Jewish parents, into Jewish cousinages and associations? Those Jewish meritocrats are strangely like the *ancien régime*'s aristocrats, they have taken the trouble to get born; except that the aristocrats realized it, and the Jews do not.

Hence the entente of the Establishment—the Ford Foundation, the Urban Coalition, the Mayor—and "the community" against the New York teachers. A friend of mine says the entente thought it was taking on Jews, and was confident it would win handily. It *would* have won handily—if those Jews had not been organized as a trade union. (More exactly: if many of the Jews had not belonged to the teachers' union.) To everybody's surprise, including their own, they fought like a trade union, instead of capitulating like educated, liberal Jews—almost as if they worked for the sanitation department (mostly Italian) or the transportation authority (once mostly Irish).

But after all, how many educated, liberal Jews are organized as a union? Will Jewish parents, college applicants, students, and professors wage a comparable fight against quotas?

Many Jewish students have shown a liking for what we politely call confrontation, and many Jewish parents and professors either approve or *understand*. But the confrontation is always in the name of universalist reform or rebellion. For Jewish students taking part in confrontation the first requirement is that they shall not think of themselves as Jews or of their purposes as Jewish. That would be parochial, out of the question. Jewish students will occupy a university building, or approve its occupation, to support the demands of blacks, but not to prevent or abolish quotas that will hurt Jews.

The class of Jewish universalists is one, with two distinguishable segments. Toward Center Left in ideology are those who make their livings in business or the professions and live on Park Avenue or in the prosperous suburbs. They have large views, responsibility, concern for the general good, impatience with parochial, particular interests. They are not like those unclassy Jews in Brooklyn, who went so far as actually to heckle the idealistic young WASP mayor of New York.

For me heckling is more than just distasteful. But when I consider how public discourse is conducted nowadays, and what one hears and sees every day on TV, in the news broadcasts, and discussion programs; and when I consider that the classy Jews *understand* these; then I have to conclude that classy Jews horrified by Jewish hecklers are like a civil libertarian who defends the public use of language that yesterday would have been called obscene, but resents someone saying "hell" to his wife. In New York the classy Jews, to dissociate themselves from those other ones and show their likeness to the idealistic young WASP mayor, invite him to talk to them on Park Avenue, where they can applaud him demonstratively. It remains to be seen what they will think and do when the quotas and community control and all the rest of it begin to be applied to their businesses and professions.

Further to the Left is the other segment of the class of Jewish universalists—the writers, editors, publishers, and professors. They too are proud of their responsibility, but this is to the radical vision, or revolution, or the new world struggling to be born. I. F. Stone is one; and it was he who admiringly described the mayor of New York as idealistic and young. (Humorously—but not really humorously—he has pitied the mayor as a downtrodden WASP.) When Jews heckled, Stone could not contain himself and wanted them slapped. Jews bother Stone. It is hard to imagine him filled with revulsion at the news that student rebels or black militants had heckled a Republican. It is not hard to imagine what he would say if someone else, in that other circumstance, got all smarmy over the idealism and youth of a

Republican politician pushing fifty. And if you wanted to slap any heckler but a Jew, Stone would call you a fascist.

It remains to be seen what the radical intelligentsia will say and do when quotas and community control are applied to writing, publishing, editing, and professing.

All that distaste for Jewish parochialism is nothing new. Deutscher has told us about "the non-Jewish Jews" he is proud to be numbered with: like Rosa Luxemburg, who said she had no room in her heart for Jewish troubles; and Trotsky, who said he was not a Jew, he was a revolutionist. On the whole, these thought they were rejecting Jewish particularity in the name of a philosophy and a vision that rejected all particularity. They thought they saw history moving to universalism, and they gave their lives to that movement. They failed, but not without some measure of honor.

What is newer is that the successors to those non-Jewish Jews are anti-Jewish Jews. Toward the end of the century, universalism is not what it was at the beginning. Nationalism, not internationalism, is the new reality. Not only in Asia and Africa: could Rosa Luxemburg have imagined Scottish, Welsh, and Breton separatisms? You can no longer say you oppose Jewish particularity because it is a particularity. That is an obsolete luxury. You have to oppose Jewish particularity because it is Jewish. You have to favor the particularities of the Jews' enemies. The journal of the French Jewish community, *L'Arche*, has reported on a book about the Middle East by a young French Jewish revolutionary. Because Israel is—as is well-known—a racist state, she did not visit it. She did visit the Arab countries, where she saw and heard much that ordinary people would take to be antisemitism, but her revolutionary wisdom tells her it is to be ignored. Her book is of such a kind that Ahmad Shukairy, the ranter-in-chief at the UN who was finally too much even for the Saudis who had employed him, has rewarded her with honorary citizenship in his Palestine of the future. *L'Arche* comments that in former centuries the enemies who hounded us most implacably were the Jewish apostates, and now they are the *progressistes* of Jewish parentage. (An exaggeration, but a small one.)

Isaiah 49:17 is a prophecy of consolation: " . . . those who ravage and destroy you depart from you." In the Middle Ages Jewish preachers interpreted this verse not as consolation but as lament. In a linguistically permissible way (compare Isaiah 39:7, for instance), they took it to mean: " . . . those who ravage and destroy you issue from you"—your own children are your enemies. The preachers meant the apostates: Petrus Alfonsi, Pablo Christiani, Abner of Burgos, Paul de Santa Maria, Pfefferkorn. As *L'Arche* implies, in this interpretation the verse can refer to the anti-Jewish Jewish *progressistes*.

Most Jews, if universalist, leave room for particularity; if we are for others' particularities, we are not against our own. What are *we* to do? What are we to think?

De Gaulle is now the enemy of the Jews. He dislikes us, but that is not his reason. He is our enemy in France's interest. As he says, nations have no permanent friends, they have permanent interests. In the United States every other group but ours understands that it should not be taken for granted, that it should encourage competing parties and candidates to bid for its support. Black nationalists and moderates have been telling Negroes that. But we Jews vote our fixation, not our interest. Why did I contribute to that 81 percent the last time out? Would 70 or 75 percent not have been liberal enough? It would still have been higher than the working class's percentage.

We esteem the left-of-center intellectuals and public figures. Why? Take the civil libertarians. They have helped to bring about a state of affairs that frightens not only the white middle class but also the Negroes. The civil libertarians (and the black nationalists) protest police brutality and the discriminatory harshness of our penal laws, but the Harlem NAACP fears criminal brutality more than police brutality. The Harlem NAACP wants police and laws and enforcement and imprisonment. Otherwise, it says, the prey of the criminals who now go uncaught or unprosecuted will be forced into something like vigilantism. They do not want to be vigilantes, but if there is no change they will have to be. Of course the roots of crime go deep. For the long term, basic social reforms are needed. Meanwhile, the NAACP says, criminals must be caught and punished.

Harlem's irreverence for the civil libertarians is not diminished by this implausible story: A court authorizes the police to tap a racketeer's telephone for evidence about one of his rackets; they hear a policeman offer to make pistols available for the murder of someone who has displeased the racketeer; the policeman is tried for conspiracy to murder; the trial court orders him freed, because the wiretap was authorized for evidence about a racket, not for evidence about a conspiracy to murder. (A question to lawyers: in what other country would a court have freed the policeman for that reason?)

The civil libertarians have always told us that due process, as for that policeman, is what civil liberties mean. Then, suddenly, we find the same civil libertarians—not exactly a *judenrein* aggregation—less fussy about due process for the New York teachers. Here the civil libertarians' old obsession with procedural justice has disappeared. Here their cry is for substantive justice, as they interpret substantive justice.

There is a scholar with a good reputation, at a good university. Just before the election he writes in a newspaper what he has learned about white workers who say they are for Wallace:

> . . . four out of five of Wallace's supporters contend that the assassinations of the Kennedys and of Martin Luther King were carefully planned by a group of people. One half blame the Communists for the riots in many of our large cities. They see a hostile environment surrounding themselves. . . . 80% fear riding buses without police protection, and fully 92% believe that safety in the streets represents the major problem facing the country today.

> This pattern of perceiving conspiracies and hostility in the surrounding environment . . . characterizes the perspective of many marginal groups in the American past: the Free Masons [he means the Anti-Masonic party], the Know-Nothings, the Populists, the Coughlinites, and the Joseph McCarthyites.

Everything is explained—explained away. It all stems from the traditional kookiness, culturally and racially if not economically reactionary, of bewildered provincials. No need to take it seriously. In his campaign Wallace kept telling the crowds: "The pointy-headed pseudo-intellectuals look down their nose at folks like you and me." That scholar seems almost to have been trying to prove Wallace was telling the truth.

Is it right-wing or racist to worry about crime? The Harlem NAACP does not think so. Is it provincial? Embassies in Washington and UN diplomats—including East European and African ones—complain to the American authorities about crime. Is it uneducated to worry? About the events preceding the Columbia unpleasantness, Daniel Bell writes: "The Columbia faculty . . . living on Morningside Drive facing Morningside Park . . . felt a strong apprehension . . . about . . . muggings and thefts, largely unreported. . . ." Is it unrealistic to worry? The reported crime rates are high enough, and, as Bell suggests, most crime goes unreported.

Is conspiracy thinking right-wing and dumb? From the Left and the academy we have a copious Fu Manchu literature, especially about the murder of President Kennedy, that makes Birchite maunderings look soberly rational by contrast. Is conspiracy thinking anti-

Negro? After the murder of Robert F. Kennedy, Negroes tended to feel that "They" were responsible, that "They" were killing off the Negroes' friends and leaders: the President, Martin Luther King, the Senator.

Jews are anxious about antisemitism, and a Jewish social scientist says we are crazy. A newspaper notes that he is the author of a study which concluded that "Negroes probably were less antisemitic than white Christians. But now, [he] suggests, the antisemitic statements of some Negro militants may be changing attitudes at the grass roots." No matter; the same paper quotes him as saying, "Jews are incredibly paranoid." He himself tells us that a minority of anti-semitic activists are affecting the Negro majority that was formerly rather well-disposed to Jews; in Germany the courts are still trying antisemites for what they did when they had the chance; Anne Frank would not yet be forty; but he says the Jews are mad to worry. (A question to psychiatrists: What is the technical name for the delusion that it is insane to be concerned about reality?)

Today it is approved knowledge that our welfare practice disserves the poor and threatens to bankrupt cities and states. Governors, mayors, a cabinet officer, commissioners of welfare, academic experts tell us that the South is dumping its problems into the North. The Southern states give the poor little, the Northern states more. Naturally, the poor go where they will get more. The solution proposed to us is a national welfare system, about the same everywhere. Then the movement of people between the states will be free and un-coerced, not the *de facto* deportation it is today. No one disagrees with what George F. Kennan says of "the great urban ghettos," but since Kennan is not in the compassion business he is able to speak in uncloudy language: ". . . you cannot cure the poverty that is already there unless you can prevent the constant importation of new poverty from somewhere else."

All this sounds reasonable. But if reasonable now, why not a few years ago? A few years ago you were not supposed to talk that way. When the New York State legislature considered a bill that would have made newcomers ineligible for welfare, everybody who was any-body exclaimed in horror. If you were for the bill, you were a bigot. That was official; and the governor, who is now complaining how unfair everything is, vetoed it. The official line was that welfare had nothing to do with migration. The New York City commissioner of welfare, now dean of a school of social work, testified at a legislative hearing that "the availability of public assistance did not affect the flow of population from state to state." He also said that if a residence requirement of six months were passed, he would do what he could to find loopholes in it.

That was in the early 1960s. At the end of the 1960s we were told this about welfare in New York City:

	1958–1959 (12 MONTHS)	1969–1970 (12 MONTHS; PROJECTED)	1969–1970 PERCENTAGE OF 1958–1959
Cost	$235,400,000	$1,700,000,000	722%
Number of people	240,000	1,300,000	542%

In the rich United States, should people be hungry and homeless? That would be an infamy. Should the residence law have been passed? Probably not. But have governors, commissioners, chairmen of community councils, and deans the right to tell us lies? Have they now the right to assert, with full and assured confidence, what they denied with the same confidence a few years ago?

How about us? Have we the right to be angry? We acquiesced in the humbug. That testimony, about higher relief standards not attracting migrants, was absurdly false on the face of it. From one side of the ocean to the other or from one side of the street to the other, people move because where they are going to is more attractive (or less repulsive) than where they are coming from; they are pulled or pushed, or both. We knew that then as well as we know it now. We wanted to be lied to.

And now we are dismayed by more than the costs, and the numbers, and their seemingly endless growth. Now it is we who are held responsible for the poverty and ignorance of those many poor and ignorant who have been pushed and pulled here, and who have borne children into conditions that favor *their* being poor and ignorant. Those children tend not to do well in school, and the schools in which they predominate are not good schools. The same kind of people—or sometimes actually the same persons—who testified then that the push-pull principle of migration had been abrogated declare now, their expertness and sincerity intact, that the schools have failed. Not employment policy, or agricultural policy, or housing policy, or welfare policy, or migration policy, or anything silly like that

—not these are at fault. The schools are at fault, the schools have failed. Some of the sincere and expert add that the Jewish teachers are busy at genocide; and few say no. They used to be our friends.

In self-interest maybe we should do an about-face. But we are not the kind of people to whom that would come easily. Prosperous people do not vote with the poor: that is the rule. Jews want to continue being the exception.

We are unable to change without injury to our sense of who we are and of what justifies us; but our inability to change leaves us vulnerable to our enemies.

In Beirut the Israelis earn the world's stern reprobation for their attack on—*horresco referens*—empty aircraft. American clergymen, the French president, and Soviet diplomats are moved by damage to things.

So are the custodians of art and culture. The Metropolitan Museum, directed by an eminent member of the Establishment, stages an exhibition about Harlem. Some Negroes do not like it, and picket. Someone scratches ten or eleven paintings, among them a Rembrandt. That is very bad, but fortunately, as an editor tells the public, "the damage is comparable to a light scratch on a piece of varnished furniture that does not go into the wood and can be removed with a little polish." No matter. "In a voice choking with anger" the museum director cries out: ". . . poisonous . . . unbelievable poison. . . ."

The Harlem exhibition is provided with a catalogue, sold at the museum and in bookstores. The introduction to the catalogue is notable for two things: (1) the authority who wrote it was a girl all of sixteen years old; (2) it is antisemitic.

Life has staged an unsubtle play, with typecasting and campy lines. Naturally, the museum director is upper-class WASP. Naturally, subordinate parts are played by Jews—*class*, classy; *occupation*, culture middleman; *habitat*, between liberal money and radical art.

In the first act the heroes stand up against a hysteria that would have us believe antisemitism is antisemitic.

Museum Director: ". . . not bigotry . . . not slander. . . . It states a fact. And if the truth hurts, so be it! . . . I condemn the tenor of the times which forces a young person who has lived in Harlem all her life to have these opinions."

First Jew (publisher of catalogue): ". . . not . . . our function to censor . . . contribute to the understanding of a difficult problem. . . ."

Second Jew (organizer of exhibition, arranger of catalogue, selector of introduction): ". . . member of the . . . Jewish community* . . . face the realities of the world in which we live . . . merely drawn attention to the facts."

The first act has a rude vigor about it, and little ambiguity. It shows how a representative of culture and the upper class weighs damage to things and harm to Jews; the entente between upper class and lower, WASP and black; how this entente sees Jews; and the function of a certain category of Jews in relation to the entente. From now on we will be unable to say we were taken by surprise.

In the second act it turns out that the hysterical Jews have a sting left. (*Cet animal est très méchant,/Quand on l'attaque il se défend.* This animal is bad indeed,/Defending itself in case of need.) The mayor puts more and more pressure on his friend the director. To be re-elected the mayor needs Jewish votes. He knows he probably will not have as many of those votes as before, but he can try to keep his losses down; having begun to squeak, the Jewish wheel now gets some of the mayoral oil. Other things, too, may have happened between the acts. Has there been a conversation in a board room about a stockholder's frown? Is a museum trustee uneasy? Has a contributor come down with writer's cramp as he was about to sign his check? All we know is that this act is about the courage which is grace under pressure: heroes adding guile to strength, yielding on the periphery but holding fast at the center. They agree to a formula that concedes nothing essential, giving less to narrow-minded, mean-spirited obscurantism than the fabled Galileo gave, voicing out loud the *eppur si muove* he only whispered. The formula concedes an error in judgment about public relations, the error of underestimating just how hysterical hysterical Jews can be. Nothing more.

First Jew: ". . . deeply regret . . . we were not more alert. . . ."

His boss (naturally, a Jew too; of the same kind but older): ". . . no harm . . . intended . . . blown out of all proportion . . . don't feel . . . a matter of life and death . . . worse things happening in the world."

Director: " . . error in judgment . . . controversy . . . has threatened to mar . . . entire project . . . has deeply disturbed certain groups of people . . . failed to sense . . . racial undertones that might be read into portions of it. . . ."†

---

* Note the confusing influence of television. This line is in the play to elicit Maxwell Smart's response: "Of course! The old I. F. Stone 'us-Jews' trick."

† For some reason, in my college days there was a brief fad of composing insolent imaginary apologies. The one I remember best is this: "If I have done anything you think I should be sorry for, I will not object to your excusing it."

Mayor (about director's statement): ". . . brave . . . how fortunate . . . to have . . . him at the Metropolitan Museum. . . ."

The third act is yet to be staged.*

We are cast as the heavies. In a city that our older kind of enemy was not long ago calling Jew York, we have been fobbed off with mock apologies for offense and haughtiness which neither that upper-class WASP nor his Jewish associates would think of committing against anyone else. In New York our remaining years in the civil service, and above all in the schools, are not many: if policy does not drive us out, terrorism will. (It has started.) In the United States we have not yet begun to experience what quotas must do to us. But oddly, after the second act of *Black, WASP, and Jew at the Museum* I think I feel a shade less discouraged than before.

Politics are still democratic. The calculus of votes and grievances still operates, the normal officeholder still hesitates to write us off. Jews are not quite so lacking in the instinct of self-preservation as I supposed, and some of us are even asking to examine the credentials of the doctors who brusquely diagnose our complaint as hysteria. What we will need for a while is a little bit of luck.

—March 1969

.13.

Class Conflict

In no American election was "the Jewish vote" so central to the strategy and tactics of the candidates, or so prominent in the news, commentaries, polls, and analysis, as in New York in 1969. It was clear that Mayor Lindsay would get most of the votes at the bottom and the top: at the bottom the poor—Negroes and Puerto Ricans; at the top the prosperous and well-educated. In the middle, it was clear that he was not going to get the votes of the Catholics, mainly Italian and Irish, of the working and lower-middle classes. The question about the middle was whether he would get enough Jewish votes to

* After this was written, the Metropolitan Museum announced the withdrawal of the catalogue from sale. It remained on sale in the bookstores.

put together a plurality. He did. Or rather, his Democratic opponent failed to get enough. It was less that Lindsay won than that Procaccino lost.

Of the white Protestant minority, most voted for Lindsay: not as the liberal candidate—they are not extraordinarily liberal—but as the fellow-Protestant, the *landsman*. Jews voted more than other whites for the liberal candidate. So what else is new? Jews always vote for the liberal candidate—notoriously in Presidential elections, as in 1968, but also locally, as in Los Angeles. There they voted not only more than other whites but actually more than the Mexicans for Bradley, the Negro who was defeated. From one point of view, little has changed.

From another point of view, much has changed. Liberalism is comparative. That Jews vote liberal means that dollar for dollar and year of school for year of school, they vote more liberal than others. It does not mean that there are no class differences in the voting of Jews. Prosperous Jews gave Kennedy a higher proportion of their votes than prosperous Christians did, Catholic as well as Protestant, but a lower proportion than less prosperous Jews, and so in all four Roosevelt elections. In New York as in Los Angeles, that has been reversed, and it is the more prosperous Jews who have been voting more liberal. The reversal began in 1966, in the New York voting on a civilian review board for the police, when Jews split fairly evenly between what were conventionally regarded as the liberal and the conservative choices, and the well-off made the liberal choice more than the less well-off. (And then too, as a group the Jews were substantially more liberal than other whites.)

One way of interpreting the reversal is to say that liberalism has new tasks. These require a capacity for sympathetic, imaginative, even abstract understanding. Naturally, the educated, who also tend to be the more prosperous, are better fitted for that understanding than the uneducated. When liberalism was fighting for social security, it was fighting for the bread-and-butter interests of working people, so of course working people supported it, or its party and candidates. Now, the argument goes, the victories of the old liberalism have deprived the new liberalism of programs comparably appealing to its old clientele. Now the old supporters of liberalism—the famous New Deal coalition—have or think they have an interest in the status quo. They have become conservative. They oppose the new liberalism with its new responsibilities, imposed upon it by time and change.

Class Conflict

This interpretation may be self-serving, and is self-righteous. In the New York campaign, the most telling bit of rhetoric was the name the Democratic candidate gave to the prosperous who accused him of conservatism: "limousine liberals." Earlier was it chiefly education that prompted Jews to vote for the civilian review board, and lack of education to vote against it? Perhaps it was prosperity and lack of prosperity. The prosperous could afford their vote. The unprosperous (and elderly), living in apartment houses without doormen and riding subways rather than taxis, may have voted as they did not because of ignorance but because of concerns explicable by the reality of their lives—a reality against which prosperity shields the prosperous. Similarly with education. Characteristically, in New York, Jews who send their children to private schools have approved for the public schools central educational parks and decentralization, integration and Black Power—whatever, at any given moment, has been the fashionable liberal thing. Jews who send their older children to expensive private colleges approve of transforming the free municipal colleges.

Less prosperous Jews do not think they are defecting from liberalism. They think they are being made to pay the bill for the limousine liberals' kind of liberalism. And they think that as if that were not enough, salt is rubbed into their wounds. First the upper class makes the others pay for upper-class notions of liberalism, and then the upper-class liberals are contemptuous. They make jokes. At a rally of Lindsay people, a comedian describes Procaccino—and by implication anyone who would want to support Procaccino—as sitting in his undershirt, drinking beer, and watching Lawrence Welk on television. Presumably Lindsay—and by implication the typical Lindsay voter— is the sort of man who, in dinner jacket, is photographed drinking a martini with Lennie at Lincoln Center, during the intermission of Pierre Boulez's premiere as conductor of the New York Philharmonic.

Especially must Italians wonder where contempt for a class leaves off and prejudice against Italians begins. People who would not dream of telling Negro jokes regale each other with Italian jokes. Was that a joke against undershirts or against Italians in undershirts? In Washington a political comedian amused his public with something he must have picked up from his set in New York: Mario is so sure of winning that he dropped by the mayor's official residence the other day to measure the living room for linoleum. The jokes that do not get into print are gamier still. If I were Italian I might imagine that the humorous liberals are not conspicuously partial to Italians. But I am not Italian, so I can understand the undershirt-beer-television-Welk joke to be as much about class and taste as about *Italianità*.

In contempt for non-upper whites, many liberals agree with the young radicals, or have learned from them. It was the campus revolutionaries from the rich suburbs who first exposed that fascist pig, the average union member—a potbellied oaf, undershirted, swilling beer, staring at the boob tube. Whether or not New York's white clods heard Lindsay's comedian's joke, they got the message, and it did not enhance Lindsay's popularity with them. Since many Jews, too, stare at the boob tube, and even drink beer, they hardly needed specifically Jewish reasons to vote against him.

In fact Lindsay, or his twins—his men on the Board of Education, that museum director, that university chancellor—had provided in abundance reasons to conclude that he was anti-Jewish: not, or not necessarily, antisemitic, but anti-Jewish.

For the Jewish members of the pro-Lindsay liberal elite such accusations, or such thoughts, were narrow, tribal, grotesquely passé, not to be entertained privately, let alone uttered publicly, by an enlightened, modern person. The liberal Jewish politicians, amateur or professional, had their own motives for supporting Lindsay. Though with the same tastes and beliefs as the other top people, yet they more urgently and personally needed him to win. Reform Democrats, they could not afford a Procaccino victory. That would lose them more than the mayor's office, it would lose them control of their party. However liberal and reform, politicians act on the principle laid down long since by a reactionary, Senator Boies Penrose of Pennsylvania: if you have to choose between losing an election and losing control of your party, you lose the election.

The most interesting voters were that small group of Jews who by education, income, and habit could be thought of as belonging to the liberal elite but who nevertheless voted *against* Lindsay, and that larger group of middling Jews who voted *for* him.

Some of the anti-Lindsay liberal Jewish elite were not especially conscious of themselves as Jews. In general, like their pro-Lindsay brothers, they rarely think about Jewish interests as such. Among these not very Jewish Jews would be some school principals, some professors in the municipal colleges, and a few intellectuals continuing an old, running fight with the kind of middlebrow outlook represented by the editorial columns of the New York *Times*. But these were a minority of their minority, because to be anti-Lindsay it helped to be a Jewish Jew. At the municipal colleges, for example, it was noticeably the Jewish-Jewish professors who took a position that could be translated as anti-Lindsay, i.e., "conservative." (There is a complication. Professors of hard subjects tend to be more "conservative" than professors of soft subjects, and the Jewish Jews seem to bunch in the hard subjects.) Of course, that those professors are "conservative" does not imply that they had probably voted for Nixon. It implies that they were worried about the Jewish future, whether in their colleges or in the city, that they saw a threat, and that they thought the threat came from Lindsay—Lindsay the agent or Lindsay the symbol.

Since, as is well-known, parochialism, narrowness, and prejudice are more usual below than above, the conviction that Lindsay and what he symbolized were against the Jews was widespread in the lower middle and middle middle class. Lindsay's strategy was to weaken this conviction, to lessen the number of people who held it. In two months he saw the inside of more synagogues than a Jew will see in ten years. He apologized, over and over again: not for having been anti-Jewish—he could not reasonably be expected to concede such a thing explicitly—but for having "made mistakes." If they wished, Jews could interpret that as an apology for acts which had inadvertently injured or offended them. Enough Jews in the middle wished to accept the apology, and to understand it as a promise to mend his ways, for Lindsay to win.

Not that they liked Mordecai, says the Talmud, but that they disliked Haman: not that Lindsay won those Jews but that Procaccino lost them. If the plurality in the Democratic primary had gone, say, to Wagner—with all his air of fatigue and his redolence of the past—Lindsay would not have had those Jews, or the election. Jews could have voted for Wagner without great enthusiasm, to be sure, but also without feelings of unworthiness, and above all without going against a powerful and still operative Jewish tradition that most are probably not even aware is Jewish. That is the tradition of being attracted by the *edel* ("refined") gentile and repelled by the *prost* (common) one.

I can give personal testimony, both to the attraction of the *edel* and to our unawareness that we are attracted because we are Jews. During Kennedy's Presidency I read a newspaper report of something that seemed to me splendidly patrician—the President with elegance and wit welcoming as his guests some artists or scholars, or his wife addressing gracious words of appreciation, in French, to a ballet company that had danced at the White House. Something like that. I was on the train, and turning to Tom O'Hanrahan, an active Republican despite his name, I told him, more or less: "Tom, forget about politics. Look at this news item. I don't care what your politics are, you've got to admit the Kennedys have class." To which he replied: "Yes, I know that's what you people think." I had thought I knew about the relation between being a Jew and having the tastes and outlooks Jews are apt to have. (I had written about it.) In saying what I said to O'Hanrahan, I had tried to discount that Jewish particularism which likes to regard itself as universalism. He educated me. He was not being anti-Jewish or offensive. He was only saying that my admiration for the Kennedy style was less universal than even I had thought—more Jewish—and less detached from politics. Would I have responded as warmly as he to a newspaper account of Ike enjoying a golf reunion with an old comrade in arms?

Lindsay was *edel*—or at any rate urbane. Procaccino was, or increasingly seemed, *prost*. It was so hard for many Jews to vote for Procaccino that Lindsay won. When they entered the booths, numbers of that great majority of Jews who earlier had told the pollsters they detested Lindsay found they could not pull the lever for anyone else. Because Procaccino repelled them, they were prepared to believe Lindsay's apologies and promises. The Jews who stayed with Procaccino were those who found it harder to believe in the new Lindsay.

As for the Jewish-Jewish middle-class Lindsay voters, Lindsay had worked hard to appease their resentment. He had eaten crow. Like the Emperor Henry IV, he had gone to Canossa—or to Canarsie. These Jews concluded that he had apologized enough, that he could be trusted not to backslide, and that his experience would warn him and his successors against making the same mistakes. Other things being equal, they thought, it would be better to vote for someone else, in the Jewish interest; only, as things stood it was in the Jewish interest to keep New York from the greater chaos into which it would fall with Procaccino. (But if only they had a Wagner to vote for!)

The Procaccino voters asked themselves the same questions but gave different answers—or alternatively, agreed about the factors in the equation but weighted them a little differently. Lindsay would not be that much better, they thought, nor Procaccino that much worse: whoever won would be mayor of an impossible city. And they thought it beside the point to speculate whether Lindsay was or was not a reformed character. Grant what was debatable, that he had truly reformed. It was still necessary to vote against him, as Voltaire said of the British government's reason for shooting Admiral Byng, *pour encourager les autres*. It is risky for Jews to show that we readily forgive injuries and slights. For Jews to forgive, to prefer the general good to our particular good—that is admirable, but also dangerous, and maybe suicidal. Among all the groups in the body politic, if there is only one which shows it is prepared to renounce its interest, which group will go to the wall in the clash of interests? Will a sensible politician hesitate to make such generous, yielding people bear more than their share of the common burden, or pay more than their share of the total cost—especially if he knows that later they will not even punish him for it at the polls? Globally, the misfortune of the Jews is that for fifty years we have had no bargaining power. Our enemies have been so inimical that our friends have not had to be very friendly to be able to count on our support. In New York now, these anti-Lindsay voters could have said, we do have bargaining power, we are at last free to choose. Let us use our freedom prudently. To vote for Lindsay would be imprudent, so let us vote for Procaccino. (But how much better it would be if there were a Wagner to vote for!)

Only about 10 percent of the Jews voted for Marchi. That is curious, because if any of the three candidates could legitimately be considered as *edel*, it was Marchi. He was superior to his rivals in learning, intelligence, and wit. His personal manner was pleasant. If he had been only the Republicans' candidate, many more Jews would have voted for him. Because he was also the Conservatives' candidate, they could not bring themselves to vote for him.

By now the top people's scorn for the slobs is no secret. The warnings have gone out and a certain amount of literature has even begun to be produced, interpreting the beer guzzlers to their betters. It reminds me of the understand-your-neighbor, one-world, antiethnocentric literature that used to be common: do not look down on the Sinhalese cultivator, he has not had your advantages—that sort of thing. One of the best-known pieces of this new kind was Pete Hamill's "Revolt of the White Lower Middle Class," published in *New York* magazine. Really, Hamill writes of the Irish and Italian working and lower middle classes in New York. He takes them seriously, he respects them. He is frightened of what they may do in their rage, and he makes it clear that he will not vote as they will, but he does not condescend to them or poke fun at them. But then, I think Hamill is not a Jew, and he is not writing about Jews. When a man called Rosenbaum writes in the *Village Voice* about the Jewish lower middle class, he is amused by those vulgar people, expects us superior readers to be amused, and all in all has a fine time telling us how funny their talk and dress are, and how irritable their narrow minds and pinched souls. The very title of his report—an account of Lindsay campaigning—is a nudge: "When in Brooklyn, Play Gimpel the Fool." Not one of the people Rosenbaum interviewed, unlike one that Hamill interviewed, was quoted as having said he had bought a gun. If we take Hamill's people seriously, as we should, we should take equally seriously Rosenbaum's people. But Hamill wants us to and Rosenbaum does not.

For the first time since 1932, or maybe 1928, the class differences among American Jews are showing signs of emerging as class conflict. The without-a-second-thought Lindsay voters are one class, the Procaccino and the hold-your-nose Lindsay voters the other class. The first is mainly upper and upper-middle, the second mainly lower-middle and middle-middle. (Mainly, not exclusively.) In the second the proportion of Jewish Jews is higher than in the first. It is members of the first that have dominated the mainstream Jewish institutions and have been prominent in the civic organizations that appeal disproportionately to Jews and rely on their disproportionate moral and financial support, like the civil-liberties unions. Until now the absence of a formal mandate has not kept the mainstream institutions from factually representing most Jews—in things like civil liberties, civil rights, separation of church and state—and therefore from having the implicit confidence of most Jews.

Now growing numbers of non–upper-class Jews have begun to suspect that when it comes to the things that they are most concerned and anxious about, and that affect them most directly, the upper-class Jews could not care less, or are actually hostile, and contemptuous in the bargain. The split between the two classes would have come more fully into the open in the New York election if in the end enough non-uppers had not felt they must vote for the uppers' candidate (for want of a Wagner). If the uppers want to regain the other Jews' confidence, they will have to be more attentive and respectful than they have seemed to be. They will have to show they care.

—January 1970

III

A PARENTHESIS ABOUT BIRTH, MARRIAGE, AND WORK

. 14 .

Population Implosion

In the *American Jewish Year Book* Erich Rosenthal shows that American Jews have stood aside from the baby boom. In 1957, when the average American married or formerly married woman of child-bearing age (fifteen to forty-four) had 2.2+ children, the Catholic rate was 2.3—; the Protestant, 2.2+; and the Jewish, 1.75—. With the average woman forty-five and over having had 2.8— children, the Catholic rate was 3+; the Protestant, 2.75+; and the Jewish, 2.2+. Jewish fertility, current and completed, is therefore about 20 percent less than the Protestant and about 25 percent less than the Catholic.

Professor Rosenthal explains that Jews rank high in everything that makes for low birth rates: living in or near the largest cities, white-collar occupation of the husband, education of the wife, income, and rapid social and economic advance. Since Jews are similar to Presbyterians in most of these things, the two birth rates are also similar. The completed fertility of the Presbyterians is one percent less than the Jews', and the current fertility of the Jews is 11 percent less than the Presbyterians'. (The Presbyterians have the lowest rate of any Protestant denomination for which we have data.)

Rosenthal dismisses the old idea that there is a specifically Jewish factor at work in lowering the Jewish rate, or more generally a minority factor—discrimination heightening the need for a good education for the children, and a good education being possible only when there are few of them. It is true that the Princeton Fertility Study, trying to account for what a friend of mine calls the contraceptive virtuosity of American Jews, points to the "perceived incompatibility between sending children to college and having large families"; but since Presbyterians apparently perceive the incompatibility too, the Jewish case can be explained without bringing in antisemitism.

I am not sure how seriously we ought to take those Jews' stated perception of an incompatibility between the number and the education of children. When people justify their behavior, they may be telling the real truth or they may be trying to fool the pollsters, or themselves. I do not know about the Presbyterians, but with the middle-class Jews of America something else is probably there, too. Economizing on luxuries would yield enough to send more children to college, but who wants to economize? Big cars and expensive vacations are fun. Besides, money is not the only cost in raising a third or fourth child. There is also the physical and emotional cost. A generation or two ago the Jews of the Western world—this is not an only-in-America matter—decided to enjoy themselves. For many Jewish women, especially, modernity has meant a kind of consumer feminism, opposed alike to the Victorians' producer feminism and to the *yidishe mamme*'s self-sacrifice ideology.

According to Donald J. Bogue's standard *Population of the United States* (1959), American Jews are "scarcely reproducing themselves." Rosenthal cites this as well as a Census Bureau finding for 1957 that "on the basis of American fertility and mortality levels, replacement of the white population required 2,100 live births per 1,000 women, single as well as married," and he observes that "the fertility rate of 1,749 per 1,000 ever-married Jewish women of childbearing age is considerably lower." Still, he refuses to say that American Jewry will not reproduce itself. He has learned caution from the failure of the low American forecasts of the 1930s.

Everyone condemns the recklessness of overcrowding the planet by engendering large families. (It is all so different from when I was in college, and everyone was worried about late marriages and small families in the educated middle class.) Where does a Jew's obligation lie? Should he absent him from paternity awhile, for the good of the human race? Or should he be of good courage, and play the man for his people?

—*September 1961*

. 15 .

The Vanishing Jew

Some years ago a book called *The Vanishing Irish* worried about the future of Ireland, but since then the Irish have stopped vanishing. The Jews have not stopped. Erich Rosenthal has told us that our birth rate is so low that the number of Jews in the United States is likely to decrease. Now to the news of loss by infertility he adds the news of loss by intermarriage. The *American Jewish Year Book* features a study by him showing that the rate of Jewish intermarriage is higher than has been generally assumed, and is rising.

Jewish intermarriage, precisely defined, refers to one of two things: a wedding in which either the bridegroom or the bride is not a Jew at the time of the ceremony, or a couple in which either the husband or the wife is not a Jew at the time of the inquiry or census. (If the husband or the wife is a convert to the other's religion, it is not an intermarriage.) Only about 30 percent of the children in Jewish intermarriages are raised as Jews or are considered to be Jews by their parents.

Professor Rosenthal's data suggest that intermarried Jewish wives are more likely than Jewish husbands to disappear as Jews, probably without the formality of conversion to Christianity, and their children more likely than the children of Jewish men not to be considered as Jews. Since intermarriage is more normal, so to speak, for Jewish men than for Jewish women, it may be that when it is the woman who intermarries she has decided somewhat more firmly to cut her Jewish ties.

Both traditional rabbinical law and contemporary rabbinical policy are inadequate to these realities. Rabbinical law declares as a Jew the child of a Jewish mother. The reason for that principle of the *halakhah* is not so much that maternity is certain while paternity is putative—it's a wise child, etc.—as the biblical finding of fact that the child takes his religion and culture from his mother. The Bible prohibits marriage with both the men and the women of the Israelites' neighbors, but in the narratives it is the women who are especially to be feared. (In Ezra-Nehemiah the Judaeans' gentile wives are said to raise their children as idolators, and are banished.) But in the United States today, the odds are that if a child born of intermarriage is brought up as a Jew, he has a Jewish father.

As to the policy of the American rabbinate, it is less a policy than habits and reflexes. The rabbis, more than anyone else, are worried about our survival, but they seem to prefer not to know that we are failing to reproduce ourselves. When they do turn their attention to Jewish fertility, it is to invoke the support of Jewish tradition or law for birth control. There are famous Reform and Conservative responsa of that kind, and recently a well-known rabbi felt it necessary to say the same thing again—as if we needed the encouragement.

Some years before Hitler came to power, the doom of the German Jews had already been pronounced. Their birth rate was so low by the 1920s, the ratio of old to young so high, and intermarriage so common, that only an impossible average of seven children in every German Jewish family could reverse the trend to extinction. We are more fortunate. To pass from minus to plus all we need is to raise the number of children in the average Jewish family to something like 2.5 or 3—not a great rise, but a rise nevertheless. If the rabbis wanted us to have more children, would they make a point of telling us that Jewish law favors birth control? They must imagine that we are unrestrained breeders.

It is on intermarriage that the rabbis center nearly all their concern for the Jewish future. Coolidge's preacher was against sin, and they are against intermarriage. But clearly, fewer Jews are listening. What the rabbis say against intermarriage might be more compelling if what they say and do not say about a closely allied question, conversion to Judaism, were less puzzling. Most of them are unenthusiastic about conversion. They believe that it is untraditional, that the would-be convert is probably a disturbed personality, or that before trying to convert others to Judaism we should convert the Jews.

The argument from tradition is that since the Roman Empire of Constantine and his successors made converting Christians to Judaism a capital crime, it has been un-Jewish to proselytize. Though the *Neture Qarta* are not popular with most of us, our reasoning about conversion is like their reasoning about Israel. They and other ultra-ultra-Orthodox Jews oppose the State of Israel as rebelliousness against God. When He decides to restore the Jews, they say, He will have no need of presumptuous mortals; He will send His Messiah. We end the *'Alenu* doxology (which Solomon Schechter called the Jewish *Marseillaise*) with the great verse from Zechariah: "And the Lord shall be King over all the earth; in that day shall the Lord be one and His name one"; but to try to bring that day a little nearer would apparently be un-Jewish.

The appeal to tradition and history has other peculiarities. For one thing, according to Blumenkranz's *Juifs et chrétiens* . . . the Jews in Christian lands in the Middle Ages proselytized as hard as they could, law or no law, until the disaster of the Crusades. When our ancestors' oppressors forbade converting Christians to Judaism, they had to enforce the edict with the death penalty. Now it is we who do the forbidding, in the name of fidelity to tradition.

The second argument, the alleged maladjustment of would-be

converts, is only an excuse for inertia. Almost by definition, a convert to any religion is likely to be maladjusted; but few religions refuse converts. Besides, maladjustment does not inhere in the genes, and the children of a convert can be as adjusted as anyone else. And anyway, the facts are in dispute. A rabbi with some experience of intermarriage and of conversion to and from Judaism tells me that if he were to generalize, he would judge our imports to be better than our exports—and, perhaps, better than the average of our domestic market, too.

The third argument, priority for the home mission over the foreign mission, is another excuse for doing nothing. Are the resources withheld from the foreign field being used for a Jewish mission to the Jews? And it is untrue that the foreign mission weakens the home mission. There is nothing like success abroad for arousing enthusiasm at home. The Anglican John Henry Newman's reception into the Roman Catholic church not only began a series of conversions to Catholicism that has not yet ended, it also strengthened the morale and devotion of Catholics by birth. Testimony, and above all the testimony of a life, rightly has much force. A few years ago a friend, a university teacher with notable gifts of learning and personality, was a supply rabbi in my congregation on Rosh Ha-shanah and Yom Kippur. Before *Ne'ilah* a woman told me how impressed she had been: "I said to myself, if someone as intelligent and scholarly as he is can be so sincere about it, then we must have a pretty good old religion after all." If he had been a congregational rabbi, she would have discounted his testimony. (What else should a rabbi be if not a sincere Jew?) If he had been a convert she would have been even more impressed.

In the face of a rise in intermarriage, rabbis keep using arguments that clearly have been ineffective and may actually be offensive. When they warn against intermarriage, they might think of doing it in a way that will allow them to continue in some such fashion as this: "It is best not to intermarry, but probably some of you will. If you do, try to persuade your fiancé(e) to become a Jew. Why withhold our tradition and religion from someone you want to marry?" If aggressive proselytism really is un-Jewish, that would not be very aggressive.

Even with the rabbis passive, there is a fair amount of conversion to Judaism in the United States, nearly all of it before marriage. Whereas in Europe conversions to Judaism seem to have been rare enough to become anecdotes, here they are common enough to make a statistical difference. In the past ten years alone we have probably received as many converts as there are Jews in Minneapolis or Cincinnati. With some rabbinical initiative, conversion might offset our losses by intermarriage, or actually produce a gain. And once we try it for demographic reasons we may find that we like it for its own sake.

—*September 1963*

. 16 .

Wanderers

In 1950 Chandler Brossard's "Plaint of a Gentile Intellectual" in *Commentary* opened with a plaintive assertion: "There is a new Alienated Man around. He is the gentile intellectual in New York City." For Brossard, the gentile intellectual was more cut off from community, family, and even his own childhood than the Jewish intellectual. The gentile had been harshly taught that you can't go home again, while the Jew regularly took the subway from Greenwich Village—this was some time ago—back to his parents and the old apartment in the Bronx. Hard to be a Jew? It was harder to be a gentile.

In another part of the forest, we find rootless gentiles of quite another sort—business executives. A doctor who lives in a rich suburb said to me not long ago, in passing: "Of course, my street is mostly Jewish, so nearly all the houses are still owned by the people who owned them when I moved here, ten years ago. The big turnover is in the gentile neighborhoods." Jews of his class typically work for themselves, or for a family firm. If they are doctors or lawyers, they cannot move any real distance without losing the clienteles they have slowly acquired. If they are businessmen, they may sell afar, but their base is close to home. By contrast, the gentiles are likely to be executives of corporations like General Electric or Standard Oil. Seven years ago they were in the Chicago office and lived on the North Shore, four years ago they were transferred to San Francisco and lived on the Peninsula, and last year they were sent to New York, to live where New York executives live. They will be shifted again, and again: IBM, for its employees, stands for I've Been Moved.

Which means, for wives, a constant change of houses and neighbors, and for children a constant change of schools and friends. Jewish wives and children are likely to have more stability in their lives. We are told, and it seems reasonable, that stability is good for a family.

What has happened to the Wandering Jew? In Europe, from the Right or the Left, antisemites have denounced the Jews as rootless and homeless—Barrès: *déracinés* (about the time of Dreyfus); Stalin: cosmopolitans, passportless wanderers. In America one hears rather less of this, because in the end traditional imagery cannot avoid contamination by reality. The wayfaring stranger on this side of the Atlantic has not been conspicuously or usually a Jew.

If the man who works for a big organization moves a lot, it is because the organization tells him to. The organization tells him many things. He is dominated by apparatuses that make decisions about him, and it is all the same to him whether those decisions spring from bureaucratic rationality or bureaucratic arbitrariness. Even his skills may not be able to sustain or satisfy him when he is on his own, but may be useful and valued only when brought together with those of many other men in a large enterprise. A carpenter or a teacher or a pants manufacturer or a doctor has no difficulty explaining to his young children what he does; an employee morale analysis coordinator—organization English, an isolating language, hates prepositions and loves nouns, the more abstract the better—can hardly explain to himself what he does.

Now, the alienation of such a man is not apt to be of the kind that moralists and social critics like—a refusal of commitment to the prejudices of the tribe. Rather, it is apt to be of the kind that they deplore—estrangement from the self, lack of authenticity, anxiety that seeks relief in conventionality. Here, too, the organization man has to pay a high price for being upper-middle-class. Why envy him? Yet on my train I observe that a middle-level Union Carbide executive outranks a partner in a small accountants' firm (though, on top of everything else, I suspect the accountant earns more). This may be an aspect of the new feudalism, where, as in the old, the retainer of a great baron lords it over the freeholder. A sensible man will take the cash and let the credit go.

What about the enforced absence of Jews from the executive ranks of the great corporations? Jews have a right not to be excluded, and we should insist that our names shall appear on the invitation lists. Omission from the lists is a bad sign. Who do they think they are, and what do they think *we* are, to leave our names off?

But the right to an equal chance at living the organization life does not necessarily mean that it would be wise to exercise that right. For Jews, would it require becoming rootless again, in obedience to a corporation's orders? Would our politics move to the right as we made the corporation team? William James said that it took a long time for him to realize that he could not be both a preacher and a pirate. He had discovered what economics knows as opportunity cost: the cost of being a preacher is having to forgo the opportunity of being a pirate, the cost of being a pirate is having to forgo the opportunity of being a preacher. What would be the opportunity cost to us of executive careers in big business?

In the 1920s, during the turmoil in the Soviet Union over Socialism in One Country, the Russian Jews told this story. Uncertain whether to believe Stalin that socialism could be built in one country or Trotsky that it could not, one man did what anyone would do: he asked the specialist in hard questions, the rabbi. The rabbi thought and then delivered his judgment: "It is possible to have socialism in one country, but it is better to live in another country."

—*July 1965*

. **17** .

A Plague of Children

I

We must turn to a course of reducing the size of the human population over the next few centuries . . . as rapidly as possible. . . . 100% effective contraception available to all would not halt population growth. . . . People want too many children.
—*Paul R. Ehrlich*, Encounter, *December 1970*

This is not the Professor Paul Ehrlich of Salvarsan, the Magic Bullet, but this one, too, leader of the movement for ZPG—Zero Population Growth—is an eminent scientist. Therefore he sees things as they are, not as he would wish them to be. He knows that people want what they should not want, what is bad for them and us, what for their good and ours they must be kept from having. Not only children: Professor Ehrlich also knows that "people want to enjoy massive consumption" and that "people are aggressive and xenophobic." No humane person could have a laissez-faire attitude toward aggression and xenophobia. He would want to curb them. And so with massive consumption, and with too many children.

Curb those dangerous passions and desires by education? Of course, but it would be folly to rely on education alone. Since antiquity the wise have known that people must be educated against greed, whether greed for money or for distinction; but that appetite has no limit, and that most people live to gratify appetite. Against murder we shield ourselves by other means besides education. Community is protected by the state, the state has police power, and police power compels by using or being manifestly ready to use force.

Perhaps murder is not the best analogy for the evil of too many children. Plague may be a better one. Both childbirth and plague are biological phenomena, and society entrusts the management of both to the medical profession. Reasonably advanced countries deal with plague by education, to be sure, but also by sanitation, by vigilance; above all by compulsory inoculation and vaccination. Against the plague of children the way to inoculate and vaccinate is to sterilize.

Many in ZPG are already educating us by the best method of the best teachers—not by telling but by showing, by setting an example. They have been sterilizing themselves voluntarily and demonstratively, so that we may be helped to leave our irrational prejudices behind. We always have to be shown. We had to be shown before we could welcome universal inoculation and vaccination.

Here the analogy ends. Inoculation and vaccination ideally should be irreversible, permanent. With sterilization, on the other hand, we could have too much of a good thing. We do not want total childlessness, only fewer children than parents, and only for a century or two. Afterward, when the population of the world has fallen to a tolerable level, we shall want as many children as parents (but no more).

So the scientists will have to be able to reverse sterilization if it is to be universal. Won't selective sterilization do? Not if "selective" means "voluntary." That would put us back to where we started: our problem is, precisely, that people are volunteering for ("people want") too many children. Then how about selective *compulsory* sterilization, more or less like the draft, which is selective compulsory military service? That won't work, either. Sterilize some, and the unsterilized may make up for them—perhaps by selling, directly or indirectly, the fruit of the womb to those whose wombs have been made barren.

Neither voluntary nor selective, therefore, but compulsory, universal, reversible, *female* sterilization. It is not men who have babies. For any quantum of effort or resources that we put into the program, female sterilization will be decisively more effective than male. Assume a hundred men with a hundred women, and assume a male-only sterilization program so good that it is 99 percent effective. With a hundred unsterilized women, one unsterilized man can produce a hundred children a year. A hundred unsterilized men, five hundred, could produce no more. Which is to say that a good male-only sterilization program is not, at the margin, any better than no program at all. But assume the same hundred men and hundred women, also with a sterilization program 99 percent effective, and this time female rather than male. Now those two hundred people can produce no more than one child a year (barring a multiple birth). Women's *ressentiment*, the single-standard ideology, what you will—these may exert pressure for male sterilization. Effectiveness requires female sterilization.

The method will be simplicity itself. Today every six-year-old has his inoculation and vaccination before being allowed to enter school. Tomorrow every ten-year-old schoolgirl will have her sterilization. When she is older and wants a child, she will apply to the Population Optimization Administration (POA) to have her fertility restored. After her child is born, the obstetrician will resterilize her. Needless to say, licenses will be fewer for second children than for first, and no licenses will be given for third children.

This is more rational, more efficient, than sentimentally allowing every woman a first child whenever the fancy takes her, and only after the damage is done having POA remove her from active fertility. The welfare of all depends on POA's smooth achievement of the Plan's annual production quotas.

II

Elected officials can no longer evade debating the ideologic issue of whether the individual right to procreate, to the detriment of society, is a basic human right and a fundamental freedom and whether it can be legally halted without damaging the fabric of freedom. The limitation of family size by law seems less an infringement than a boon to individual civil liberty.

—Edgar Berman, "We Must Limit Families by Law," New York Times, *December 15, 1970*

But what is freedom? Rightly understood,
A universal license to be good.

—Hartley Coleridge, Liberty

The *Times* identifies Dr. Berman as a noted research surgeon who served as special assistant on health problems to Vice President Humphrey. On the evidence he is also a political philosopher, in that great tradition Coleridge *fils* compressed so ably into the couplet above. Aristotle reproved the tendency of people in democracies to think that freedom means everyone doing what he likes. For the Stoics the bad and ignorant are slaves, only the good and the wise and those who suppress their desires are free. (Freedom is the recognition of necessity. The gods themselves do not fight against necessity.) For John Milton none can love freedom heartily but good (or, wise and good) men; the rest love not freedom, but license. Spinoza called that man free who is guided by reason. Montesquieu thought freedom was the power to do what we ought to will, or alternatively the right to do what the law permits. Rousseau thought so too, and he so loved liberty that he would compel us to be free.

Still, a few difficulties remain. The same Milton who made freedom the exclusive property of the good and the wise suggested that Necessity is the tyrant's plea. And there is the other tradition, represented by John Stuart Mill, for which the only freedom worthy of the name is that of pursuing our own good in our own way. There is also the difficulty of passing from general principles to particular cases.

I do not know Professor Ehrlich or Dr. Berman, but I should not be greatly surprised if they belonged to a civil-liberties union, or at least sent it their contributions. I should not be surprised if they were repelled by the Nixon-Mitchell no-knock legislation. I assume they think it a disgrace, and a threat to our liberties, that a police force should be empowered to break into someone's home without first knocking at the door.

Let us project our imaginations three years into the future. (Things move rapidly nowadays. Five years ago, who would have prophesied that our governments would now be so enlightened as routinely to provide abortion on demand, in public hospitals?) Universal, compulsory, female sterilization has been enacted into law, the Demographic Plan has been adopted, the Population Optimization Administration is in business. Defiant lawbreakers—naturists in the East Village or a New Mexico commune, Amish in Wisconsin—are reasonably believed to present a clear and present danger of conceiving, or even of giving birth, in contravention of the Plan, of the Annual Production Target (APT), and of the POA regulations, as authorized in the Universal Female Sterilization Act (UFSA). To knock or not to knock? If the police have to knock, they will find a man and woman playing rummy, or praying; or else a window suspiciously open and a bed suspiciously rumpled. If the police are allowed to kick the door in, they can well prevent a conception, or even a parturition, and nab the criminals in the act.

Or the POA police may know that antisocial physicians are issuing false sterilization documents. Shall a woman in possession of a document, but suspected with good cause of not having really been sterilized, be allowed to stand on the Fifth Amendment and escape examination by an honest, public-service physician?

In strict logic it may not be easy to choose between no-knocking to catch a dealer in heroin and no-knocking to catch an unlicensed procreatress or parturient. Practically, however, the choice is less difficult. Measured against the civil-libertarian principle, probable heroin-dealing is trifling; measured against the enormity of willful childbearing, the civil-libertarian scruple must give way: *salus populi suprema lex*, the people's safety is the highest law. Let the wise guys inscribe their jeering graffiti, their "Pushers sí, mothers no." The stock in trade of the old-fashioned politician was flag and mother. Luckily for us, both have become obscenities, equally.

So much for some of the difficulties uncovered in a legal approach to ZPG. Difficulties of another order are uncovered in an economic approach. An elated ZPG scientist has told me that recent research shows intelligence to contain only a small hereditary element. This scientific finding—which I must admit surprised me—will be helpful for appealing to the intelligent, who may have been thinking that it is their eugenic duty to have children. Now they may be told, in good conscience, not to procreate but to adopt. Adoption by the intelligent will accomplish two useful things: it will reduce total births, and it will transfer some infants from less satisfactory natural parents to more satisfactory adoptive ones.

But the intelligent (or at least the educated) are likelier than others to have incomes high enough for a substantial measure of discretionary spending. Convince them it is their duty to adopt, and when they go into the adoption market they may bid up the price of children, thereby stimulating producers to increase their production. Make that illegal and you could get a black market. Prohibition made liquor illegal but did not end liquor. Instead it brought about corruption, high prices to drinker and high profits to bootlegger, and a low, even dangerous, average quality of the product. And there is the additional possibility that after UFSA, some illegal purchasers may be brought into the market by people's ancient propensity to regard stolen water as sweet.

One more economic point: as Professor Ehrlich shows, reduction of children goes hand in hand with reduction of massive consumption. Today we can spend on Cadillacs, or houseboats, or rising college-tuition fees. Not for long, though. With only one child permitted to a couple, even the tuition fees of the future may not sop up those discretionary dollars of ours; while Cadillacs and houseboats will be in short supply. We will have the spare cash to buy children with.

Consequently, it is prudent to assume that all the ingredients will be there for a vigorous black market in children, or in childbirth licenses. We cannot foresee its details, but we should get set for the ingenuity of eager buyers and sellers. This usually exceeds the ingenuity of honest officials, if only because a good part of the black market's ingenuity is exercised in turning honest officials into corrupt ones. Seized by the authorities, moonshine and contraband narcotics have nevertheless been known to escape destruction and find their way back into the hands of illegal traffickers. What assurance have we that that will not also happen with contraband neonates?

All the more reason, then, why our scruples, which merit the greatest respect in the case of minor things like pushing heroin (or murder confessions), will have to be put aside in the case of the major thing, population.

III

. . . man in primitive societies has always controlled his own reproduction by custom. His customs in primitive, and to a less extent in advanced, societies have . . . always tended to produce not a maximum increase but an optimum density. Abortion, infanticide, restricted intercourse and various contraceptive devices are the means employed. . . . Those who are prevented from marrying or mating by warrior grading or postponed initiation . . . are forced into homosexuality

which then becomes a major agent of family limitation. The old are
generally left to die. And in extreme crisis the infants are eaten.

—C. D. *Darlington,* Evolution of
Man and Society, 59

. . . the [Cretan] lawgiver has made many wise provisions . . . for the
segregation of the women, so that they shall not bear many children;
and he instituted male congress. . . .

. . . other practices too have been reinvented over and over again, in
the long course of time . . . for necessity is the mother of invention. . . .

As to whether the children who are born shall be put away or brought
up, let there be a law against bringing up anyone damaged; while
from the point of view of the quantity of children, if the customary
arrangements prevent any of those born from being put away, a
limit must be set to the amount of child-production; and if any have
coupled and a child in excess is conceived . . . abortion is necessary.
. . . Let it be decided also for how long it is fitting that man and
woman shall do their public service by producing children. . . . anyone more than four or five years older than [fifty] should be relieved
from procreation . . . and thereafter any congress they may perform
must clearly be for health's sake or for a similar reason. As to congress
with another woman or another man, simply let it be ignoble for
anyone to be disclosed as engaging in it in any way at all, so long as
he is a husband and has that title; while if anyone is disclosed to be
doing anything of the sort during the time of his child-production,
let him be amerced by deprivation of privilege commensurate with
his error.

—*Aristotle,* Politics *1272a, 1329b, 1335b–1336a*

Isn't it in a futurist novel by Anthony Burgess that government
counters overpopulation by drumming it into the citizenry that gay is
beautiful, gay is better?

The Pill, legal abortion, Women's Liberation, Gay Liberation—all
have begun their careers of conquest pretty much at the same time.
An old-fashioned moralist will say that separately and together these
represent the triumph of the new paganism. The new pagans (so
called) will say that those things which frighten the fuddy-duddies
are only ideas whose time has come asserting themselves against the
Establishment.

Maybe the credit lies elsewhere. Maybe the new pagans are forcing
an open door. If there is such an essence as "government," maybe in

the last third of the twentieth century government is not at all displeased with ideologies, enthusiasms, movements, and behaviors that hold the population down.

IV

Then a new king arose over Egypt, who had not known Joseph, and he said to his people, "Why, the Israelite people are too many and too strong for us. . . ." So taskmasters were put over them to oppress them. . . . But the more the Israelites were oppressed, the more they multiplied and spread, until the Egyptians could not stand them any more. . . . Then the king of Egypt said to the Hebrew midwives . . . , "When you deliver the Hebrew women, . . . if it is a boy, kill him. . . ." But because the midwives were Godfearing, they did not do as the king of Egypt had ordered them. . . . So Pharaoh commanded all his people as follows: "Any boy that is born, throw him into the Nile. . . ."

—*Exodus* 1:8–22

In 1726 and 1727 the [Hapsburg] Emperor Charles VI issued two decrees, as a result of which in both Bohemia and Moravia the existing right of permanent residence of the long-settled Jewish families was allowed to be bequeathed to only one of the sons in a family. As the heir, that son was allowed to establish a new family; but as soon as he got married his brothers and sisters lost the right to remain. The purpose of this cruel law, worthy of the ancient Pharaohs, was to block the natural increase of the Jews and thus to effect a "*Reduktion*" in their numbers. . . .

—*Simon Dubnow*, Weltgeschichte des jüdischen Volkes, VII, 299–280

(Prosecution Exhibit 1544)
Top Secret
Memorandum

On 6 March I attended a meeting in the Reich Main Security Office concerning the further handling of the Jewish problem. The purpose of the meeting was to clarify how the general directives laid down in the "meeting of the State Secretaries" of 20 January 1942 [editor's note: the Wannsee Conference, on the Final Solution of the Jewish Question] are to be carried out actually in practice. The question of the sterilization of the persons of mixed blood amounting to approximately 70,000 individuals was considered to be particularly difficult. According to a report by the Supreme Medical Authority, this would be equal to 700,000 days spent in hospitals. As the hospitals are occupied by the wounded, this method does not seem practicable, at least during the war. As an alternative to the solution mentioned in section IV/1 of the minutes of 20 January it was, therefore, suggested to assemble all persons of mixed blood (first degree) in a single city . . . and to postpone the question of sterilization to the period after the war. . . .

> [signed] Rademacher (Berlin, 7 March 1942)
> —Trials of War Criminals before the
> Nurenberg Military Tribunals . . .
> October 1946– April 1949, XIII, 221–222

Under the patronage of the SS and Police, sterilization experiments were conducted on Jews in the killing center of Auschwitz, and from time to time the experimenters sent in reports to the effect that a technique for large-scale sterilizations was about to be "perfected."

. . . [in Holland] by February 1944, only 8610 intermarried Jews were still living in their homes. These Jews were accorded complete exemption from anti-Jewish measures, to the point of permission to dispose of the [yellow] star, if they could prove their sterility. A total of 2256 Jews had submitted such proof; hundreds of them had acquired it by subjecting themselves to an operation. . . . It appears that sterility of the Christian partner was not an acceptable ground for releasing restrictions. It was the Jewish partner who had to be sterile.

> —Raul Hilberg, Destruction of
> the European Jews, 273, 377

Long before the proclamation of the Jewish State, the She'erit Ha-peletah ["the surviving remnant"] established miniature Jewish states within the [Displaced Persons'] camps. . . . Tens of thousands of new families were established, resulting in a birth rate of 75 to 100 for every 1,000—unsurpassed in the world.

> —Editor, last issue (Jan. 10, 1950) of Dos Vort,
> the newspaper of She'erit Ha-peletah;
> in Leo W. Schwarz, The Redeemers, 308

The keynote is the very low level of Jewish fertility. In all countries for which data are available, including the United States, the fertility of the Jews is below that of the general population. In several countries it has fallen below replacement level. After a short-lived post–World War II baby boom, Jewish birth figures declined in the 1950's. . . . In all diaspora Jewish communities . . . the proportion of . . . old people is greater. . . . This . . . affects unfavorably the balance of births and deaths.

> —Usiel O. Schmelz, "Evaluation of Jewish
> Population Estimates," American Jewish
> Year Book, 1969, 274–275

A *Plague of Children*

Long ago the Jewish parochials were put in their place by that joke about The Elephant and The Jewish Question, and now the parochials are worrying about The Population Explosion and The Jewish Question. The parochials are solemn about the Jews' uniqueness in being so much fewer, all these years after Hitler's war, than before it. They say that Russians, Poles, Germans have made up their wartime losses, and that only the Jews have not. They worry even about America, and will tell you that the Jewish ratio to the total population has dropped a fifth in one generation.

Of every 1,000 people in the world, 996 or 997 are not Jews. A concern about minorities is admirable, of course, and all that, but really! How much attention are we—even those of us who happen to have been born Jews (whatever "Jews" may mean)—supposed to give to a tiny fraction of the world's population? Explaining why his country cannot afford to be anti-Russian, a Pole has said that Russia is bad enough, but China will be impossible: the entire Polish people is smaller than a small statistical error in the Chinese census. But *all the Jews in the world* are fewer than half of the Poles in Poland. All the Jews in the world are fewer than two-thirds of the blacks in the United States, fewer than one-third of the Catholics in the United States. How can you justify a preoccupation with Jews?

If it were only a matter of the Jews as Jews, therefore, we need have no second thoughts. It is only as the Jews represent groupiness—group interests, passions, and suspicions—that we have to pay attention to them, or rather to the groupy questions that are regrettably likely to be raised. Let us restate the central principle: the philoprogenitiveness of selfish or backward individuals is at odds with the common good of the human race; and against selfish desires, or archaic values and habits of thought, the common good must prevail. That truth cannot be shaken. But the existence of groups means that individuals have sentiments and purposes stemming from their group memberships as well as from their individualities.

The first practical complication arising from groupiness is easily disposed of. That is what used to be called national interest or, from another perspective, patriotism. Some may argue that the very metaphors ZPG people use in talking about population show that population has military significance: "bomb" and "explosion." They may then go on to point out that for American ZPGers, the birth of an American baby is much worse than the birth of a Chinese or Indian baby, because Americans use up a hugely disproportionate share of the world's goods, and foul earth, water, and air with a hugely disproportionate share of the world's junk and garbage. For ZPGers, this means that ZPG is more urgently needed in America than in China or India. But with population having military significance, will not what may amount to unilateral American ZPG be a kind of unilateral American disarmament?

This is easily answered: yes. But the matter must not be allowed to rest there. Counter-questions are in order. Are you a militarist, a hawk, a cold-warrior? What kind of person are you, to oppose ZPG for narrow reasons of national interest, so called—which, at that, are nothing more than apprehensions of military (!) disadvantage?

The domestic rivalries of group interests are stickier. Take abortion, for instance. There are some (and not blacks alone) who think it a remarkable coincidence that abortion, so long illegal and so long a near-monopoly of the white middle class, should have been made legal and widely available just when the taxpayer types were making louder and louder noises about the rising cost of supporting the rising number of welfare children. If those suspicious of abortion should now direct their suspicions against ZPG, they would be misguided, of course; but given their experience and outlook, can they be convinced they are wrong?

There is more yet. Some blacks are against abortion not primarily because they resent the motives they impute to the social engineers who legislated it but because, quite simply, they want the black population to increase more rapidly than the white. Such people say that the blacks of the United States are a minority of awkward size, 11 percent—too big not to be conspicuous, too small to be strong. They want the black proportion bigger, about 25 percent. For them, ZPG will be even worse than abortion, which after all is voluntary. ZPG will be compulsory and it will freeze population ratios. Inevitably, some will say it is antiblack. Of course freezing population ratios is not what ZPG is for. We know that, but the black populationists may tell us again that white racism is not always conscious. And, unfortunately, freezing American population ratios can evoke memories. The explicit purpose of the Immigration Restriction Acts of the 1920s was, by freezing population ratios, to preserve America's Nordic character against Slavs, Mediterraneans, Asians, and Africans (and Jews).

Conscientious citizens will serve on the local Population Optimization Administration boards, and loudmouths will make life miserable for them. Has Mrs. A been denied a license for reversal of sterilization? Then the POA board is discriminating against Catholics. Miss

B? The board is against feminists. Mrs. C? Against the poor. Mrs. D? Against blacks. Mrs. E? Against the wives of policemen. The members of the board are prejudiced, arbitrary, snobbish. They are corrupt. They show favoritism. The head of the POA in Washington is corrupt and prejudiced.

To advance meaningful freedom it may be necessary to silence those demagogues.

V

The Lord spoke to Moses and said: Speak to the Israelites and say to them: I am the Lord your God. You shall not do as is done in the land of Egypt, where you dwelt, nor shall you do as is done in the land of Canaan, to which I am bringing you; you shall not follow their ordained practices. You shall keep My laws and observe My decrees. . . . : I am the Lord your God. . . . My decrees and My laws, by which, if a man obeys them, he will have life: I am the Lord. None of you shall approach anyone of his own flesh to uncover nakedness: I am the Lord. . . . You shall not lie seminally with your neighbor's wife, defiling yourself with her. You shall not give any of your children for offering to Molech, lest you profane the name of your God: I am the Lord. You shall not lie with a male as with a woman; that is an abomination. You shall not lie with any animal, thereby defiling yourself. . . . For by all such things those nations defiled themselves whom I am driving out in your favor. . . . But you, you must not do any of these abominations . . . so that the land shall not spew you out for defiling it, as it spewed out the nation that preceded you. . . . I am the Lord your God.

> —*Leviticus* 18 (*read in the synagogue Yom Kippur afternoon*)

Moses . . . gave the Jews novel religious usages, opposed to those of all other people. For the Jews everything is profane which among us is sacred, and contrariwise, among them everything is permitted which to us is unclean . . . though a people most inclined to lust, they shun lying with foreign women—while among themselves nothing is unlawful. . . . Also they are concerned to increase their population; for they think it an abomination to kill any unwanted or inconvenient child . . . the Jews understand God . . . to be one . . . supreme, eternal . . . not to be represented. . . . Therefore they display no images in their cities, not to speak of their temples; such flattery their kings do not receive from them, nor such honor the Caesars. . . . the Jewish way is senseless and filthy.

> —*Tacitus*, Histories V, *iv, v*

. . . one commandment the pagans keep is that they do not write a marriage contract between males. . . .

—*Hullin* 92a,b

[T]*hey do not write a marriage contract between males*: For though the pagans are assumed to practice homosexuality, and in fact do practice it, they are not so far gone in derision of the commandment against it as actually to write a marriage contract.

—*Rashi ad loc.*

Nero . . . married the boy Sporus with all due rites, including dowry and bridal veil; took him home, accompanied by a large crowd, and kept him as his wife. Somebody's rather clever mot is still in circulation, that it would have been a good thing for everyone if Nero's father Domitius had had such a wife.

—*Suetonius*, Lives of the Caesars VI, *xxviii*

The *She'erit Ha-peletah* witnessed the collapse of European [sc., Western] civilization. . . . We have given the world the will and testament of those who perished: "Do not put your faith in European civilization. . . . Return to the sources of Jewish morality. Live in accordance with the moral imperative of Judaism. . . ."

—*Dos Vort, January 10, 1950*

As Israel were redeemed from Egypt for the merit of having been fruitful and having multiplied, so will Israel be redeemed in future for the merit of being fruitful and multiplying. . . . Know this to be so, that Israel are redeemed only if they are fruitful and multiply; as it is said [Isaiah 54:3], "For to right and left you will increase. . . ."

—*Seder Elijah Zuta 14 ad fin.*
(*Lublin edition*)

Well, maybe at that it would be artificial, in talking about ZPG, not to talk about the Jews.

So many in the movement seem to be Jews. So many of the self-sterilizers, who are setting an example for the more backward, seem to be Jews. That is, Jews of the good kind, not like the The-Elephant-and-The-Jewish-Question ones. The latter, in a characterization once standard in Christian theology, are carnal—which is to say, fleshly, or material. The fleshly, material Jews are also the parochials, who link everything to The Jewish Question. About everything they ask, "Is it good for the Jews?" They ask that even about ZPG.

Parochial, fleshly Jews say that since ZPG is for combatting the population explosion, it is the right thing for population-exploders:

A *Plague of Children*

Indians, Chinese, Russians, Americans, what have you. But the Jews are not exploding, it is not they who have too many children. The Jews have too few children, they are imploding. For Jewish population-imploders, say the fleshly parochials, the right thing is not ZPG but MPG—Maximum Population Growth. Self-consciously Hebraic, they yet appeal to a Hellenic principle: justice is the equal treatment of equals; whereas no less than the unequal treatment of equals, the equal treatment of unequals is injustice.

Prophetic Jews, on the other hand, are not always asking, "Is it good for the Jews?" Prophetic Jews know better than to grant the parochials' plea for exempting the Jews. ZPG is the Jews' obligation not only because it is the obligation of all, but especially because it is in the highest degree a prophetic duty for Jews to take the lead and be an example. The fleshly parochials—we may as well call them priestly, too, to set them off against the prophetic—would actually say that for the Jews a devotion to ZPG is suicide. They do not even shrink from hinting that there may be something immoderate, problematic, about Jews cheerfully volunteering for sterilization, untroubled by any memory of what sterilization meant for Jews only yesterday, and of how the capacity and desire of the survivors to bring children into the world affirmed the Psalmist's "I shall not die, but live."

This sort of thing the prophetic Jews reject with the indignation it deserves; as they reject with the contempt it deserves the pedantic quibble that prophetics ought to know their Prophets.

The prophetics will not let their humanity, their very vocation for prophetism, be cribbed and confined by pedantries, or by tribal compulsions to relive old, irrelevant horrors, or by home-bound, timorous refusals to adventure forth into a wider universe of thought and concern. The prophetics understand that it does not matter if the Jews die away, so long as Jewish ideals live; that if Jewish ideals are to live, it may well be necessary for the Jews to die away; even that it may *be* a Jewish ideal that the Jews should die away.

Is it not sad that there are still some Jews deaf to a prophetic voice?

VI

So Pharoah commended all his people as follows: "Any [Hebrew] boy that is born, throw him into the Nile. . . ." Now, a man of the house of Levi had gone and married a Levite woman. She conceived and bore a son and, seeing what a fine child he was, hid him for three months. When she could no longer keep him hidden, she got a papyrus basket for him, caulked it with bitumen and pitch, placed the boy in it, and put it among the reeds by the bank of the river. His sister stationed herself at a distance to learn what would happen to him.

Pharaoh's daughter, having come down to bathe in the Nile . . . , noticed the basket among the reeds and sent a maid for it, who picked it up. Opening it, the princess saw the baby—a boy, crying—and taking pity on him, said, "He must be one of those Hebrew children." So his sister said to Pharaoh's daughter, "Shall I go and engage a nurse among the Hebrew women for you, to suckle the child for you?" Pharaoh's daughter said yes, and the girl went and engaged the child's mother. . . . When the boy was older, she brought him to Pharaoh's daughter, who adopted him as her son, and named him Moses. . . .

—Exodus 1:22–2:10

Amulius deposed his brother Numitor and reigned in his place. Adding crime to crime, he destroyed his brother's male line; and Numitor's daughter Rea Silvia . . . Amulius appointed Vestal Virgin, putting an end to her hopes for progeny. . . . Having been raped, Rea Silvia the Vestal gave birth to twins . . . and named Mars as the father. . . . But neither the gods nor men could save her or her children from the cruel king. The priestess was bound and put into prison, and the boys were ordered thrown into the river. . . . By divine chance the Tiber had overflowed its banks . . . and no one could get to the river proper. . . . Thus, imagining they were carrying out the king's order, his men put the infants into the nearest overflow. . . . The tale is told that when the flood let up, the tub containing the boys floated to a dry spot; and a thirsty she-wolf, coming down from the surrounding hills and attracted by the childish wails, was so mildened that she let down her dugs and suckled the boys. The king's herdsman, whose name was Faustulus, found her licking them with her tongue and took them home to be brought up by his wife Larentia. (But there are some who think that it was Larentia who was called She-wolf, among the shepherds, as being a common harlot. . . .) Such was the manner of Romulus and Remus's birth and upbringing. . . .

—Livy, History of Rome from
Its Founding, *I, iii, iv*

If children are to be headed off or put away, let there be no slip-ups. Sterilizations must sterilize, abortions abort (and drownings drown). One thing is pretty certain, that the world needs no new Prophets or Founders, no new Judaisms or Romes. Even now someone may be writing a novel set in the twenty-first century, complete with mythos of the child doomed, spared, endangered again, and finally revealed as Savior—whether Founder or Prophet.

What will be his equivalent of tub and caulked basket?

—April 1971

IV

JEWS WITH OTHERS

. 18 .

Two Cities

Algeria, about to become independent, had much in common with Central and Eastern Europe in the years before and after the 1914 war—the dissolution of empire, conflict between a dominant minority and a subordinate majority, and the Jews boxed in a corner. Most Algerian Jews would have preferred Algeria to remain French, just as most of the Jews in the Hapsburg lands probably would have wanted the empire intact. A minority of Algerian Jews were for an Algerian Algeria because they thought it just and progressive or because they were Algerian nationalists, as a minority of Jews in Prague or Lemberg (Lwow) favored Czech or Polish independence.

The case of the Jews of Prague is best known, on account of the interest in Kafka. They were part of the Jewry of the German *Kulturkreis*, whose grandfathers had spoken Yiddish. But one thing that made Prague so Kafkaesque for the Jews was that there German was the language and culture of a hated minority. The peasants in the country and the workers and servants in the city spoke Czech and, led by a nationalist elite, dreamt of the overthrow of German lordship. For the Czechs the Jews were hateful Germans, all the more to be despised because they were not really German. (The real Germans were not very fond of the Jews either.) When Czechoslovakia was established, the Jews were uneasy, briefly, until they came under the shelter of Masaryk's liberalism.

In western Galicia the assimilating Jews were attracted to German rather than to Polish and in eastern Galicia to Polish rather than to the Ukrainian of the peasantry. In Riga the Jews who had given up Yiddish and did not care for Hebrew were partisans of the Russian language and culture against Lettish, even after the creation of Latvia. In Slovakia the emancipated Jews preferred Hungarian to Slovak.

Of two contending gentile cultures, therefore, Jews were attracted to the more advanced one. The attraction was understandable and natural, but it made trouble. The success of Zionism in Prague and of Hebrew or Yiddish school systems farther east was partly—not primarily—due to a growing Jewish belief that when gentile nationalities were in conflict it was more dignified for Jews to assert a kind of autonomous neutrality than to side with either. It was more prudent, too, because partisanship would mean the heightened enmity of one nationality and the ingratitude of the other, while neutrality, though it would not make friendships, might keep enmities tolerable.

In Algeria the Crémieux decree gave French citizenship to the Jews in the nineteenth century. Their equivalent of Yiddish was a Judeo-Arabic tongue, written, like all Jewish languages, in the Hebrew alphabet. It was abandoned, like Yiddish in Prague, because it seemed to the Algerian Jews that only by a Western citizenship, language, and culture could they lift themselves from superstition, ignorance, disease, and poverty to enter the world of modernity and achievement. Giving up rabbinical law—including the right to polygamy, only Ashkenazim being affected by Rabbenu Gershom's ban a thousand years ago—was not felt as a hardship. The Algerian Jews became zealous Frenchmen of the spirit-of-'89 and the liberty-equality-fraternity school.

Unfortunately, not all Frenchmen were of that school. In Algeria most of the *colons* and many of the lower-class Europeans were reactionary and antisemitic. During the turmoil over Dreyfus there was violence against the Jews and aggressive antisemites kept winning at the polls. A half century later the Vichy regime—which has been called the anti-Dreyfusards' revenge—revoked the Algerian Jews' French citizenship, to the delight of the Pétainist mass of Europeans. Of the Moslems, not all were so delighted as Vichy had hoped. Many rejoiced, but the more thoughtful did not want citizenship withdrawn from the Jews. They only wanted it extended to themselves.

For decades the Algerian Europeans vetoed all proposals to make it easier for a Moslem to become a Frenchman, until they woke up to find that the Moslems were no longer interested. As soon as it was French nationality and nationalism against Moslem-Algerian nationality and nationalism, the position of the Jews of Algeria ceased to be merely potentially like that of the Jews of Central and Eastern Europe forty or fifty years earlier. Only, the Algerian Jews had even more reason to worry about the Moslem Arab majority than the Jews of Prague about the Czechs.

The agreement between the Algerian revolutionary leadership and

Paris had guarantees for French citizens, including the Jews. (For a long time the provisional government had insisted that the Jews, being as native as the Moslems, should not be deprived of their Algerian status merely because imperialists in the nineteenth century had thought it useful to make them legally French. The Jews were touched, but chose to go on being legally French all the same.) Guarantees notwithstanding, and even if, impossibly, the hatreds and guilts of the recent and distant past were forgotten, few non-Moslems imagined that they would be able to stay after there had been time to develop a native intelligentsia, to use Krhushchev's phrase about some Soviet republics.

Who knows? The Algerian Jews might have done better as Jews in a candidly triple society than as legally French in a make-believe dual society. In Belfast a Jewish boy was caught one Orange Day between a gang of Protestants and a gang of Catholics, each demanding to know which he was. He had never been so glad to be able to say he was a Jew, but then they asked whether he was a Protestant Jew or a Catholic Jew. That question would probably not be asked where the Jews were one element of three.

—*May 1962*

. 19 .

The Moroccan Vote

When Disraeli spoke of England as two nations, the rich and the poor, he was not denounced for it. Perhaps that was because he was an Englishman, in the thick of politics. Otherwise, unflattering things might have been said about his understanding and especially his motives, as were said in Israel about the understanding and motives of the cultural anthropologist Alex Weingrod after his "Two Israels" was published. The two Israels, Ashkenazim and Sephardim ("Easterners"), are a commonplace in Israel itself, but Weingrod was handled roughly.

In particular, Weingrod's critics made much of his being an American Jew and of the psychological needs presumably arising from that circumstance, which presumably impelled him to say harsh things about the dominant Ashkenazim. Shelomo Grodzensky also entered into the discussion. While not acquitting Weingrod of all the charges of misunderstanding against him, Grodzensky tried to situate him in a tradition of cultural anthropology, influential in America, that refuses to see the fact of cultural difference as meaning the superiority of one culture over another, and especially of the people of one culture over the people of another. Affirming that tradition for himself, Grodzensky hoped it would become influential in Israel too.

I am not sure that cultural anthropology is the dominant influence on us. If we have been educated at all, it is by American politics and American society. Not very long ago the intellectual and moral elite here was saying things about the Irish that today we can hardly believe were said even when we see them on the printed page. Low nature, imperviousness to American ideals—there was no end to the bill of particulars. By now it is not hard to see that the accusations tell us as much about the accusers as about the accused, or as little. American Jews, who have been similarly complimented from time to time, know there is something wrong when the same sort of thing is said about the newer lesser breeds in this country, like the immigrant Puerto Ricans and the in-migrant Negroes.

The immigrants' children or grandchildren finally make it. Sometimes they make it by using means that are conventionally regarded as distasteful or even un-American, such as the famous so-called bloc vote. But we know now, better than ever, that their success has not been at the expense of the common good. The late President Kennedy's irreducible power base was Irish Catholic Boston. Was he a worse President than, say, Harding and Coolidge, who were not of more or less recent, self-conscious immigrant stock and religion?

In the United States the son of a Protestant immigrant from England or Canada is in some sense old-stock, a realer American than others. The others resent that here. In Israel an immigrant from Poland can be a realer Israeli than other, native-born Israelis. The others resent that there. An American Jew may be the cousin of an Israeli, both having a Polish grandfather in common. All kinds of emotional difficulties are likely between the two, from both sides. Still, it is not those difficulties so much as the American's American experience that would lead him to sympathize with the resentment of the non-Ashkenazi Israeli.

Whether it will lead him to sympathize with non-Ashkenazi group voting in Israel is something else again. American Jews are uneasy about group voting here, mostly because the universalist ideology that expresses the vision of the good society—and the self-interest —of nearly all modern Jews, almost everywhere, coalesces in America with the individualist ideology that expresses the interest and the values of the enlightened, chiefly Protestant, upper middle class. But our American experience and consciousness may be changing, slowly. Since there was a distinct group element among the forces that brought Kennedy to the White House, group feeling in politics cannot be all bad. To the extent that his election had the effect of narrowing the gap in status between the old and the new stock, it is seen to have been mostly good for the society. And when we think of the Negroes and what the country owes them in justice alone, we begin to discern that individualism, like patriotism for Edith Cavell, is not enough.

Favoring "one of our own" seems to be more evident than before among the non-Ashkenazim in Israel. By electing the fellow Near Easterner or North African one assures one's self not only the kind of gratification that Italians used to get from Joe DiMaggio here, but also the tangible rewards, and respect, that success in politics normally brings. The Israeli government is doing all it can to raise the living standards, the vocational skills, and the education of the Easterners; but let them show disenchantment with the existing parties and elect some of their people on their own ticket, as they did last year in Beersheba and Ashdod, and the government may do even more. How much a government must do sometimes determines how much it can do.

After the elections in Beersheba and Ashdod the expected cries of outrage were heard—"appeals to communal prejudice" and "communalism." Communalism, especially in India, means the desire of religious and linguistic communities for states of their own, with some damage to the authority of the central government and to the national unity. The *Jewish Chronicle* (London), the Thunderer of the Jews, gravely warned the Israeli government not to temporize or compromise by "patronage . . . on a communal basis," but instead to "train young Oriental immigrants in the duties and privileges of citizenship." The words are old, familiar, and therefore comforting. A generation or two ago the uptown Jews here addressed them regularly to the downtown Jews.

Why the fuss? The charge of communalism, in its Indian sense, is silly. Both the Easterners and the Ashkenazim are Jews and both speak Hebrew, or would like to speak it. (Today we can see how right the Hebraists were and how wrong the Yiddishists when, decades ago, they debated the proper language for the Yishuv. How would the Easterners feel now about an Israel, and their place in such an Israel, whose language was Yiddish? And we can see that the Ashkenazi Hebraists were right, too, in adopting an approximately Sephardi pronunciation for the Hebrew that they ordained.) In these matters Israel is more like the United States than like India, and the experience of the United States is that if groups, so defined by origin and by exclusion from the Establishment, vote as groups, they are voting to become equals in one nation, not to form separate nations. It is also the experience of the United States that the groups within the Establishment, not conscious of themselves as groups, think the outsiders are immoral to behave as they do. Ideology not only justifies interest, it also veils reality.

I have never been able to understand how people in the United States can persuade themselves that it is proper and even desirable to vote for your interest as a worker or a storekeeper or a manufacturer but improper to vote for your interest in achieving equality of treatment and regard as an Italian or a Negro or a Catholic. Is the precise size of your bank account so much more intimately related than your parentage and memories to who you feel you are and how you would like to be treated? In 1960 Irish Catholic businessmen tended to vote for Nixon. To hear some of them talk then—they probably do not want to remember it now—Kennedy was out to destroy business. If they had to err about Kennedy, it would have been a more amiable error to favor him as one of their own, the man whose election would help to affirm the equality of Irish Catholics, than to oppose him as the businessman's bogeyman.

In the same way, I find it hard to understand why in Israel a Moroccan laborer is thought to be acting with civic virtue and wisdom if he votes for one of the labor parties, but not if he votes for a Moroccan who campaigns on a platform of greater regard and opportunity for Moroccans and Iraqis, and whose very election on an Easterners' slate will hearten his supporters. The labor parties—or the parties representing lower-middle-class shopkeepers, etc.—will be displeased, of course, and take a high moral tone. That does not mean that such a vote is the disservice to Israel that everyone seems to agree it is. In the long run, by exerting pressure on behalf of the second, non-Ashkenazi Israel, it may help to make the two Israels one. Voting for your own can become less tempting when enough of your own have been elected.

—*January 1964*

· 20 ·

The Twelve Weeks of Christmas

The last decorations will surely have been taken down from the lampposts by Lincoln's birthday, so the end of the Christmas season is in sight. The Jews of America are completing another cycle of ease and unease—in November, Thanksgiving; in December, Christmas.

Thanksgiving seems made to order for Jews. As a friend and colleague has noted, it is celebrated by eating, and Jews eat rather than drink. Again, what one eats then is not the flesh of an unclean animal or a fish without fins and scales, but a thoroughly kosher bird. And what comes out of the mouth on Thanksgiving is equally Jewish —both the message and the tone. Thanksgiving is the great point of intersection between Judaism and the sacral tradition of America. The Spanish and Portuguese Congregation's Thanksgiving rite, which goes back to the eighteenth century, consists largely of psalms, including two from the Hallel.

In my town three Jewish and two Protestant congregations came together in a Conservative synagogue on the night before Thanksgiving, and aside from having to cover their heads and turn pages from right to left, the Christians seemed to find nothing exotic or inapposite about what was done and said. After all, the Methodist minister said in his sermon, thanksgiving psalms were recited in the Temple at Jerusalem long before the rise of Christianity. "We Gather Together" was also sung. It, too, is at home in a synagogue.

A rabbi told me it was the Protestant ministers who had suggested a service on Wednesday night. In their experience attendance was likely to be unsatisfactory Thursday morning, because of the greater attraction of golf or of sleeping late. They had heard that Jewish congregations did better on Friday night than Saturday morning, and for Thanksgiving they wanted to try Wednesday night. The experiment was successful. The 'erev-Thanksgiving service next year will be held in one of the churches and the sermon will be preached by a rabbi.

Reform Judaism in the United States has tried two alternatives to its Saturday-morning service, which is not well attended: Sunday morning and Friday. People found it as easy to stay away on Sunday as on Saturday, but late Friday night worked. Afterward the Conservatives took over the emphasis on Friday night, and now their Saturday-morning service can be so much the private domain of Bar Mitzvah boys, families, and guests that anyone else is apt to feel like a gate-crasher. Protestants have been complaining for years about their Sunday-morning attendance. Will they follow the Jewish example? And, since Saturday night will not do, will it be Friday night for Methodists and Baptists too? That would be a significant Jewish contribution to American religious life.

In the old days, say ten or fifteen years ago, Christmas did not start until after Thanksgiving. Now the merchants seem to be starting it earlier (and ending it later), and in the midst of our Thanksgiving weal we taste our Christmas woe. As Thanksgiving represents the convergence of the Jewish and the American, so Christmas represents their divergence. Christmas is inherently problematic for Jews—and ex-Jews—while it is not problematic in the same way even for ex-Christians. A Jew can have a tree, hang stockings on the mantelpiece, and send out cards, but if he chooses "Merry Christmas" cards he will have an uncomfortable moment when he asks himself whether "Season's Greetings" would not be in better taste, and if he does his best for his children with tree and Santa Claus, he may still find it necessary to draw the line at a wreath on the door. The two or three months of Christmas remind us every year, against our will, that there is an America of people and things and custom that is not the same as the America of the great documents of freedom; and not the same, either, as the America of Thanksgiving. In Christmas America, whether we are of the second or of the seventh generation, it is easy to feel that we are not quite native.

It is all there in "America," the usual anthem when I was in school. "Sweet land of liberty" is ideological America, the country of the mind, whose doctrines are the Declaration of Independence and the Bill of Rights and Enlightenment and liberal Supreme Court decisions, to which one gives intellectual assent. In that America, Jews, not as the seed of Abraham or even as the children or grandchildren of immigrants from Central and Eastern Europe, but as adherents of the Enlightenment philosophy, are rooted citizens, while it is Madison Grant and Lothrop Stoddard—and perhaps Henry Adams, as he himself said, bitterly, about his place in the America of bustle and ambition—who are aliens.

"Land of the Pilgrims' pride" is good for the Jews too. It is the America of Thanksgiving, and the Pilgrims stand for all the immigrants who have ever come here, drawn to the new country and driven out by the old. Jews have had more cause than most to give thanks for that America, not least because its Thanksgiving has such a Jewish spirit about it and speaks in such a Jewish idiom. Still, "Pilgrims" can also mean the real, physical Pilgrims, Mayflower Anglo-Saxons. Then it leaves us on the outside, because it merges with "land where our fathers died."

That is the opposite of ideological America. It is ancestral, hereditary, almost biological. Few Jewish families have been here long enough for most of us to be able to say with any conviction that this is the land where our fathers died, but even those of us who are or could be Sons or Daughters of the American Revolution must perceive a fatal ambiguity in the words. We have our handful of Haym Salomons, but no Founding Fathers. In the America of the Christmas months Jews cannot spontaneously enjoy the family celebration. We feel like children who were adopted, so late in life that we cannot pretend to ourselves that it makes no difference. Time has not controverted the prediction made a generation ago by Warner and Srole in their *Social Systems of American Ethnic Groups,* that an honorary birthright would be granted less readily to Jews than to others of European stock.

Since one of the three Americas, and not the least important, is a land of family (or clan) and memory, I am always startled when critics, often Jews, explain something about American literature by the standard assertion that rootlessness, or lack of tradition, or Americanness as an act of will rather than a matter-of-fact and natural identity, is the essential clue to America. In their own lives the critics might not want to belong to the societies revealed to us by Faulkner or Auchincloss or Cozzens or Marquand or O'Hara, but would they be accepted in those societies even if they wanted to be? Jewish literary intellectuals sometimes deplore America's traditionlessness, but it may be that their definition of America as personal-volitional is not less optative and contrary to fact than the desire of ordinary Jews to believe that America is the sweet land of liberty and the land of the Pilgrims' pride, but not the land where our—which is to say, *their*—fathers died.

—January 1963

. 21 .

Two Decisions

As the Romans said about books, so about Supreme Court decisions: they have their destinies. Justice Black's majority opinion in the Regents' Prayer case suffered no lack of public attention or comment, whereas a year earlier a decision (or cluster of decisions) in four cases arising out of Sunday-closing laws had gone relatively unnoticed. Because it struck down the Regents' Prayer as an impermissible breach in the wall of separation between church and state, the Supreme Court stands high in Jewish esteem. Most Jews apparently do not know that in two of the Sunday-closing cases the Court ruled against Jews who wanted an exemption because they close their businesses on Saturday.

In one of those cases, having to do with a kosher market in Massachusetts, Chief Justice Warren's majority actually reversed a lower court which had held that the state law was sectarian and discriminatory in enforcing the Christian Sabbath at the expense of the Jewish one. In general, the majority found that Sunday-closing laws are neither sectarian (though in the Massachusetts law Sunday is always "the Lord's day") nor discriminatory; that to be sure, they had their origin in Christianity and Christian influence upon government, but that now they are secular; and that if forbidding work on Sunday to those who abstain from work on Saturday forces them to go out of business, too bad, they must take their loss. Justice Frankfurter, who took no part in the Regents' Prayer decision, concurred with the majority in the Sunday cases—perhaps, in some measure, because his doctrine of judicial restraint teaches reluctance to overrule legislatures. But Warren, like Black, is a judicial activist, and his ruling against the Jews in the Sunday cases is unlikely to have arisen from the reluctance.

The dissenting opinions were impressive. Justice Douglas said that Sunday laws are by their nature religious, that they violate the separation of church and state, and that everyone should be allowed to do business on Sunday. Justices Brennan and Stewart upheld the restriction on those who wish to do business on Sunday for merely com-

154

mercial reasons, but were indignant about the refusal to exempt observers of the Jewish Sabbath. Brennan declared that the "effect [of Sunday laws without exemptions] is that no one may at one and the same time be an Orthodox Jew and compete effectively with his Sunday-observing fellow tradesmen. . . . What overbalancing need is so weighty in the constitutional scale that it justifies this . . . limitation of appellants' freedom? . . . It is not even the interest in seeing that everyone rests one day a week, for appellants' religion requires them to take such a rest. It is the mere convenience of having everyone rest on the same day. . . . In fine, the Court, in my view, has exalted administrative convenience to a constitutional level high enough to justify making one religion economically disadvantageous. . . . The Court forgets . . . a warning uttered during the congressional discussion of the First Amendment itself: ' . . . the rights of conscience are, in their nature, of peculiar delicacy, and will little bear the gentlest touch of governmental hand. . . .' "

Stewart, in turn, denounced "a law which compels an Orthodox Jew to choose between his religious faith and his economic survival. That is a cruel choice. It is a choice which I think no state can constitutionally demand. For me, this is not something that can be swept under the rug and forgotten in the interest of enforced Sunday togetherness. I think the impact of this law upon these appellants grossly violates their constitutional right to the free exercise of their religion."

In the Regents' Prayer case Stewart was the lone dissenter, and Douglas concurred but did not join with the majority. Both in that and in the Sunday cases each was consistent with himself and each delivered an opinion that had internal coherence and logic—unlike Warren's majority in the Sunday cases and Black's (which included Warren) in the Regents' Prayer.

Douglas's position, explicitly or implicitly, is this. Whatever may be the historical and contemporary relation among culture, society, and religion in the United States, our law and government must be secular. There must be no legal or governmental support or encouragement of religion, or aid to religion. This means that not only prayers in public schools, however nonsectarian, are unconstitutional, but also chaplains in Congress and the armed services, chapel at the service academies, religious services in federal hospitals and prisons, religious proclamations by the President, use of the Bible for administering oaths, "In God We Trust" on our coins, the mention of God in the Pledge of Allegiance, tax exemptions and postal privileges for religious organizations, tax deductions for contributions to religious organizations, and the words that are part of the ritual for convening the Supreme Court itself: "God save the United States and this honorable court." (He mentions these, and more, in the Regents' Prayer case.) Similarly, law and government have no business remembering the Sabbath day, Christian or Jewish, to keep it holy. Douglas is insisting that law and government should be religion-blind, much as liberals used to insist that in matters of race, law and government should be color-blind.

Stewart, on the other hand, does not believe that government and law can or should be separated from society and culture. The no-establishment and religious-freedom clauses are foundation stones of American democracy, he would say, but the adjective is as significant as the noun. In America religious freedom and the mutual independence of church and state have not been threatened by such things as tax deductions for contributions to religious institutions. On the contrary, Stewart believes, they have been strengthened. And it is precisely because he considers governmental benignity toward religion (but not toward any denomination) as permissible or actually desirable that he is concerned about the unfair treatment of any religious minority. Realizing that the Christianity of most Americans and the Christian influences on American culture and institutions must affect the public life, he is especially careful to protect the right of Jews not to be made to conform to Christian usages.

In the Regents' Prayer case the Warren-Black majority refused to go as far as Douglas, but the distinction they drew between the Regents' Prayer and the Supreme Court prayer—the former religious, the latter ceremonial or patriotic—is unconvincing. Douglas has the better of that argument, and so has Stewart: the Regents' Prayer and the Supreme Court prayer must be offensive or inoffensive together. But not only are Warren and Black inconsistent within their decision on the Regents' Prayer, they are also inconsistent between their Regents' Prayer and their Sunday-closing decisions. If a nonsectarian prayer is unconstitutional, *a fortiori* so should a state's enforcement of "the Lord's day" be. Yet the majority could bring itself to deny that "the Lord's day" is the Christian Sabbath! (". . . the objectionable language is merely a relic.") It is not hard to imagine how they would have dealt with that relic if they had wanted to rule against the Sunday law rather than for it.

One lawyer told me that he welcomed the decision against the observers of the Jewish Sabbath because, in his opinion, a decision for them would have established a bad precedent, encouraging all sorts of exceptions for minority religions and thus weakening the separation principle. I am sure that other Jews besides him assign less value to protecting observers of the Jewish Sabbath against discrimination than to rejecting all sectarian special pleading, so called. Their admiration for Warren has not abated on account of his decision in the Sunday cases.

The immanent logic of Warren and Black's Regents' Prayer position must lead them to Douglas's, though they have stopped short of it. Then tax deductibility for contributions to Harvard will be unconstitutional, as aiding the Harvard Divinity School; together with deductibility for contributions to UJA and Jewish federations, because these are, after all, sectarian. Thanksgiving may be unconstitutional. I doubt that that is what we really want. And I doubt that we really think that the Supreme Court majority can go much further toward full agreement with Douglas before the Congress and the state legislatures and the people amend the Constitution to legitimize breaches in the wall of separation that will retrospectively make the breaches we now complain of look like pinholes.

But even an uncontested definition of church-state relations in the spirit of Douglas, which raises higher the wall of separation, will not produce true religious neutrality in our public life. Sunday will still be the primary day of rest in the civil service. And there will always be a Christmas.

In a way, history has provided us with a laboratory experiment. Between 1905 and 1940 the Third French Republic had as much separation between church and state, legally and institutionally, as has ever been known in the West. France was committed to a religious neutrality sometimes indistinguishable from irreligion. Yet in that France, where all religions were ignored, Judaism was more ignored than Christianity. Children went to school—and still go—on Saturday, not Sunday. In England, with much less separation between church and state, there is more regard for the religious sensitivity of Jewish children, or simply their dignity.

Suppose an America with a religious neutrality something like that of the Third French Republic, and suppose another day added to the school week. Which will it be, Saturday or Sunday? A society truly neutral about religion, or even a truly neutral legal and institutional structure, never was and can never be.

—January 1963

. 22 .

Those Catholic Schools

Everyone knows that most Jews oppose federal aid to parochial schools. Institutional pronouncements do not always mirror popular opinion, but in church-state matters among Jews they do. This is all the more striking because the central Jewish tradition clearly favors religious education and practice for non-Jews, provided their religion is not pagan. That tradition used to be as much a part of the popular consciousness as of the elite's learning.

When I was a boy my mother told me a story about my grandfather in the old country, which I later discovered had been told about more illustrious figures and which should be reckoned as belonging to the folklore and psychology of the Jews of Eastern Europe. The story is that he once engaged a peasant coachman to drive him to another town. In a few miles they passed a church, but the driver did not cross himself. My grandfather waited a while and then, on the pretext of having forgotten something, told the driver to return home. When they got back my grandfather dismissed him and explained to my grandmother: "A peasant who does not cross himself does not believe in God. What is to prevent him from murdering me when we are alone in the woods?" One of the few spokesmen for federal aid in the Jewish community—though he is not really *of* the community —Rabbi Schneersohn, the venerated leader of the Habad (Lubavitch) school in Hasidism, has reasoned that since to will the end must be to will the means, Jews should therefore support federal aid.

Yet only in a part of the Orthodox section of the Jewish community does one find some support for federal aid; and even there, it is due to the needs of the Jewish day schools, which is what we call our counterpart of the parochial schools. If the Jewish community supported the day schools more adequately, as by subventions from its welfare funds, the Jewish voices raised for federal aid would be even fewer than they are now.

All of which means that a newer tradition has largely replaced the older one. And in fact, in these questions the effective tradition of most Jews today, not only in the United States but also practically everywhere else in the Western world, is a strong, rather unified set of beliefs and attitudes that have grown out of the history of the Jews in the past two hundred years or so, since the Enlightenment and the beginnings of Jewish civic equality.

It should not have to be said that to Jews the adjective Christian does not mean or suggest what it does to Christians. In ordinary usage among Christians, it often means good, moral, admirable; sometimes it can even be a synonym of human. That is why the apocryphal chairman of the Brotherhood Week banquet could say, "Protestants, Catholics, Jews—we're all Christians together." (When the late Warren Austin represented the United States in the U.N., he once declared that Jews and Arabs ought to be able to settle their differences in a Christian spirit.) Jews, on the other hand—out of their European memories, to be sure, more than their American experience—can think of another anecdote. Soon after the end of World War I, it is said, an American Y.M.C.A. secretary attached to a relief mission in Hungary was introduced to the regent, Admiral Horthy. Told that the initials stood for Young Men's Christian Association, Horthy shook hands and said, "Glad to meet a fellow antisemite." For many years *christlich* in European politics usually meant, among other things, antisemitic.

In the French Revolution, when the more modern-minded Jews responded eagerly to civic equality, on the whole the church and churchmen were against it. In England it is not much more than a hundred years ago that the first Jew was allowed to take his place in the House of Commons, against Anglican opposition. England must remain a Christian nation and state, the argument went, and therefore no Jew should be an M.P. Since Cromwell readmitted the Jews, England has been a more tolerant and pleasant place for them than almost any other European country, and it has been happily free of the continental strife between *laïques* and churchmen. Yet to this day English Jews are especially quick to see the point of the old joke that the Church of England is not the nation at prayer, as the Anglican theory had it, but the Tory party at prayer; and even now few of them can bring themselves to vote Tory.

Before Hitler the most disillusioning and frightening thing that happened to the Jews of the West—and to those Jews of backward countries like Russia who aspired to the status of their brothers in the West—was the Dreyfus case. It turned Theodor Herzl, who had once thought of leading a parade of Jews to the baptismal font, into the founder of Zionism. In France the mob and Society bayed for blood, while throne-and-altar Catholicism denounced the Jews as gnawing worms and the Republic as a Judeo-Masonic conspiracy to subvert religion and morality. The Dreyfus case accounts in part for the kind of separation between church and state that was established in France when the anti-Dreyfusards were discredited, and it reinforced the attachment of Jews throughout the West to strict separation.

In the United States itself it was to protest a Catholic act of persecution in Italy that Jews created their first nationwide organization, just before the Civil War. In Bologna, a Jewish child called Edgar Mortara was baptized by a servant without the knowledge of his parents. When they dismissed her, she told the authorities what she had done and the papal police took the little boy away. It was a worldwide scandal, but the church, including the American hierarchy, closed ranks. Nothing could persuade Pope Pius IX to return the boy to his parents. (He died, a priest, in 1940.)

Once the rabbi of my congregation asked me to tell an adult study group why I believed that Jews should modify their dominant opinion on church-state matters, which I think is becoming a bit anachronistic. After I had spoken, a normally kind and friendly man rose to answer me, but he was so upset that he stopped after a few sentences and ran out of the room. (He later apologized.) He was born and educated in Czechoslovakia, and has never forgotten the taunts and occasional beatings he suffered on the days when the clergymen came to give religious instruction in school.

Any Jew with immigrant parents is likely to have heard of the fear, and sometimes danger, that their communities had to endure in Holy Week and especially on Easter, and there are many of my generation who remember the hazards of walking home from public school past the Polish or Irish parochial school. Today, even those Jews who know about recent trends in Catholic thought have probably had occasion to regret the lag between the new spirit on top and actual practice in the parish. Once I overheard my daughter's friend tell her that the Jews killed Christ—that was what she had learned in released-time religious instruction—and I cannot suppose that I am an exception.

And of course most Jews, like most other non-Catholics, are unhappy with the church's record on issues like divorce and birth control.

All this is to explain why Jews are not convinced that what the church does and teaches is necessarily good and why they are not enthusiastic about proposals that public funds should be used to strengthen the parochial schools. Are they anti-Catholic? They are suspicious of the church, but they are not against Catholics.

In 1928, when an anti-Catholic binge was America's answer to Al Smith's candidacy, Jews gave him a large majority of their votes. In 1960, probably a higher proportion of Jews than of Catholics voted for President Kennedy, and certainly a higher proportion of prosperous Jews than of prosperous Catholics. Later, in New York City the Catholic Wagner first got more Jewish votes than his Jewish opponent in the Democratic primary, Levitt, and then more than his Republican Jewish opponent, Lefkowitz.

In the 1920s, when the very life of the parochial-school system was at stake and Catholics were contesting the Oregon statute which made public education compulsory, the Jewish community sided with them. Louis Marshall submitted to the Supreme Court an *amicus curiae* brief challenging the constitutionality of the statute; and in those days the Jewish community was said to be under Marshall law.

Anti-Catholicism, in Peter Viereck's famous aphorism, is the anti-semitism of the liberals. If that is so, then Jews are not anti-Catholic. An antisemite is not a man who is skeptical of Judaism or the synagogue; he is a man who hates Jews.

It is not only that most Jews are to some degree repelled by, or negative to, the church and parochial schools. They are also attracted by, or positive to, the public schools. They think public schools are good and desirable in themselves.

On the whole, the history of the Jews in the United States is a success story, and they know it. Most are a generation or two removed from immigrant origins, and in that short time they have done fairly well, having become a predominantly middle-class community. Education is what helped to make this possible. Jews have been particularly grateful for free, universal education in the United States because where most of their parents or grandparents came from, the government tried to keep them out of whatever schools there were.

But the American public school did rather more for its Jewish students than help them to get ahead in the world. It also helped them to become part of America and of American culture, with unexpected speed and completeness. And for that the Jews are doubly grateful to the schools.

In the early years of this century Henry James saw the Lower East Side and worried about the national and cultural future of America. By a singularly apt irony of history, the grandchildren of the immigrants who worried him—graduates of the public schools—are today captains of the Henry James industry. Jewish professors are no new phenomenon in the Western world. There were many in the Kaiser's Germany and later in the Weimar Republic, but in both Germanies there were no Jewish professors of German history or literature. Those subjects were too close to the German "essence" to be entrusted to Jews, who were told to concentrate on mathematics or biology or art history. In the United States, Jews teach English literature and American history at our greatest universities. The difference is appreciated even by the many Jews who, if you asked them to identify Henry James, would guess that he was Jesse's brother.

For Jews, America is the open and hospitable country that it is because the public school expresses its true spirit. They see the public school as simultaneously an instrument for individual progress and the symbol of a benign, inclusive national ideal. They take *e pluribus unum* seriously and they take pluralism seriously, and for them the public school is a kind of quintessential America which has succeeded remarkably well in reconciling the two.

Which is why Jews do not want anything to weaken public schools, in principle or practice. But they fear that that is what federal aid to parochial education would do. They go further. A chief reason why most Jewish welfare funds do not subsidize Jewish day schools is the common feeling that that would be a betrayal of the public schools.

Actually, it is on this point that the Jewish day-school movement differs most revealingly from the Catholic parochial-school system. Everyone knows that the United States is where Catholic schools are for all Catholics rather than for an elite minority, and where half of the bold ambition to have every Catholic child in a Catholic school has been achieved. That is an impressive ambition and an impressive achievement. It is quite otherwise with the Jewish day schools. They are rather new in having any statistical significance at all, and they enroll fewer than 10 percent of all Jewish children in school. What is more, the very advocates of the Jewish day schools do not dare, or do not even wish, to think that most Jewish students will attend them. The day schools are for a minority, a kind of saving remnant. Some of the warmest words I have ever heard for the public school, as institution and ideal, were spoken—sincerely, I am convinced—by an Orthodox rabbi who presides over one of the largest and best Jewish day schools in New York.

Many parents of day-school students express something akin to guilt over not sending their children to a public school, as well as explicit regret for the educational loss that their children incur by not being there. (So do many Jewish parents of children in nonsectarian private schools.) The guilt is because they fear they are helping to weaken the public schools. The regret is because in a public school their children would be learning, directly and by personal experience with children of various sorts and origins, what pluralism is and how to live in a pluralist America. Day-school educators answer that they are careful to teach understanding and respect for all religions, races, and nationalities. The educators do not question the principle, they merely do not like to think that they go against it.

There is an old Jewish story that I shall permit myself to tell. A rabbi, in his judicial capacity, heard a plaintiff and said that he was right. Then he heard the defendant and said that *he* was right. When the rabbi's wife protested that they could not both be right, he told her she was right too.

I think that the parochial schoolers are right and that fairness, an ungrudging acceptance of Catholics as real equals in the American community, and the educational needs of the American people require public aid to parochial schools. I also think that the public schoolers are right and that the public schools have deserved well of the country, should be defended in their integrity and primacy, and might be threatened by measures that would make it too easy to expand the nonpublic sector.

The rabbi and his wife agreed that both sides could not be right. Must that be true also of the two sides in the dispute over federal aid, or can we help the parochial schools without hurting the public schools? For such a solution to be at all possible, as I hope it is, people will first have to give up self-righteousness and familiar and comforting watchwords.

I have not spoken here of constitutional arguments, though the friends and enemies of federal aid are fond of them. I know practically nothing about constitutional law, and I suspect that I am not alone in my ignorance. From what I have observed, even those who speak with knowledge are apt to be advocates rather than jurisconsults—that is, they advance legal arguments to defend ends and values which engage their loyalty on other than legal grounds. That is natural and honorable, but not persuasive. For myself, I assume that if we can arrive at a consensus on what is just and is good for the country and its people, it is likely to be constitutional.

—January 31, 1964

. 23 .

The Wall

The Jews are probably more devoted than anyone else in America to the separation of church and state. At times, hearing some of us talk about separation, or reading the statements of our organizations, one has the impression that we also think ourselves more loyal to the Constitution and more skilled in its interpretation—although of course nobody ever says that in so many words. Thoughts protected against expression, as this one is, can be foolish. We are not more loyal to the Constitution or more skilled in its interpretation, we are only more separationist. And with every passing year our separationism comes closer to being part of the "old order" that Tennyson, in those verses that used to be so popular, wanted to see "yielding place to new;/ . . . Lest one good custom should corrupt the world."

The case for the regnant Jewish ideology or emotion goes this way: Granted, there must be something special in our own experience and memory, and some strong feeling about what is in our interest, to account for our separationist fervor; but we perceive and intend separation to be for the good of all as well as for our own good. More than anyone else the Jews warned against Hitler and Nazism. Afterward, everybody could see that we had been right, that we had not merely been pleading our own cause when we said that resistance to Hitler and Nazism was not a Jewish interest alone but the interest of all. Similarly now in church-and-state matters.

Because the Jews have had to pay for the lesson—so the case continues—we know that separation of church and state is good and the absence of separation is bad. A country with separation is democratic, tolerant, open, free; a country without separation is despotic, persecuting, closed, unfree. The greater the separation, as in America and France, the more democracy and tolerance; the less the separation, as in Spain, Tsarist Russia, and the Papal States before the unification of Italy, the less democracy and tolerance. Of course Jews do better in an America and a France than in a Spain and a Tsarist Russia. Doesn't everyone? In wanting America to be ever more separationist, which is to say ever more American, we want it to be ever better for all. "Religious freedom," in the words of the canon, "is most secure where church and state are separated, and least secure where church and state are united."

A good, strong case—or it would be if not for the vice of faulty enumeration. Where do you put England, Denmark, Norway, and Sweden, with their state churches? No one can deny that Great Britain and Scandinavia are free and democratic and that religious freedom is closer to being most secure there than least secure. Nor can any Jew deny that those countries are, as we used to say, good for the Jews. On the other hand, in the Soviet Union church and state are constitutionally separate, but the Soviet Union is neither free nor democratic nor good for the Jews, and so far from making religious freedom secure—let alone most secure—it persecutes religion.

It may be argued that Soviet persecution does not fairly come under the head of separation and that state persecution of religion is a kind of negative mode of state establishment of religion. Without conceding the argument, let us return to the Soviet Union when we consider secularism and for the moment instead compare state-church England with separationist France. In democracy and freedom, the two are alike (or used to be, before de Gaulle's somewhat authoritarian Fifth Republic); in openness and tolerance to Jews, the state-church country is better than the separationist one. Which is not to say that establishment is better than separation, but only that other things—notably democracy as it is inclined by national culture and tradition—make the issue of separation/establishment quite secondary.

In the Fifth Republic the Ecole Normale Supérieure, the nursery of the French intellectual elite, tried to keep out a qualified Jewish student because he observed the Sabbath. Why, he was asked, should he be admitted to an institution that trains *lycée* professors? A *lycée* has Saturday classes, like all state schools in France. Would not his Sabbath observance prevent him from teaching? The Ecole Normale Supérieure has been traditionally on the side of the French Revolution—republican, anticlerical, anti-antisemitic—and since before the university careers of the Reinach brothers and Léon Blum, it has had Jewish students. But unlike the other Jewish students before him, this one was religious. Keeping in mind the distinction between secularist and religious Jews may help us to understand something about ourselves in the United States.

For a long time the distinction was blurred in the American Jewish community because in this country, church-state issues tend to be school issues. Our separationism goes back to the time when the public school was in many ways a common-denominator or inter-sectarian Protestant school. In that age of Protestant imperialism, as it has been called, the virtues and standards of America were so widely held to be the same as the virtues and standards of Protestant-ism that a public school had to be a basically Protestant school. One reason why the founder of American Reform Judaism, Isaac Mayer Wise, was a Copperhead in the Civil War was that he resented the Protestant imperialism of the abolitionists. (Lincoln needed the sup-port of the Know-Nothings and did not condemn them publicly. Elijah Lovejoy, the abolitionist martyr, printed anti-Catholic tracts.) It was Wise who began the unbroken Reform tradition of opposing public-school Protestantism in the name of separation. Whether he would have opposed religion-in-general in the schools is unclear. In Germany his masters and colleagues took it for granted that the state should favor religion.

Sometimes Wise's tradition was a well-kept secret among his dis-ciples and successors, because the laity was in no mood to attract attention by protest; yet while Reform rabbis now disagree about God, Torah, and Israel, they still do not disagree about the separa-tionist article of faith, though Protestant imperialism has gone the way of so many other imperialisms. And just as the Irish taught the rest of the Catholics how to be American, so Reform Judaism taught Orthodoxy and Conservatism. Separation became the common plat-form of the major varieties of Jewish religion in America. (The Or-thodox have begun to go their own way, but that is a long story.) Wise would have been happy with no Lord's Prayer in the schools, but only yesterday we were unhappy even with the Regents' prayer in New York State, certified desirable by the Lubavitcher Rebbe himself.

As for the Jewish secularists, they have opposed religion in the schools for a simple reason. They are secularists. For a secularist, religion is infantile and infantilizing, the enemy of enlightenment, science, progress, freedom, and peace. The less religion a society or community has, he says, the better it is.

But religionists and secularists do not live apart in the Jewish community. They have in common ideas and, above all, emotions. Few Jews of Central or East European origin or parentage, whether Orthodox or Reform, religious or secularist, have been able to think well of the church. The church was Pobedonostsev, with his vision of a third of the Jews of Russia converting, a third emigrating, and a third dying of hunger. The church was the threat of pogroms in the

Easter season. The church was the Mortara case, the Dreyfus case, the Beilis case. "Christian" was part of the name an antisemitic party would give itself, in Protestant Prussia as in Catholic Austria. To Christians, Theodor Reik wrote when he still lived in Austria, Judaism was uncanny (mostly because of circumcision) and therefore fearsome. To Central and East European Jews, the iconic, sacramental, and sacerdotal Christianity they saw about them was uncanny, and it still is to their children and grandchildren. Until a few years ago, the common memories and emotions and sense of danger tended to obscure the differences between Jewish religionists and secularists. So united was the Jewish front that only occasionally would a mainstream rabbi be bold enough to advise his confreres that they would do well, if only for the sake of public relations, to phrase their separationist statements in rather more religious-sounding language.

In Isaac Mayer Wise's Midwest, the Christian environment was Protestant. For most Jews today, who live in and near the great cities, the Christian environment is apt to be mainly Catholic. Wise's separationism was a defense against what he saw as a Protestant threat; ours is mostly against what we see as a Catholic threat, and especially what we see as the threat of the parochial school.

Traditions die hard, even the traditions of the untraditional. A man will say that the United States must rethink its foreign policy from beginning to end because the world has changed. Ask him to rethink his own policy because the world has changed and he will tell you he is no trimmer or opportunist; let the weaklings and conformists veer with the winds of popularity, he will remain loyal to his principles. Everyone thinks he is a dissenter and nonconformist—in good faith, because there are always communities of opinion and fashion in opposition to which he can honestly see himself as one. What he prefers to overlook is that there are also communities of opinion and fashion—or, more honorifically, of thought and style—to which he relates positively, and in that relation his nonconformity can be quite conformist. In our own community, the informal and private one or the organized and public one, separationism is not a bit nonconformist. (It is curious that dissent/dissenter, nonconformity/nonconformist should come to us from the language of English ecclesiastical history.)

As things are today, religionists and moderate secularists have one interest and radical separationists another, and our separationism now serves the radical interest. (Radical is generally not an O.K. word, but

I cannot think of anything better. Extreme is even less O.K., consistent is not what I mean, and fanatical is insulting.) Whether a secularist is moderate or radical depends on whether his secularism is one of several more or less equal goods or whether it is his chief good; whether it is a means as well as an end, to be judged in part by its usefulness in furthering other ends, or whether it is more like an ultimate end. For the moderate, separationism is a strategy more than a philosophy, and if new conditions call for a change in strategy he will be ready to make the change. For the radical, the strategy goes so closely with the philosophy that change can only be betrayal. As integralist Catholics are convinced (notwithstanding Vatican II) that the marriage of Throne and Altar is God's will, so radical secularists are convinced that root-and-branch separationism is Reason's dictate.

What are the considerations that should induce a moderate secularist, and all the more a religionist, to question his inherited separationism? The first of these may by itself not be strictly probative, at least about America, but it points to something. For secularists the example of the Soviet Union should teach skepticism about the secularist faith itself. The Soviet Union is the most secularist society in what used to be Christendom (or Islam, Judaism never having controlled any territory to speak of). In that most secularist society, separationism has gone so far as to become persecution of religion; and in that most secularist society, secularism is not the companion or handmaiden of freedom, intelligence, and all the other good things of man's mind and spirit, as secularists once thought it must be. Rather it is the companion or handmaiden of the jailer of art and literature, science and scholarship and philosophy, honest thought and honest feeling. Not church-state England or Sweden vilifies and imprisons Sinyavsky and Daniel, but the Soviet Union, which calls itself the guardian of enlightenment and the scourge of obscurantism. For a Jew it should also matter that nowhere else in what used to be Christendom are Jews and Judaism persecuted—alone among the Soviet nationalities, including the Germans, and more than the other Soviet religions.

In America a state church on the English or Swedish model is out of the question, and that is all the more reason why the separation decreed by the Constitution should be defended against mutation into separationism. For separationism can be tyrannical even here. No citizens of this country are more peaceful and inoffensive than the Amish, yet agents of the Iowa public schools have been photographed pursuing Amish children through the fields to drag them into schools that the parents reject for religious reasons. In New York it took a decision by the superintendent of schools himself to allow a high-school boy to cover his head in class. A Board of Education lawyer had ruled that if the boy wore a *kippah* he would be breaching the wall of separation between church and state! (The superintendent's name was Donovan.)

Almost as alarming is the growing isolation of Jewish separationism from the social liberalism of which it used to be part. On every side, President Johnson's aid-to-education and antipoverty legislation is recognized as a major advance, and if liberals have a complaint, it is that the legislation does not go far enough. Liberal Protestants, accustomed to suspicion of Catholic designs on the public treasury and critical of Johnson on foreign policy, marvel at his achievement in bypassing the kinds of church-state objections—or rationalizations—that invariably killed similar bills in the past. The congressional opponents of Johnson's legislation, who went down continuing to profess indignation over the breach in the wall, were mostly reactionaries and racists.

Together with these stand the radical separationists, although theirs is a true and not a feigned indignation. They are unreconciled to educational benefits being extended to children in nonpublic (mostly Catholic parochial) schools, and to churches being included among appropriate neighborhood institutions for conducting antipoverty programs. As the separationists see it, the child-benefit theory is a mere device for benefiting parochial schools by the back door while evading the (presumed) constitutional prohibition of benefits by the front door, and churches and church-related institutions have no business in antipoverty programs or anything else that gets public money.

What if the benefits cannot readily be extended to children outside their nonpublic school? What if excluding a church or a church-related institution in this or that neighborhood weakens the effort to help the poor raise themselves out of poverty? Your single-minded separationist, after first trying to deny that your questions are real questions, can say nothing. Creditably, American liberalism in general does not accept this kind of hard-heartedness. The separationists make the usual defense in such cases: it is not really we who are hard-hearted but the other fellow, to whom we refuse to pay blackmail and who has maneuvered us into a false position. They may believe this, but whenever I hear or read Jewish separationists weighing the claim of the poor against the claim of separationism, their emotion goes to separationism. Yet we are still fond of thinking ourselves *rahamanim bene rahamanim*, the compassionate sons of compassionate fathers.

If not even regard for the poor moves the separationist to condone back-door dealings and aid, it is easy to imagine what he thinks about the front door. But here, too, his single-mindedness is beginning to isolate him. He cannot bring himself to look upon his favorite doctrine as one of many good things, not necessarily compatible in its fullness with the other good things in *their* fullness, and subject, like all of them, to compromise and give-and-take.

Of late some remarkable voices have been heard for governmental aid to the nonpublic school: the *New Republic* and Walter Lippmann, among others. Their purpose is not to help the Catholic schools but to help American education; or better, to help bring about the conditions in which all Americans can have the best possible education. Since the quality of the nation's life will depend so greatly on education, Lippmann and the others say, education has a more urgent claim on the nation than separationism. This means helping the Catholic schools, because so many children are educated there—about one in every seven. The Catholic schools need money, in quantities that can come only from government, to hire more teachers so that classes will be smaller, to get good teachers by paying good salaries, to improve classrooms, to build up libraries.

The First Amendment does not command, "Thou shalt not give governmental aid to parochial schools," it commands that there shall be no establishment of religion and no curtailment of the free exercise of religion. The Rabbis said that the gates of interpretation of the Torah are not closed, and the Supreme Court has shown that neither are the gates of interpretation of the Constitution closed. If the justices think the nation needs education more than separationism, they can easily decide that the Constitution permits aid to nonpublic education. If they think otherwise, then it is the turn of the gates of amendment not to be closed. Having had an amendment prohibiting liquor and another annulling the prohibition, the Constitution can have an amendment allowing aid to religious or church-related schools.

This kind of talk is hardly daring any more, but to most separationists it is novel and perverse wickedness. That is not liberal openmindedness. It is more like the outrage of a nineteenth-century, Herbert Spencer liberal confronted with the immoral proposal that the government should take taxes from him to support a school for educating his neighbor's children. There are still such liberals, only for many years now they have been called, by general agreement, reactionaries.

To Jews, Jewish separationists like to say that separationism is necessary for our safety and well-being. I think this argument is a second thought, invoked to justify a decision already taken on another ground. Those who invoke it remind me of a businessman who wants to contribute corporation money to a university or a community chest or the symphony orchestra. Possibly he wants to do it because he is a decent, generous man, but he has to justify his decency, to himself as well as to the other officers and the stockholders, by giving businesslike reasons for the contribution: it will be good for public relations, or it will help to make the environment so healthy that the corporation will be able to thrive.

There would be nothing wrong about consulting our interest when making up our minds whether to support governmental aid to church schools in the name of better education or to oppose it in the name of separation. If we consulted interest, we would estimate advantages and disadvantages by applying the appropriate calculus. That is how a man runs his business, or he is soon out of business. It is how the Defense Department chooses between missiles and manned bombers, between submarines and aircraft carriers. But though I follow the Jewish discussions, I recall little that resembles a true weighing of alternatives. We prefer incantatory repetition of the dogma that separationism is our interest.

It is time we actually weighed the utility and cost of education against the utility and cost of separationism. All the evidence in America points to education, more than anything else, influencing adherence to democracy and egalitarianism. All the evidence points to Catholic parochial education having the same influence. (And all the evidence points to Catholic antisemitism as probably less than Protestant.) Something that nurtures a humane, liberal democracy is rather more important to Jews than twenty-four-karat separationism.

There is another thing related to the Catholic parochial schools that we ought to weigh in the balance of Jewish interest. Outside the American consensus stand the far Right and the antisemites. (There is antisemitism on the outside Left, too, and among some of the young Jews in it.) It is good to broaden the consensus, to bring inside those who are outside. They change when they come inside.

Why are some people outside? Usually because they have a grievance. They feel they are disregarded and treated unfairly. The sociologists call this feeling *ressentiment*; let us call it sullenness. When statesmanship becomes aware that a social group is sullen, it tries to remove the causes, if that can be done without unacceptable cost to the other participants in the competitive cooperation of political society. In part it is because the Negroes have finally been seen to be sullen, in this sense, that the government is trying to make room for them in the game and bring them into the consensus. Sometimes, of course, a group's price for giving up its sullenness is too high for everybody else, and it has to be left outside—like the Birchers, who just for a start want the political and social game to return to the rules of the 1920s or the 1890s. But it must be conceded that some people, disoriented and bewildered by the passing of the America they were comfortable in, are needlessly being driven into the Radical Right. Some good libertarians are saying that such symbolic victories for separationism as making Bible reading in the schools illegal have been won at too high a real cost—the sullenness of the defeated and the departure of some of them from the consensus.

Many Catholics are sullen. For a non-Catholic it should not be unreasonably arduous to pretend for a moment that he has children in a parochial school. Call it role-playing. For the average Catholic, affluence is either a figure of speech or what someone else has: he is less affluent than the average Episcopalian, Congregationalist, or Jew. The taxes he pays to the public schools keep rising. So do his parochial-school costs, but the parochial school continues to fall behind the public school—in the size of classes, in salaries to attract good teachers, in equipment and amenities. He can hardly afford to pay once, but he has to pay twice; and in return his children get an education that he fears may not be good enough. This, when the diploma society is already here and his children's chances of making it depend more than ever on the education he can give them.

He asks for aid, and a coalition of Protestants and Jews, far from respecting him for having done the hard thing so long, answer coldly that private education must be paid for privately; if he can't afford it, let him not complain, let him use the public schools. At the same time he sees that in the cities many in the coalition, whether businessmen or intellectuals, do indeed pay to send their children to private schools. Apparently they believe nonpublic education is like a Cadillac: just as it would be ridiculous to subsidize a poor man's purchase of a Cadillac, so it would be to subsidize his purchase of nonpublic education. He suspects that this uncharacteristic enthusiasm of theirs for the principles of Ayn Rand is due rather to their distaste for Catholic education specifically than for nonpublic education generally.

Then, in self-defense, or out of resentment, or as a means of exerting pressure, the Catholic votes against higher taxes for the public schools, and the coalition is confirmed in its opinion of him. He is narrow-minded. But tolerant and understanding, and proud of it, they tell each other that it isn't really his fault. It is the priests who make him send his children to the parochial school, the priests who make him sullen about the inevitable, unalterable consequences. *We* do not need a priest to make us prefer a nonpublic school, only *he* does. Tell them of the evidence that the average Catholic parent prefers the parochial school of his own accord; they answer: never heard of it, propaganda. If I were that Catholic parent, I could be pretty sullen.

Catholics, therefore, have a real grievance. To remove the grievance would be just. It would also be statesmanlike, and would help to improve the education of a significant part of the American population. People are coming to see that. The public-opinion polls have shown a steady rise in the proportion of respondents favoring governmental aid, until now there are more for it than against it.

What then will happen to the public schools? Probably not much more than has already happened. Whoever asks this question must come into court with clean hands. Are his own children in a public school? Are the tax-supported schools of Scarsdale or Highland Park as public as the tax-supported schools of New York and Chicago?

Jews have special reason for being grateful to the public school: it helped make the America of opportunities for newcomers, and it trained us to seize the opportunities. It has also helped to make American culture receptive and inclusive, with everything *that* has meant to us. So we are all for the public school. At the same time, we tell each other horror stories about what it has become. If we can, we either send our children to private schools or move to where the public schools are not too public. Meanwhile, out there, some others are less attached than we to the public-school idea and system and are asking rude questions about it, aloud. They are even suggesting that the attachment is a cultural lag, unsuited to the new times.

When this is suggested on behalf of the Catholics, we find it easy to dismiss the suggestion as illiberal. But now it has been suggested on behalf of the Negroes, and we cannot so easily dismiss that. Christopher Jencks, for instance, has argued that the public-school systems of the big cities are so diseased with bureaucracy and inertia that they cannot reasonably be expected to recover and do the job they are supposed to do. In their place, he proposes, the government should give parents the money needed for educating their children; and then the parents, having formed suitable associations, can set up their own schools and hire their own teachers.

Whatever the merits of that particular proposal, Catholics might want to use governmental tuition payments for parochial-school education. What objection could there be then?

To repeat: It is not true that freedom is most secure where church and state are separated; separation and separationism are not the same; even in America, separationism is potentially tyrannical; separationism needlessly repels some from the democratic consensus; it is harsh to those who prefer nonpublic schools for conscience' sake; and it stands in the way of a more important good (and a more important safeguard of Jewish security), the best possible education for all.

The final reason for rethinking separationism is connected in some ways with what has been said about tyranny. The reverence of right-thinking people for the Supreme Court and the Constitution is quite old now, but I still find it a bit strange. When I was coming of age, my elders and betters regarded the Supreme Court as the Nine Old Men and the Constitution as the horse-and-buggy document that Charles Beard had debunked—or so it was thought—in his *Economic Interpretation*. The cause of the change is obvious and to be grateful for: the Court and the Constitution (as the Court reads it) have been more decent and libertarian than government by plebiscite would be, or than a direct democracy of the people at large. But I continue to be put off when modern types speak of the Constitution as a fundamentalist does of Scripture, and when they speak of the Court as Jews once did of the Sanhedrin.

Especially strange is the concentration on (some of) the *ipsissima verba* of Thomas Jefferson, so that an unofficial metaphor about a wall of separation comes to have the sacred character of the specifications for the Tent of Meeting. Jefferson's more important words tend to be ignored: his enmity to the empire of the dead over the living and his caution against excessive deference to ancestral documents and dicta, including his own. It was Jefferson, after all, who advised posterity to water the tree of liberty every now and then with the blood of revolution—at the very least, a more forceful way of saying what Tennyson was to say in those verses I quoted.

It is a truism that the problems of freedom have changed since Jefferson's time. When we worry now about freedom of the press, we do not have in mind primarily censorship by government or intimidation by a mob. Those restraints have grown fewer and weaker, but we are not at all sure we have more freedom of the press. What bothers us is that not very long ago a man with a few thousand dollars could start a newspaper, and there were many papers. Today it takes millions of dollars, and every year we have fewer papers. Neither censorship nor intimidation has caused the multiplication of one-newspaper cities. What has caused it is that nowadays everything is complicated and expensive. For solving that problem the First Amendment, necessary as it is, is not nearly enough.

In Jefferson's time the press was exactly that—the printing press. Except for earshot speech and handwritten letters, there was no other means of communication. Now we have electronic media, and above all radio and television, which influence opinion probably more than print. In our time unhindered communication of opinion and information depends on a freedom of the press that includes freedom of radio and TV. But the relation of government to radio and TV has to be totally different from its relation to the printing press.

The libertarian's conception of the ideal relation of government to the press is that there shall be no relation at all: government and press have nothing to do with each other, nobody needs a license to publish. In principle there is no limit to the number of newspapers or presses. With radio and TV, on the other hand, the laws of physics impose a limit. Two stations cannot operate on the same wavelength at the same time in the same place, so someone must determine that A shall operate and B shall not. That is, the government; and it is to government that A and B come to plead for a license. A government that respects freedom of the press finds itself having to license the radio-and-TV part of the press. What would Jefferson have thought?

In deciding whether to license A or B, the government has first to decide which of the two will probably better serve the public interest and the needs of society. But these include religion in its many forms. Consequently, when the government examines the record of a radio or TV licensee it must ask, among other things, how he has served his community's religious interests and needs. If it did not ask this question, if it asked everything else but not this, a licensee could exclude religion entirely from his programs; or give his own sect a monopoly of the time he allowed for religion; or set aside all that time for attacking a religion he disliked, or some religions, or religion in general; or sell all of it to the highest bidders. Yet Marcus Cohn, a friend of mine, considers that the government's asking about the religious programming of licensees breaches the wall of separation. He has written:

> While the U.S. Supreme Court has been gradually strengthening Jefferson's "wall of separation between church and state," the Federal communications Commission has been doing its best to persuade people to go to church. . . . The commission has held . . . that the proposed religious programming of one applcant for a television station . . . was superior to another because it afforded "a more positive proposal for providing time to diverse religious faiths." In another case, it gave a comparative—although not a disqualifying—demerit to . . . [a] proposed program schedule [because it] failed to include "any strictly religious programs" and thus left a "void in . . . over-all program structure."

Radio and TV are not the instruments of the state, they are the instruments of society. The state is there, has to be there, only because a technology Jefferson could not dream of has made rationing the airwaves necessary. If Cohn's principle were followed, the FCC would not be protecting the separation of church and state, as he thinks. It would be promoting the separation of religion and society— something else again.

The late Theodore Leskes, a lamented colleague and an authority on First Amendment questions, was rather more convinced than I of the need for a wall. Nevertheless, when I asked him whether he objected to military chaplains, he answered that he could not object in principle. The army, he said, is a surrogate society. When the army drafts a man it is obligated to make available to him, insofar as possible, what he has had in the civilian life from which it cuts him off— including the opportunity for religious worship and guidance. Otherwise the government's maintenance of a conscript army would mean the government's exclusion of religion from the lives of some millions of young men.

And so with education. As late as the end of the nineteenth century President Garfield could say that a college education was a log with Mark Hopkins at one end and a student at the other. If no longer entirely true when he said it, it still had a certain verisimilitude. Now it would be absurd—not only about our colleges, but also about our high, junior-high, and even elementary schools. These demand ever more costly laboratories, closed-circuit TV, equipment for teaching languages, psychological testing, vocational guidance.

When logs were cheap, it was rather widely possible to maintain nonpublic schools of the same quality as the public schools, even without governmental aid. Not any more. No violation of the First Amendment is needed to reduce freedom of the press substantively, by the disappearance of one paper after another; the only thing needed is for economic law to be allowed free play. Allowed free play, economic law would have the same effect on the nonpublic schools, but with an even worse effect on society.

In the political and social thought that has least to apologize for, despotism is understood to prevail when state and society are all but identical, when the map of the state can almost be superimposed on the map of society. In contrast, freedom depends on society's having loci of interest, affection, and influence besides the state. It depends on more or less autonomous institutions mediating between the naked, atomized individual and the state—or rather, keeping the individual from nakedness and atomization in the first place. In short, pluralism is necessary.

Given that a shriveling of the nonpublic must fatally enfeeble pluralism, especially in education; and given that the agent of that enfeeblement is the unchecked operation of economic law, the remedy is simple: check it. Let the government see that money finds its way to the nonpublic schools, so that they may continue to exist side by side with the public schools. That will strengthen pluralism, and so, freedom.

Arguments for nongovernmental pluralism have to overcome the obstacle of their popularity with conservative immobilists. From Social Security to Medicare, unfeeling rightists have been quick to warn that the omnicompetent state is upon us. Nobody listens any more, the boy has cried wolf too often. But in the fable a real wolf finally appeared, and for us the state coextensive with society may yet appear. Technology encourages it. The simple fact that there are now so many people encourages it. The time when the state took little of the room of a man's life is gone. Happily, one can favor the welfare state and still oppose the omnicompetent state.

Can government be expected to subsidize the nonpublic sector, to pay for keeping vigorously alive centers of influence and power whose very existence will limit its own influence and power? If government is democratic, the expectation is altogether realistic. American governments routinely subsidize the nonpublic sector: the deductibility provision in the federal and state income taxes is nothing but an indirect subsidy to nonpublic institutions—community chests, universities, theological seminaries, churches, synagogues.

Historically, establishment has gone with monarchy: throne and altar, crown and mitre. Separation has gone with a republic: no king, no bishop. And in fact England, Denmark, Norway, and Sweden have established churches and are monarchies. Republicanism was once even more of a fighting creed than separation, but who in Great Britain or Scandinavia is excited by republicanism any longer? It has become an irrelevance, an anachronism. While monarchies have shown that they can be decent and democratic, republics have shown that they need not necessarily be either decent or democratic. In America separationism may soon be just as anachronistic, if only because our establishmentarians are not much more numerous than our monarchists.

Even the metaphors are coming down with mustiness. "Wall of separation" may have sounded good once, but if you say it to a young man now he is as likely as not to think you mean the wall that separates Berlin. Leave it to a poet: "Something there is that doesn't love a wall."

—July 1966

.24.

Reply to Two Critics

Why is my critic's libertarian separationism especially common among Jews of the same kind as he? His views, he says, are not part of his heredity. Which is to say, being a Jew is not much more than a biological datum. If this obtuseness is uncharacteristic of him from one point of view, from another it is entirely characteristic of the group to which he belongs—without his wanting to recognize that he belongs to it.

By an individual pursuit of universal reason, he thinks, he has arrived at his beliefs and conclusions. So think other Jews like him. They are a regiment of individualists marching in step, each assuming that the rhythm is his own. Granted that it is universal reason

which beats the drum, why is the beat heard with such disproportionate acuity by people of a certain kind? To others they appear as
only one group of marchers among many, each with its distinctive
manner and banner, and not a few with conflicting pretensions to
universalism.

In *Commentary* Daniel P. Moynihan once wrote about Reform
and Regular Democrats. The Reformers, he said, were liberals, mostly
Jews. They were incapable of conceding legitimacy to others' habits
of thought, or putting themselves in the others' shoes, or realizing
that in the others' eyes they were a cohesive self-interest bloc—for
instance, the speaker at a conference on legislative issues in New
York State who

warned that a higher-education bond issue . . . would permit building
loans to *parochial* colleges. The regulars react to this much as the liberals
would react to a speech by a Bronx Italian protesting that an increase
in competitive state scholarships for higher education would only give
further advantages to the children of middle-class Jews—a view not unknown in Albany, but emphatically not expressed.

Remove Christian religious influence from the public schools as
completely as you wish, you are not going to change the fact that in
the best circumstances a Jew is sometimes going to feel like an outsider—and therefore, in my critic's view, punished—in an English-
language culture of Chaucer and Shakespeare and T. S. Eliot and
Ezra Pound, of Milton and Hawthorne. Or take culture in the anthropologist's sense. Having removed Christmas from the schools, if
that were fully possible, you couldn't remove it from the street or the
stores or television. The message of American culture to a Jewish
child is, Yes, Ruthie, there is a Santa Claus; and, No, he isn't Jewish.

If you think of our minority status as punishment, you will naturally want to escape it. What can help? The Revolution? No; witness
Russia. The conversion of multitudes to Judaism? For that you may
have to await the Messiah. Going to Israel? That would work. But
here in America, the only thing that can help and is in your power to
do is to go over to the majority, to become or pretend to become a
Christian; then at least your grandchildren will not feel punished.
That is what is implied in equating minority status with punishment.

On the other hand, you could see unpopularity—which these days
is less than it used to be, anyway—as a price, and minority status as
the good for which you pay the price; and well worth it. Moderns do
not like to be caught quoting the *Rubaiyat*, but some of us remember

those verses: "I wonder often what the vintners buy/One-half so precious as the stuff they sell." What is a possible Jewish symbolism here? The vintners are some Jews; the wine they are eager to rid themselves of is Judaism, or the state or quality of being a Jew; what they buy is something they regard as more valuable, freedom from a minority condition experienced as punishment; but the poet knows they are getting the worse of the bargain.

For my critic, nonpublic education is something of a vice when too accessible for the common people. It cannot quite be declared illegal, but sound public policy requires that we shall limit it to their betters by making it expensive. Equal justice, above all: nonpublic=nonpublic; parochial school=private school. We give no aid to the stockbroker with a child in a private school, we give no aid to the workman with children in a parochial school. Thus is justice not only done, but manifestly seen to be done.

The name of this philosophy is libertarian separationism.

It is the ease even more than the fact of our separationism's victory that I object to. A man I have known and respected for a long time has written me:

I was a member of the [appropriate] committee of [an important Jewish organization]. It was an interesting experience. One of the most extraordinary happenings was the debate on the poverty and education bills. The passion with which the Wall was upheld would have been unbelievable to me if I had not been present. [X] made an appeal as vehement as if he were admonishing us to fight Hitler or Stalin. Dean Keppel, then the U.S. Commissioner of Education, was received at the luncheon meeting at which he was the guest of honor with such cool, formal courtesy and was asked such hostile questions that I was ashamed of myself for being present.

Passions spin the plot.

In his peroration, my critic is angry with "divisive, frequently undemocratic special-interest groups." That is strange language for a liberal. It is intolerant, authoritarian; it is how the Know-Nothings and the American Protective Association spoke of those sinister Catholics in the nineteenth century, it is how some people speak of the Negroes now.

For the damage from bigness, pluralism is, if not a preventive, at any rate a mitigative. I can understand why fearless spirits engaged in a critique of pure tolerance should be scornful of liberal democracy and therefore of its corollary, pluralism. What I cannot understand is why a liberal democrat should be scornful of pluralism.

We must thank another critic for a remarkable theorem, that religious freedom in Great Britain is insecure, as well as for a highly original proof: the "quite shocking" difficulty in which Jewish children find themselves if they want to get into "good" schools. His own quotation marks tell us he is not talking about good state schools, or even schools like Manchester Grammar, which technically qualifies as what the English call a public school; he is talking about schools like Eton and Harrow. He means there are Jews who are denied a good old-school tie, not a good education. That is to say, he is talking of social discrimination. The reason why there is social discrimination against English Jews, he says, is that England has no separation of church and state. Presumably it is because the United States *has* separation of church and state that American Jews have never been kept out of neighborhoods, clubs, hotels, prep schools, colleges, or fraternities.

About the argument that released or dismissed time, by making children aware of religious differences, is divisive, and produces discomfort in Jewish children, the psychologist Samuel Flowerman, a deceased colleague, said—and this is probably written down in some learned journal—that the facts alleged are not facts at all: it is an illusion of the *Konfessionslos* that a child is unaware of religious differences if his teacher does not bring them out. The child is not initially uncomfortable, Flowerman said, but uncomfortable parents project their own discomfort onto him, and later still he may catch it from them. The pathology is less in the situation and the child than in the parents.

—December 1966

. 25 .

Negroes, Jews, and Muzhiks

Can anything still be said about Negro and Jew in the United States that has not already been said—by Fiedler, Glazer, and Podhoretz; by Baldwin, Clark, and Rustin; in conferences, speeches, books, and articles? The relation between American Jew and American Negro has even been examined in the perspective of Israel and Africa. Let us add the perspective of Belorussia and the Ukraine.

European and European-born scholars like Yves Simon and Bruno Bettelheim have shown that the American relation between white and Negro is similar in some ways to the European relation between bourgeois and proletarian before 1939. Like Negroes and whites here, proletarians and bourgeois there were two nations. Like Negroes here, proletarians there were exploited, alienated, feared, seen as primitive and unclean: George Orwell's shabby-genteel parents used to say, "Workingmen *smell.*" In Europe the moral and intellectual elite sided with the workers, here it sides with the Negroes.

All this is clearly true, but I think a better comparison might be with the European peasant, especially before 1914. There are psycho-sexual reasons, among others, for this: Lady Chatterley's lover was a gamekeeper, the personified principle of opposition to the death-in-life of the factory and the office, choosing to be neither proletarian nor bourgeois. In European folklore the depraved noblewoman recruits her lovers from among coachmen, grooms, and goatherds. Their closeness to animals gives them an animal potency, they are stallions; and in their primitiveness and social inferiority she gratifies her taste for lowness, the *nostalgie de la boue.* In the American imagination, of course, the man-stallion is Negro. On the female side, the serf girl was the sexual property of her master and his sons, and so was the Negro slave girl: Edmund Wilson reads Mrs. Chesnut's *Diary from Dixie* and is reminded of what Tolstoy said about Russia. Like the Negro slaves in America, the muzhik serfs, emancipated at almost the same time, are then perceived as ignorant, improvident, violent, drunken, incontinent—id figures, embodiments of the untamed instincts.

The association of the Jew with the muzhik was older and more intense than that with the Negro. With the Negro the association does not go back, essentially, before the memory of men and women still living. For Jews here, the Negro has not been the only Other (though he is most other); and notwithstanding Negro talk of the Jewlandlord and Goldberg, proportionately few of us in America deal chiefly with Negroes. By contrast, Jews in numbers had lived and dealt with the Slavic peasantry for the better part of a thousand years —in Poland, in the Polish-Lithuanian empire, and finally in the Tsarist Russian Pale of Settlement. Enough time has passed since Khmelnitski led Ukrainian Orthodox peasants in a massacre of the Polish Catholic landowning gentry and their Jewish estate agents and men of business for his name to have become, in the language of our grandparents, a synonym for antiquity. For the Jews of the East European villages and small towns—not the cities, like Warsaw or Odessa—from whom most American Jews are immediately descended, the muzhik was the Other, statistically and psychologically. The muzhik was the Jew's external environment and, more often than not, his livelihood. In the dictionary the Yiddish word for "peasant" is *poyer* (German *Bauer*), but in fact the Russian or Polish Jew was likely to say *goy*: the muzhik was the consummate gentile.

When we consider that the history of relations between Jew and muzhik is so old and intense; that muzhik and Negro have been alike, not least in the culture's perception of them; and that even in plural America the Negro is nevertheless most Other—when we consider all this, we may reasonably expect that current Jewish feelings and ways of thinking about Negroes will be affected by older feelings and ways of thinking about muzhiks.

The Jews of the Pale of Settlement thought themselves superior to the muzhiks, feared them, felt guilty about them, pitied them, envied them, and, while distrusting them, wanted to see their lot bettered.

The Jews did not hate the muzhiks. In general, we are poor haters —partly, I suppose, because we have had so many enemies that hatred is pointless. What Jew hates Spain? Of Titus, a traditional Jew will still say, when he has occasion to mention him, "may his name and memory be blotted out" (thus preserving the name and memory), but he does not hate Rome. At most he has a fixed epithet that goes with Rome, "the wicked kingdom." We do not even hate Germany. I still look twice when I see a Volkswagen or Mercedes in the parking lot of a synagogue, and I will make an effort to avoid buying a German article, but I have not taught that to my children, and when they notice what I am doing they regard it as a cute eccentricity; nor can I altogether blame the Israelis for their heavy imports from Germany. If I do not readily work up enthusiasm for Rumania, Hungary, the Ukraine, Lithuania, and Poland, that is not hatred. The emotional relations between Jews and East European Gentiles were asymmetrical. Nothing with the Jews corresponded at all closely to the hatred against us felt—and acted on, murderously—by Rumanians, Hungarians, and the rest.

To return from this digression—I have said that Jews thought themselves superior to muzhiks. On the Jewish scale of values, Jews ranked high and muzhiks low. As between *shabbat* and *ḥol*, *ruḥaniyut* and *gashmiyut*—sabbath and weekday, spirituality-intellectuality and corporeality—the Jews, in their own eyes, stood for the first term of each set, and the muzhiks for the second. Typically, Jews could read and muzhiks could not, and literacy and illiteracy have their distinctive corollaries.

Jews feared muzhiks—for the same reason, basically. The muzhiks were so *physical*, so patently the sons of Esau. Jews remembered that their ancestor Jacob had feared his brother Esau and that only a blind man could be persuaded that the hands of Jacob were the hands of Esau. Muzhiks could kill you—either individually, in a passion or for gain, or collectively, in a pogrom. More than most, Jews have cause for fearing violence.

Jews felt guilty. When a merchant (the word is much too grand) is almost as poor as his very poor customer and when he has the upper hand in such things as simple arithmetic, he is apt to take advantage. He shouldn't, but sometimes he does. The rabbis' insistence on the biblical commandment of just weights and measures and on the sacrilege of violating this commandment in dealings with gentiles is proof that there were violations. The violators rationalized their conduct: "The muzhik steals me blind, but even when I catch him at it I have to make believe I don't see anything because I'm afraid of him, so the only way I can get my own back is to juggle the figures a little." Or else they took their ability to fool the muzhik as further proof of their cleverness and his stupidity. But they also felt guilty. They knew that what they were doing was not right.

An Israeli joke: Jews from a Polish village have survived Hitler and have established themselves as an egg-and-poultry cooperative in Israel. They are grateful to their friend, the peasant elder, for helping to save them from the Nazis, and they are proud of having made themselves into productive, progressive agriculturists. As the Zionist song has it, they came to Israel to build and to be built, and they have succeeded. So they pool their money and send a ticket to the old peasant, who eventually comes from Poland to visit them. They show him their modern equipment and methods, and he is impressed. Then they show him how artificial light twenty-four hours a day keeps the hens laying without interruption. He shakes his head and says, "Ah, *Zhidy, Zhidy!* You have no honest Poles to trick any more, so you trick chickens."

Jews pitied the muzhik: he had to bear on his back the weight of the gentry, the bureaucracy, the army, the church, the absolute monarchy. He labored and suffered so that these need not, and so that they could lord it over him. He was a man, by definition created in the image of God, and they had made him less than a man.

Jews envied the muzhik: the other side of revulsion is attraction, even fascination. People under the firm rule of the superego must hanker, whether they know it or not, for instinctual anarchy. As soon as the sovereignty of Torah and the rabbinocracy had been breached, the attraction could express itself: Isaac Babel rides with the Red Cavalry Cossacks, for reasons that Lionel Trilling has finely explained, and the Second and Third 'Aliyot bring with them to Palestine a Tolstoyan peasant-and-soil romanticism. In I. B. Singer's *The Slave*, when the peasant Wanda becomes the Jewish Sarah she is more admirable than the homeborn Jewesses. What all modern Jews in Eastern Europe had in common, transcending any difference of formal ideology, was that they valued action, forcefulness, masculinity, and saw the old Judaism as passive, weak, feminine. They liked Esau more than their parents did, and Jacob less.

As the Jews did not hate the muzhik, so they did not blame him. They blamed the system, or the authorities—priests, government. I remember the late Hayyim Greenberg writing that the ordinary Jew would say, "The peasant is really a good fellow, if he's left alone and if he doesn't get drunk"—exactly what I used to hear at home when my parents spoke of the old country. If only the priests and officials didn't incite the muzhik, if only they cared enough to make him educate his children, if only the social and political system were decent, all would be well, for muzhik and Jew alike.

But Jews believed that the muzhik needed help and guidance and could not be trusted to do things for himself. Without guidance, his childishness, impulsiveness, and propensity to violence would spoil everything. In the 1870s and early 1880s some young Jewish revolutionaries joined the *narodnik* (populist) movement and "went to the people," that is, to the peasant masses. Then came the pogroms. Some Jewish narodniks tried to excuse these as the first stirrings of the revolutionary spirit in a formerly inert mass, but most Jews were strengthened in their conviction that while to do something for the people was just and necessary, to trust them to do it was folly. In the Jacobin formula, the people were to be compelled to be virtuous.

After Hitler and all that the Nazis had done to the Poles, there was a pogrom in the Polish town of Kielce against the handful of Jews who had escaped the crematoria and returned. Most Jews took the pogrom as the signal to leave forever, chiefly for Israel. Those who chose to remain—above all, the polonized and assimilated—were tempted to rely on Stalin and the Red Army to implant virtue in the Poles, and some became agents of the Stalinist Polish Communist police. That suited Stalin and the Stalinists: let the Poles hate the Jews instead, as always.

Usually, the Jewish distrust of the masses has included a distrust of the leader who comes from the masses, and who is all too likely to share their prejudices and weaknesses, including antisemitism. Better by far the patrician liberal, cultured, above plebeian uncouthness. Whether a Jew is modern or traditional, if he has any political theory at all it is apt to be classical: the state must have a monopoly of violence, it should be just, and it should be in the hands of enlightened men. Rule by an establishment can be bad, but in the Jewish experience it is generally less bad than rule by men from the masses, appealing to their emotions.

Raw antisemitism is more a plebeian and populist phenomenon than an establishment one. Lueger, the late-nineteenth-century antisemitic mayor of Vienna, was the populace's man. Between him and the Jews, protecting them, stood the Emperor Francis Joseph; and the Jews of the Hapsburg empire loved their emperor. Hitler was a kind of tribune of the plebs. (In literature Céline speaks their rancor, with their voice.) Centuries earlier, in the late Middle Ages and the early modern period, expulsions of the Jews had accompanied the nationalisms and the formation of the national states of Western Europe, in England, France, and Spain; and the impulse for both the nationalisms and the expulsions had come more from the rising new men than from the established old ones. The Spanish Inquisition was populist in its origins, and normally Jews had more to fear from the lower clergy than from the higher.

In the United States, Tom Watson was a Populist, and he helped to lynch Leo Frank. The historians debate whether the Populist movement was really antisemitic or only seemed so, but Jews can be forgiven for uneasiness about several things associated with the Populists, including the frenzy aroused by a speech against crucifying mankind upon a cross of gold. For Christians, crucifixion was the Jewish crime above all others; and about the time when Bryan was declaiming, the Tsarist secret police was forging the *Protocols of the Elders of Zion*, according to which there was a gold power out to conquer the world, and that power was Jewish.

McCarthyism was populist and popular. Its target was the establishment—Harvard, the State Department, the Supreme Court, even

186

the Army—and it could be defeated only by the establishment. Civil liberties and the rights of minorities are not characteristically cherished by any populism, which tends toward an intolerant majoritarianism: the Soviet prosecutors of the intellectuals who fail to think wholesome thoughts are able to appeal to popular sentiment. Early in this century American populism won a great victory for democracy, the initiative and the referendum. Today, from coast to coast, these are used with almost invariable success against the civil rights of Negroes. In California, where a large majority voted to put racial discrimination in housing beyond the reach of law, it had to be left to the courts, elitist by their nature, to uphold decency against the electorate speaking through the polls.

On the whole, therefore, we have had some justification for our distrust of populism and men from the people, and for our preference for the cultivated, liberal, patrician leader. Sometimes, though, we overdo it. We gave and still give to Franklin D. Roosevelt more devotion than he earned, by any cool, political measure of favors done and benefits conferred. But at least Roosevelt was a President, and a great one. What can explain our infatuation with Adlai Stevenson? (I am entitled to ask the question. I voted for him twice.) He was not especially favorable to Jewish causes or interests, nor was he even much of a New Dealer. It was enough for us that he seemed to incarnate all that is enlightened, cultured, and well-bred. (Another good sign: he was obviously no athlete.) To most other Americans, he was not nearly the man Eisenhower was. We were a little tardy in getting to like President Kennedy, because Stevenson was in the way, but when we could perceive Kennedy, too, as enlightened, cultivated, and patrician, we were his—again, a little more than his objective merits or accomplishments warranted.

On the other hand, we have consistently underestimated Truman, and fewer of us voted for him than for any other Democratic Presidential candidate since 1932. Nothing patrician about him. Rather, something folksy-populist, and so a bit disquieting. Twenty years from now, someone may write that we underestimated Johnson, for similar reasons.

What are some of the differences between our present attitude toward Negroes and the older attitude toward muzhiks? Negroes are not so exclusively the Other as the muzhiks used to be: Negroes are 10 percent or so of the population of America, muzhiks were probably 90 percent in old Eastern Europe. If there had been psychoanalysts in

Zhitomir or Grodno, they would have found that the id figures of their Jewish patients' dreams and fantasies were muzhiks, and only muzhiks. Here psychoanalysts no doubt find their Jewish patients dreaming and fantasizing about Negroes, but not only about Negroes. Our society and our culture offer additional possibilities for representing the id.

We also feel less guilty about Negroes, I think. For the sake of argument, let us concede what should not be conceded: to deal with = to exploit. But even of the so-called Goldbergs, even of the Jewlandlords, not all are Jews. Some are actually Negroes. They are called Jewlandlords because they are landlords.

In what way are the two attitudes the same? About Negroes, Jews fear what our grandparents feared about muzhiks, violence. We know in our bones that the civil peace is always fragile, that a habitude of violence is easily established, and that then Jews and people like Jews had better watch out.

In our distaste for violence we differ hardly at all from our grandparents. When they were displeased they did not hit, they acted *broygez* (Yiddish, "offended" or "sulky," from Hebrew *berogez*, "in wrath"): they did not speak to the person who had offended them, they avoided his—often her—company. (In his wife's presence, a man would say to his child, "Tell your mother the soup is cold.") The characteristic response of Jews to an unpleasant situation is still avoidance, flight not fight. If a Jew does not like Negroes moving into his neighborhood, he moves out. He does not band together with his neighbors to burn a cross—of course not—or to throw bricks and bottles. That may be why Jewish neighborhoods turn into Negro neighborhoods fairly easily. It was not where Jews live that Martin Luther King's marchers for integrated housing needed massive police protection in Chicago. It was where Ukrainians, Lithuanians, Poles, and Italians live—the children and grandchildren of muzhiks (and other peasants).

If I were a Negro I would resent a Jew's acting *broygez*, but I would surely prefer it to someone else's violence. Still, that may only prove I am unable to rise above my Jewish thinking. Malcolm X once said on television—publicly, emphatically, to many thousands— that he liked Sheriff Clark of Selma, Alabama, the man with the dogs and the electric prods, better than Jewish liberals and supporters of the civil-rights movement. Malcolm said: Clark is a wolf but the Jewish liberal is a fox, and the wolf is better because with him you know where you are. Now it appears that Malcolm is a great man in his death, and not only among the young generation of Negroes. A university journal has published a rhetorician's effusion about his rhetoric, which purports to demonstrate—*le style c'est l'homme même*—that Malcolm was good and noble and honest, attacking only those people and things that were wicked and base and false. The rhetoric of the wolf and the fox was not mentioned.

As for populism, we like it in Negroes no more than in muzhiks or in white Americans. Once more, violence or its aura of violence worries us, as well as its encouragement to indulge prejudice and dislike of outsiders and to suspect and resent elites, whether good or bad. Everyone says harsh things about "the power structure," but the non-power structure is usually worse. Most judges are better than most citizens, most mayors than most voters, most union leaders than most of their members, most presidents of chambers of commerce than most businessmen. I do not say intrinsically good, but relatively better. A study of American thinking about civil liberties showed that the average chairwoman of a DAR chapter and the average commander of an American Legion post were usually better than their rank and file.

Black power? For what it represents of violence-populism, no. But it also represents something that modern Jewish history knows, favorably, as self-emancipation (Pinsker's auto-emancipation). Emancipated Jews know self-hate, though it seems to be our good fortune now to know less about it at first hand than only a generation ago. We know or knew enough about it for the books on it to be written by Jews, about Jewish examples. (Who can forget the case of Otto Weininger?) In some form, black power has to precede or accompany black self-acceptance and self-esteem. Otherwise, there will be black self-hate.

When a Negro demands better education for his children, it must be intolerable for him to hear himself saying that a predominantly Negro school is necessarily an inferior school. Negroes must feel better when they say that white is not better than black, white is only richer than black; with money, Negro schools can be as good as white schools, and better. Now this may be a myth, but if so, it is of that species of myth which, by transforming men, transforms itself into reality. Herzl's Jewish state was a myth of the same species—about which he prophesied, truly: "If you will it, this need not be a myth."

—*October 1966*

V

JEWS AND CHRISTIANS, JUDAISM AND CHRISTIANITY

. 26 .

On Reading Matthew

Judeo-Christian?

Does the Judeo-Christian tradition exist? There has been much talk about it, especially since the Vatican Council, but to talk about a thing does not necessarily mean that the thing is real. A Judeo-Christian tradition, if it existed, by its nature would have to be ancient and Palestinian-Mediterranean; but the talk seems to be mostly modern and Western, not to say American. One is apt to be suspicious.

From the Jewish side it is generally the Orthodox and the Zionists who are most suspicious. For the Orthodox, a Christian who talks about a Judeo-Christian tradition is now trying to seduce Jews by gentleness and fair words, after the failure of violence and threats to compel them; and a Jew who talks about it, sinfully denying the uniqueness of Judaism, is helping the Christian seducers. For the Zionists, the talk has nothing to do with theology or sacred history, but is only another of the many stratagems Jews in the Diaspora have used to protect their civic equality and to fool themselves into believing that they need not go up to Israel for their safety and dignity.

Both the Orthodox and the Zionist suspicions may be examined in *De'ot*, an Israeli quarterly that describes itself as the publication of the religious (i.e., Orthodox) academics. In one number I have seen, there is a comment by Eliezer Livneh. Livneh, who must be respected for his independence above all, is neither an academic nor, I am pretty sure, Orthodox, but he is a Zionist. Denying "a common Judeo-Christian heritage," he tells us that Christianity was really "only one of the currents of late Hellenism, which succeeded in becoming a world religion. . . . Besides innocent causes for discovering a Judeo-Christian 'partnership,' there enters into the picture conscious apologetics. . . . This is not at all innocent: it is a Diaspora-Jewish [*yehudit-galutit*] propaganda instrument, especially in the United

States, for 'public relations.' Its spiritual worth is nil." *Galuti* can have about it something of the contempt that American Negroes give to "Tom."

Livneh is advancing two arguments here: that Christianity is not Jewish but Hellenistic in origin, and that "the Judeo-Christian tradition" is a Diaspora-Jewish ideology. The first is more serious than the second. An ideology arises to justify the interests and aims of those who hold it, but it is a fallacy—the genetic fallacy—to believe that knowing about the birth and function of an idea proves its untruth. Equality is the ideology of those who have been kept inferior. May we conclude that equality is a false idea?

Livneh declares flatly that Christianity's origin is Hellenistic, not Jewish. As they say, everyone is entitled to an opinion, but his is only that. Intertestamental literature, early Christianity, late Hellenism, and contemporaneous Judaism are not his fields. They are the fields of David Daube, the Regius Professor of Civil Law at Oxford who is also a traditional Jew, and Daube sees Christian origins as very Jewish indeed. Even more persuasive is the testimony of David Flusser of the Hebrew University, the Israeli scholar Edmund Wilson wrote about in his book on the Dead Sea Scrolls.

According to Wilson, Flusser was irreligious then, but he does not seem to be now, if we may judge from his two pieces in the issue of *De'ot* Livneh was in. Livneh appears to be unaware that in the *Festschrift* for Isaac Fritz Baer, Flusser published a study, uncompromisingly titled "The Jewish Origin of Christianity," that was impatient with the Enlightened commonplace about Hellenistic origins. Flusser's person deflects arguments based on the genetic fallacy. About the thing itself, the relation of Christianity to Judaism, the English summary of this study says this:

> . . . paganism had very little effect on the origins of Christianity. . . .
> The tension between Christianity and Judaism can better be explained by
> the operation of Jewish centrifugal forces in the new religion . . .: (1) Rab-
> binic Judaism, which was the origin of the religious personality of Jesus
> and of the mother-church of Jerusalem; (2) the Essene movement, which
> influenced the second stratum of Christianity, dominated by the religious
> personalities of Paul and John the Evangelist, and (3) Hellenistic Judaism,
> which influenced Christian apologetics.

In the first note to his text, Flusser cautions: "Of course this does not mean that Christianity is Jewish, or a Judaism of a certain kind. . . . The forces that led to the rise of Christianity, though their origin was in Judaism, brought about Christianity's independence and separation from the body of Judaism."

Of course. Christianity is distinct from Judaism. What would be the point of asking about a Judeo-Jewish tradition?

Matthew: Language and Text

Ever since Wilson's essay "On First Reading Genesis," I have wondered how it would be to examine the Greek New Testament as he examined the Hebrew Bible. I got around to it only with the current debate over the Judeo-Christian tradition. *Ad fontes*—back to the sources. This is a report on the first book, Matthew.

Wilson's fondness for deducing a people's timeless character and mentality from language must impress a linguist pretty much as a fondness for phrenology would impress a psychologist. Reading a text in its original language will not lay bare the soul of a people—or even, for most of us, reveal nuances blurred in translation. The first advantage of reading in a foreign language, above all if you do not know it well, is that you must slow down. Nowadays we have to make our way through such masses of print that all of us are speed-readers. With an important text, read slowly; but that is hard to do when its language is yours and the text seems easy. Until I read Matthew slowly, I thought I remembered the argument in Chapter 15 as being against the prohibition of nonkosher food. In fact it is against having to wash the hands before eating.

The other advantage of reading in the original language is that ambiguities are preserved. Translations have a way of being more definite than originals. For instance, in the Lord's Prayer (6:13) the Authorized (or King James) Version has ". . . deliver us from evil"; so has the Revised Standard Version, but adds a note: "Or *the evil one*," while the New English Bible has ". . . save us from the evil one." Slightly earlier in the Sermon on the Mount (5:39), KJV had "But I say unto you, That ye resist not evil"; RSV, " . . . Do not resist one who is evil," and NEB, ". . . Do not set yourself against the man who wrongs you." On the basis of the language alone, "deliver us from a wicked man" and "do not resist the Devil" are as possible as what the versions give us. (Context makes the second a bit less likely than the first.)

Ambiguity goes beyond language, to the text itself. RSV's translators say explicitly that they often prefer other Greek manuscripts to the ones King James's translators worked on. Words, phrases, even entire verses differ. Three examples: (1) KJV ends the Lord's Prayer with "for thine is the kingdom, and the power, and the glory, for ever. Amen." RSV does not include this. (2) In 19:9, according to KJV it is adulterous to marry a divorced woman, but not according to RSV. RSV: "And I say to you: whoever divorces his wife except for unchastity, and marries another, commits adultery." KJV: "And I say unto you, Whosoever shall put away his wife, except it be for fornication, and shall marry another, committeth adultery: *and whoso marrieth her which is put away doth commit adultery*." (But compare 5:32. Luke [16:18] does not recognize Matthew's exception for unchastity: "Every one who divorces his wife and marries another commits adultery, and he who marries a woman divorced from her husband commits adultery." Matthew may have been edging away from Luke's uncompromising doctrine. The End of Days kept receding and life had to go on.) (3) In 24:36 it is KJV that omits and RSV that adds. KJV: "But of that day and hour knoweth no man, no, not even the angels of Heaven, but my father only." RSV: "But of that day and hour no one knows, not even the angels of heaven, *nor the Son*, but the Father only." The theological significance of saying the Son is inferior to the Father is obvious.

For a Jew the instability of the New Testament is all the more striking because he is accustomed to a stable Hebrew Bible (*christiane*, "Old Testament"). The differences between the text of Kittel's Biblia Hebraica and the Hebrew Bible lying before King James's translators are minute, but the differences between Nestle's Novum Testamentum Graece and KJV's New Testament are many and weighty.

But even a stable text does not do away with ambiguity. Take the *Shema'*: "Hear, O Israel, the Lord our God, the Lord is one." Its conclusion can be translated, and has been, in at least three more ways: the Lord is our God, the Lord is one; the Lord our God is one Lord; the Lord is our God, the Lord alone. (As if that were not enough, *shema'* itself can be not only "hear" but also "understand" and "obey.")

The first effect of Matthew's language is a kind of amazement. Why should Jews be talking Greek? All those polysyllables—e.g., *katadikasthēsē(i)*, "you will be condemned" (12:37)—so unlike Hebrew and Aramaic. But immediately one hears the Jewish language under the Greek. "And it came to pass," which KJV retains faithfully, is not Greek but biblical Hebrew: *wa-yehi*. "Answering he

said"—e.g., 3:15. "And Jesus answering said unto him"—is also biblical: *wa-ya'an wa-yo'mer*. When the angel said (1:20–21): " . . . Mary
. . . shall bring forth a son, and thou shalt call his name Jesus: for
he shall save his people . . . ," he was not talking Greek. "Call his
name" (rather than "call him") is Hebrew, and it is in Hebrew that
the name corresponds to the reason for the name: Jesus is *Yeshua'*
(in the English versions of the Hebrew Bible, Jeshua, a later variant
of Joshua), and "he shall save" is *yoshia'*. Compare Genesis 16:11:
"And the angel of the Lord said unto her [Hagar], . . . thou . . . shalt
bear a son, and shalt call his name Ishmael; because the Lord hath
heard [*shama'*]. . . ."

Or consider some nonbiblical expressions and formulas. A good
Greek compound, *oligopistoi* ("men of little faith," as in 6:30),
turns out to be rabbinic: "R. Eliezer the Great said, Anyone who
has bread in his basket and asks, What shall I eat tomorrow?, is but
of the men of little faith" (*mi-qetanne amanah*; Sotah 48b). In 10:13
"let your peace come upon it [the house]" is "say, 'Shalom 'alekhem,
peace (be) upon you,' to the people in the house." For 11:26 RSV
gives as the more literal rendering, in a note, "so it was well-pleasing
before thee." That is still the liturgical Hebrew of the synagogue:
with a change of tense and mood, *ken yehi razon* and *yehi razon
mille-fanekha*, and even *ken yehi razon mille-fanekha*. In 12:32 KJV's
"this world . . . the world to come" and RSV's "this age . . . the age
to come" are transparently *ha-'olam ha-zeh, ha-'olam ha-ba'*.

"Scribes and Pharisees, hypocrites!" is Matthew's special contribution to what has been called the teaching of contempt. It has cost us
dearly. Yet even this is of Jewish origin; and not only Jewish, but
actually Pharisaic. There is a famous story in Sotah (22b) about
Alexander Jannaeus, who killed thousands of Pharisees almost a
century before Jesus was born: "Said King Jannaeus to his queen, Be
afraid neither of the Pharisees nor of those who are not Pharisees, but
of the hypocrites who seem like Pharisees. For their deeds are like the
deed of Zimri, but they seek the reward of Phinehas." (The reference
is to Numbers 25. Calling a Jew Zimri is something like calling a
Christian Judas.)

Now I come to what may be—I am not sure—an original thought.
It seems to me possible that Jesus (or Matthew's source) liked
"hypocrite" so much because it was a pun, and punning was an
accepted mode of scholarly-religious discourse among the Jews. Thus
the prayer book quotes from Megillah (28b): "It was taught in the
school of Elijah: Whoever studies laws every day is assured of life in

the world to come, as it is said (Habakkuk 3:6): 'His ways are ever-lasting.' For 'ways,' *halikhot*, read 'laws,' *halakhot*." This last almost seems to be debating by pun across the centuries. Though I have forgotten where, I remember reading some years ago that one of the Dead Sea writings was bitter about the *ish ha-ḥalaqot*, the man of smooth things, the man of flattery. Is there an attack here against the *ish ha-halakhot*, the man of the (novel, Pharisaic) laws?

"Hypocrites" is *zevu'in*, as in the statement attributed to Alexander Jannaeus. An honorific word associated with the Pharisees was *zenu'in*, "modest, retired, chaste"; or, in relation to such matters as tithes, "scrupulous, meticulous." In Demai (6:6) we read about a fine point of tithing, that "the more meticulous [*zenu'in*] of the school of Hillel used to observe the words of the school of Shammai." If there was one thing not calculated to impress Jesus and his followers, it was fussiness about tithes. Do the Pharisees like to be called *zenu'in*, modest, meticulous? Rather call them *zevu'in*, hypocrites—especially since Pharisees use the word themselves, for men who have the show but not the substance of Pharisaism.

Matthew's references to the Hebrew Bible and quotations or paraphrases from it are abundant, if only because he causes so many prophecies to be "fulfilled": a common formula is "that it might be fulfilled which was spoken of the Lord by the prophet" (RSV, "to fulfill what the Lord had spoken by the prophet"). Almost always the quotations are apposite and show a good knowledge of the original—by heart, and thus sometimes not quite accurate in detail. The few I have compared with the Septuagint lead me to believe that Matthew need not rely on the existing Greek translation but can translate directly from the Hebrew. For instance, 7:23 quotes Psalm 6:9 (8), "Depart from me, all you workers of evil"; but where the Septuagint has *apostete* for "depart," Matthew has *apochōreite*; and Matthew, unlike the Septuagint, omits "all." He can also differ from the Septuagint when quoting from the Pentateuch, the first part of the Bible to be translated, whose Greek text was therefore more established than that of Psalms.

Besides quotations, Matthew has pseudo-quotations. A fine pseudo-quotation is in 27:9–10, an alleged fulfillment of prophecy about the thirty pieces of silver, supposedly from the book of Jeremiah. In their notes Nestle and RSV give pride of place to Zechariah 11:12–13, but even that does not quite fit. As for Jeremiah, the verses they suggest, hesitantly, are out of the question. In Nestle's critical apparatus we learn that some ancient manuscripts have Matthew quoting not Jeremiah but Zechariah; and some, Isaiah! It was an embarrassment from the beginning.

Finally, there is deliberate tendentiousness. From the Sermon on the Mount Christians have learned for centuries that a Jew is commanded to hate his enemies. In Nestle's edition typography shows up the tendentiousness beautifully. Since Nestle uses distinctive type for New Testament quotations from the Hebrew Bible, 5:43 would look like this if he were giving us Matthew in RSV's English: "You have heard that it was said, '*You shall love your neighbor* and hate your enemies.'" Visibly, the first part is a quotation, the second is not. The margin refers us back to Leviticus 19:18: " . . . you shall love your neighbor as yourself: I am the Lord."

To paraphrase a saying of Jesus', it is easier for a camel to go through the eye of a needle than for a Christian translation of the New Testament to be entirely satisfactory. Witness Matthew 1:20–23 (RSV):

> . . . an angel of the Lord appeared to him in a dream, saying, "Joseph, son of David, do not fear to take Mary your wife, for that which is conceived in her is of the Holy Spirit. . . ." All this took place to fulfill what the Lord had spoken by the prophet: "Behold a virgin shall conceive and bear a son. . . ."

Let us look closely at "virgin." The Revised Standard Version so renders Greek *hē parthenos* here, like the King James Version before it and even the New English Bible after it. The Hebrew word in Isaiah 7:14, which the Septuagint translates as Matthew was to do later, is *ha-'almah*. Now KJV is at least consistent: its Isaiah also reads "virgin." Not so RSV's Isaiah, which, unlike its Matthew, reads "young woman"; but then, to make things even worse, it adds one of the most disgraceful notes I have ever seen in a scholarly enterprise: "or *virgin*." Disgraceful, because it has been many years since anyone has so understood *'almah*. Brown, Driver, and Briggs were Protestant clergymen as well as professors of Hebrew or Bible (at Union Theological Seminary and Oxford), and their *Hebrew and English Lexicon of the Old Testament*, published in 1907, was only stating what had long been accepted by all scholars when it defined *'almah* as "young woman (ripe sexually; maid or newly married)."

Why did the Septuagint translate *'almah* as *parthenos* in the first place? Perhaps for the same reason that modern translators—including

RSV!—*refrain* from translating *parthenos* as "virgin" in another part of Matthew. In Chapter 25 KJV's five foolish and five wise virgins are maidens for RSV, and in the New English Bible they are five foolish and five prudent girls. Hellenistic *parthenos* was no longer exclusively or necessarily "virgin." What had happened to this word in the course of time was something like what has happened to English "maid," but less than to German *Dirne*—"damsel" first becoming "wench" and then "strumpet." ("Wench" itself has a similar history.) So it used to be that a lover was a suitor, and his mistress the girl or woman he wanted to marry; while now, lover and mistress are —well, lover and mistress. When T. S. Eliot wrote a letter to the *Times Literary Supplement* complaining about NEB's girls and asking for the return of the virgins, the scholars put him in his place: *parthenos* in Hellenistic usage *might* be a virgin; she *was* a girl or young woman. Which did not prevent RSV and even NEB from translating *'almah-parthenos* in Matthew's Isaiah as "virgin."

A question to the scholars: Is "the young woman" the best rendering for Isaiah's *ha-'almah?* Perhaps it should be "the Crown Princess," wife of the heir apparent to the throne? *Ha-gevirah* means "the lady," but as a title it is "the Queen" or "the Queen Mother." (Monsieur and Mademoiselle were the styles of specified members of the French royal family.)

Jews and Gentiles

For Jesus, the gentiles (Greek *hoi ethnikoi* or *ta ethnē* = Hebrew *ha-goyim*) are to be avoided. What they do is bad; and if they do something good, that proves it is so to be taken for granted, so much a mere human instinct, that no merit attaches to it. In 10:5–6 he charges his disciples: "Go nowhere among the gentiles, and enter no town of the Samaritans, but go rather to the lost sheep of the house of Israel." And in the Sermon on the Mount:

> For if you love those who love you, what reward have you? Do not even the tax collectors do the same? And if you salute only your brethren, what more are you doing than others? Do not even the Gentiles do the same?

(The tax collector—KJV's publican—was the lowest of the low, enriching himself at his people's expense while serving the voracious foreign oppressor.) A contradictory verse, 28:19, is manifestly late and not Jesus' at all: "Go therefore and make disciples of all nations, baptizing them in the name of the Father and of the Son and of the Holy Spirit."

Antigentilism persists in a Christian *halakhah* that must have arisen to govern internal church discipline after Jesus, though it is attributed to him (18:15–17): "If your brother sins against you . . . but . . . does not listen to you . . . [or to] two or three witnesses . . . [or] even to the church, let him be to you as a Gentile and a tax collector." The law is based on Deuteronomy 19:15: ". . . only on the evidence of two witnesses, or three witnesses, shall a charge be sustained."

What then of "their synagogues," so frequent in Matthew? It may mean "the synagogues of those others, the Jews." Or it may mean *their* synagogues—the synagogues of those who do not follow Jesus, as opposed to *ours*, the synagogues of those who do follow him. So, in modern times, Hasidim and Mitnaggedim could say "their" about each other's synagogues.

Christianity's passage from the Jews to the gentiles has left its clearest traces in the contradiction between the New Testament's account of Jesus' descent and its account of his birth. In the genealogical part Jesus is descended from David. Only a Jew would say this, and only to Jews. For them David was the great king, from whose line would come the Messiah: in the *Shemoneh-'esreh* Jews still pray (three times a day, most days), "Speedily cause the scion of David, Thy servant, to spring forth, and exalt his horn [strength, glory] by Thy salvation; for we await Thy salvation all the day. Blessed art Thou, etc." But what was David to the heathen? An obscure shepherd-chieftain who had once attained some local eminence, according to the Jews, in a minor outpost of the civilized world. The Davidic descent is by and for Jews.

That being so, the conception by the Holy Spirit must be gentile; for how can Joseph transmit a descent from David if he is, emphatically, not Jesus' father but only the husband of Jesus' mother? In 22:41–46 there is a would-be proof from Scripture (Ps. 110:1) that the Messiah is not the scion of David. The proof is feeble, being ignorant of the Hebrew. (Again RSV is shifty, translating the Hebrew as "The Lord says to my *lord*: Sit at my right hand . . ." but translating the Greek of Matthew as "The Lord said to my Lord. . . .") In any event, these verses have to come from a source other than the early one that gave Jesus a Davidic lineage.

Law and Spirit

Not until I read Matthew closely did I see how literally Jesus is to be understood when he says, in the Sermon on the Mount (5:18–19):

> . . . till heaven and earth pass away, not an iota, not a dot [KJV: one jot or one tittle] will pass away from the law. . . . Whoever then relaxes one of the least of these commandments and teaches men to do so, shall be called least in the kingdom of heaven; but he who does them and teaches them shall be called great in the kingdom of heaven.

And in fact, Jesus is stricter than the Rabbis—except about tithes and levitical purity.

Do these verses give us the words of Jesus himself? If not his words, then his thought. They do not represent the ideology of a church that was becoming unobservant of the Torah ("law"). Such a church would have preferred to delete them. If it retained them, that could only be because they were universally known and universally attributed to Jesus.

Jesus is represented as not acting in accordance with his affirmation of the Torah in Chapter 12, where he justifies to the complaining Pharisees his disciples' plucking ears of grain on the Sabbath:

> . . . if you had known what this means, "I desire mercy, and not sacrifice" [Hosea 6:6], you would not have condemned the guiltless. For the Son of man is lord of the sabbath.

But this does not sound like Jesus. It sounds like Jewish followers of Jesus after his death, who are attributing the justification for their practice—a sectarian *halakhah*—to their master (but who do not dare to go so far as to say Jesus himself plucked ears of grain on the Sabbath). Later in the same chapter Jesus' defense of healing on the Sabbath, in opposition to the Pharisees, is also improbable.

We can be most sure of Jesus' conviction about something when he speaks in passing, by the way. Then the author or editor of Matthew, his attention concentrated on the main point, may fail to bring the incidental reference into line with his own purpose. Such a passage is 24:15–21:

> When you see the desolating sacrilege . . . in the holy place . . . let him who is in the field not turn back to take his mantle. . . . Pray that your flight may not be in winter or on a sabbath. For then there will be great tribulation. . . .

He is saying, by the way and as a matter of course, that you should keep the Sabbath even at the cost of impeding a flight for your life. Holding that you might not violate the Sabbath to save your life, he could not have held that you might violate the Sabbath, by plucking grain, to allay your hunger at once; and he is unlikely to have held that you might violate the Sabbath by initiating a cure for a chronic illness (as opposed to a sudden or acute one).

In contrast, a *midrash* (Tanḥuma to Mas'e) teaches:

> One who is attacked by robbers may break the Sabbath in order to save his life. Once letters from the Roman government, containing evil tidings for the Jews, reached the elders of Sepphoris. They asked R. Eleazar ben Perata [about 90–135 C. E.] what to do. It was the Sabbath, and they said: "Shall we flee?" He . . . said, "Danger to life annuls the Sabbath, for man is to live by doing God's commandments, and not to die by them. . . ."

During the Maccabean wars, Jews had died unresisting on the Sabbath, until the Rabbis' predecessors ruled in the spirit of R. Eleazar three hundred years later. If this leniency had sunk into the people's consciousness, the elders of Sepphoris would not have had to ask him for a ruling. Jesus was closer to the conservative folk than to the Rabbis.

On the question of oaths Jesus seems to have a position midway between people and Rabbis. He agrees with the folk that an oath is an oath and that if a man means his utterance to be one, he should be bound by it, without regard to technicalities about oath-formulas. The Rabbis, who disapproved of oaths, sought by technicalities to narrow the range of utterances that were legally binding as such. In doing so, they left themselves open to Jesus' sarcasms (23:16–22), with which the folk probably agreed:

> "Woe to you, blind guides, who say, 'If any one swears by the temple, it is nothing; but if anyone swears by the gold of the temple, he is bound by his oath.' You blind fools! For which is greater, the gold or the temple that has made the gold sacred? . . ."

He disagrees with the folk in that he reproves oaths: " . . . you have heard that it was said to the men of old, 'You shall not swear falsely. . . .' But I say to you, Do not swear at all. . . . Let what you say be simply 'Yes' or 'No' . . ." (5:33–37). "I" was saying this in agreement with the Rabbis, not in opposition to them. To this day a traditionally pious Jew has at least one thing in common with a pious

Quaker: he will not take an oath. The late S. Z. Cheshin of the Israeli Supreme Court—once my teacher in a Talmud Torah here—tells in *Tears and Laughter in an Israel Courtroom* about plaintiffs and defendants who, rather than testify under oath, choose to lose lawsuits in which they are in the right.

Jesus is said to defend his disciples' failure to wash their hands before eating (15:1–20). The defense has two parts, of which the better-remembered is this:

> Then Pharisees and scribes came to Jesus and said, "Why do your disciples transgress the tradition of the elders? For they do not wash their hands when they eat." . . . he called the people to him and said to them, ". . . not what goes into the mouth defiles a man, but what comes out of the mouth, this defiles a man." [And to the disciples,] "Do you not see that what goes into the mouth passes into the stomach, and so passes on? But what comes out of the mouth proceeds from the heart, and this defiles a man. For out of the heart come evil thoughts, murder, adultery, fornication, theft, false witness, slander. These are what defile a man; but to eat with unwashed hands does not defile a man."

This part by itself is complex enough. As with plucking ears of grain on the Sabbath, Jesus himself is not represented as doing what the Pharisees complain of, only as justifying his disciples' doing it. Again, this sounds like a rationalization of a sectarian *halakhah* of the early church, and we may doubt whether Jesus ever said it, at least in this form.

What is more, the argument shows an antinomian tendency, a contempt for law in the name of spirituality and morality, which must be even later. Note how cleverly it is done. Hand and mouth belong together: the hand brings food to the mouth. But here the mouth is made secondary, a mere entrance to the stomach—which is promptly forgotten—and an agent for the heart, and the relation between hand and mouth is transformed into a distinction between what goes into the mouth and what comes out of the heart. That this is illegitimate we may see from the kinds of immorality that are made to issue from the heart by way of the mouth: not only false witness and slander, which are indeed oral, but also evil thoughts, murder, adultery, fornication, and theft, which are not. (Nor need the stomach have been forgotten, since Jewish law condemns gluttony.) The inference is that people who worry about their ritual obligations are unconcerned about murder, etc. The argument is so massively disproportionate to the occasion—which is after all only a reproach that a tradition of the elders, not the Torah itself, is being ignored—that I can understand why I thought I remembered it as justifying something like eating forbidden meats. If Jesus had accepted the argument, he could never have said what he did about observing every jot and tittle of the law.

In actuality, those who are careful about the ritual washing of hands before meals sin less than others, not more, in murder, adultery, fornication, and theft, and perhaps less in evil thoughts, too; while the logic of antinomianism—Paul himself later discovered this, to his dismay, and we learn it from the history of spiritualizing enthusiasms of all kinds—is that immorality tends to become as trivial as not washing the hands. Or rather, immorality tends to become either a higher good in itself or a necessary means to a higher good. Shabbethai Zevi's followers, for instance, had a doctrine of the good deed that comes by way of transgression.

What we can retain of this part of the story is that Jesus said to the Pharisees, more or less: "Why are you concerned about conveying ritual impurity to the mouth through neglect of washing the hands? Why are you not concerned about the moral impurities that issue from the mouth: false witness and slander?" Jesus could very well have said this—though in saying even so little he would have been rather less than fair. Perhaps because the Jews are a verbal people, and therefore particularly exposed to the temptation of sinful speech, the classical rabbinical literature and our liturgy—composed by men who took very seriously the washing of hands and the purity of what goes into the mouth—incessantly, and often in a most exaggerated fashion, denounce *leshon ha-ra'*, evil speech. So do medieval ethical wills. A saintly rabbi who died as recently as 1933 was known not by his own name but, in accordance with the tradition, by the name of his work, the *Ḥafeẓ Ḥayyim* ("Who Desires Life"), subtitled "Laws Prohibiting Evil Speech [*leshon ha-ra'*] and Slander [*or gossip; rekhilut*] or Any Suggestion [*avaq*: dust] of Them." (Ps. 34:13,14 [12,13]: "What man is he that desireth life, and loveth many days,/that he may see good? Keep thy tongue from evil,/and thy lips from speaking guile.") Other works of his, with similar titles, taught the same lesson. The Ḥafeẓ Ḥayyim was ritually punctilious in a measure beyond our understanding, but his life's work was against evil speech, gossip, and slander; while we antiritualists are not conspicuously free of those things. As a friend of mine puts it, we call them character analysis.

The second part of Jesus' argument about washing the hands (15:3–5) has to do with the primacy of commandment over tradition:

He answered them, "And why do you transgress the commandment of God for the sake of your tradition? For God commanded, 'Honor your father and your mother,' . . . But you say, 'if any one tells his father or his mother, What you would have gained from me is given to God, he need not honor his father [or his mother—Nestle].' So, for the sake of your tradition, you have made void the word of God. You hypocrites! . . ."

In the New Testament the Pharisees are straw men, easily knocked down. If they had had a fair hearing, they would have answered that to honor father and mother is not an absolute commandment. To honor God is a greater commandment, and clearly father and mother should not be honored by obedience if they order their children not to honor God, as by worshipping idols. Abraham did not, in this sense, honor his father, and the Psalmist had said (27:10); "For my father and my mother have forsaken me,/but the Lord will take me up." The decision the Pharisees had made in the case Jesus cited was open to discussion, but the principle underlying it was one that he himself must accept. And, relying on the evidence of Matthew (8:18–22, 10:34–37, 12:46–50), the Pharisees could have gone further and turned Jesus' "hypocrite" against him:

1. Now when Jesus saw great crowds around him, he gave orders to go over to the other side. And . . . [one] of the disciples said to him, "Lord, let me first go and bury my father." But Jesus said to him, "Follow me, and leave the dead to bury their own dead."

2. "Do not think that I have come to bring peace on earth; I have not come to bring peace, but a sword. For I have come to set a man against his father, and a daughter against her mother. . . . He who loves father or mother more than me is not worthy of me. . . ."

3. While he was still speaking to the people, behold, his mother and his brothers stood outside, asking to speak to him. But he replied to the man who told him, "Who is my mother, and who are my brothers? . . . whoever does the will of my Father in heaven is my brother, and sister, and mother."

These hard sayings show something less than devotion to the commandment of honoring father and mother. Elijah, who in Christian typology is a forerunner of Jesus, was patient with a disciple whose filial duty was less urgent than burying a father (I Kings 19:20–21): " . . . 'Let me kiss my father and my mother, and then I will follow you.' . . . Then he arose and went after Elijah. . . ." And Mary's son snubbing her and his brothers, letting them stand waiting outside while he discourses on the superiority of spiritual to fleshly kinship, is hardly edifying. Abraham is not shown behaving toward his idolatrous father Terah as Jesus behaves toward his mother Mary.

On Reading Matthew

Any zealotry brings not peace but a sword, setting sons against fathers and daughters against mothers. We have seen politics do it, and Hasidism did it. But even for a zealot Jesus' behavior is unlovely.

Jesus' annoyance with the Pharisees over their insistence on washing hands is real. On either side, hygiene had nothing to do with the question. The Pharisees taught that since a man's hands inevitably touch impure things or things that have touched impure things, he must wash before meals so as not to transfer impurity from his hands to his food. For the Jewish peasantry, the 'am ha-arez, tilling the soil and tending the flocks, it was hard to meet the Pharisees' elaborate requirements for avoiding transferred impurity, and they resented the Pharisees' refusal for that reason to eat with them or associate with them. They also resented the Pharisees' finickiness about produce: had it been certainly tithed properly?; was it fit to be eaten by a pious man? Just as Jesus expresses the 'am ha-arez's impatience with having to wash the hands of transferred impurity, so he expresses their impatience with a burdensome tithing code (23:23):

Woe to you, scribes and Pharisees, hypocrites! For you tithe mint and dill and cummin [=you worry whether even small herbs have had a tithe properly set aside], and have neglected the weightier matters of the law, justice and mercy and faith; these you ought to have done, without neglecting the other.

The last clause, so unsubversive of the Torah, recalls not only the jot-and-tittle injunction but also 23:3: " . . . practice and observe whatever they [the Pharisees] tell you, but not what they do; for they preach, but do not practice."

As distinguished from the Sadducees, the Pharisees were the popular party. The people supported them and accepted their leadership. This having been said, it must also he said that the Pharisees—and the Rabbis after them—alienated the peasant 'am ha-arez by distance and contempt: for one disgusting expression of that contempt, see Pesaḥim 49b. That the 'am ha-arez responded appropriately we learn from R. Akiba himself, who remembered the murderous hatred he had felt, when an unlettered young shepherd, for talmide hakhamim. As a champion of the 'am ha-arez against their contemners the Pharisees, Jesus is attractive.

(In our time, when the first religious kibbutzim were being established, the founders had to ask a rabbinical authority about some difficult points of law: for instance, are cows to be milked on the

Sabbath?; and if so, what is to be done with the milk? [Yes, because though milking is work, and Sabbath work is forbidden, yet a cow would suffer pain if not milked, and we are explicitly commanded to succor a distressed creature on the Sabbath. But the milk is to be poured out, because though we are forbidden to waste or destroy wantonly, the prohibition against profiting from Sabbath work removes the pouring from the category of wanton destruction.] Point after unusual point was raised with the rabbi, until finally he demanded: "You're good Jewish boys. Why can't you be storekeepers, like your fathers?")

To sum up, the conflict between law and spirit, as we know it in Christianity from Paul to Luther, is not Jesus'. For him, as for Judaism, the law was the protection of the spirit. Two final examples under this head:

1. " . . . when you give alms, sound no trumpet before you, as the hypocrites do . . . that they may be praised by men. . . . But . . . let . . . your alms . . . be in secret; and your Father who sees in secret will reward you" (6:2–4). He is talking about *mattan ba-seter*, "a gift in secret" (elevated in Jewish practice from its meaning in Proverbs 21:14). Some Jews still practice it, in spite of the tax code and the ways of modern philanthropy, for the reason Jesus gave—so that their Father who sees in secret will reward them. After my grandfather's death, the family discovered he had been a secret giver.

2. As RSV's note suggests, "our daily bread" in the Lord's Prayer is rather "our bread for the morrow": *ton arton hēmŏn ton epiousion*. The adjective *epiousios* comes from *epiousa*, "morrow," formerly the participle in *hē epiousa hēmera*, "the coming day, the following day." So the prayer is "Give us this day our bread for tomorrow." (Note the Jewish plurals: "our" Father, not "my" Father; give "us," not "me.") But R. Eliezer the Great said: "Anyone who has bread in his basket and asks, 'What shall I eat tomorrow?', is but of the men of little faith." Jesus is closer to R. Eliezer in saying (6:31), " . . . do not be anxious, saying 'What shall we eat,' or 'What shall we drink,' or 'What shall we wear?' " than in instructing his followers to pray for the morrow's bread.

Was R. Eliezer, then, a man who exalted spirit over law? Not at all. Although of the school of Hillel, by temperament and outlook he seems closer to the school of Shammai. He was so inflexible and opposed to innovation, so insistent that nothing should be taught or instituted which had not been formally handed down from master to disciple, that his colleagues had to put him under the ban. They continued to respect him—he remains "the Great"—but in the crisis after the destruction of the Temple his ultraconservatism was a danger. Nor was R. Eliezer a lover of the *minim*, the heretics, the Jewish Christians. Since he was the traditionalist he was, the doctrine he taught must have come to him from his masters, and from *their* masters before them—Pharisees of Jesus' time and earlier.

The Gentle Carpenter

It was from elements of Renan's *Vie de Jésus* that the secularized, sentimental picture of a tender and "progressive" Jesus was drawn. Of all the strange pictures of him over the centuries, this is the strangest. In reality he is often violent in speech or action. And either he is unwordly—since the end is near, very near—or he is satisfied with things as they are.

Not once does he hold God to His justice—unlike Abraham (Genesis 18:25: "Far be it from Thee to do such a thing . . . shall not the Judge of all the earth do justice?") and Job and Jeremiah (12:1: "Righteous art Thou, O Lord, when I complain to Thee;/yet would I plead my case before Thee") and Levi Isaac of Berdichev. Jesus likens God to a king or to a householder (*oikodespotēs*; perhaps better "owner of an estate") who behaves in an arbitrary, cruel, or greedy way; and then it is not the arbitrariness, cruelty, and greed that Jesus condemns, but their victims, cautioning us to avoid their fate. Four examples:

1. The parable of the king who wished to settle accounts with his servants (18:23–35) ends as follows:

"You wicked servant! I forgave you all that debt because you besought me; and should not you have mercy on your fellow servants, as I had mercy on you?" And in anger his lord delivered him to the jailers [*basanistai*; RSV's note: "Greek *torturers*"; KJV, less euphemistic than RSV's text: tormentors], till he should pay all his debt. So also my heavenly Father will do to every one of you, if you do not forgive your brother from your heart.

Agreed; each of us should forgive his brother. But if we do not, should a just and merciful God hand us over to the torturers? And if Jesus were indeed gentle and compassionate, would he approve?

2. "For many are called, but few are chosen" (22:14): first a king commands his servants to waylay travelers and to make them go as

wedding guests to his palace, and then he casts one such guest into outer darkness for not having a wedding garment.

3. The wise maidens (NEB's prudent girls) are commended for a piece of selfishness like the morality of La Fontaine's ant—prudential, but hard to admire—and the bridegroom's rejection of the foolish girls, eager to be guests at the wedding, is not questioned (25:1–3):

> . . . the foolish said to the wise, "Give us some of your oil, for our lamps are going out." But the wise replied, "Perhaps there will not be enough for us and for you; go rather to the dealers and buy for yourselves."
> . . . Afterward the . . . [foolish] maidens came . . . saying, "Lord, lord, open to us." But he replied, "Truly, I say to you, I do not know you."

4. In the parable of the talents (25:14–30) the so-called slothful servant says: "Master, I knew you to be a hard man, reaping where you did not sow, and gathering where you did not winnow." Which the master confirms by his reply: " . . . you ought to have invested my money with the bankers, and at my coming I should have received what was my own with interest." The moral is equally noble: " . . . to every one who has will more be given . . . but from him who has not, even what he has will be taken away." The prophet Nathan was less complaisant, denouncing King David in the parable (II Samuel 12:1–6) of the rich man who could not bring himself to butcher one of his many sheep, and instead took the poor man's one ewe lamb (Bathsheba).

Blessed are the poor; but there is no need to get excited about them (26:6–11):

> Now when Jesus was at Bethany . . . a woman came up to him with an alabaster jar of very expensive ointment, and she poured it on his head, as he sat at table. But when the disciples saw it, they were indignant, saying, "Why this waste? For this ointment might have been sold for a large sum, and given to the poor." But Jesus . . . said to them, ". . . you always have the poor with you, but you will not always have me."

His "you always have the poor with you" is quite different from its source, Deut. 15:11: "For the poor will never cease out of the land; therefore I command you, You shall open wide your hand to your brother, to the needy and to the poor, in the land." Similarly, when Jesus counsels the rich young man to sell all he has and give to the poor (19:21), he is concerned not with the poor but with the rich man's chances of going to heaven.

Christianity is never less able to rely on the New Testament, never more in need of the Old, than when it tries to do something about justice and mercy.

There is much that is arbitrary and willful in Jesus himself. We have the enigmatic 21:18–19:

. . . he was hungry. And seeing a fig tree by the wayside he went to it, and found nothing on it but leaves only. And he said to it, "May no fruit ever come from you again!" And the fig tree withered at once.

This may be another attempt to show that prophecy has been fulfilled, since tree, fruit, and leaves point to Jeremiah 8:8–13:

How can you say, "We are wise/and the law of the Lord is with us?"/ . . . from the least to the greatest/every one is greedy for unjust gain;/ from prophet to priest/every one deals falsely./They have healed the wound of my people lightly,/saying, "Peace, peace,"/when there is no peace./Were they ashamed when they committed abomination?/No, they were not at all ashamed;/they did not know how to blush. . . ./when I would gather them, says the Lord,/there are no grapes on the vine,/nor figs on the fig tree;/even the leaves are withered. . . .

(This last verse, about grapes on the vine and figs on the tree, begins the ominous Prophetical lesson for the morning of the fast of the Ninth of Av.)

The author of Matthew seems puzzled about the meaning of the story he tells. He has the disciples asking, not why Jesus did what he did, but "How did the fig tree wither at once?", and he has Jesus answering that if they have undoubting faith they will be able to do more than wither fig trees, they will be able to command mountains to be cast into the sea. Whatever the meaning that has escaped Matthew, this story seems small and peevish, especially when read beside the Jeremiah it echoes.

In general, the miracles in Matthew are frivolous. The things Moses does at the parting of the sea, Joshua at Jericho and Gibeon, Elijah at Mount Carmel—these are large and public, decisively affecting the people of Israel at turning-points in their history, and mankind through them. But when Matthew has Jesus walking on the sea and encouraging Peter to walk on the sea, in Chapter 14, is that necessary? What would be different in the working out of God's plans for men if the miracle did not happen? What is Matthew's Jesus doing if not showing off? And so with the story told twice (in Chapters 14 and 15), with some statistical variations, about feeding the multitudes. As the disciples say, the crowds will not starve in the absence of a miracle; they can go into the villages and buy food for themselves. But he sees to it that the five thousand (or four thousand) men, besides women and children, are amply fed with five (or seven) loaves and two (or a few small) fishes, and that twelve (or seven) baskets full of broken pieces are left over. A miracle unnecessary for the multitudes, unnecessary for the disciples, unnecessary for hallowing the Name and establishing the kingdom.

Finally, Jesus' character as a faith-healer and expeller of demons must be taken seriously. Much later Israel Ba'al Shem Tov was also a faith-healer, and exorcizing a *dybbuk* was no laughing matter for him and his contemporaries. How large and central a place the casting out of demons and healing occupy in Matthew—this I did not realize, again, until I read slowly.

Judeo-Christian

A friend once told me that if I wanted to get an idea of Jesus and his disciples, and what they were with each other, I should observe Hasidim in Jerusalem or Brooklyn and try to reconstruct what Hasidism had been in its glory. And indeed there are many similarities between early Christianity and Hasidism: faith-healing and exorcism; the breathless expectation of wondrous things; tales of the master's miracles; the elevation of the master's *logia* and behavior to the rank of Torah; superiority of master to father; vying for place among the disciples; the sacred meal of master and (male) disciples, with the master giving them bread; appeal to a folk accustomed to suffering the scorn of the learned; observing the law, but in a manner irritating to the authorities (as in the Hasidim's way with the time of prayer and with sectarian slaughtering)—and more. There is even the possibility, in some branches of Hasidism, of an esoteric doctrine of the master as Messiah.

I do not believe in a timeless mentality or character, but it is hard not to believe that something immanent in Judaism brings forth such movements and enthusiasms from time to time. Besides Hasidism as a parallel to early Jewish Christianity (or Christian Judaism), we have had Shabbethai Zevi and his teachings and followers; and who knows how many other sectarianisms of like nature remain buried under the sand of the Jewish past.

Matthew is not all of the New Testament, as the New Testament is not all of Christianity, but Matthew by itself is enough to persuade me that speaking of a Judeo-Christian tradition is different from speaking of a Slavic-Patagonian tradition. Christianity grew away from Judaism, and no Jew can believe that that was for the best. But it did not grow away altogether, and a desire on the Christian side to speak of the Judeo-Christian tradition must mean, among other things, a desire rather to return closer than to depart further.

Why, then, is the talk about the tradition so recent? When men perceived only Christians and Jews (so many of them, so few of us), they saw the differences. Now we live in a perceived world that is mostly neither Christian nor Jewish—not so much that it is secular as that it is non-Western. Becoming aware, in that world, of a nearness formerly not thought of we begin to speak of the Judeo-Christian tradition.

There is nothing unusual about social realities influencing how men think about religion. Because Byzantium had its kind of emperor, it thought of Jesus as Pantocrator; and the Jews' vision of hell, as Saul Lieberman has demonstrated, reproduced the particular kinds of torture they experienced at the hands of their gentile rulers. The distance between Judaism and Christianity led to distance between Jews and Christians, but it is also true that the distance between Jews and Christians led them to want to believe that Judaism and Christianity were distant. Now, naturally, men ask themselves whether the religions are truly alien from each other totally. Social circumstance suggests the question, it does not provide the answer. Theology and historical scholarship can alone do that. But that raising this religious and historical question is due to the situation of Jews and Christians in the Western world today, or even in America primarily—what is so sinister or discreditable about that?

—*October 1965*

· 27 ·

Rome and Jerusalem

Orthodox rabbis, Reform rabbis, the National Community Relations Advisory Council, the World Jewish Congress—all were scornful of active Jewish interest in having the Vatican Council issue a declaration on Christian relations with the Jews and Judaism. The cry was that antisemitism is a Christian, not a Jewish problem, for Christians to solve on their own and for self-respecting Jews to stay away from. Though no offender was mentioned by name, the newspapers made it clear that the self-respecters had the American Jewish Committee in mind.

The Orthodox, if not entirely candid, at least were unmoved by institutional envy. Basically, and with ever-lessening dissent, they oppose a softening in the ancient hostility between Christians and Jews. They now believe, almost to a man, that Judaism can survive only behind ramparts; and that if Jews are to keep the ramparts strong and to avoid venturing out from behind them, they must either be or expect soon to be under siege. But improved Catholic attitudes toward the Jews and Judaism, decreed from the Vatican itself, would weaken the Jewish sense of being besieged and might lead to a crumbling of the ramparts. For the Orthodox, then, a Jewish contribution toward improving Christian attitudes would be wrong not as sinning against self-respect—that is only useful rhetoric —but as weakening the appeal of the ramparts policy. The dwindling minority who disagree are not highly regarded.

The other critics' equation of Jewish self-respect with leaving it to the Christians to deal with their antisemitism has its comical side. A week after the New York *Times*, covering the World Jewish Congress, had reported that "Goldmann Criticizes Jews for Seeking Pope's Aid," *Civiltà Cattolica* recalled a visit and "a long memorandum" by Dr. Goldmann to Cardinal Bea. (But that was in another country. . . .) Reform Judaism has the Jewish Chautauqua Society, founded in the last century, to enlighten Christians about Jews and Judaism, and its seminary boasts of the Christian divines enrolled in its graduate courses. Conservative Judaism, one of whose spokesmen led the attack on deficient self-respect at the NCRAC, later, at a meeting of its World Council in Mexico City, formally expressed the hope that Vatican II would issue the right kind of declaration. That antisemitism is a Christian problem is what Jews have been saying for as long as anyone can remember. If it is the kind of Christian problem that self-respecting Jews do not meddle with, why are all those self-respecting Jewish defense agencies prolonging their existence?

It is normal politics to deprecate what someone else did that you would have liked to do yourself, but there is a worrisome possibility that the punch-line of the old joke applies here: "Rabbi, that fellow doesn't understand subtleties, he means it." Can it be that some Jews, and even rabbis, really believe that antisemitism is a Christian problem—believe it, that is, as something more than a tautology?

Nazism was a German, not a Jewish problem: manifestly, to embrace such nonsense and to be devoted to a Hitler could only mean that Germany had a real problem, as we say of a severely disturbed person that he has a problem. In the German case the psychotic's problem meant his neighbor's death. In the United States the denial of justice to the Negroes is not a Negro, it is a white problem, but the Negroes suffer. They are constantly aware of the problem, and we only occasionally. It was Negroes who had to demonstrate, North and South, before some whites started to demonstrate, too. They are only about one in ten of the American population, but they were about three of four in the March on Washington. Were they lacking in self-respect because their share of the Washington marchers was so disproportionate to their share in the American population?

One way of trying to make sense of those statements about self-respect is that we Jews in America have been leading such a quiet and comfortable life lately that we may have begun to believe that antisemitism is not even a Christian problem. Perhaps the calculation goes something like this: Christian thinking about Jews and Judaism has changed so greatly for the better in the last generation—with some encouragement from the Jews, when the need was desperate—that we can now depend on the Christians to be carried by their own momentum, without our continued encouragement.

I hope that that is not what we think, because I would rather believe us disingenuous than foolish. John Maynard Keynes said that businessmen tend to have little memory of the past or imagination for the future but to live in an eternal present, expecting that tomorrow will be much as today is. With Sholem Aleichem's tailor, Keynes's businessman is like a human being: most of us live in an eternal present. But our rabbis should not be like most of us. Of them especially we have the right to expect a sense of history—as the presentness of the past—and an awareness of mutability. Christian attitudes toward Jews and Judaism are better than they used to be, but they are not good enough, and the line on the chart can turn down as well as it can keep going up.

The best declaration by the Vatican Council must still fall short of removing the grounds for Jewish uneasiness, because the essential scripture of Christianity is the New Testament, which is ineradicably anti-Jewish. And even if Christians, with all the good will in the world, try to mute the anti-Jewish animus, it must constantly be reintroduced from what can be called the New Testament culture.

What could be more innocuous than a Greek grammar? Tennyson thought poorly of Jowett, the Plato translator and Master of Balliol who was also an Anglican clergyman, for not knowing Hebrew: "Fancy a priest unable to read the scriptures of his own religion as they were written!" By the same reasoning, Christian ministers should know Greek too. A standard textbook used in Protestant seminaries is J. Gresham Machen's *New Testament Greek for Beginners* (published 1923, *thirty-fifth* printing 1962). By the 1920s classical studies had so declined in the United States that large numbers of college graduates were entering the seminaries Greekless. The book continues to meet their need, not even assuming some knowledge of Latin.

A learned Fundamentalist and something of a reactionary, Machen seceded from the faculty of Princeton Theological Seminary to protest against the growing liberalism and modernism of most of his colleagues and helped to found Westminster Theological Seminary. He regarded theological liberalism as soft-headed and dangerously anti-intellectual, and H. L. Mencken himself, not noted for a partiality to the Fundamentalists, thought that Machen had the better of it in controversy.

Of course this does not appear in the textbook, which would not have been very different if Machen had been a liberal. What the book does is to present the grammar and some of the vocabulary of the New Testament. Instead of being asked to translate "My aunt's pen is on the table" (or its equivalent for classical Greek, "Why did the triremes not flee more rapidly?"), the student is asked to translate "The Lord will come to His Church in glory." But here and there one also finds translation exercises like these: "After the Lord was risen, the Jews persecuted His disciples. . . . When they have killed Jesus, they will cast out of their synagogues those who have believed on him. . . . This is the race that killed those who believe on Jesus. . . . The king of the Jews was doing these things because he wished to kill the children in the village."

Suppose that every last professor of theology or New Testament or history goes out of his way to soften the anti-Jewish import of his material, and every professor of Christian education to warn against biased lesson materials for the young. That is not only unlikely, it also would be inadequate. Learning neither theology nor history but only grammar and vocabulary, while their guard is down, so to speak, well-intentioned future ministers and prelates of a religion that for sixteen centuries has been dominant rather than dominated, who study and reside in stately, well-endowed edifices, come to identify themselves once again with a Church poor, pure, and persecuted by a Synagogue big, bad, and bullying. Rulers of the earth see themselves as the poor in spirit whose kingdom is in heaven; builders and occupants of cathedrals are still, in their own minds, being cast out of synagogues. If it does not happen when they are learning theology, it can happen when they are struggling with the New Testament Greek verb.

Christian antisemitism is going to be with us for some time to come, and Christians will always need nagging to accept it as their problem.

—September 1964

. 28 .

Catacombs

Cyprus is in the news and His Beatitude Makarios III is in the news pictures, with his archiepiscopal vestments and beard. Yet the one thing people do not seem to talk about when they talk about him is that he is an archbishop. It is not clear why that should be so. Perhaps it is because he is not only Archbishop but also Ethnarch of Cyprus, the leader of his people in their national character, as the chief ecclesiastics of the Greek, Armenian, and other national churches have long been in that formerly Ottoman part of the world. Possibly we now refrain from asking what an archbishop is doing in an uneven war against the Turkish Muslim minority for the same reason we once refrained from asking what he was doing in a war of ambush against the British: it hardly occurs to us that ethnarchs should be squeamish about means that may be useful for national liberation or domination.

As for the Sermon on the Mount, that is a text. It is not expected actually to govern behavior, but only to prove that Christianity's words are better than other religions' deeds. A bishop of William the Conqueror's rode into battle with a mace instead of a sword, thus honoring the prohibition of bloodshed by priests; and Makarios does not even carry arms.

The prelate-ethnarch's doubleness or ambiguity of role is not confined to the Orthodox Levant. In Catholic Ireland, Quebec, and Poland, the Church has comforted and protected communities distressed in their nationality as much as it has administered the sacraments and taught the faithful. That is probably why the Church commands greater loyalty there than anywhere else.

We Jews look on with admiration and envy as advanced Protestant and Catholic thinkers here and in Western Europe denounce culture Christianity and call a defeat what the Christian generations before them called a great victory and the sign of God's favor—the Emperor Constantine's establishment of Christianity as the state religion of the Roman Empire. "Back to the Catacombs" is the new slogan. For the anti-Constantinians, Christianity was never so healthy as when it was poor and oppressed, and its success in the world was the beginning of a prolonged illness. They say that culture Christianity has to be infected with tribal idolatries, cannot prophetically condemn a sinful state or community, and loses its soul by trying to make worship which in fact is offered to Molech or Baal look like worship offered to the Lord. Therefore, they tell us, it is not enough merely to sever the last ties between church and state. For its own good, Christianity must go further, and exile itself from the community's culture. A well-known Catholic priest disagrees with the usual exhortations to put Christ back in Christmas. What he favors is to take Christ out of Christmas altogether.

So many Christian clergymen and seminary professors speaking and writing so impressively, and so few rabbis and professors in our seminaries! If our religious thinkers and spokesmen object at all to Judaism's involvement in culture, it is to involvement in Gentile culture. The comparison seems to be all in favor of the Christians.

Our admiration and envy may be a little excessive, because Makarios is a more typical Christian leader than the late H. Richard Niebuhr. That is certainly true of the lands of hardship. American Christians do not know, nor do most West Europeans, what it is to be under siege in the decisive respect of religion *and* nationality (which is to say, religion and culture). They have not the harsh and still living traditions of Catholic Poles crushed between Protestant Prussians and Orthodox, now Communist, Russians; of Catholic Irish under the Protestant Ascendancy, or of Orthodox Greeks hating the Sultan in his turban only a little less than the Pope in his tiara. But even in America and Western Europe the churchman is an ethnarch more often than he thinks, or we recognize.

In short, the anti-Constantinian thinkers in Christianity are neither numerous nor influential. When Charlemagne convinced the pagan Saxons of the truth of Christianity by having 4,500 of them beheaded in one day, he was acting in a Constantinian manner, and students in Catholic schools are still taught that he did well. Western Christians who speak against the involvement of religion in culture are a little like the rich man who tells us that to be poor is better than to be rich. He says it because he is rich, and the Catacombs thinkers say what they do because they are Western. Their Christianity is so deeply rooted in the culture and so well nourished by it that they can afford to make light of the culture. They can ask that Christ be taken out of Christmas because Christ is in Christmas—or half in, anyway. (Jews could tell them that.) If Christ were out of Christmas altogether, there would be no Christmas. No Christmas, and Christianity in the West would really be so close to the Catacombs again that the Catacombs would lose their charm. It is because the anti-Constantinians know there will always be a Christmas that they can afford to speak against it.

About the time when the State of Israel came into being, W. H. Auden was asked whether he thought the new state would be a good or a bad thing and whether Jewish nationalism was good or bad. His answer was something like this:—I am against states and nationalisms, but that may be because I am of British birth and American citizenship, and a poet writing in English. England and America have been independent for a long time and have spread their language and literature all over the world. If I had been born to a people dominated politically and culturally by others, I should probably value political and cultural independence.

However it may have been in antiquity, in modern times a Catacombs existence has in fact not been advantageous to the life of the spirit. Consider the Protestants who stayed in France between the revocation of the Edict of Nantes and the French Revolution. By 1789, as Herbert Luethy has written, a century of persecution had deprived them of a learned ministry and of religious education, so they retained little more of the content of Protestantism than hatred of the Catholic church. (Naturally, they were all for the Revolution.) To the powerful, powerlessness may seem an aid to grace. The powerless know better.

Usually the anti-Constantinians also say that we are living in a post-Christian culture. From some points of view it *is* post-Christian, but not so much as they think it is, or as non-Christians and ex-Christians would like to believe it is. Anti-Constantinian Christian thought is popular with these because it feeds an illusion they need— that Christianity, or sometimes religion generally, is about to disappear as a massive fact. That is a hardy illusion, at least two hundred years old now.

The Orthodox Churches belong to the World Council of Churches, and in the United States to the National Council of Churches of Christ. While Protestant liberals blamed the Catholic church for persecuting Buddhism in Vietnam, which may or may not have been true, they are not blaming their allies for overpowering the Cypriote Muslims. And while they raised their voices against the persecution of Protestants in Catholic Colombia, the Protestants were rather less clamorous about the persecution of (Protestant) Jehovah's Witnesses in Orthodox Greece.

Constantine and Charlemagne, therefore, are still the representative Christian figures. All that the anti-Constantinian talk has done is to give Christianity a spiritual gloss adapted to the modern sensibility, but without effect on the actual business of Christendom. Makarios remains archbishop.

He assumed the name when he became *Makariotatos* ("His Beatitude"), as a Roman Catholic cardinal assumes a regnal name upon elevation to the papacy. In fact, the Archbishop's style and name mean Most Blessed Blessed, because *makariotatos* is the superlative of *makarios*, and *makarios* is how the Septuagint and the New Testament render Hebrew *ashre*, "blessed, happy, fortunate." Thus the first verse of the First Psalm is: "Blessed [Septuagint, *makarios*] is the man who walks not in the counsel of the wicked. . . . " In its plural form, the word recurs in the Beatitudes (*Makarismoi*) of the Sermon on the Mount: "Blessed [*makarioi*] are the meek . . . the merciful . . . the peacemakers. . . ."

—*May 1964*

.29.

Unitarians, Trinitarians

In Bernhard E. Olson's *Faith and Prejudice* what is particularly striking is his discussion of the treatment of Jews and Judaism in the materials prepared by the liberal Unitarian and the Neo-Orthodox Presbyterian educators.

American Jews are apt to know, or we think we know, more about Unitarians than Presbyterians: "Unitarians believe in the fatherhood of God, the brotherhood of man, and the neighborhood of Boston," or "Unitarians believe in one God—at most." Even since Moses Mendelssohn, Unitarianism has been the Christian persuasion that Jews have found it least distressing to pass into; in 1799 Mendelssohn's disciple, David Friedländer, anonymously proposed to a Berlin clergyman that the Jews would become Christians if they were allowed to subscribe to a unitarian rather than a trinitarian credo. (In the Unitarian church of an Episcopalian friend and her Catholic husband—both agnostics—between a quarter and a third of the congregation are Jews.) We remember that the young Emerson was a Unitarian minister, and we remember the *Education of Henry Adams:*

> In uniform excellence of life and character, moral and intellectual, the score of Unitarian clergymen about Boston, who controlled society and Harvard College, were never excelled. They proclaimed as their merit that they insisted on no doctrine, but taught, or tried to teach, the means of leading a virtuous, useful, unselfish life, which they held to be sufficient for salvation. For them, difficulties might be ignored; doubts were waste of thought; nothing exacted solution. Boston had solved the universe; or had offered and realized the best solution yet tried. The problem was worked out.
>
> Of all the conditions of his youth which afterwards puzzled the grown-up man, this disappearance of religion puzzled him most. The boy went to church twice every Sunday; he was taught to read his Bible, and he learned religious poetry by heart; he believed in a mild deism; he prayed; he went through all the forms; but neither to him nor to his brothers or sisters was religion real. Even the mild discipline of the Unitarian Church

was so irksome that they all threw it off at the first possible moment, and never afterwards entered a church.

About Presbyterianism most of us do not know much more than this: that Princeton was originally a Presbyterian institution; that the ethnic background is Scottish; that the theology is, or used to be, Calvinist; and that Milton, punning etymologically, said: "New Presbyter is but Old Priest writ large."

From Dr. Olson we learn that the educational materials of both the Unitarian and the Presbyterian churches are against antisemitism, but that the Presbyterian materials are more affirmative about Judaism. The Unitarians:

> The liberal's universality is predicated on a "many roads to truth" approach. . . . Mankind is bound together by its common search and by the oneness of truth. . . . "If you exchange ideas with a liberal of the Jewish faith, you will find him close to your own. . . . You will not be surprised if one of your friends calls himself both Christian and Buddhist, if you know something of the essentials of each faith. . . . And you will appreciate the Hindu affirmation that truth shines more brilliantly when it shines from many angles, like the diamond with its many facets." . . .

> The natural is prior to the historical, and for the liberal those experiences which antedate others are considered to be controlling in religion as in life. For example . . . the antecedents [of Hanukkah and Christmas] are found to be mid-winter festivals, celebrating the yearly cycle of death and rebirth symbolized also in the equinox. Seen in this way, it is recommended that in educating the young child Jews and Christians can unite in stressing those natural similarities which make sense and have value for all children rather than the particular historical meanings which tend to set off these holidays, and Jews and Christians themselves, from each other. . . .

> There are . . . ideas which liberals feel they must surrender because they stand in the way of the emergence of a world faith. . . . [It is wrong for] Judaism and Christianity to regard themselves as proclaiming unique messages, therefore implicitly contradicting the unitary conception of reality and truth. . . .

> "The children . . . found that it [the Bible] was about ancient beliefs which somehow were not very different from the beliefs of the primitive people they had already studied."

The Neo-Orthodox (Presbyterians) speak differently:

> Although they also have a respectful, if critical, attitude toward other faiths, the neo-orthodox writers unqualifiedly identify with the Judeo-Christian tradition. In this respect, neo-orthodoxy is particularistic; it places itself in one specific tradition in the world, and not in many. From

within this tradition, however, it seeks to establish a firm basis for positive and responsible relations with other religious groups. . . .

"The God of the Hebrew-Christian tradition is a God who has acted in history. This accounts for the superior quality of Judaism and Christianity over other religions that have worshipped a god who is primarily a nature deity." . . . This understanding of God's reality comes to man through a specific religious history, namely the history of the Jewish people and the church. . . . As one writer asserts: "and in understanding the history of Israel, we gain an understanding of mankind."

Essentially . . . prejudice and intergroup hostility is a rejection of God through the substitution of personal, cultural, and tribal gods.

If everyone acted in the future as Unitarian or Presbyterian children are now being taught, all would be well, and in that sense the Unitarian and Presbyterian materials are equally good. Dr. Olson is objective and impressively successful in thinking himself into the other man's "faith perspective." Yet it is clear that he likes the Presbyterian outlook better than the Unitarian. So do I, though as a Jew I am bewildered by trinitarianism.

Whatever the statistics of affiliation may be, Unitarianism approximates closely to "the American religion"—what most Americans really believe, as distinguished from what the several churches tell their members they ought to believe. On the Jewish side, Unitarianism is often seen as not much different from Ethical Culture; and Ethical Culture was a kind of left-wing Reform, created by Jews, where ex-Jews and ex-Christians could unite in honorable equality. Only somehow, to this day, Jews remain more eager than Christians to be ex.

For some Jews, therefore, the Unitarians' lack of regard for Judaism is unlikely to be a fatal defect. (That lack of regard originates with the Socinians, in the sixteenth century.) It goes with a perhaps even greater lack of regard for traditional Christianity. More importantly, it points toward a future when both Judaism and Christianity have dwindled away. Since Mendelssohn, that has been the form that messianism has assumed among many of us. For those attracted to a revolutionary variant of this kind of messianism, the favorite verse in the "Internationale" has been "No more tradition's chains shall bind us": the modern, acceptable equivalent of Paul's "neither Jew nor Greek."

Conversely, the Neo-Orthodox Protestant insistence on the special place of Judaism and the Jewish people in the divine economy repels rather than attracts such Jews. But it does not repel only the un-Jewish

Jews. Reconstructionists, for example, certainly do not want the Jewish people and tradition to disappear, but they are theologically not very different from Unitarians and Ethical Culturists. And even Jews more traditional than the Reconstructionists could apply to Christian esteem for Judaism and the Jewish people an aphorism of the Rabbis: *la mi-duvshakh we-la me-'uqzakh*—"don't kiss me and don't kick me" (literally, "neither your honey nor your sting"). For while the Presbyterian educators are exemplary people, historically there is a line that connects the special place of Judaism in Christian thought with the persecution of Jews. Even pious Jews, in their anguish, have sometimes debated with themselves whether the destiny for which God chose us—as we say when we thank Him, "Thou hast chosen us from among all the peoples"—is a blessing or a curse. That was one reason why Zionism wished to "normalize" the Jews, i.e., to make them less special.

Having said all this, knowing that the curse has been the verso to the blessing's recto, I still think that the Neo-Orthodox position is better for the Jews—hallowed phrase!—than the Unitarian. Why are the African intellectuals and their European and American friends so concerned to discover and reveal a glorious African past? In principle, it should be enough for Africans to know that Europeans and Americans respect them for the humanity that we all have in common. So Melvin Lasky has argued, questioning the need for rehabilitating the African past and suggesting that in their enthusiasm some of the Africans and pro-Africans may be mixing invention with discovery. But for the Africans, obviously, equality with other human beings, as human beings, is not enough. They need to know for themselves, and they need to have others know, that the African past is not empty, let alone contemptible. They feel that their present, human as well as African, cannot be suspended over a past that is void or worthless. They want their ancestors and their ancestors' achievements to be respected, and they will not believe you if you tell them that you respect them and their present but not their fathers and their past. I hope the Africans are successful in uncovering and making public a past they seek. For myself, I resent know-it-all teachers who encourage know-it-all children to judge my tradition as primitive.

I doubt that Arnold Toynbee is a dues-paying Unitarian, but he might as well be. In his religious syncretism, in his preference for Oriental religion (which in occidentals is often a sign that something nasty is about to be said of Judaism), in his distaste for the Jewish tradition, and in his harsh judgments upon us, he does not differ greatly from the Unitarian writers. As late as in *Reconsiderations*, Toynbee could say: ". . . in the Jewish Zionists I see disciples of the Nazis." Similarly, after the Israelis had caught Eichmann a Unitarian minister wrote in the *Unitarian Register*: "In the ethical sense I can see little difference between the Jew-pursuing Nazi and the Nazi-pursuing Jew." A Neo-Orthodox writer would not say that, if only because he would feel himself implicated in the corporate sin of Christendom against the Jews. The Unitarian, for whom sin is a primitive concept and who may not identify with Christendom, has no scruples about saying it—especially since his ethical sense is so uniquely well-developed.

The invincible self-righteousness and self-satisfaction are not new. Adams, reflecting on the Unitarian Boston of his childhood, said:

> . . . that the most intelligent society, led by the most intelligent clergy, in the most moral conditions he ever knew, should have solved all the problems of the universe so thoroughly as to have quite ceased making itself anxious about past or future, and should have persuaded itself that all the problems which had convulsed human thought from earliest recorded time, were not worth discussing, seemed to him the most curious social phenomenon he had to account for in a long life.

Of the educational materials that Dr. Olson examined, he writes:

> Liberal teachings are more *abstractly* relevant and the neo-orthodox more *concretely* relevant to the given situations. . . . The liberal's monistic view of reality leaves little place for the fundamental cleavages in society, for a recognition of basic conflicts which may perpetuate endless pluralisms, for the prime importance of the particular as against the universal and the uniquely historical as against the natural. On the other hand, the neo-orthodox faith centers in a personal God who has acted in a specific history. . . . This . . . view of reality, revealed to a particular people, makes a much larger place for deep and fundamental cleavages in society, for basic conflicts, for differences, concreteness, and specificity than does a monistic faith. . . .
>
> Does anti-ethnocentrism make a place for all by affirming some common denominator, or does it do so by affirming the right of each group to its own particular existence, its uniqueness, or its right to be different and to contradict the assumptions of those who affirm a common core? . . . There are a variety of ways of crossing group lines, and there are different kinds of antidotes to ethnocentrism. . . .

For the 1,600 years or so between Constantine and Hitler, in the Western world, our persecutors were Christians. It has remained for the twentieth century to produce anti-Christian persecutors of Jews, worse than all their Christian forerunners—Hitler and Stalin. The historical record now shows that neither the religion nor the irreligion of gentiles, nor gentile religious liberalism, guarantees friendship or even minimal humanity toward Jews. Hitler's theologians included liberals, who despised Jewish (or Judeo-Christian) particularity and who saw themselves as being enlisted in a crusade to liberate Christianity from an unbecoming and constrictive attachment to its Jewish origins.

The liberals offer me friendship because I am a man, but slight my tradition and memories. The Neo-Orthodox offer me friendship because God is my father, and the father of all men; and they also honor my tradition. If most Jews nevertheless prefer the liberals, as I believe they do, that may tell us something about our modernity.

—*May 1963*

VI

NO MORE TRADITION'S CHAINS?

. 30 .

The 1961 Commentary *Symposium*

The symposium on Jewishness and the younger intellectuals in *Commentary*, with all that talent, all that verve, all that candor and concealment—what is one to make of it?

Norman Podhoretz has noted a central tone very similar to the tone of the *Contemporary Jewish Record* symposium in 1944—rejection of the Jewish community as it is and as it probably can be. Still, as the old proverb has it, even in bad luck it is nice to have good luck. The present symposium showed a rather uniform respect, however shy and obituary, for the Jewish tradition. (Many sounded like the two Viennese Jews in the good old Dollfuss days. FIRST JEW: What do you retain of Judaism? SECOND JEW: I still read the *Neue freie Presse* [= New York *Times*]. And you? FIRST JEW: I'm still afraid of dogs.) And while the symposiasts successfully dissembled their love for the Jewish community, they did not quite kick it downstairs. If we compare what they said with what the Jewish angry young men were saying in England recently, and with the responses of Jewish university students to a questionnaire in France some years ago, the American Jewish community could have fared worse, and so could the religion and tradition which the community is supposed to embody.

There is irony here. All the symposiasts find it hard to forgive American Jewry for its success, its thorough Americanization. Yet it is that very success which is responsible for their (grudging) respect. Jewish existence in America has affected American thinking. "The Judeo-Christian tradition" is more than a formula that serves the civic peace. It is taken seriously by serious people. An eminent New Testament scholar of foreign birth and education now teaching in the United States has been quoted as saying that until he came here and saw all those Jews he never fully appreciated Judaism and the Jewishness of Christianity, though he had certainly studied Strack and Billerbeck. Reinhold Niebuhr's ideas about Judaism have been strongly influenced by the many Jews he has known—most of them not very Judaic Jews, at that. Part of the respect for the Jewish tradition expressed by the symposiasts is to be traced to the prestige of Judaism in America, and that prestige reflects the numbers and achievements of the Jews in America.

Some Random Observations:

1. Why so much admiration for the older generation of socialist intellectuals? Orwell should have helped us to see that there was something ambiguous about the radical intelligentsia of the thirties and what it stood for and worked for. Rereading the literature, I incline to believe that the best of the Jewish socialist intellectuals in this country—those with the clearest conscience and the least arrogance, those least prompted to apocalyptic political gestures by a kind of aesthetic and emotional fauvism—were the tiny minority associated with the Labor Zionist *Jewish Frontier*. Why did no one mention Hayyim Greenberg? And why, when the *New Leader* was once mentioned, was it dismissed with a sneer? At least the *New Leader* has no blood on its conscience. The older generation of socialist intellectuals deserve to be an example, but an equivocal one, a warning as well as a model—often wrong, disastrously; always cocksure.

2. Several say that the Jews (everywhere?) are now so prosperous and secure, so tainted by complicity in their own success, that active sympathy can no longer go out to them. A generation ago most intellectuals were saying that to worry about the Jews was parochial and was to mistake the symptom for the cause. The thing to do was to abolish capitalism.

3. All agree that the world is changing very rapidly. Their wave of the future, as fact and as desideratum, is Afro-Asian. Why are they so happy? How does one reconcile a passion for such a future with a stated allegiance to the values of John Stuart Mill and E. M. Forster? Perhaps this is a time for caring about the Western tradition and how to keep it from being made into an archaeological relic.

4. Elihu Katz says: "The trouble with Israel is that it is such a big idea in the perspective of world history and such a little idea in the perspective of modern history." I am not sure that Katz means land of Israel to the exclusion of children of Israel, or even religion of

Israel. Perspective is a tricky thing, and so is world history. Greeks and Romans did not consider Israel to be a big idea at all. Neither did H. G. Wells, and neither, probably, would the Chinese or Hindu thinker. Voltaire was savagely contemptuous of the spiritual and intellectual state of the Jews just when Hasidism was being born and just before—as time should be measured in the perspective of world history—Veblen wrote his essay on the "Intellectual Pre-eminence of Jews in Modern Europe."

Early in the last century Archbishop Whately, satirizing the new Bible criticism, wrote in biblical language a true chronicle of the French Revolution and Napoleon. Then, applying the best historical and philological analysis to his narrative, he was able to show that it must be a tissue of lies, myths, and errors. If anyone today were to write in biblical language the story of the Jews in the past hundred years, it would seem as incredible as what happened between Joseph and Joshua. On any proper scale of measurement that is not little but big.

5. Werner Cohn does not like "cigar-smoking B'nai B'rith gentlemen." His great Jewish model is Freud—a cigar-smoking B'nai B'rith gentleman.

Security will not come with shuddering at the round, smooth faces of the vulgar. Form a community of the happy few and Mary McCarthy will be around to expose it.

6. It must mean something that the Jewish saint most often mentioned in the symposium is Marx. Alfred G. Aronowitz's brother-in-law likes Hank Greenberg because he is a Jew. At least he *is* a Jew. Heine may have regarded himself as a Jew, even Disraeli may have regarded himself as a Jew, but not Marx. Certainly not Marx.

They should find themselves a better Hank Greenberg.

7. There is a kitchen culture that teachers of foreign languages, especially, are familiar with. A son of Italian parents takes Italian in high school because he thinks it will be a snap. The teacher discovers, as he expected, that the boy knows only the familiar form of address, imagines that certain Italianized English words are part of Dante's vocabulary, and assumes that a regional dialect, as spoken by the untutored, is standard.

Most of the symposiasts have a smattering of Jewish kitchen culture—a peculiar position for intellectuals to be in. Yet most are not backward about declaring flatly what Judaism is or is not. For instance, they speak confidently about Jewish messianism. Now Jewish messianism is a subtle, complex thing—activist and quietist, utopian and restorative, cosmic and national, immanent and circumstantial, antinomian and juridical. Gershom Scholem has written some remarkable things about it, and J. L. Talmon has discussed it too. No one would talk about, say, the Protestant ethic and capitalism without knowing something about Weber and Tawney. I rather doubt that most of the contributors know something about Scholem and Talmon.

Of course, their notions of Judaism come from something else as well, besides kitchen culture—the prestige of Judaism in American culture generally, mentioned earlier. (A colleague has pointed out to me how curiously little most of them seem to know or want to know about Christianity.)

8. They agree that it is not tradition but persecution that accounts for Jewish sympathy with the downtrodden. Nat Hentoff puts it this way: "Growing up as a Jew, I very early and involuntarily acquired some understanding of and empathy with other minorities. . . . my concern with civil liberties was first stimulated by being beaten up as a child because I was Jewish." But the premise is false. Minorities do not necessarily or even typically sympathize with other minorities.

Reinhold Niebuhr knows the reluctance of Jews to attribute their generosity or social decency to their tradition, and thinks they are wrong. I am reminded of something that Jacob Viner once wrote in a study of mercantilism. Discussing the origins of an eighteenth-century war, he noted that economic causationists were delighted by contemporaneous justification of the war as designed to increase trade and fatten the treasury. What more explicit proof could there be of its economic causes? But, Viner asked, why should we assume that there was not then the same difference between good reasons and real reasons as now? Trade was then a good reason. The real reason may have been dynastic.

I agree with Malcolm Diamond, who agrees with Nathan Glazer, that we should guard against self-righteousness in explaining the way we are about justice and compassion. Still, it is just possible that Jewish tradition, even though a suspiciously good reason, may be as real a reason as being beaten up.

9. The symposium produced a scientific discovery of some moment. Dynamic psychologists tell us there is a birth trauma, and some would also say there is a weaning trauma. Ned Polsky has disclosed the Bar Mitzvah trauma, and has shown how serious it can be.

—*May 1961*

.31.

East Side, West Side

For ex-Jewish moderns the alternative to Jewish tradition has nearly always been one or the other of the legitimate children of the Enlightenment: science, Culture and Art, or some variant of left-of-center politics. Of ex-Christian moderns, most seem to have gone in the same direction politically, but the proportion has been somewhat lower than among Jews. Among ex-Christians there has been a good deal of cultural elitism joined with reactionary politics: Yeats, Maurras, Pound. There has also been some turning to the wisdom or religions of the East: Schopenhauer, Aldous Huxley, Toynbee. (T. S. Eliot, a Christian and of the Right, was also pro-East.)

Now Donald Nugent writes, in *Cross Currents*:

Several years ago I was at a gathering where Allen Ginsberg, the patriarch of the hippies, was the center of attraction as he ecstatically chanted a mantra to the accompaniment of his finger-cymbals. The atmosphere was exotic and Oriental. The author asked him what seemed an appropriate question: "Have you completely repudiated Western civilization?" I was astonished when, without hesitation and with a look of perfect candor, he replied in a manner so strangely reminiscent of Augustine: "No. The Sacred Heart is enough." I will never forget his answer.

Once I said that when we view some of the family histories of modern Jews—Mendelssohns, Ehrenbergs, Bergsons, Weils, Pasternaks—we must conclude that other things being equal, for Jews occidental secularism is a propaedeutic to Christianity. Today Ginsberg tells us that for Jews even a turn to the Orient can be a propaedeutic to Christianity. What else can it mean that a man called Ginsberg, no less, the author of a *Kaddish*, no less, ecstatic chanter of mantras yet man of the Left, answers, so memorably, that the Sacred Heart is enough?

For the Jewish Reformers, chanting (as of the Pentateuch and Prophets) was Oriental, so they did away with it.

—April 1970

. 32 .

"And Many Peoples Shall Come . . ."

In the Israeli journal *Molad* Professor E. E. Urbach of the Hebrew University has written: "In our contact with the new nations of Asia and Africa, we do not appear as the people which gave the world the belief in one God, nor as the adherents of a religion [with a vision of] one world united by faith in one God, but as a people of efficient technicians and energetic businessmen. What do our many guests hear about our religion and Torah? . . . I am not urging a missionary effort, but we must find ways of bringing Jewish religion and Torah to the world." If I correctly understand Vittorio Lanternari, the Italian author of the *Religions of the Oppressed*, Professor Urbach need not be so hesitant. There are many who would respond to a Jewish mission. For a hundred years or so, Judaizing sects have been arising spontaneously among peoples rebelling against the rule of oppressive strangers.

Judaizing is only one form of religious rebellion for them, other forms being Islamizing and Christian-pagan syncretism. What has been happening in Africa and Polynesia is more or less what has been happening with, say, the Black Muslims of the United States. On the one hand, the culture of the alien ruler is powerful and attractive; on the other, it is hated as the instrument and symbol of oppression. The solution is to take over many of the new values, but to organize them in such a way as to turn them against the oppressor and his culture. In the United States the Black Muslims, while rejecting the world of the white slaveholder and his religion, Christianity, are devoted to the so-called Protestant ethic (which, by the time the popular magazines started writing about it, possibly had become more historically than actually Protestant): sobriety, industry, frugality, responsibility, and the like. The Islam of the Black Muslims is Christian sectarianism. The Father Divine movement was in some ways much the same kind of thing, and we are told that that is how we must view the Judaism of some Negro congregations in New York.

And so in the white man's colonies. The education received in missionary schools makes the old-time, unproblematic pagan religion impossible. Theological enlightenment aside, the people who have been to those schools see in the old paganism a backwardness they can no longer accept. It is a religion for people who cultivate by scratching the earth with a stick, not for men who want tractors. But the new religion goes with the hateful foreign domination. So one combines parts of the old with parts of the new in a Christian-pagan syncretism, which is in itself rebellious; or, having been influenced by contact with *this* high religion, Christianity, one declares for a related high religion, Islam or Judaism. According to Professor Lanternari, the rapid spread of Muslim influence in Africa, which Christian missionaries have been lamenting for some years now, is perhaps more antiwhite (or anti-imperialist) than it is authentically Muslim.

Judaizing is even more directly related than Islam to what the rebels have learned in the missionary school. Quite simply, to them what a Christian calls the Old Testament means more than the New Testament. One Christian explanation, of a transparently sour-grapes character, is that this is because they are too primitive for the spirituality of the New Testament. Especially for Protestants, that is a grotesque thing to say.

In *Encounter* an article by Herbert Luethy has reviewed the old debate over Max Weber on Protestantism and capitalism. Luethy calls the Protestant Reformation, approvingly, "the first occasion in the history of Western Christendom that the spirit and the speech of the Old Testament prophets was heard again," and he goes on to speak of the Protestants' self-identification with the people of Israel and their prophets, "who rose against unjust princes and false prophets and who believed that the children of God should be concerned not only with holiness but also with justice and sanctification *here on earth*." In the Roman Church, he says, "that tradition had lain completely buried for more than a millennium beneath the Roman imperial and gentile heritage." (The idea is old, but evidently not obsolete.) Lanternari, for his part, shows that the Jewish Bible speaks as directly to the colonial oppressed as it once spoke to the Protestant Reformers of Europe, and additionally that the history of the Jews—persecuted but triumphantly surviving their persecutors—is a history that Africans and Polynesians want for themselves.

Uncle Tom was nobler than his modern detractors believe, but he was also submissive, in the New Testament fashion. Hence the use of his name as a supreme insult in the Negro community. For their songs of freedom and redemption his people used the language of the Jewish Bible—Moses, Egypt, "Let my people go." That is why Judaism can be attractive, even in the absence of Jewish missionaries—as it was, for that matter, to the peasants of San Nicandro, in Italy.

The motives of the modern Judaizers should be no less acceptable to official Judaism than the motives of the Khazars, whose conversion to Judaism in the Middle Ages has traditionally been a proud consolation for us. Not all the Khazars were converted, only the royal house and the aristocracy; and whether these became Jews or whether they were Judaizers is still unclear. What is clear, or what the modern historians agree on, is that the Khazars probably chose Judaism out of need and expediency as much as for its own sake. Contact with the high religions of Christian Byzantium and the Muslim Caliphate had made the old paganism untenable, but they wanted to preserve independence and neutrality between Constantinople and Baghdad.

The remarkable thing about Lanternari's work is that we owe it to an Italian from Bari, when there are so many Jews in anthropology and so many Israelis in Africa. It must have been hard for the Jewish anthropoligists and the Israelis to avoid becoming aware of what Lanternari is now telling us—especially the Israelis. The African nations are important for them. Nasser, in part to counter Israeli influence, set up a Muslim missionary organization for sub-Saharan Africa as a branch of his foreign operation. If only to counter Nasser, we might suppose that the Israelis would at least think about the Jewish religion in the new nations of Africa. But, as Urbach says, even when the Africans are in Israel the Israelis show them everything and talk to them about everything except Judaism.

That is not a failing of Israelis, it is a failing of modern Jews. Diffident about our religion and tradition among ourselves, we can scarcely be expected to commend them to others. And yet we must surely have some regard for our religion and tradition—enough, at any rate, to prefer them to Christianity. In the United States we could probably welcome a fair number of Negroes into our midst, if we wanted to. That would be good for them—so a Jew ought to assume—and especially good for us. By putting our rhetoric to the test, it would make us try to turn moralizing into morality. We would not succeed brilliantly, but at least we would be doing something serious. Evading the test while saying fine things, as we do now, is not serious.

—*May 1964*

. 33 .

Subject or Object?

For Mr. Ben Gurion, the seventeen centuries between Bar Kokhba's rebellion (132–135 C.E.) and Zionism are not Jewish history but a cessation of history. In those centuries the Jews are seen as having been objects, not subjects; acted upon, not acting. Having lost their state, and then the will and the capacity for a state, they became slaves. Their prayers for restoration and their messianic dreams were not so much stimulants as tranquillizers, reconciling them to exile and justifying passivity. In this view, they were enslaved by their own slavishness as much as by their masters. Slavish slaves, as we have been told by the philosophers since antiquity, are objects. They have not the stuff of citizenship in them.

Mr. Ben Gurion, therefore, can appeal to a respectable tradition when he says that to turn those slaves and objects into citizens and subjects, a state was needed—and, perhaps more, the will for a state. A merely conferred equality would not do. Even before the First Zionist Congress, Ahad Ha'am had told the French Jews that theirs was a psychology of slavishness in the midst of freedom.

But is a state the essential thing? For the Greeks, man is a being of the *polis* (the famous *politikon zōon*) not only because the *polis* is the city-state but also because it is community and society. My former colleague Professor Leon J. Goldstein has told me that we would understand Hegel better if we realized that his "state," too, can have the social and communal meaning, besides the political.

The Jews never lost community and society, or the feeling for community and society. In their own society and community they were active not passive, citizens not slaves. Mr. Ben Gurion came of age when most historians still thought history was past politics. In the centuries he dislikes, Jewish history is social (and religious) far more than it is political, but increasingly the study of history, generally, is social. However valid the subject-object distinction, to regard the Jews between Bar Kokhba and the nineteenth century as objects is a nineteenth-century prejudice.

· · ·

This must have been the last thing James Q. Wilson and Edward C. Banfield of Harvard had in mind when they wrote their "Public-regardingness as a Value Premise in Voting Behavior" (*American Political Science Review*, December 1964). Their purpose was to test a hypothesis: "That some classes of voters (. . . 'subcultures' constituted on ethnic and income lines) are more disposed than others to rest their choices on some concept of 'the public interest' or 'the welfare of the community.'" The test was an analysis of the votes in twenty elections, between 1956 and 1963, on thirty-five proposals in seven cities—Cleveland, Chicago, Detroit (and their counties), Kansas City, Los Angeles, Miami, and St. Louis—for things that would cost money, like hospitals, parks, roads, and schools. The authors conclude:

> . . . we reject . . . [the] theory . . . [that] the low-income Polish renter who votes against expenditures . . . that would cost him nothing and would confer benefits upon him and the high-income Anglo-Saxon or Jewish homeowner who favors expenditures . . . that will cost him heavily without benefiting him would both behave differently if they thought about the matter more or if their information were better.
>
> . . . voters in some income and ethnic groups are more likely than voters in others to take . . . the welfare . . . of "the community" into account as an aspect of their own welfare. . . . Each subcultural group, we think, has a more or less distinctive notion of how much a citizen ought to sacrifice for the sake of the community as well as of what the welfare of the community is constituted; . . . of what justice requires and of the importance of acting justly.
>
> . . . upper-income people tend to be more public-regarding than lower-income people. We do not think that income *per se* has this effect; rather, it is the ethnic attributes, or culture, empirically associated with it. It happens that most upper-income voters belong . . . to an ethnic group (especially the Anglo-Saxon and the Jewish) that is relatively public-regarding in its outlook. . . .

"The Anglo-Saxon and the Jewish." There is no mystery about the Anglo-Saxons: people who have long been subjects of history are apt to be civic ("public-regarding"), with a code of stewardship and *noblesse oblige*. But the Jews, according to Mr. Ben Gurion, were objects. Yet they are civic. How can objects be civic? And it is civicism that is the problem here, not ideology. The issues voted on were this hospital or that park, not liberalism or welfarism. If it were a question of ideology, the Anglo-Saxons and the Jews would not be linked. Most of the Anglo-Saxons were for Eisenhower and Nixon, most of the Jews for Stevenson and Kennedy; and so on.

If we wish, we may interpret Wilson and Banfield's findings as showing that some groups have a tradition (a living past) of subject-hood and others a tradition of objecthood, and that those traditions affect outlook and behavior. For instance, in Cleveland proper there was

> a negative correlation . . . between the percentage of voters . . . of foreign stock and the percentage of the total vote . . . that is "Yes." . . . the Poles and Czechs have the strongest distaste for expenditures . . . the percentage of Poles and Czechs is . . . more important . . . than median family income. . . .

And in a note:

> A person is of "foreign stock" if he was born abroad or . . . one or both of his parents. . . . We believe that the reason why a significant [negative] relationship does not appear for the suburbs is that there is a considerable number of Jews among the foreign stock of the suburbs. In the central city, there are practically no Jews. Like other Jews, Jews of East European origin tend to favor expenditures proposals of all kinds.

But those Poles and Czechs are of East European origin, too—East European peasant origin. As nations, they were oppressed by alien Romanoffs, Hapsburgs, and Hohenzollerns; as a class and as men, by the nobility and squirearchy, native or foreign. So far, not much difference between them (or the Italians, essentially) and the Jews. The crucial difference is that in the old country the Jews had a community, and with it a sense of community.

The historians and sociologists of American immigration—notably the immigration of the Poles and the Irish—have had to take into account peasant pessimism, or mistrust. For mistrustful peasants, government is a racket, society is a racket, taxes are extortion, social institutions are a fraud and a cloak for graft. You can depend only on your own family—a little.

The Jews, also oppressed, had no such racket theory of society. Living in the midst of hostile nations and empires, among themselves they lived in a community. The governments they knew were rackets and worse, but society was not a racket. Jewish society, Jewish community, was what made it possible for a man to live a Jewish life— which is to say, a human life. It was because of community that you had synagogues to pray in, a rabbi to adjudicate your disputes and tell your wife whether her egg or chicken was kosher, opportunities and incentives to study; above all, fellowships for good works both to help you in your need and to allow you to give and work, so that you might win honor on earth and merit in heaven.

All that was no racket. To a Jew it was as necessary as the *polis* had been to a freeman of Periclean Athens. The Jew complained about the leaders of the official community, their subservience to the government, and their unjust distribution of the tax burden; but he also taxed himself. He could hardly tell where discipline left off and his own sense of obligation began. One Passover, Levi Isaac of Berdichev, addressing himself to God, told Him: "The nations of the world have kings and ministers, generals and armies, but the land is full of violence and theft. Thy people Israel have neither kings nor ministers, neither generals nor armies, but no leaven will be found these eight days in all their habitations." (That was when he was speaking *for* the Jews. Another Passover, having seen labor conditions in the communal matzah bakery, he spoke *to* the Jews: "The nations of the world accuse us of baking our matzot with Gentile blood. That is a lie. We bake our matzot with Jewish blood.")

Psychologists believe that the infant's experience determines whether trust or mistrust will be the man's basic attitude toward life. By analogy, we may say that Polish and Czech peasants brought with them to America, from their experience of life in Europe, a tradition about how to understand the world, a prevalent attitude of basic mistrust. Jews brought a tradition or attitude of basic trust.

Emigrants are not usually the old country's elite, and neither were the Jews who came to America. Yet even these carried in their baggage habits and ways of thinking that made it easy for them, without hierarchy or authority, to create an unbelievable number and variety of institutions, from synagogues and free-loan societies to home-town relief and family circles. As before, the Jew who asked another for money or participation was not turned away and told that it was all a racket; the burden of justification was on the refuser, not on the asker—who, more often than not, was a demander. That has not disappeared. The University of Michigan Survey Research Center has reported that a higher proportion of Jews than of others give to persons and institutions, and give more, even when differences in income are taken into account. (Perhaps this ought to be put negatively: fewer do not give and fewer give little.) They could save a lot of money by saying that philanthropy is a racket, or by voting against a county hospital they are unlikely to use.

Subject or Object?

So far from the Jews being objects, from one point of view they excelled all others as subjects. The individual Jew felt personally responsible for the collective future. An Italian could become something else without worrying about the life-expectancy of Italy and Italian culture; the land and the people would always be there. A Jew, on the other hand, could rarely leave without feeling guilty about his failure to honor an obligation that he could not entirely deny. Marshall Sklare has noted that feeling in the work of a social scientist who thought he was writing impersonally, about a subject larger than the Jews: ". . . the individual who consciously wishes to . . . 'move away' feels . . . personal guilt. . . ."

A widely shared, internalized responsibility is not the mark of an object people; yet it was the very absence of a state that caused the Jews to internalize responsibility.

Where did the Jews get their favorable attitude toward government, if not toward particular governments?

The system of Jewish law incorporates Mar Samuel's principle (Babylonia, about 250 C.E.; Bava Qamma [113b]); *dina de-malkhuta dina*, a civil law of the state (or government; lit., kingdom) is the law for Jews, taking precedence over the corresponding Jewish civil law. (Especially in the Middle Ages, the rabbis and the communities they led made it clear that an oppressor's edict was not *dina*. This was good medieval political theory, much like Bracton's *rex est sub Deo et lege*, the king is under God and the law. The divine right of the absolute monarch came later.) Again, if there was one part of rabbinical literature that the ordinary Jew knew, that was Pirqe Avot, and there (3:2) he read an echo of Jeremiah (29:7): "R. Hananiah the Vice-High Priest said: Pray for the welfare of the government [*malkhut*], for if not for the fear it inspires, a man would swallow his neighbor alive."

A digression: modern scholars are likely to see in R. Hananiah's dictum the conservative outlook normal in troubled times, especially for a man of his class; or a justification of the sacrifices on behalf of Rome in the Temple, perhaps polemically against the Zealots' ideology, "No king but God"—as Jesus may have been arguing against the Zealots with his "render therefore to Caesar the things that are Caesar's and to God the things that are God's." Two centuries later the Rabbis are preaching patience under the foreign yoke in a manner that we can understand, given the circumstances, but that also lets us understand Mr. Ben Gurion's displeasure. In Ketubbot (111a) a political interpretation is made of the three occurrences, in the Song of Songs, of "I adjure you, O daughters of Jerusalem, /by the gazelles or the hinds of the field,/ that you stir not up nor awaken love,/until it please" (2:7, 3:5, and, without the gazelles and hinds, 8:4):

> . . . in accordance with R. Yose the son of R. Ḥanina [Palestine, about 250 C.E.], who said: Why these three adjurations? One refers to an oath that Israel would not mount upon the wall [in Palestine, to take arms against Rome]; one refers to the oath that the Holy One, blessed be He, made Israel [in the Diaspora] swear, that they would not rebel against the nations of the world; and one refers to the oath that the Holy One, blessed be He, made the nations of the world swear, that they would not subjugate Israel too much [*shello' yishta'bedu bahen beYisrael yoter middai*].

"Not subjugate Israel too much"!

Jews came to the United States, then, with an actively positive attitude toward society and community, growing out of their life in their own society and community; and a potentially positive attitude toward government, growing out of a Jewish tradition that affirmed the worth of government and out of their strong feeling for the social and communal. Already civic, they wanted to be citizens. They had been waiting for a chance to find a legitimate state, whose law would be their law, and it is as if they had also been waiting for a chance to enlarge the boundaries of the society that was society for them. Happy to have found those chances here, Jews from Europe behave in a major respect much like Anglo-Saxons and little like others who came here at the same time from the same places.

If these Jews had not had the capacity for civicism in the United States, other Jews would not have had the capacity for state-building in Israel. Perhaps the two capacities are one. Whether one or two, they grew from traditions and institutions that go back to the centuries Mr. Ben Gurion would like to forget.

—July 1965

· 34 ·

Our Fundamentalists

An outward and visible sign of the new Orthodox aggressiveness in the United States is the English-language publication of Agudath Israel, *Jewish Observer*. Agudath Israel was founded in Europe before the First War, an uneasy coalition of East European Hasidim and Mitnaggedim, unfriendly to each other, who spoke Yiddish and disliked secular education, and Germans of the Hirsch-Breuer school, who had a good secular education. Here nearly all the Agudah's followers are of East European origin or background, but in the circumstances of American life and in the publication of an English journal, the German precedent naturally tends to be somewhat emphasized.

In principle, Agudath Israel's great enemy is secularism and apostasy; in practice, an Orthodoxy that is not intransigent enough for its taste. The Agudah is harsh to assimilationists, harsher to secular Zionists, still harsher to Reform and Conservatism, and harshest of all to the Orthodox who in one way or another cooperate with or merely recognize other Jews—Mizrachi Zionists; rabbis and synagogues in organizations (like the Synagogue Council or rabbinical boards) where non-Orthodox rabbis and synagogues are also represented; and, unmistakably though not quite explicitly, Yeshiva University and the more or less moderate Orthodoxy that is staffed by the graduates of its seminary. The message is simple and repeated like an incantation: total opposition to all that does not totally oppose what is not totally Orthodox.

The first time I read that R. Moses Schreiber (Sofer), better known as the Ḥatam Sofer, had raised against the nascent modernization of his day a talmudic principle about something else, *"ḥadash asur min ha-Torah"*—what is new is forbidden by the Torah—I was suspicious. It seemed to me that this must be an invention of his enemies. Later I learned I was mistaken. *Jewish Observer*, proclaiming its fidelity to the Ḥatam Sofer's tradition, repeats the slogan. It has reprinted a comparison of Prague and Bratislava (formerly Pressburg) by Rabbi Meir Shapiro of Lublin, who died in the 1930s. In Bratislava, where the Ḥatam Sofer was rabbi, a relentless war was fought against the modernizers and anyone who would compromise with them. Not so in Prague. A hundred years after the Ḥatam Sofer's death, Bratislava was still a fortress of Jewish piety and learning, while Prague——Q.E.D., on the assumption that the only significant difference between Prague and Bratislava was that the Ḥatam Sofer was rabbi of one and not of the other. But what an assumption! As well compare Odessa with Shnipishok. Yet this is the sort of thing that can be published for devotees who are shown by letters to the editor to include an Air Force officer and a college teacher.

The attack is on the Orthodox who refuse to declare war on the

243

non-Orthodox, and the logical step is taken from attacking them to questioning their Orthodoxy. Of course, the Agudists never give the title of rabbi to Rabbi Louis Jacobs of England—though he was ordained at a yeshivah of the kind they like, it would be astonishing if they called him that. But they also withhold the title from a congregational rabbi who is both a Yeshiva University professor and a former president of the rabbinical association of Yeshiva's alumni. He, too, becomes Doctor. In effect, therefore, non-Agudah Orthodox rabbis are being threatened with contemptuous rejection of their qualifications, as if they were Conservative or Reform rabbis. (A parallel: in the thirties Communists, Socialists, and connoisseurs understood exactly what Earl Browder was doing when he addressed Norman Thomas as Mister, not Comrade.)

But let the Orthodox of the Yeshiva kind take heart. Though the Agudah complains of heresy, what bothers it more than anything else is the inclusive communal policy of Yeshiva's alumni. If they accept the Agudah's exclusive policy, much will be forgiven. Today Israel Azriel Hildesheimer has an implicit near-equality with Samson Raphael Hirsch as a spiritual ancestor of the Agudah, but in his lifetime he had trouble with the scions of the Ḥatam Sofer. Before establishing in Berlin the rabbinical seminary that came to be called by his name he was active in Hungary-Slovakia, and there the Soferim gave him a hard time. For them his school, or rather the very type he represented, was a Torah-forbidden novelty. They denounced the school to the government and hounded him in every way they could. Even when he sided with them against the reformers, they would have nothing to do with him, until finally he had to organize a bloc of his own. (He called it *kulturorthodox*—civilized Orthodox.) But in Berlin he stood for the *Austritt* (secessionist) Orthodoxy that Hirsch stood for in Frankfurt, and today Hildesheimer has been rehabilitated, to borrow a term. Which shows, like Hasidism itself, that one generation's forbidden novelty can be a following generation's ancestral tradition.

The strikingly new element in the way Agudath Israel talks now, in the United States, is its sharpness about the Catholic church. In Central and Eastern Europe the Agudah got along rather well with the Catholics in politics. (It also entered into understandings with the Jewish bourgeois assimilationists.) The old tone is heard in the Agudah's support of federal aid for parochial education—in the interest of its own schools as well as out of a desire for governmental encouragement to religion generally—while the new tone is heard in the insistent repetition that Christianity has always been antisemitic and that the Catholic church aided Hitler. *Jewish Observer* was pleased with Hochhuth's *Deputy*, has quoted at length from Professor Guenter Lewy's *Catholic Church and Nazi Germany*, and has said some strong things about the popes and a cardinal or two.

Why the difference? The Agudah in Poland then was hardly likely to be unaware of Christian antisemitism, of which it is so aware in the United States now. Once again, the real fight is with the near rather than the far. Among Jews, the Agudah disputes most fiercely with the Orthodox to its left; and as between Christians and Jews, more fiercely with Jews. The attack on the church is not so much on the church as on the Jews who hope to encourage an improvement in the church's attitude, and the derision that greets anti-antisemitic statements by pope or cardinals is a derision of the Jews who welcome such statements. In Poland, Agudath Israel could be pro-Catholic because that was politics, not influencing private relations or intimate attitudes, but in the United States it fears that relations and attitudes will be influenced. That would be bad for the policy of retreat behind the ramparts.

There is something else, too. The Agudah probably feels let down by the church. As long as Catholicism represented intransigence on the great scene, the Agudah did not feel alone in representing intransigence within Jewry. The church's nineteenth-century Syllabus of Errors condemned as an error the proposition that "the Roman Pontiff should and can reconcile himself with progress and modern civilization." In a Jewish frame the Ḥatam Sofer had already said the same sort of thing, and Hirsch was condemning proposals "to bring Judaism up to date, to adapt it to the needs of the time. . . . Instead of complaining that it is no longer suitable to the times, our only complaint must be that the times are no longer suitable to it." Now the church is bringing things up to date, and the Syllabus of Errors has turned into an error.

If I had lived when the Enlightenment was clashing with the Hatam Sofer's kind of Orthodoxy, I would have been of the enlighteners. (A Marxist historian now shows them to have been rather less attractive than we their heirs have been brought up to think.) If now the Orthodoxy of Agudath Israel were able to affect how I have to live, I would fight. Yet I feel a certain reserve in my opposition to the Agudah and what it stands for.

I have heard a distinguished Israeli man of letters praise the Jewish and humane worth of modern Hebrew literature. He remembers young men and women in the Russian Revolution who killed in the cellars of the Cheka, so devoted were they to the revolutionary ideal; yet, though Hebrew was beginning to be regarded as counterrevolutionary, in secret they still read the poems of Bialik and Chernikhovsky. For him that proved the attraction and power of Hebrew literature. For me, though to say so would have been offensive, it proved the weakness of literature or culture. That some of the Nazis who kept the crematoria burning were moved to tears by Beethoven does not prove that music is evil, but neither, certainly, does it prove that music has great power for good. The idealistic Cheka killers who loved Hebrew poetry were not pious Jews. Piety would have kept them from such idealism; culture—whether the Hebrew poetry of Bialik or the Russian of Pushkin—did not keep them from it. They helped to establish the reign of pitilessness. They also helped to suppress Jewish culture, and to oppress Jews.

Throughout our history it has been the stubbornly pious who have resisted the persuasions of self-interest and idealistic universalism, and it is that resistance which has kept them and their descendants from becoming idealistic killers. The moral account of those who yielded to self-interest or what seemed to be idealistic universalism—the two temptations often appear to be one—is not so clean. Spanish apostates from Judaism wanted the Inquisition, to prove their good faith. Among their descendants, we are told, were a St. John of the Cross and a St. Teresa of Avila, but among them also, or such of them as were somehow able to merge with the Old Christians, were men who helped to make Spain what it is, a country whose history is called a tragedy—of fanaticism, hatred, and blood. The intransigent Jews have no guilt for that tragedy, either for themselves or for their descendants. They chose to be victims of oppression, not oppressors.

In another place and at another time, Heine paid the price of baptism for a ticket of admission to Western culture. If he had had descendants, even by the Nuremberg standard they would have been *echt* Aryan, and some, therefore, would have been Nazis. That cannot be said of the followers of S. R. Hirsch. Whether we look to Spain or Germany or Russia, and whether from the point of view of Jewish or of universal values, we are in no position to laud ourselves above the intransigents.

That may help to explain a change in historical outlook. It is my impression that while the nineteenth-century medieval Jewish historians were essentially pro-Sephardi, the twentieth-century ones are pro-Ashkenazi. In the nineteenth century the Sephardim of the Middle Ages were an attractive model for Jews who wanted to be modern. They showed that Jews could remain Jews and still be at home in the general culture, or even do remarkable things in philosophy, literature, and science. That was necessary for reassuring the modernizing Jews, half-suspicious of their own motives, and was also thought useful for persuading the gentile authorities to take the last step toward full emancipation.

In the twentieth century we are less impressed with Jewish achievements in general culture. The edge is off our hunger and we worry now about the cost of the achievements. German Jews from Heine and Moses Hess to Kafka (culturally German) and Franz Rosenzweig respected backward East European Jewry for its Jewish and human authenticity more than they did German Jewry, with all its modernity. In the same way our historians today, looking back to the Middle Ages, have noted virtues in medieval Ashkenazi Jewry and vices in medieval Sephardi Jewry that their predecessors were not prepared to see. The philosophically naïve Ashkenazim of the Middle Ages—so the picture is now seen, broadly—preferred a martyr's death to apostasy; the Sephardim were too philosophical for that (that is to say, those who were most essentially Sephardi, i.e., most philosophical). During the Crusades the Jews of the Rhineland went to the stake rather than to the baptismal font. In 1492 more than a century of pogroms, threats, and accommodations had baptized most of Iberian Jewry; and then, in turn, only a minority chose expulsion over baptism.

Throughout the late Middle Ages, among Jews, Christians, and Muslims, there was a kind of underground skepticism and free thought of the philosophically enlightened. It was in the cosmopolitan Sicilian court of the Emperor Frederick II that the *De tribus impostoribus* seems to have had its origin. (The three impostors were Moses, Jesus, and Mohammed. The Three Rings of *Nathan the Wise*, a less negative statement of that idea, go back to the Middle Ages, too.) Earlier, in Golden Age Spain, an unfriendly Muslim had reported a conversation overheard among three Jewish physicians. The three agreed it was best to remain loyal to your own tradition: the first because he thought Judaism, Christianity, and Islam equally true; the second because he thought them equally false; and the third because he thought only one could be true, but no one could tell which.

From mid-fifteenth-century Spain there has come down a kind of handbook for Jewish religious polemic—polemic was not yet impossible—by the physician R. Ḥayyim ibn Musa. *Magen wa-romaḥ* ("Shield and Spear") tells the following story at the expense of the philosophizing preachers, whom it accuses of having "led Israel astray from within":

In the days of my youth I once heard a certain preacher expounding God's unity in the analytical manner of the philosophers. He would say repeatedly: "If He is not one, then such and such must follow." Finally a certain householder rose, of them that tremble at the word of the Lord [Isaiah 66:5], and said: "In the massacre in Seville [in 1391] they robbed me of everything I had and beat me and wounded me and left me for dead. All this I bore for my faith in *Hear, O Israel, the Lord our God, the Lord is One*. Now you attack the tradition of our fathers by way of philosophical analysis, saying, 'If He is not one, such and such will be the case.'" And the householder said: "I believe more in the tradition of our fathers. I do not wish to listen to this sermon." Then he left the synagogue, and most of the congregation with him.

Skeptics are not the martyrs' breed. The Jewish philosophizers were friendly with Christian philosophizers and thought it foolish for skeptical Jews to die or flee rather than become skeptical Christians. (Not all of Christianity in Spain was fanatical. Erasmus had a Spanish following.) How they and their descendants fared, we know. It is not so much that they were shamed and terrorized as New Christians; it is that the best of the descendants of those prudent, skeptical Jews, especially if they were lucky enough to escape the New Christian trap, were Christian fanatics.

In the Soviet Union possibly the noblest Russian of our lifetime was Boris Pasternak. He was born a Jew, but he lived and died a Christian, and he had a Christian's irritable impatience with Judaism. The revolutionary freethinkers did not expect that the best spirit in the land of the revolution would be a Jew who was consciously, deliberately Christian. The Jews who worked for the revolution—because it would at last make Judaism equal with Christianity, as outmoded superstition?—expected it least of all. Still, they helped to bring it about, though that was the least of their crimes. Of all those crimes the faithful Jews were innocent. And when the story is finally told, we shall learn that many were more than innocent: they were heroic, prolonging over the year a *qiddush ha-Shem*—hallowing the name of God—that makes our enlightened reasonableness, and especially the particular sorts of idealism into which it sometimes boils over, look shabby.

Writing about the tensions between European and "Oriental" (North African and Asian) Jews in Israel, Nissim Rejwan, a journalist of Oriental origin, has quoted a historian:

. . . what the Jews of Eastern Europe in Israel really dislike about their fellow Jews from the Orient is . . . that the latter tend to remind them of the social and cultural conditions prevailing only a few decades ago in their own now rejected *shtetls* and ghettos in Russia and Poland. It is this . . . eagerness . . . of most East European Jews in Israel to forget and disown their own past, their own selves, almost, which has led, on the one hand, to their present rejection of the "Sephardo-Orientals," and, on the other, to the dangerous drift away from their own traditions and culture.

The Orientals are not alone in reminding us of what we would like to forget, and being resented for it. There are also the devout. Their presence reminds us that from Philo of Alexandria's nephew, Titus's staff officer in the destruction of Jerusalem, to the Chekists, they that tremble at the word of the Lord have played a more honorable part than we or our predecessors. Today the intransigents' zealotry is a nuisance, but even as we strike back, something stays our hand. We would like to forget, but in a part of ourselves we remember.

—September 1964

. 35 .

The State of Jewish Belief

One of the ironies in all the recent discussion about the "death of God" is that, in many intellectual circles at least, God has not been so alive since Nietzsche wrote His obituary almost a century ago. The editors of *Commentary* were curious to know whether this might also be true among Jews, especially since so much of the talk about Jews in past decades has been about Jewishness—that is, Jewish identity, understood historically and sociologically—rather than about Judaism, the system of belief and practice to which Jews are presumably obligated. Accordingly, a list of questions was submitted to some fifty-five rabbis (not all of whom, however, have congregations). Thirty-eight responses were received: fifteen Reform, twelve Conservative, eleven Orthodox.

Reading the responses, one sees that the true division is between Orthodox and non-Orthodox. Cover the identifications of the non-Orthodox and what they write will not usually give you a clue to a Reform or a Conservative affiliation: few call themselves Reform, none Conservative. (Yet when a Conservative wants to pray in a synagogue and has no Conservative synagogue to go to, he is much more apt to go to an Orthodox than a Reform one—especially if he is a rabbi.) Of the twenty-seven non-Orthodox, I come up with this census: more or less classical (or serene) Reform, four or five—including a borderline case whose affiliation is Conservative; Reconstructionists, six or seven—including one who takes his lead not from Dewey but from Sartre and Camus; disciples of Franz Rosenzweig—fifteen to seventeen, mostly youngish. The single greatest influence on the religious thought of North American Jewry, therefore, is a German Jew—a layman, not a rabbi—who died before Hitler took power and who came to Judaism from the very portals of the church. Obviously we have not given Nahum Glatzer and Schocken Books anything like the thanks we owe them for telling us about Rosenzweig in English. Obviously, also, since even his name is unkown to most of us, the rabbis have not spoken about him loudly enough.

Any other group of non-Orthodox North American rabbis would probably show a similar distribution, but it is uncertain that the Orthodox respondents in this symposium are equally representative of the Orthodox rabbinate. The uncertainty does not derive from the ratio of so-called modern Orthodox rabbis; modern Orthodoxy is not a theological category, it is a sociological one. Nor does the uncertainty derive from the absence of some of Yeshiva University's young critics of Orthodoxy from within, since their criticism basically is of strategy and style. It derives, rather, from something that is hinted at in one of the more uncompromising responses. To be able to write English passably well; to have earned a doctorate in English literature, or analytical philosophy, or biology; above all, to teach those subjects—for Orthodox Jews of a certain kind, such interests and achievements and occupations are, if not sinful, then capable of inciting to sin. At the very least, the old-school Orthodox say, a man who studies Milton or Mendel or Wittgenstein is guilty of *bittul Torah*, the transgression of wasting on frivolities the time he could give to studying Torah. Of course this is not an unchallenged Orthodox doctrine, or rather attitude; but of course, equally, this symposium cannot adequately represent those whose doctrine or attitude it is. Still, some of the Orthodox respondents are in a certain measure spokesmen for Orthodoxy of this traditional East European type. They may even think of themselves as sacrificially risking the world's slow stain in order to shield the purity of those whose study of Torah is never diluted or diminished by the study of anything else.

Two or three give this impression. One is wild, not easily classifiable. The rest stand in the tradition of another German Jew, this one of the nineteenth century, Samson Raphael Hirsch. For him a guiding principle was *Torah 'im derekh erez*, Torah together with secular studies. Thus he irritated the modernizers, for whom Torah was outmoded, and the old-fashioned, for whom secular studies were unclean. I say that most of the Orthodox rabbis here stand in Hirsch's tradition—though some would prefer to say they are the disciples of Elijah Gaon of Vilna—because Hirsch had studied in a university. That was why the Polish and Lithuanian rabbis regarded him as a bad example for their own people, though no doubt useful enough for the fallen-away Jews of the West.

Hirsch and Rosenzweig, Germans. All modern Jews—insofar as they are modern, or even postmodern—walk in the footsteps of German-speaking Jewry, the pioneers of Jewish modernity. Besides Hirsch and Rosenzweig, there are Mendelssohn and Heine and Frankel and Freud and Herzl and Kafka and Zunz and Hess and Baeck and Buber. Most of us, children or grandchildren of Jews from Eastern Europe, have inherited a dislike of German Jewry. We still chuckle when we remember Chaim Weizmann's mot, that the German Jews combined the best elements of both cultures, having all the modesty of Jews and all the charm of Germans. It is time we did the handsome thing and acknowledged our debt.

What has been Buber's influence on Jewish thought in America? From the evidence of these statements, not much. That is strange and needs explaining. Buber was the first Jewish religious thinker since Maimonides eight centuries ago who was able to influence Christian theology, and his thought might therefore have been expected to benefit among Jews not only from its own merit but also from its prestige among Christians. Yet as between Buber and Rosenzweig, close associates in the 1920s, it is Rosenzweig, fated to die young, and ignored by Christians, who dominates non-Orthodox Jewish theology; and it is Buber, who died full of years, and honored in Christian theology, whose influence on Jews is less. Some Jews read his books on Hasidism, more flocked to his lectures, and a few respected his work for rapprochement between Arabs and Jews. That seems about all.

Buber was for encounter and openness, not for law. His opposition to *halakhah* as the enemy of openness and spontaneity made him unusable for the Orthodox, of course; but also for the non-Orthodox who affirm the principle of *halakhah* (though not the *halakhot* specifically) on either Rosenzweigian or Reconstructionist grounds. Classical Reformers, while not put off by Buber's antihalakhism, can be made uncomfortable by his talk about encounters between God and man. Reformers of this type like to say that "the essence of Judaism" is contained in Micah 6:8: ". . . what does the Lord require of you/but to do justice, and to love kindness [*or* mercy], /and to walk humbly with your God?" When they use their own language, the essence is apt to be worded in some such way as this: ". . . a religion [that] affirms ethical monotheism, rejects idolatry, makes central the sanctity of man and the significance of the task of bringing about a just society . . . is a true religion." The part about walking humbly with your God tends to get lost.

What impression does this symposium give of the present state of Jewish religious thought? In general, that there is far less theological ferment than among Christians and that there are few new ideas about Judaism. Mordecai M. Kaplan's system was all but complete thirty years ago, Rosenzweig's forty years ago, Hirsch's a hundred years ago. What is a novelty to some Christians is, as many of the rabbis here remind us, old-hat to Jews. The Anglo-American "death of God" corresponds in a way to the slogan—and title of a book—that preceded the worker-priest movement in French Catholicism in the 1940s: France, missionary territory. This was shorthand for the discovery that France, once the Eldest Daughter of the Church, had become so dechristianized that it had to be won back for Christianity almost as if it were *in partibus infidelium*. With Jews, the large-scale defections and indifferences go back before that, and before Nietzsche and Feuerbach, to when Jews were first becoming modern. From this point of view, at least, Spinoza was the first modern Jew.

Those modern Jews who want to be religious, including rabbis, have such a long familiarity with modernity-godlessness that they are less apt to be shocked by it, for good or for ill, than the Christian clerical "country boys," as one of the rabbis calls them. Biblical criticism, for instance. Most of the non-Orthodox (and perhaps a few

Orthodox, too, privately) would say that Rosenzweig said: Wellhausen may be right, and the Torah may be composed of four independent documents, J, E, D, and P, brought together by R; only for me, R does not mean Redactor, as for Wellhausen; for me it means *Rabbenu*, our master, or teacher, or rabbi. (*Rabbenu* is Moses' fixed epithet.) Living in tension with modernity, embracing and repelling it, doubting and believing—these are old experiences for religious modern Jews.

On the whole, therefore, the relative absence of newness was to be expected, together with the dominant intellectual, if not emotional, calm. After all, Judaism is rather old. Intellectually—if it is decent to make such a distinction—even the crematoria are not qualitatively new. Before Hitler the Jews knew Hadrian and Khmelnitzki and how many others. Intellectually, Auschwitz should shake the secular humanist at least as much as the theist.

In any case, theology is not the same as religion or faith, and Jews have normally theologized less than Christians. It was not Jews but Christians who, to use an old illustration, massacred each other for an iota: is the *Son homoousios* with the Father, of the same substance, or *homoiousios*, of like substance? Even when bloodless, Christian theologizing has often led an independent life of its own, with no effect on deed or creed but serving ultimately as little more than raw material for dissertations in *Dogmengeschichte* or some other branch of intellectual history.

The typical Jewish attitude is embodied in the story about a German Jew who had returned to Judaism and was lecturing on the philosophy of prayer one afternoon at an Agudath Israel convention. After he had been talking for some time, his auditors began to drift out in twos and threes, until he was all but alone with the fidgeting chairman. "Have I offended them?" he asked. "No," said the chairman, "they're leaving to say the afternoon prayer."

When others say that to me, in defense of the minimal theological activity in our rabbinical seminaries, I become suspicious. I am not a follower of Buber, but once, when everybody at one seminary was sneering at Buber-*mayses* (a pun on the Yiddish *bobbe-mayses*, old wives' tales), I almost wanted to enlist on Buber's side. They were really sneering at the theological enterprise itself. Historically, some Jewries were more theological than others. The more advanced the culture they lived in and the more vigorous its philosophical life, the more they had to theologize. Medieval Spanish Judaism was more theological than Franco-German Judaism, Maimonides more than Rashi. In those terms, we live in Spanish and not Franco-German conditions, and we too need theology. How much? More, I would say, than we are getting.

—August 1966

. 36 .

Going to Shul

In the past months, since my father died, I have been in the synagogue twice a day to say the Kaddish. Other congregations would regard mine as observing bankers' hours, but even so its morning schedule requires arising in the dark and cold, especially in the winter. For afternoon-and-evening prayer the hour varies, depending—at least in principle and in Orthodox synagogues—on the time of sunset, but going every evening is not easy, either.

Which is why not even the devout necessarily frequent the synagogue every day, contenting themselves with private prayer, particularly on weekdays. It is the man who is saying the Kaddish who must have a *minyan*, public worship. In most American synagogues nearly everyone you see at prayer during the week is a mourner, together with most of those who are there from the beginning on Saturday morning. Inconvenience also helps to explain the tenth-man problem, quite apart from the big explanations we like better: the difficulty of belief, the difficulty of prayer. In few synagogues where the speech is English is it unnecessary to have a list of volunteers who can be telephoned in an emergency to round out the required number of ten.

In the Middle Ages it was thought that saying the Kaddish for a year was especially helpful to the dead if they had been wicked. Since no one wanted to imply that his father or mother had been wicked, today we say the Kaddish for eleven months. I do not know what proportion of Jewish men observe the full eleven months, but I suspect it is fairly high, especially when put beside our known propensity for staying away from the synagogue.

If this is so, why? Well, feelings about death, especially the death of a parent; guilt and anxiety, and the need to relieve them; ritual— all these can be interpreted along conventional Freudian lines and

254

have been, often. For Freud, religion was a kind of public, collective neurosis. I take this idea seriously. It tells me better than anything else why the very inconvenience of saying the Kaddish morning and afternoon-evening every day for eleven months, and thereafter on anniversaries—normally at least two in a man's life—becomes a virtue, perhaps an attraction. It is expiatory, it is almost punitive, and we have been taught that guilt seeks punishment.

It is more, of course. Much has been said in dispraise of Jews who obey the rules of the Kaddish though otherwise they hardly ever pray at all. The contempt is unwarranted: the Kaddish must meet their needs better than anything else in the synagogue. And these are not only needs of the kind we have learned about from Freud, but also needs for style and tradition. Freud said that the collective neurosis of religion spares us the trouble of developing individual, personal neuroses. With the Kaddish, Judaism spares each Jew the trouble of developing for himself a style—etiquette, ritual, mode of expression, symbolic action—at a time when he wants it and when he knows he cannot devise something personal that will be as good.

If each of us were accountable for his own ritual of mourning, who would escape censure? Who would escape his own censure? The Jewish rites—the burial, the seven days at home, the Kaddish—have the advantage of being a tradition, a style. We need assume no responsibility for them, as we would for any personal or private symbolic action, nor can there be any question of their appropriateness. They are appropriate almost by definition, because of their antiquity, their near-universality, their publicness—*quod semper, quod ubique, quod ab omnibus.* Yet their publicness, so far from making them exterior and impersonal, makes them all the more appropriate to the particular relationship between mourner and mourned: the Kaddish I now say for my father, he said for his; and so back through a recession of the generations that exceeds what my imagination can grasp. Acting as my father acted, I become conscious that I am a link in the chain of being. Nor am I hindered from expressing particular, local, present emotion.

One of the things a Jew is supposed to say about someone who has died is the prayer that Abigail said for David (though in his lifetime and in his presence), that his soul may be bound up in the bundle of life. Saying this is of a piece with the rest of our ritual. Whatever its efficacy may be for the dead, it binds *me* up in the bundle of life, situates *me* in the procession of the generations, frees *me* from the prison of now and here.

Although we have been born when it is hard to believe in immortality, the Kaddish helps us to believe, a little. I know that it makes me think of my father often, more than forty times a week; and it will keep reminding me of him after I have stopped saying the Kaddish daily, when I hear someone else say it and I make the appropriate response. To think of my father, to recall him, is to hold off his mortality—and because ritual is eloquent, to hold it off still one generation further. Where has Daddy gone? To shul, to say Kaddish for Grandpa. By doing what allows my children to ask this question and receive this answer, I also allow myself to hope that my own mortality will similarly be delayed.

A Kaddish-sayer and shul-watcher can learn something even if his experience, like mine, has been limited to not many more than a dozen synagogues, Orthodox and Conservative, mostly in or near New York.

With our past and present confusingly simultaneous, many of us are not in the category we should be in. Of the elderly and immigrant, for instance, it is to be expected that they will use a Polish-Russian Ashkenazi pronunciation of Hebrew; of the middle-aged, the standard Ashkenazi that was taught in our Hebrew schools a generation ago; and of the young, the more or less Israeli, more or less Sephardi pronunciation that is now taught in most schools—for instance, *yitbarákh* "may (he/it) be blessed": standard Ashkenazi, *yisborákh*; Polish-Russian, *yisbórekh, yisbúrekh*. With eyes closed, you can usually know the man by his Hebrew. Usually—but I have opened my eyes after hearing *yisbúrekh* to see a youngish man who could be in advertising or public relations. And as with pronunciation, so with the atmosphere and the ways of a synagogue. In any synagogue you are apt to find people who by all the rules belong more properly in a different one.

Jews who are Americanized (or Anglicized, or Gallicized; before Hitler, Germanized) want restraint in their synagogues, in the officiants as well as the laity. The virtuoso cantor, I had thought, came into his own at a certain time in history, when Jews from the traditionalist villages were moving to the big cities of Europe and America, and he disappeared when their children learned that his kind of singing was out of place in a church. I have not heard really gaudy *hazzanut* anywhere recently, but I have heard other survivals from the bad old days where there was no reason to expect them: a kind of falsetto throating; stretching or repeating some words and swallowing others; singing as if the text consisted of vowels alone, without consonants.

If bar-mitzvahs are a horror, as everyone says, they are normally not so in the synagogue itself. That may come later, somewhere else. Still, the accumulation of bar-mitzvahs, two or more a week, week after week, can be too much of a good thing. By now I can do without the high voices, and the slow chanting, and the charge to the boys, and the congratulations to the parents, and the benediction, and the presentation of kiddush beakers and prayer books, and the boys' pledges and thanks. If I am querulous, put the blame on lingering shock. Not long ago I heard a bar-mitzvah boy double as cantor when the Torah scroll was being returned to the ark. At that point the cantor summons the congregation with a verse from the 148th Psalm: "Let them praise the name of the Lord, for His name alone is exalted." Instead of *yehalelu et shem*, however, the boy sang *yehallelu* . . . , "Let them profane the name . . ."! (The identical phrase is in Leviticus, negatively of course: ". . . lest they profane My holy name," *we-lo' yehallelu et shem qodshi*. "Profanation of the Name," *hillul ha-shem*, is the rabbinical term for blasphemy specifically or conduct unbecoming a Jew generally.)

Sometimes I wonder about the bar-mitzvah guests. The occasional woman in a sleeveless, near-décolleté dress—where does she get her notions of seemliness? The uncle for whom the Hebrew blessings are practically nonsense syllables but who accepts being called up when the Torah is read—why does he do it? Since his abject stammering is surely as painful for him as for the rest of us, he might at least rehearse the syllables a day or two earlier.

In my wanderings I have discovered an argument, new to me, against the Orthodox segregation of the sexes. It is still true that when women sit by themselves they talk, and in shul they have to be shushed—one of the few things our grandmothers have in common with their college-graduate granddaughters. When in a Conservative synagogue and dispersed among the men, the same women seem to talk less than when in Orthodox isolation. After one deafening Sabbath morning near the divider between the men and women, I could appreciate the answer of the great Rabbi Israel Salanter—I think it was he—when he was asked what should be done with some bricks left over from repair work on a synagogue: "Use them to wall up the entrance to the women's gallery." In a way, that is what Conservative and Reform Judaism have done.

I have a research project for a specialist in the social psychology of small groups: examine a daily *minyan*. It is an ideal opportunity for a participant-observer, especially if one moves about from time to time and gets to see how others are.

Take the *minyan* in the congregation I belong to. When you consider that its members are unhappy about having to be there in the first place and that its composition changes, veterans departing as newcomers enter, its morale is remarkable. On the whole they are not conspicuously pious Jews, but most make it a point of honor to disregard bad weather and hazardous driving to get there on time. Clearly they believe that the *minyan* must go on, that it would be wrong to let the side down.

So strong is this sentiment that it makes some who have finished their eleven months keep coming, if not every day then one or two mornings during the week. That is when it counts, because Saturdays and Sundays are no problem. Getting up early when they want to sleep a little longer, and could, their own daily Kaddish-saying now behind them, they show a devotion and self-sacrifice more to be respected than the writing of a check or the signing of a petition. These men do the inconvenient thing so that the other men, who need the *minyan*, will have it. And though they may be too bashful about this motive even to admit it to themselves, I suspect they do it, too, because of what they think a shul should be: a place from which the praises intoned by Israel ascend, as is said of the *Shema'*, "evening and morning, twice every day always, lovingly"—or thrice, if you take the afternoon prayers (which lack the *Shema'*) and the evening prayers to be separate in fact as well as principle.

I have the impression my *minyan* is something of an exception in its morale. At any rate, I find it more attractive than others I have seen. It has little of the prevalent mumbling combined with sprinting that is another survival from the bad old days. In my *minyan* we sing. Not only that, but also I can actually finish one prayer before the next is begun. We are out at the same hour every day, because it is the starting time that varies, not the leaving time: we start early on Mondays and Thursdays, when the Torah is read, and earlier still on a New Month. With the time for leaving calculated and fixed, we do not race the clock. For the kind of people we are, the singing and the deliberate pace ratify our being engaged in what we recognize as suitable prayer. It may even make us a little more prayerful than we would be otherwise.

Not many of us have or attain *kawwanah*—inwardness, concentration, the merging of the pray-er with his prayer. They say it used to be common. Whether or not that is so, I can hardly recite a verse of six or seven words without my mind wandering. (I can hardly listen to three bars of music at a concert without my mind wandering.) Beside *kawwanah,* decorum and singing and pace and every other occidental propriety are trash. Unfortunately, though, their absence does not guarantee its presence; and if we are going to have to do without *kawwanah,* we may as well have niceness. Let a man be free enough from haste to be at least aware of the plain meaning of the words he is saying or singing. When he leaves, hurrying to his car, let him not have a bad taste in his mouth.

I still catch myself daydreaming about the things I would do if I were rich. Lately, one of those things has been to have my own shul, with the legislative, executive, and judicial powers all mine. I would make some radical reforms, of a generally reactionary character.

As among the Sephardim, I would have the reader read every word aloud, from beginning to end, except for meditations intended to be silent or those minatory admonitions that are traditionally muted, like Deuteronomy 11:17 after the *Shema'.* As Maimonides decreed for the Jews of Egypt, I would have the Standing Prayer said only once, aloud. Every biblical text that is more than one or two verses long would be chanted, like the Torah and the Prophetical lessons and the Megillot. (The prayer book includes many psalms, but I have yet to hear one chanted that way.) I would have the musical emphasis that is given to a prayer, or even a phrase, correspond to the doctrinal or liturgical emphasis it ought to have. I do not pray for the restoration of the sacrificial cultus, nor does the prayer book I use (on the Sabbath) include a prayer for it; and the Conservative theologians who edited that *siddur* even refrained from translating the biblical prescription for animal sacrifice incorporated in the Standing Prayer for *Musaf.* Yet the congregation is encouraged to sing that very passage, in an almost fondling sort of way: "And on the Sabbath day, two he-lambs. . . ."

The Sabbath service is on the long side: in my congregation three hours—not unusual—and in another I know of, four. The other is the Orthodox synagogue of Sons and Daughters of the American Revolution. It may be that the four-hour Sabbath worship is one of the reasons why the Sons and Daughters stay away from their synagogue so religiously.

The length of the synagogue service, on the Sabbath and festivals and even weekday mornings, is only a sign of the contradiction or tension in our worship. On the one hand, the Rabbis enjoin us not to make a perfunctory routine, *qeva'*, of our prayer. On the other hand, our liturgy consists, with some expansions and additions, of prayer-texts that the same Rabbis declared to be *hovah*, obligatory. It is hard to keep the repeated and obligatory from becoming routine. Even in the age of faith only a small elite could have succeeded.

But to make the service short will not help us much. I have felt most untouched and unmoved in short services, Reform or near-Reform Conservative or Reconstructionist; and my neighbors have seemed to me equally untouched and unmoved. In fact, length has certain advantages. In a way, a long service is like a long poem. You do not want unrelieved concentration and tightness in a long poem; they would be intolerable. Length requires *longueurs*. A good long poem is an alternation of high moments and moments less high, of concentration and relaxation. In our synagogues the heights may not be very high, but the long service does provide some ascent and descent. The short service tends to be of a piece, dull and tepid.

If I shortened at all, it would be at the end rather than the beginning—the *Musaf*, not the introductory hymns and psalms. Time would also be saved by a total ban on bar-mitzvahs (let them go somewhere else), but twenty minutes or so would continue to be reserved for the sermon. The sermon would not be consistently topical, because I can acquire on my own the approved attitudes toward whatever the approved topics may be at any given time, from the approved sources: New York *Times Magazine*, *Saturday Review*, public-service television. It is less easy to acquire Torah.

My most reactionary radicalism would be reserved for the Friday-night service: back to Orthodoxy, almost all the way. Almost—because I would substitute some other reading from rabbinical literature for *Ba-meh madliqin*, which, besides being boring, is offensive in the reasons it gives for women dying in childbirth. Job should forever have put an end to that kind of theodicy.

How to recruit a good congregation of respectable size is a problem I am unable to solve even in a daydream. A bare *minyan* is not quite right for a Sabbath, let alone Rosh Ha-shanah and Yom Kippur. "In a multitude of people is the glory of a king." For the Rabbis that verse from Proverbs proved that Jews should worship together, the more the better. A large number of worshipping Jews assembled together can generate a kind of heat—analogous to the physical heat that people generate when they are closely assembled—that will affect each one individually. I have heard about it but I have not experienced it. On Rosh Ha-shanah and Yom Kippur a large number of Jews are assembled where I go, only most of them are not what anyone would call worshipping Jews. They are there, they bring their warm bodies, but they are a kind of inert mass and they deaden rather than quicken the worship. They are an audience—not an especially understanding one—rather than a congregation. According to Ninotchka, Stalin wanted fewer but better Russians. That is a cautionary precedent, but I would still be glad to exchange some Jewish quantity for quality.

Now, as to the prayer books I would use: something on the order of Birnbaum's excellent *siddur* and *maḥazor*, but different in having an English facing page that does not give the impression it was written by a hand in a woolen mitten. (For Ps. 24:1, "The earth is the Lord's and the fulness thereof," he has "The earth and its entire contents belong to the Lord.") Conservative variations should be presented, besides the Orthodox text. I would not particularly mind additional readings and meditations from modern work, provided they were additions not substitutions, and provided I could continue to ignore them. Either the modern lends itself with difficulty to what a prayer book should be or editors have usually made the wrong choices—probably both. A warning: if "insight" appears anywhere in the book —except perhaps in the introduction, and preferably not there, either —I will not buy it.

A good *siddur* is particularly useful during those necessary and soothing low-keyed stretches in the service. You may decide, for instance, to read a psalm or a rabbinical prayer more closely than you could if you were trying to keep up with the cantor and congregation. You can read for anything you wish—plain meaning, literary effect, doctrine, allusion or suggestion, historical placing, or even praise and supplication. If there are good notes and a good translation, you have most of the help you need.

For astigmatics like me, make sure the Hebrew characters are large and distinct, and more especially watch those vowel signs: I often have trouble telling a *qamez* from a *segol* or a *pataḥ* from a *zere*. To Hebrew editors and printers everywhere I commend the example of David de Sola Pool in his edition of the Sephardi prayer book, who for short *qamez* uses the left-hand half of the sign. Unlike the Ashkenazi, the Sephardi-Israeli pronunciation distinguishes between long and short *qamez*, and a visual marking of the distinction is something to be grateful for. Without it, in hard or doubtful cases it becomes necessary to see whether the Kittel-Kahle Biblia Hebraica has a *meteg,* for example; and then what if the verse or word is not biblical? But even Dr. Pool is not to be completely relied on in these difficulties, because the Sephardi *siddur* is far from identical with the Ashkenazi. What is more, the Sephardim's tradition is unacceptable about such matters as the length of the *qamez* preceding *ḥatef-qamez:* for instance, instead of *ṭohorah,* "purity," they say *ṭahorah,* and Dr. Pool so points it.

My *siddur* would go to the Sephardim for variety, as in the Kaddish. The Kaddish is a doxology, of which the substantial and historical kernel is the congregation's response: "May His great name be blessed/praised (forever and ever)." Formally, it is not a prayer for the dead; only the graveside Kaddish mentions the dead, and then not specifically but generally, in its praise of God as the future author of resurrection. The four forms of the Kaddish said in the synagogue—two by the cantor or reader, two by mourners—are, as it were punctuation marks in the service, setting off one part from the next. As far as "may He establish His kingdom" the Ashkenazi Kaddish is the same as the Sephardi one; but then the Sephardim (and Hasidim) add, ". . . causing His salvation to spring forth and bringing near [hastening the advent of] His Messiah." Why not take that over into, say, the reader's Kaddish *Titqabbal* or the mourner's Scholars' Kaddish? It would make somewhat more explicit the messianic hope that the Kaddish has expressed from the beginning.

In the *Kedushah,* with the reader repeating the Standing Prayer and reader and congregation saying a doxology built around "Holy, holy, holy," there are slight differences between the Ashkenazi and the Sephardi-Hasidic texts. Every now and then we might want to follow the Sephardi usage, and the *siddur* ought to have it for us. In the *'Alenu* we should take from the Sephardim the passage that the Christian censors deleted from our text.

The story is told about a Hasid—the same story in its essentials no doubt exists in other religious traditions, too—that people complained of his frequent absence from the synagogue. "I start to go," he answered, "but when I leave the house I see God's world testifying to the majesty of Him who in His goodness renews every day, continually, the work of creation. So I recite some psalms, like 'The heavens declare the glory of God,/and the firmament proclaims his handiwork' and 'How great are Thy works, O Lord!/Thy thoughts are very deep!' And then, by the time I remember where I am and where I was going, it's too late, and I don't get to shul. But," he said, brightening, "sometimes I don't get distracted by thinking about God, and then I go."

Does the moral apply to us? Of course, but not entirely. We are different from that Hasid. We do not bless the Creator for His creation, because we have learned that the argument from design is a fallacy. Both for him and for us the synagogue is a distraction, but for us the distraction is unlikely to be from thinking about God.

Another story about Hasidim: In the presence of their sleeping master, two disciples were talking low about how hard it was to resist temptation, and how the *yezer ha-ra'*, the Evil Desire, kept running after them. Their master, who had not been asleep after all, opened his eyes and said: "Don't flatter yourselves. The Evil Desire isn't running after you, you haven't reached that height. You're still running after the Evil Desire."

Even when a man has arrived at a high degree of spirituality, we are informed, he has problems. I suppose an analogy might be with the rich, who have problems that the poor are either ignorant or skeptical about, and certainly in no position to complain about. The frail spirituality of the synagogue must be a real problem—for the spiritually rich. Who will believe us, paupers and groundlings, if we pretend that it is our problem and that we have reached that height?

—*April 1966*

. **37** .

Relevance in the Synagogue

Everyone, especially the young, seems to agree that the synagogue is irrelevant. When Jewish college students (and youthful or wishfully youthful college teachers) are asked whether the synagogue is relevant, they answer no. In all that interests them—peace, race, poverty, the meaning of morality, freedom—the synagogue says and does little that seems to them useful or important. It is not unexpected that they should say this. Most of them are uncommitted or, as they are sometimes called, un-Jewish.

What may be unexpected is that even those young people who consider themselves to be committed Jews are apt to say the same thing.

In effect, they say they are committed Jews, synagogue Jews, not because of the synagogue but in spite of it. They are disappointed when they turn to it for encouragement, help, or advice in those things that to them are most important—which are not greatly different from the important things of the uncommitted. Members of a self-conscious youth generation tend to have similar ideas about what is important; and particularly now, when you don't have to be young to be convinced of the importance of peace, race, poverty, and the rest.

There is a certain ambiguity in this criticism of the synagogue. Are the young people saying that the synagogue is as irrelevant as the church, or that it is more irrelevant? If the critics wanted to, they could argue, plausibly, that the synagogue is more irrelevant. They could point to the far-out nuns and priests, the new-morality and secular-city theologians, the community activism of the mainline Protestant denominations, the traditional peace and service activities of the Quakers. In image, at least, and probably also to some extent in deed, the synagogue is substantially to the rear of the churches in these matters. Yet the critics of the synagogue generally avoid the comparison. I think they avoid it because they want to make believe that a big, obvious fact does not exist: that America, though it is a secular society and has more separation of church and state than practically any other country in the world, is also a Christian society. I shall come back to this later.

Provisionally, let us regard the criticism of the synagogue as a criticism of religion generally—that is, one which assumes an equal unsatisfactoriness of church and synagogue. What is new about this is that it is made at all. Criticism arises from expectation. In the *entre deux guerres*, enlightened, progressive people did not make the criticism. They did not have the expectation. They simply took it for granted that religion was so thoroughly stupid and out of the question that it need not be thought about at all. We all say and believe that the world is more secular than it has ever been. Simultaneously, enlightened, progressive people are more disillusioned with irreligion and more expectant of religion than they have ever been. If a New Leftist can bring himself to think of coalition at all, he will include not the trade unions but the churches.

As for the synagogue, it may be less relevant than it used to be, but I am not sure. The social-justice phase of Reform Judaism in the 1930s seems to have been chiefly a matter of resolutions by the

Central Conference of American Rabbis and of a certain idea that the Reform rabbinate, or part of it, had of itself. It does not seem to have had much effect on the Jewish consciousness, let alone on the social reality. Looking back, some are inclined to think social justice was emphasized then not only because that was what America was thinking about but also to help the rabbis feel they were not superfluous. A friend of mine, ordained at a Reform seminary in the 1950s, has told me that a professor once explained to his students: "In those days we had rabbis of two sorts: there were the social-justice ones, and then there were the ones who knew Hebrew." (My friend speaks Hebrew with his children; and he was jailed in the South when jail was not yet fashionable.)

As it happens, the synagogue did have serious and important things to say then to Jews about social questions, but those were Jewish—notably antisemitism. We are thankful to have fewer such problems now, but we still have some: antisemitism in the Soviet Union and Poland, the incomplete disappearance of antisemitism in the United States, the curious rise of an antisemitism on the American Left. About these, most young Jews are not greatly concerned. They are likely to deny, impatiently, that such things exist. That is all so parochial, they say; so limited, so—so Jewy.

I have read to Jewish college students poems by LeRoi Jones which *mutatis mutandis* are Nazi, and have asked the students what they think. They look at me with bewilderment and incomprehension. What am I talking about? Why do I want to talk about antisemitism? What has it to do with them? Besides, Jones isn't really an antisemite. If he hates Jews who exploit, they deserve to be hated.

It is as though Hitler were no more recent than Haman.

For a universalist, antisemitism is not an important problem. There are few Jews in the world, and a universalist will worry about the problems of the many. Yet if you are a Jew, antisemitism can kill you though you are also a universalist. It killed Jewish universalists on the other side of the ocean in the other half of the century. If you think antisemitism unworthy of your notice, think again.

Much has changed, but here little has changed. A generation ago the fathers and uncles of the young critics were equally impatient. For them, antisemitism was a symptom, a by-product, of capitalism. To abolish antisemitism, you had first to abolish capitalism. You had first to institute socialism. Antisemitism was rampant in Germany, where capitalism had attained its pure or ultimate form of Nazism, and in the United States. In the Soviet Union antisemitism had been uprooted and had disappeared. Worrying about antisemitism only distracted you from what was really needed, the struggle against capitalism.

As we can see now, that reasoning was not exactly scientific. It proceeded from essence, or from definition: capitalism was wicked, producing wicked things, and socialism was good, producing good things. The logic was scholastic—decadent scholastic at that, not greatly different from the logic of decadent scholastic medicine that Molière allows us to overhear: *Quare opium facit dormire?—Quia habet quandam virtutem dormitivam.—Optime!* Why does opium put you to sleep?—Because it has a certain power that causes sleep. —Very good!

Today in the United States students wonder what you are talking about when you talk about antisemitism, but in the Soviet Union and Poland they know. In capitalist-Nazi Germany 600,000 Jews were held to be at the same time Bolsheviks and bankers, assuming those roles in a fearsome Jewish conspiracy to subvert the German nation and the Aryan race. In socialist-Marxist Poland the few thousand Jews are held to be at the same time Zionists, cosmopolitans, and Stalinists, assuming those roles in a fearsome Jewish conspiracy to subvert the Polish nation and its socialist order.

So the synagogue did not talk too much about antisemitism (Nazi and fascist) then. Maybe it is not talking enough about antisemitism (Soviet and leftist, and generally contemporary) now. But that is hardly the sort of thing that universalist critics normally mean by relevance.

Actually, are the critics saying that they are perplexed, that they do not know what to think or do about peace, race, poverty, and that they want the synagogue to advise and lead them? Not usually. They are saying that the synagogue should tell them what they want to hear, that it should support and strengthen them in what they are already doing. And they want the synogogue to transmit the truths understood by the enlightened to its members, so deficient in enlightenment.

A year or two ago I heard a scholar describe the typical sermon in an up-to-date American synagogue as the rabbi's review of a bestseller. He did not know what he was talking about, probably not having been in a synagogue in thirty years. The book-review sermon is not typical any more. When it was typical, that was because rabbi and congregation wanted to be relevant.

266

Relevance in the Synagogue

Can there be any similarity between social-action deeds and sermons, on the one hand, and popular book reviews, on the other? It may be said that popular book reviews are only an expression of what religionists themselves, especially such Christian theologians as H. Richard Niebuhr, condemn as culture religion (the anthropologists' culture, not Matthew Arnold's). Such religion, whatever it may call itself, is a tribal idolatry, echoing the prejudices and self-love of the secular community, whereas the duty of true religion is to stand apart and judge. Those who agree that book-review sermons were out of place in the thirties but insist that social-action sermons are needed now would transpose to the sphere of society and politics the distinction often made in literature and art between high culture (Arnold's) and popular culture: book-review sermons are bad, belonging to popular culture; social-action sermons are good, belonging to high social thought.

But escape is not that easy. Lionel Trilling has shown us how blurred the old distinctions have become. In the old days high culture was for the happy few, and the man who adhered to high culture could realistically see himself as set apart from the vulgar. That is no longer so. The adversary culture, as Trilling calls it, is now as established as what used to be the official, established culture: in that *New Yorker* cartoon the artist's girlfriend asks him, "Why must you be a nonconformist like everyone else?" Niebuhr's judgment can apply equally to religion that affirms what used to be the established culture and to religion that affirms what used to be the adversary culture; equally to religion that affirms popular politics and to religion that affirms adversary politics.

With Jews, what is more, adversary has long been as popular as popular. In the fifties how much courage did a rabbi really need, or how much distinctive moral leadership did he exercise, when he criticized Senator Joe McCarthy to his congregation? This year how much courage does he need, and how much leadership does he exercise, when he praises Senator Gene McCarthy?

The advice to be relevant comes most vocally from students and teachers. From them, is it good advice? Professor Leonard J. Fein has written:

Around the country, rabbinic groups and individual rabbis have spoken and speak vigorously on social issues. I applaud their vigor. I believe the community cries out for that sort of leadership. But . . . I do not believe that the image of the rabbi as a social-protest activist or as a literary critic is going to inspire either the students or the academic community. The rabbi, as he moves from his specific field of competence—which was, of course, always . . . Torah . . .—becomes a dilettante. . . . He must be *au courant* with literature, politics, psychology, sociology, history, anthropology . . . and necessarily dilettantish.

A sermon on Black Power . . . may be all the information a rabbi's congregants will get . . . and therefore he is obligated to give it. . . . If a student of mine came to me to find out about Black Power, I would either send him up to Tom Pettigrew at Harvard or I would urge him to take my seminar on race in America.

. . . the rabbi, in ministering to the needs of the pants manufacturers, is boring the academic. If he were to minister to the needs of the academic, he would violate his responsibilty to the pants manufacturers. That is what makes this a dilemma. . . .

But it may be worth suggesting what my conception of ministry to academics by rabbis might mean. . . . The rabbi as Judaic scholar becomes the peer of the academic, and only as Judaic scholar . . . whether by Judaic studies one means biblical exegesis or Jewish demography. . . . I would more readily attend a sermon on historical analogies to Old Testament literature, perhaps, than a sermon in which a rabbi purported to inform me about Black Power or, I might add, about Vietnam.

Professor Fein implies, but it remains to be said explicitly, that a rabbi speaking about or from Torah can also say something significant about Black Power or Vietnams—something that only he can say, and therefore that we must hear from him rather than from Pettigrew or Fein. No rabbi imagines that the Torah gives unequivocal commands about Black Power or Vietnam; yet, struggling with the problems or demands of this day, he can be helped by what the Torah says that is not of this day.

Once rabbis were not skeptical enough about the usefulness of sermons. Now they are too skeptical.

The synagogues I go to are not extraordinary. The rabbis who preach there are not the most famous, but they are good rabbis, and I hear good sermons from them. Usually the sermons instruct me, sometimes they stir me, and sometimes they move me to do what I might otherwise not want to do or lack the will to do.

One such sermon was about Negroes and Jews, and was taken seriously because the congregation knew that the rabbi takes antisemitism seriously, including the antisemitism of black nationalist intellectuals. The rabbi told us our attitude toward Negroes was wrong. It was like that line from *My Fair Lady*, Why can't a woman be more like a man? We ask, Why can't Negroes be more like Jews?

Relevance in the Synagogue

We should remember, he said, that in the Passover Haggadah the answer to the questions asked by the child begins, "We were slaves in Egypt." It is easier for slavery to produce a rabble than a people: the Torah tells us that many who left Egypt with Moses were *'erev rav* and *asafsuf*. Our ancestors had a revelation at Mount Sinai, and Ten Commandments. After having been so uniquely favored, they went on to the golden calf. If we insist on criticism of the Negroes, the rabbi concluded, it should be not that they are too little like the Jews, but too much.

Another sermon, by another rabbi, related even more directly to Passover. On the face of it, the sermon was unworldly, half ritual detail and half eschatology. The Prophetical lesson on the last day of Passover, from Isaiah, sees a transformation:

. . . There shall come forth a shoot from the stock of Jesse,/and a branch shall grow out of his root./And the spirit of the Lord shall rest upon him. . . ./with righteousness he shall judge the poor,/and decide with equity for the humble of the earth. . . ./The wolf shall dwell with the lamb,/and the leopard shall lie down with the kid,/and the calf and the lion and the fatling together,/and a little child shall lead them./The cow and the bear shall graze;/their young shall lie down together; and the lion shall eat straw like the ox./The sucklng child shall play over the hole of the asp,/ and the weaned child shall put his hand on the adder's den./They shall not hurt nor destroy/in all My holy mountain;/for the earth shall be full of the knowledge of the Lord/as the waters cover the sea./. . . and there will be a highway for the remnant of His people/that remains from Assyria,/as there was for Israel/when they came up from the land of Egypt./. . . with joy you will draw water from the wells of salvation./And you will say in that day:/"Give thanks to the Lord,/call upon His name;/ make known His deeds among the nations,/proclaim that His name is exalted. . . ./Shout, and sing for joy, O inhabitant of Zion,/for great in your midst is the Holy One of Israel.

The rabbi told us that there is a link between that prophecy and a kabbalistic usage in the Seder. When we break the middle matzah we put aside the larger half for the *afiqoman*: first we eat the smaller half and only later do we eat the larger. This is to signify that the future redemption will be greater than the redemption Passover celebrates, of the Jews from Egyptian slavery. There is yet to come the redemption of all men, and of nature itself, from the slavery of hurting, destroying, and ignorance of the Lord. Our Past Passover (*Pesaḥ de-'avar*) is of the lesser redemption. The Future Passover (*Pesaḥ de-'atid*) will be of the greater redemption. Celebrating the Past Passover, we long for the Future Passover. Prefiguring the Future Passover, we do the little we can—which is all we can—to lessen hurting, destroying, and ignorance.

The third rabbi has a sermon he repeats from time to time, with variations, about America, the Jews, and Jewish education. In America, he says, more than in any other country where Jews have lived as a minority, we enjoy freedom and opportunity without having to pay the price of abandoning Judaism. What we shall make of ourselves depends entirely on us. Precisely because America is so accepting, many are tempted to forget about Judaism—to want the best colleges for their children while being content with a few years of Sunday school, or not even that. In quality and quantity, Jewish education must begin to match our ever-rising general education. Our responsibility, he concludes, is to assure Jewish education for our children (and ourselves).

None of these sermons is irrelevant. All, in different proportions of universalism and particularism, speak directly to us. They are relevant in the synagogue for the very reason that they would not be relevant anywhere else. If we did not hear them there, we would not hear them anywhere. The synagogue in which they are preached and the rabbi who preaches them are not irrelevant.

Now to return to what was mentioned earlier: on the whole, the critics ignore the simple, big fact that America is a Christian country. What it amounts to is that they ask the synagogue to behave as if most Americans were Jews. Asking synagogues to pretend they are the majority church does not mean asking them to be more relevant. It means asking them to be more irrelevant. (Now, in Israel it would be different.)

Whether as individuals or through our institutions, we enter into programs for dealing with racial inequities as if the relation of white Jews to Negroes were the same as of white Christians to Negroes. But most Negroes are, or have been, Christians. That must be our starting point. What would a Jewish congregation's remedial-reading program for Christian Negro children amount to? Would Negroes not see it as Lady Bountiful's condescension? Of that they have had all they want. But might they not feel differently if they were members of the congregation, or invited to become members?

People have been asking why there are not more black faces in insurance offices, or in TV commercials. The synagogue's critics ought to be asking why there are not more black faces in Jewish congregations. And if that is for the future, right now there is a real problem that we are not dealing with as we should be. There are some black Jews in the United States. On the whole, the overwhelmingly white synagogue has not done nearly enough to welcome them. If there are black Jews who are also black nationalists, the synagogue has not done nearly enough to talk with them.

The coin has two sides. It is true, as the critics say, that the synagogue should do more to condemn the exploitation of Negroes by Jewish merchants (or landlords, or employers). It is also true, as the critics usually do not say, that the synagogue should be indignant about having merchants identified as Jews. Granted, arguendo, that those merchants are exploiters and that they are Jews. Are they merchants who exploit or Jews who exploit? And in fact, is everyone an exploiter who is so accused? Everyone? Is everything done against him justified? Everything? The synagogue would ask these questions if the accusers, or those in whose name the accusation was made, were white. It must ask these questions if the accusers are black.

Provincialism can be of time as well as of geographical space or culture. In that sense, some of the synagogue's critics are provincial. They want it to be relevant to our time, but its time is not ours alone. The synagogue's time is also liturgical time. It corresponds in a way to "seedtime and harvest, cold and heat, summer and winter, day and night"—which "shall not cease," we have been promised, "so long as the earth endures." If one wishes, it is cyclical time rather than linear. (The cycles are short: daily, weekly, yearly.) In the synagogue's rhythm of liturgical time, it is being relevant to non-linear needs. Not that the synagogue's time isn't linear or contemporary at all; just that it also consists of Sabbath and weekday, feast and fast, morning and evening.

The critics' objections to the synagogue are temporally provincial, too, in making the assumptions of our time. For us these are axioms. We assume that only innovation and "creativity" count, forgetting that most of what we do is not that sort of thing at all. Mostly, we work to hold the wilderness at bay, to preserve a clearing in the woods, to keep things going: making the beds, stopping the leak, mowing the lawn, delivering the mail and milk. Eric Hoffer calls this maintenance, and can be lyrical about it. Without maintenance, what would happen to our houses, schools, factories, farms? The cyclical time of the synagogue is something like maintenance. It is not innovative, it is merely sustaining—and altogether necessary, and worthy of honor and respect. If maintenance may be said to be feminine, and innovation (like adventure) masculine, then the synagogue, though classically it has been an institution of men, may be said to be in part a feminine institution. Is that wrong?

A girl says, "You go to the synagogue for a dance or to pray, but you never consider going there [for] social action. . . ." No Hebrew school when you were a child; no adult education (including lectures about civil rights); no meetings to protest Soviet antisemitism? And why equate prayer and a dance? If your grandfather and *his* grandfather had not prayed in a synagogue, what makes you so sure you would be so zealous for social action? Young Jews are a small fraction of all young Americans, but an appreciably bigger one of all young Americans who worry about and do social action. The synagogue—Judaism—is not a sufficient explanation of that; but neither is any explanation sufficient which disregards the synagogue. And the social action of Jews does not have to take place in a synagogue building.

There is another way in which the synagogue could fail us by being too much of our time. We would love democracy shallowly if we did not realize how problematic it is. If we took democracy as self-evidently best, we could not hope to understand what Churchill meant when he said that democracy is the worst of all forms of government—except any other form that has ever been tried. We could not understand Bishop Stubbs saying that feudalism would be best, if men were angels and archangels. We could not respond to the Shakespeare who says:

> . . . O! when degree is shak'd,/Which is the ladder to all high designs,/ The enterprise is sick. How could communities,/. . . But by degree, stand in authentic place?/Take but degree away, untune that string,/And, hark! what discord follows; each thing meets/In mere oppugnancy. . . .

Shakespeare our contemporary, yes. And our ancestor. The synagogue is, it has to be, our contemporary and our ancestor.

Perhaps because of the season, Passover is on my mind; or perhaps because Passover is central to the Jewish experience and imagination. At the time of the revolution of 1848, the leading Jewish educator in Germany was Samuel Ehrenberg (the great-grandfather of Franz Rosenzweig and his Lutheran cousins). Exulting in the emancipations decreed by the revolution, Ehrenberg wanted to remove from the Haggadah the passage which reads, "Now we are slaves, next year may we be free men." He was trying to make the synagogue relevant. Could anything have been more irrelevant?

Even politically, it is still too soon for us to stop saying, "Now we are slaves." And beyond politics, not until the Future Passover will we stop being slaves (or enslaved, or slavish). Despite Israeli independence, for which God be thanked, those Orthodox are right who say that only the Future Passover will abolish the fast of the Ninth of Av, which laments exile. The Jews' physical or political exile may be passing—let us hope so—but the passing of the exile of Adam's children from Eden is not yet on the horizon. Until then, on Passover let us say that now we are slaves and on the Ninth of Av let us lament exile, and let contemporaries think all that to be irrelevant.

On *Shabbat Ha-gadol*, the Sabbath before Passover, we read the last verses of the last Prophet, Malachi: "Behold, I will send you Elijah the prophet before the great and terrible day of the Lord comes. And he will turn the heart of the fathers back to the sons, and the heart of the sons back to their fathers, in order that I may not come and smite the land with a curse. (Behold I will send you Elijah the prophet before the great and terrible day of the Lord comes.)" Elijah is the forerunner of the Messiah. Only Elijah or the Messiah can bring about a full reconciliation of fathers with sons; only the Future Passover. In the meantime, hoping for as much reconciliation as we are capable of, we are resigned to some separation.

If the fathers are also taken to represent history (the past, tradition), and the sons to represent contemporaneity (the present, relevance), we must conclude that until the Messiah comes we have to live, uneasily, with both. Since it is not the characteristic temptation of our generations to slight the present in favor of the past, for us a call to present relevance may not be the needful thing. For us the needful thing may be to remember that relevance, unlike ripeness, is not all.

—*May 1968*

. **38** .

Yom Kippur in Nineveh

Reading the Torah is the heart of the synagogue service. That, even more than prayer, was what the synagogue was invented for, probably during the Babylonian Exile 2,500 years ago. Reading and expounding the Torah are so much the central purpose of the synagogue that the "dim religious light" of stained-glass windows is not for us. "Let there be light" is more like it.

What part of the Pentateuch shall be read on an ordinary Sabbath is determined by its place in the annual cycle—which over the centuries slowly replaced a triennial cycle—from Genesis 1:1 to Deuteronomy 34:12. For holy days, whether falling on a Sabbath or not, it was the Rabbis (and their predecessors) who determined what the Pentateuchal lesson should be, the principle then being appropriateness rather than sequence. When the *haftarah*, the Prophetical lesson following the Pentateuchal one, was instituted, it was apparently for the reader to choose. (Luke has Jesus given the book of Isaiah to read from on a Sabbath, but in the book Jesus reads what he wishes.) Gradually the Rabbis fixed the *haftarot* for certain days, and finally for all. For Yom Kippur, the most solemn day in the Jewish calendar, the Rabbis must have fixed the Prophetical lesson early.

Everything about the Yom Kippur Scriptures is unusual or unique. On Yom Kippur there is a full reading in the afternoon as well as the morning. On Yom Kippur a *haftarah* consists of an entire book, Jonah—followed by three verses from Micah. (The five *Megillot*, which severally are read on the Pilgrimage Festivals, the Ninth of Av, and Purim, are not *haftarot* or even Prophetical, but Writings; and though Obadiah, only twenty-one verses long altogether, is read by Sephardim on a Sabbath shortly before Hanukkah, Ashkenazim are then reading from Hosea.) On Yom Kippur the afternoon *haftarah* is longer than the Pentateuchal lesson. And on Yom Kippur the *haftarot* appear to contradict the Pentateuchal lessons they follow, instead of paralleling them. The Yom Kippur readings call attention to themselves in an especially emphatic way.

The morning Pentateuchal lesson, priestly and ritualistic, consists of Leviticus 16 and Numbers 29:7–11, which the Mishnah Yoma tells us the High Priest used to read or recite in the Second Temple on Yom Kippur. All of Yoma, until nearly the end, is in the same spirit, full of slaughterings and countings and sprinklings—one, one and one, one and two, one and three . . . one and seven; from above downward, except when from below upward; from northeast to northwest to southwest to southeast. But the Rabbis, who codified those laws and who ordained that those numbing passages from the Pentateuch should be read in our synagogues, also selected Isaiah 57:14–58:14 for the Prophetical accompaniment:

Yom Kippur in Nineveh

... For thus says the high and lofty One who inhabits eternity, whose name is Holy: I dwell in the high and lofty place, and also with him who is of a contrite and humble spirit. ... Is not this the fast that I choose: to loose the bonds of wickedness, to undo the thongs of the yoke, to let the oppressed go free, and to break every yoke? Is it not to share your bread with the hungry, and bring the homeless poor into your home; when you see the naked, to cover him, and not to hide yourself from your own flesh? ... Then you shall call, and the Lord will answer; you shall cry, and He will say, Here I am.

I have said that Isaiah appears to contradict the Pentateuch's priestly ritualism, but that is a modern's bias. The Rabbis saw no contradiction, only completion. In the last paragraph of Yoma they have the same kind of contradiction-completion to their own ritualism:

If a man says, "I shall sin and repent, and sin again and repent again," he will be given no chance to repent. If he says, "I will sin and the Day of Atonement will effect atonement," then the Day of Atonement effects no atonement. For transgressions that are between man and God the Day of Atonement effects atonement, but for transgressions that are between a man and his fellow the Day of Atonement effects atonement only if he has satisfied his fellow.

The Rabbis were serious about every last detail of the ritual, but they were as explicit as they could be that all that was nothing without the right inward disposition and the right conduct. So they made the reading about loosing the bonds of wickedness follow the reading about bullocks, goats, and incense; and in our Rabbinical prayer service we say: "Repentance, prayer, and works of justice and mercy [*zedaqah*] can avert the harsh judgment."

The afternoon readings are more enigmatic: Pentateuch—Leviticus 18; Prophet—Jonah, followed by Micah 7:18–20. In the morning the Pentateuchal lesson stated the ritual laws and the Prophetical lesson the spiritual or moral laws. But Leviticus 18 is about chastity and unchastity, and why single that out for Yom Kippur? And what has Jonah to do either with that or with the day?

Leviticus 18 is a unit of three parts. Exordium (five verses):

... You shall not do as they do in the land of Egypt, where you dwelt, and you shall not do as they do in the land of Canaan, to which I am bringing you. You shall not walk in their statutes. ... You shall ... keep my statutes and my ordinances, by doing which a man shall live: I am the Lord.

Body (eighteen verses): Incest is defined by enumeration and prohibited, including marriage with living sisters, and prohibitions then follow against lying with a menstruous woman, adultery, child sacrifice, sodomy, and bestiality.

Peroration (seven verses):

Do not defile yourselves by any of these things, for by all these the nations I am casting out before you defiled themselves; and the land became defiled, so that I punished its iniquity and the land vomited out its inhabitants. But you shall keep my statutes and my ordinances and do none of these abominations . . . lest the land vomit you out, when you defile it. . . . So keep my charge never to practice any of these abominable customs which were practiced before you, and never to defile yourselves by them: I am the Lord your God.

The Rabbis did not pick this chapter to remind us that it is wholesome family life which has sustained the Jews, as one embarrassed editor-translator writes. Leviticus 18 is there for more compelling reasons.

Whether or not those scholars are right who think that Rosh Hashanah, Yom Kippur, and Sukkot (which begins five days after Yom Kippur) were originally one holiday, the month of Tishri, in which they fall, was the time of harvest and autumnal equinox. In the ancient world, and even in much more modern times, to celebrate the New Year of harvest and equinox with due rites would amount to what the Rabbis euphemistically called *qallut rosh*, levity. In a well-known passage in the Talmudic tractate Sukkah an old source says that the authorities had to try three ways of separating the sexes in the Temple before they were able to prevent *qallut rosh*, and in an equally well-known passage in the Mishnah Ta'anit we are told that on Yom Kippur itself the daughters of Jerusalem used to dance a courtship dance before the young men. While that is said approvingly —they are nice Jewish girls, exhorting the young men to consider family, not beauty—at an earlier time the character of the season's jollity had disgusted the prophets. On Sukkot, in the Second Temple, there were water libations and torchlight processions, which are unmistakable fertility rites. (On one famous occasion, a Sadducee priest-king's contempt for the libation provoked a riot, which he suppressed with great cruelty. The Pharisees favored the rite, not for its intrinsic merit but because they upheld the Unwritten Law—i.e., tradition—in principle.) Tishri was a time for being wary of fertility celebrations.

• • •

Yom Kippur in Nineveh

Theologically, Leviticus 18 is about paganism. It insists that pagans—Egyptians, Canaanites—are unchaste and depraved because their religion commands them to be, not because it fails to restrain them: to "do these abominations" and "practice these abominable customs" *are* "their statutes." For the Bible, and the Rabbis, unchastity and depravity are the piety of paganism.

Were the Bible and the Rabbis unfair? We know that brother-sister marriage was an honored tradition of Egyptian royalty. We know that male cult-prostitutes—*qedeshim*, related to *qadosh*, "holy"!; "sodomites" in the King James and Jewish Publication Society versions—were an honored class of the Canaanite temple personnel. They are forbidden in Deuteronomy, where they are also called dogs and an abomination to the Lord, but in II Kings we learn that when King Josiah of Judah reformed the Temple, "he broke down the houses of the *qedeshim* which were in the House of the Lord." The scholars quote Lucian of Samosata as reporting that in the second century of our era the services of *qedeshim* were still a "very sacred custom" for the pious pagans of Hierapolis, in Syria.

In Numbers, the Israelites "began to play the harlot with the daughters of Moab. These invited the people to the sacrifices of their gods, and the people ate and bowed down to their gods." Here, as commonly in the Bible, *zanah*, "to play the harlot," is both literal and figurative. A standard metaphor for infidelity to God is marital infidelity.

But the decisive proof that Leviticus 18 is concerned with paganism rather than with sexuality as such is its prohibition of child sacrifice, in the center of the five prohibitions after the long, multiple prohibition of incest, and the only of them ending with "I am the Lord." It was not by fun and games alone that pagans celebrated or invoked fertility. Robert Graves has made us aware of this for ancient Greece, and essentially the same paganism, i.e., fertility religion, prevailed throughout the Mediterranean. The Carthaginians, who still called themselves Canaanites in St. Augustine's time, sacrificed human beings well into the Rabbinic and Christian period, centuries after their conquest by Rome. Kings and founders of cities, of course, were under a special obligation to assure the fertility of their people, the fertility of livestock and crops, and the general well-being. In II Kings, when Mesha, king of Moab, saw that his battle with the Israelites was going against him, "he took his eldest son who was to reign in his stead, and offered him for a burnt offering upon the wall." Kings Ahaz and Manasseh of Judah—both, especially Manasseh, under pagan influence—burned their sons as offerings. The prophets repeatedly accuse paganizing commoners, too, of sacrificing their children.

That seems to have been true also of the popular, loyal, unpagan Israelite religion, when it was yet unaffected by prophets or reformers and as it was practiced before the Babylonian Exile. Jephthah sacrificed his daughter to keep a vow to the Lord, as the pagan Agamemnon was prepared to sacrifice his daughter Iphigenia to Artemis at Aulis. When Hiel rebuilt Jericho, "he laid its foundations at the cost of . . . his first-born, and set up its gates at the cost of his youngest son." Above all, there is that dark saying in Ezekiel: "Moreover I gave them statutes that were not good and ordinances by which they could not have life; and I defiled them through their very gifts in making them offer by fire all their first-born . . ." (Micah 6:7 suggests the same).

The most probable time for the choice of Leviticus 18 as a Yom Kippur reading, therefore, was the period of or soon after Ezra and Nehemiah, the latter part of the fifth century B.C.E. Fertility religion was then not merely a vestige or a memory, as it was to be in Rabbinic times. It was an ever-present danger, the faith and practice of those who had not gone into exile—the Old Believers, as we might call them—and of the local women whom the returning Judaeans first married and then were forced to banish as seductresses. This Yom Kippur reading, further, is linked to the Rosh Ha-shanah reading(s), which must have been fixed at the same time—the account in Genesis of the Binding of Isaac and God's command to our father Abraham to sacrifice not his son, but a ram. It did not trouble the (post-)Ezranic religious authorities that by the standards of Leviticus 18, to which they themselves gave such prominence, Jacob was guilty of incest in marrying two living sisters, Leah and Rachel. Their indifference is further proof that the unchastity or depravity they were condemning was not, or not only, the ordinary kind, but pagan "statutes." Obviously, no one could think of Jacob as a pagan.

This does not explain Jonah as the afternoon *haftarah*. To be sure, there is a lexical tie between Leviticus 18 and Jonah, in that between them they have the verb *qy'*, "to vomit" or "to spew," four of the six times it occurs in the Pentateuch and Prophets (nine in the entire Bible). Sometimes that sort of thing seems to be the only reason why a *haftarah* was chosen—e.g., Hosea 2:1–22 for Numbers 1:1–4:20, which do not have much more in common than the noun *mispar*, "number," and the verb *paqad*, "to count" in Numbers and "to punish" in Hosea—but Yom Kippur would require a better link. If the intention was to choose a Prophetical lesson that would strengthen the Pentateuchal denunciation of unchastity-depravity-paganism, other Prophetical passages are more appropriate than Jonah—passages from Hosea or Jeremiah, for instance.

It does not matter whether, as most scholars believe, Jonah is late, dating from the fifth or fourth century b.c.e., or, as Ezekiel Kaufmann argues, considerably earlier. It does not matter that its Nineveh is an abstraction and not the real capital of Assyria that was destroyed late in the seventh century b.c.e. For the Rabbis it was the book of Jonah the son of Amittai, the prophet of the Lord mentioned in II Kings. Jonah is not about the great fish. It is about God's eagerness for the repentance of men and women, so that He may forgive them—not Jews alone, but pagans also, and not ordinary pagans, but Assyrians, "the rod of My anger," the scourge of the ancient world who destroyed the Northern Kingdom, exiled the ten tribes, besieged Jerusalem, and devastated Judah. God wants Jonah to summon Nineveh to repent and live, Jonah flees, and God, plucking Jonah from his ship, makes him go and preach. The Ninevites fast, repent, and are saved. Jonah, then, is about fasting, repentance, and salvation. So is Yom Kippur.

Whoever the author of Jonah was, and whenever he lived, he must have wanted his readers to think of Abraham too, and especially of Moses and the exodus from Egypt. Jonah identifies himself to the sailors in a puzzling and striking way: "I am a Hebrew." The only other personages the Bible calls Hebrews are Abraham, Joseph, and Moses: it was to Abraham that child sacrifice was first forbidden, and Joseph is linked to Moses in that the first leads the Israelites into Egypt and the second leads them out. Just before the exodus the last of the ten plagues strikes the Egyptians in the death of their first-born, "from the first-born of Pharaoh who sat on his throne to the first-born of the captive who was in the dungeon, and all the first-born of the cattle." The only other place in the Bible with that peculiar threefold composition of society—king, commoners, and cattle— is Jonah; but in Jonah the three classes fast, repent, and pray, and are saved.

Passover, the exodus festival, is in Nisan, and Rosh Ha-shanah, Yom Kippur, and Sukkot are in Tishri. Tishri, as we have seen, is the time of a harvest and the autumnal equinox; and Nisan is the time of another harvest, of lambing, and of the vernal equinox. A Passover Pentateuch lesson tells of the death of the Egyptian first-born, to which the Yom Kippur *haftarah* of Jonah seems to refer, negatively, by stressing that God spared the Assyrians; and a Passover *haftarah* tells how King Josiah purged the Temple of its *qedeshim*, which seems to refer to the Pentateuch read on Yom Kippur afternoon. Further, Yom Kippur is about salvation and redemption, and the great historical event and paradigm of redemption is the exodus from Egypt, which Passover celebrates.

There is still another reason why the Pharisees, or their predecessors, were conscious of Passover when they decided the Scripture to be read on Yom Kippur. Egypt was an urgent political reality for them. After Alexander the Great died, his general Ptolemy became king of Egypt and his general Seleucus king of Syria and, for a time, Mesopotamia. Judaea, contested and fought over by the two dynasties, in the third century B.C.E. was under the Ptolemies and in the first third of the second century under the Seleucids, each uneasy about the Jews' allegiance. A famous article by Louis Finkelstein in the *Harvard Theological Review* recalls those imperial rivalries to date the curious passage in the Passover Haggadah which says that Laban the Aramean, Jacob's uncle and the father of his two wives, was worse than Pharaoh. Since Laban has nothing to do with Egypt and the exodus, what is he doing in the Haggadah? And why is it insisted that he was worse than Pharaoh? For the Ptolemies, Passover must have seemed anti-Egyptian. Laban is "the Aramean," i.e., Syrian, and proclaiming the wickedness of the archetypal Syrian was an attempt to reassure the Egyptian Ptolemies about the Jews. Hence that part of the Haggadah must be from the third century B.C.E. On the other hand, Dr. Finkelstein writes in a later article in the same journal, the Haggadah's quotation of Joshua's epitome of God's dealings with Abraham, Isaac, Jacob, and their descendants, which emphasizes the patriarchs' Mesopotamian origins, must be a pro-Seleucid gesture, and is to be dated in the first third of the second century B.C.E.

In Hellenistic times, as for Herodotus earlier, "Assyria" was thought to be a variant of "Syria," and to the Seleucids Jonah on Yom Kippur must have been as reassuring as Joshua on Passover. The Yom Kippur afternoon Pentateuch has the Egyptians as an example of abominable vice, while the *haftarah* shows that the God of the Jews loves the (As)syrians. Jonah as a Yom Kippur *haftarah*, therefore, may also date from the first third of the second century B.C.E.

• • •

Yom Kippur in Nineveh

The Rabbis—to use an anachronistic term for convenience—had to reckon with suspicious foreign rulers, but they must have longed for that verse in Isaiah to become a present reality: "Blessed be Egypt My people, and Assyria the work of My hands, and Israel My heritage." It was they who chose Jonah as a Yom Kippur *haftarah*, and ideologically Jonah is universalist rather than particularist.

Jonah ends with God saying: "And should not I pity Nineveh, that great city, in which there are more than a hundred and twenty thousand persons who do not know their right hand from their left, and also much cattle?" In the *haftarah* the Rabbis append to this the final three verses of Micah, of which the last is: "Thou wilt show faithfulness to Jacob and steadfast love to Abraham,/as Thou hast sworn to our fathers from the days of old." If it is possible for Assyrians to be forgiven—pagans par excellence, and therefore practicers par excellence of all the abominations forbidden in Leviticus—how much more possible it must be for Jews!

The Rabbis regard themselves as being in the line of descent from Ezra and Nehemiah, the particularists who invoked Deuteronomy's injunction that "no Ammonite or Moabite shall enter the assembly of the Lord, even to the tenth generation" to make the Judeans banish their foreign wives; but it was the Rabbis who selected Ruth for reading in the synagogue on Shavu'ot, and many scholars consider Ruth, together with Jonah and parts of Isaiah, to be a polemic against the narrowness of Ezra-Nehemiah. "Ruth the Moabitess" she is called, five times; and we are told that she is to be the great-grandmother of David, the king whose scion will be the Messiah. The book ends with "David."

For the Rabbis, Jonah's "much cattle" must have reinforced "persons who do not know their right hand from their left." It would be too much to say that the Rabbis had a doctrine of sin that derived sin from ignorance or folly alone; but on Yom Kippur they were satisfied to plead ignorance, before the Tribunal on high, in extenuation of the people's sins. The last verse of Jonah echoes the verse from Numbers that is constantly repeated in the Yom Kippur service: "And all the congregation of the children of Israel shall be forgiven, and the stranger who sojourns among them, because the whole people did erroneously."

Is all this what the Rabbis really meant, or only what we would like them to have meant? The Mishnah being the Rabbis' own codification of the law, let the Mishnah decide. We have seen that toward the end of Yoma the Rabbis teach that Yom Kippur is nothing without true repentance and that while God will forgive us for our intentions, it is by deeds that we must win the forgiveness of our fellows. And then, at the very end, we read:

R. Akiba said, Happy are you, O Israel! Before whom are you made clean, and who cleanses you? Your Father who is in heaven; as it is said [Ezekiel 36:25], "I will sprinkle clean water upon you, and you shall be clean." And it further says [Jeremiah 17:13], "O Lord, the hope [*miqweh*] of Israel." As the *miqweh* [immersion pool for lustration] cleanses the unclean, so does the Holy One, blessed be He, cleanse Israel.

It has been argued that this is a later addition, missing from an early manuscript and inserted for the traditional purpose of ending a text with *divre nehamah*, words of consolation, in the same way that Amos, for instance, is made to end in words of consolation and Pirqe Avot in the verse from Exodus: "The Lord shall reign for ever and ever"; or for the purpose of ending with *aggadah*, the easier, non-legal dicta, rather than *halakhah*, the difficult legal matter. But George Foot Moore considered this text to be authentic, and *he* was guided by Louis Ginzberg. In any event, R. Akiba's saying is faithful to the Rabbinical spirit, down to the ritualization of the hope-*miqweh* and the spiritualization of the bath-*miqweh*. That is yet another contradiction-completion, like making Jonah follow Leviticus 18.

It is also like the relation between the 'Avodah and the 'Al ḥet in our Yom Kippur service. The 'Avodah—work, service, cultus—is a kind of long, versified paraphrase of Yoma, recalling the Temple and the sacrifices in detail. To pious Jews through the centuries, its recitation this day in the synagogue, on the principle of "so will we render for bullocks the offerings of our lips" (Hosea, JPS version), was an exalting thing, hard as that may be for us to believe. But over and over we also say the 'Al ḥet, the long, inclusive *nostra culpa*. The 'Al ḥet does not mention one ritual transgression. ("Eating and drinking" probably refers to intemperance rather than violations of *kashrut*.) The offense that recurs in it most often, under many synonyms, is *leshon ha-ra'*, an "evil tongue."

After two thousand years of liturgical expansion, the basic structure and intent of our Yom Kippur service remain what they were in the time of the Rabbis. The last word is still Akiba's.

—*September 1962*

· 39 ·

Paganism

Jews—most Jews—are modern, enlightened. Judaism is not. By Judaism I mean, for instance, the synagogue on Yom Kippur. Even of those of us who were in the synagogue on Yom Kippur, probably few are all that different from the ones who stayed away. How many really believed what we heard, read, and recited then? We are too modern. And because we are modern, we are apt to be dubious about religion. Not for scientific or philosophical reasons—most of us are not philosophers or scientists. You and I have neither the intellect nor the training to choose between Bertrand Russell and Father D'Arcy when they debate about God. What do you and I know about the ontological proof, let alone the history and present status of the argument over it? Of course we know that science is supposed to have disproved God, or religion; but then what do you or I say to an Orthodox Jewish physicist or biologist?

What you and I give weight to and feel confident about is the so-called anthropological argument, the argument from human nature and history. We judge religion by its human effects, and we do not like what we think it has done to men and women and to society. There are worse ways to judge.

What are those bad things that religion does? In antiquity Epicurus hated religion—the pagan religion he knew—for terrifying people and robbing them of peace of mind. The most complete extant statement of Epicureanism is the De Rerum Natura of the Roman Lucretius; and Professor Peter Gay, who admires the eighteenth-century Enlightenment, tells us that Lucretius was one of its two favorite classical authors. (The other was Cicero.) With ancient Epicureanism, the Enlightenment agrees that religion makes people unhappy and cruel. Lucretius lamented that *tantum religio potuit suadere malorum,* religion has been able to stir up so much evil; and the Enlightenment had its own confirming memories and experience. Additionally, the Enlightenment accused religion—Christianity, and the Judaism at its root—of despising reason, slandering human nature, and teaching a harmful sexual ethic.

Formally, at least, most of us have not moved much beyond that bill of particulars. Yet for us the criticism has become less appropriate, less evidently a matter of good faith. The original criticism of religion can now be more validly directed against what is left of the Enlightenment in our late-twentieth-century hands. As with Epicurus's peace-of-mind argument, so with the later ones: the positions have been reversed. Only, after the reversals we still feel superior to religion.

For Epicurus, religion is bad because it robs us of peace of mind; if it gave us peace of mind, it would be good. For moderns, religion gives peace of mind, and therefore is childish. For moderns, religion stands in the way of a lucid maturity—our recognizing that the universe is indifferent or actually hostile to human needs, values, and yearnings. In Russell's "Free Man's Worship," the free man refuses to delude or beguile himself. Things are as they are, and they do not make for peace of mind. So much do we take all this for granted that the better class of religionists are embarrassed by Norman Vincent Peale and Joshua Loth Liebman—remember them?—and vie with the proudly despairing atheists in contempt for peace of mind.

Persecution, hate, division? To blame religion alone, now, is a feeble joke. We know what else causes them: race, or nationality, or tribe, or caste, or class, or language, or ideology, or greed. Or simple bloody-mindedness.

The Enlightenment liked to say that Judaism invented intolerance, the mother of pious extirpations and burnings at the stake. At the same time, the Enlightenment greatly admired Rome, and the Latin authors more than the Greek. This was not only an inferior literary and intellectual taste. It was also political. The French Revolution had a cult of Roman republicanism.

The enlightened could blame the Book of Joshua for teaching the West to kill unbelievers: if not for those dreadful Jewish examples in Palestine three thousand years ago, Europe would have been spared later horrors. None chose to remember the republican Romans' coldly expedient genocide of their kin, the Samnites, carried out in the full light of history. None thought to ask why not one Roman writer had ever expressed doubt or regret about that genocide—or, for that matter, why no European humanist had ever expressed doubt or regret. Only in our time do the Romans seem to have first been indicted for the Samnite genocide. And—ironically—only the Bible criticism that arose after the Enlightenment knows that Joshua is not very historical.

Paganism

For the eighteenth-century enlightened, the jealous Jewish God had to be blameworthy and the Romans' tolerant paganism had to be praiseworthy. For us, to the evidence from ancient pagan history can be added all those fine modern things that have happened in our own century, after the decline of religion. That makes no difference. We continue to blame religion.

Religion is the enemy of reason—so the Enlightenment taught and so we still believe. Or rather, we take the trouble to believe it in the part of ourselves that still honors reason. In the greater part of ourselves, reason bores us. Two hundred years after the Enlightenment, its heirs celebrate their independence not from rationalism—for the Enlightenment was as much empiricist as rationalist—but from rationality itself. The professors tell us that the campus rebels are among the most intelligent students of all, and maybe the French and German professors say that about their campus rebels. Of those heirs of the Enlightenment the implicit slogan is "logic, shmogic." In the old days the enlightened could not find language contemptuous enough for the religious *sacrificium intellectus*. Now the campus is as fertile in myth as any conventionally preliterate culture.

The distinction between reason and unreason is called artificial, and the very concept of insanity a gimmick for imprisoning spontaneity or vision. To some in the New Left, Rabbi Morris Adler's murderer was not deranged and sick; he is a political hero, fallen in the struggle against bourgeois hypocrisy. Liberalism is fascism, permissiveness is repression—so says an elite of the intelligent and educated in the West. (In Prague and Warsaw the intellectuals are not amused.) Compared with some of the elite, it is the ignorant who seem positively addicted to reason: as a certain comedian used to say, "You can't fool me, I'm too ignorant." Professor Huston Smith has written:

> . . . as the weeks moved on . . . the students' true interests surfaced.
> . . . I cannot recall the exact progression of topics, but it went something like this: Beginning with Asian philosophy, it moved on to meditation, then yoga, then Zen, then Tibet, then successively to the *Bardo Thodol*, tantra, the kundalini, the chakras, the *I Ching*, karati and aikido, the yang-yin macrobiotic (brown rice) diet, Gurdjieff, Maher Baba, astrology, astral bodies, auras, UFO's, Tarot cards, parapsychology, witchcraft, and magic. And, underlying everything, of course, the psychedelic drugs. Nor were the students dallying with these subjects. They were *on* the drugs; they were eating brown rice; they were meditating hours on end; they were making their decisions by *I Ching* divination, which one student designated

the most important discovery of his life; they were constructing complicated electronic experiments to prove that their thoughts, via psychokinesis, could affect matter directly.

And they weren't plebeians. Intellectually they were aristocrats with the highest average math scores in the land, Ivy League verbal scores, and two to three years of saturation in MIT science.

I do not doubt it for a minute. Those were not low-I.Q. types, in that Washington march, who performed their Tibetan rites of exorcism against the Pentagon. And those others in the march, who would not be so gauche as to snicker, were not low-I.Q. types either. If only I could forget how Paul Massing's *Rehearsal for Destruction* describes a group of the intellectual forebears of Nazism in the generation before World War I: emancipated, educated or semieducated food faddists, naturists, spiritualists, lovers of conspiracy theories, *et hoc genus omne*. Massing's subjects were on the Right, while Professor Smith's (and Norman Mailer's) are on the Left. That is supposed to reassure us.

For two hundred years liberals and radicals have agreed that traditional Christianity maligns human nature; and insofar as traditional Judaism has been thought of at all, it too has been judged guilty of lese humanity. Voltaire said that Pascal had taught men to hate themselves, whereas they ought to learn to love themselves. A generation or so later, in Boston, one of the Eliots—they are still prominently associated with Unitarianism—wrote to a relative of hers, in sufficient explanation of her departure from the old, Calvinist ways, and above all from the doctrine of total depravity: "Eliza, do you kneel down in church and call yourself a miserable sinner? Neither I nor any of my family will ever do that." Yet today Voltaire's disciples are respectful about Pascal—less the Pascal who honored God, of course, than the one who was unimpressed by man.

Actually, it is not clear how many descendants Voltaire has left. Sade probably has more. To say so may distress the proper members of the Enlightenment family, but Sade *is* in the genealogy. If it is true that the new young's philosophy of life can be summarized in the question, "Why not?", then Sade is the obvious ancestor. The God-is-dead theologians may not know it, but before Nietzsche it was Sade who declared (repeatedly, Professor Robert E. Taylor informs me), "God is dead, and anything goes": *Dieu est mort, et tout est permis*. In the contemporary theater there is a serious play that takes Sade seriously. From Sade descend *Story of O* and Genet and others as well. Does their idea about humanity teach us to love ourselves? Even Calvinism is likelier to do that than our art is. Calvinism insists that a human being is a miserable sinner. At least this can be said for a miserable sinner, that he has a soul and was created in an image of some dignity.

In these days, if any thinker tells us good things about humanity, he is probably religious: Reinhold Niebuhr, say, who speaks of a "religious expression of trust in the meaning of human existence . . . recognizing and preserving the humanity of man." The irreligious will take this as further evidence of religion's childish evasion of the truth about man's total nullity.

On no point is there greater agreement than that puritanism—or religion simply—teaches a wrong and harmful sexual ethic. Commonly the argument against puritanism is the same as against chastity, or continence. Professor Gay calls the Enlightenment modern paganism, and a good bit of that paganism is rebellion against puritanism's twisting of our sexual nature.

It is a strong argument: Not only does puritan continence make us suffer, needlessly; not only does it impoverish our lives when they could be rich and fulfilled; but, as if that were not enough, it also transforms an energy that could have rejoiced us into something sour and cruel and rancorous. Frustrated in the wholesome satisfaction of our needs, misled into feeling guilty about our natural desires, we do everything we can to make others equally wretched, enviously harrying men and women wiser and healthier than we. We make our society a prison, mirroring in the large the individual prison each of us has allowed himself to be locked up in, or has actually built around himself. Delighting in death rather than life, we make misery and war the perverse expressions of the instincts we deny and suppress. Against such wicked folly the only useful counsel can be, "Make love, not war."

If any teaching of the intellectuals has become truly popular, it is this. One common theme of vicarage detective stories used to be the church-going voyeur, and another was the sanctimonious murderer. (We take it for granted that Jack the Ripper, who murdered prostitutes, must have been a victim of the puritan disease—indeed, take it for granted that prostitution itself is only a symptom of the puritan disease.) And just a little while ago I was able to read a new detective story, set in Dutch Calvinist country, in which—I have forgotten the details—either the murderess or the writer of the poison-pen letters that touch off murder is a respectable, Godfearing woman, another victim of the puritan disease.

Professor Gay's *Party of Humanity* tells us:

Diderot['s] . . . *Supplément au Voyage de Bougainville*, written in 1772, . . . may be taken as typical. Diderot seeks to integrate sexual life into the life of the community as well as the life of the individual—love-making is delightful in itself and socially useful. Diderot's Tahitians are noble, but they are not savages. They are genuinely civilized men, and they are genuinely free. Tahitian society, as viewed by Bougainville and as reconstructed by Diderot, is a rational social order.

"In our presence, without shame, in the center of a throng of innocent Tahitians who danced and played the flute [the young Tahitian girl] accepted the caresses of the young men. . . . The notion of crime and the fear of disease have come among us only with your [sc., the Christians'] coming. I don't know what this thing is that you call 'religion,' but I can only have a low opinion of it because it forbids you to partake of an innocent pleasure to which Nature, the sovereign mistress of us all, invites everybody." . . .

Christianity makes people miserable and criminal: "People will no longer know what they ought and ought not to do. They will feel guilty when they are doing nothing wrong."

Who that is modern, when he hears "Tahiti," can fail to see in his mind's eye an edenic existence—sun, and breeze, and waves, and handsome, happy people whose life outside the skin is continuous with the life inside? To a modern what Diderot says is self-evident. I have read neither Bougainville's *Voyage* nor Diderot's *Supplément*, only what Professor Gay says about them. Whether it is a blessing or a curse I do not know, but I cannot help being modern. Modernity is the station in history in which it has pleased God to set me. Tahiti can cast a spell on me, too.

Like the Maoris and Hawaiians, the Tahitians are Polynesian. I became a bit uneasy about this Bougainville-Diderot-Gay picture of genuinely free and civilized men, and their rational social order, and their life harmonious with reason and a benign nature, when it occurred to me that except for "aloha" and "luau," the only Polynesian words I knew were "taboo" and "mana"—not quite the sort of words usually associated with freedom and reason. So I went to the encyclopedia (where I discovered I knew another freedom-and-reason Polynesian word, "tattoo") and read:

Paganism

The Polynesians, because of their simple life and natural graces amid enchanting island surroundings, have long exercised a romantic appeal for the outside world. . . . The worship of the greater gods was in the hands of an organized priesthood, serving the ruling chiefs. Some of these gods required human sacrifices. . . . The chiefs, as descendants of the gods, possessed *mana*. . . . All the land of the island or district under [a chief's] jurisdiction was his. Over the people he had absolute power. . . . In some of the islands, human flesh was included [in the diet] at times.

And if the Tahitians were like the Maoris, they too had "slaves . . . mainly prisoners of war [who] performed much of the menial labor."

Are these Diderot's happy consequences of paganism? Though Bougainville may have misinformed him about the Polynesians, he knew about Rome. Knowing about Rome, could Diderot really believe that paganism, or pagan sexuality, is delightful in itself and socially useful? The one thing no one can say about the Romans, at least after the Punic Wars, is that they subjected themselves to the rigors of anything resembling a Jewish or Christian ideal of chastity. It was not puritanism that made the Romans what they were.

Even today it can be unpleasant to read about the gladiators. Gladiatorial combat was not a product of Roman corruption or decadence. It was well established long before the end of the republic, when Augustus could boast that he had entertained the people by providing them with ten thousand gladiators to fight in the amphitheaters: butchered to make a Roman holiday. The Emperor Commodus—the son of Marcus Aurelius no less—personally engaged in a thousand gladiatorial duels, and staged fights between cripples. (Other examples are even more sick-making.) Only when the Roman empire had been Christian for a hundred years could the gladiatorial shows be abolished.

As for Rome's treatment of slaves and her means of putting down the servile rebellions that that treatment incited—those do not bear thinking about.

Today the vanguard no longer even pretends to believe in the benignity of pagan sex. It is not against pagan sex. Not at all. It just is not much for benignity. Thus "theater of cruelty" is not an insult, by hostile outsiders. In the New York *Times* of all places, Elenore Lester, who likes what is going on in the advanced theater, can write the following:

Today's near-copulation is likely to give way, in the not-too-distant future, to the real thing, fulfilling a prediction Kenneth Tynan made about two years ago. And after actor-to-actor copulation, will it be actor-to-audience? . . . surely the next step must be programmed rape of the audience.

Of course, sexual relationships are not the only kind possible. . . . Violence is also interesting. . . . Polish drama theoretician Jan Kott observed that, because of all the shocks that are being given by the real world these days, there is a need for real shock in the theater. "We get that from sex and violence," he said. "It is possible to show lovemaking on the stage today, but," he added with a tinge of regret, "it is still impossible to murder." But of course, that was last year.

Surely Mr. Kott knows about the Roman theater. In a recent Roman history we read that "the Colosseum was the scene of theatrical performances in which the murders were not fictitious but real. Under Domitian the public was able to see plays in which one criminal plunged his right hand into a fire, and another prisoner was crucified. . . . In this period, too, Tertullian saw a performance of the *Death of Hercules*, in which the actor representing Hercules was actually burned to death as part of the show."

Only yesterday we thought of hippies as flower people. Their apparent gentleness could be taken to prove that if you satisfy the sexual instinct, you will be peaceful and mild. Today they, or their slightly younger brothers and sisters, are not more frustrated sexually, they are only less gentle. Similarly with college students. Granted, we exaggerate the degree to which they are sexually freer than their parents were when *they* were in college; but if there is a difference, it is in the direction of greater freedom. Yet we do not find that the more violent students are also the more repressed sexually. Their violence is of speech and thought and appetite as well as of action.

Soft-boiled modern pagans have for some time been turning to Eastern pagan spirituality—music, meditation, texts, and so on. How long is it, as these things go, since the British in India had forcefully to suppress suttee, the burning-alive of widows? And in our time the Associated Press can receive the following dispatch from India:

Prime Minister Indira Gandhi has demanded an example be made of those responsible for the ritual slaying of a 12-year-old boy in Rajasthan state. A contractor is reported to have slashed the boy's neck to appease the gods at the laying of the foundation stone for an irrigation project.

The soft-boiled Western pagans may have only a partial understanding of Eastern paganism.

In our time, though, an intellectual or style-setting elite has to be hard-boiled. Its violence is not comic-book or television violence—that is for kids and the lower middle class—but something a little more thoroughgoing. There is the Sorbonne philosopher who is reported to have proclaimed, at the time of the French student uprising, that it was not enough to develop a philosophy of terror, it was necessary to replace philosophy by terror. There is the American literary review that helpfully ran a front-page diagram of a firebomb. Like the Enlightenment ancestors, the vanguard despises puritanism for its sexual repressions; but while the ancestors condemned puritanism for encouraging cruelty, our vanguard should be condemning puritanism for repressing it.

At this stage of the evolution of modern paganism, where you get your kicks is unimportant, as long as you get them. Both bed and Colosseum are groovy. If the Colosseum—whips and chains—is groovier for you, O.K. Do your own thing. In fact, if we could only stop being hypocritical long enough to admit it, maybe the Colosseum is groovier for everybody. Isn't death the ultimate kick? (Someone else's death, that is; but maybe your own, too.) Unfortunately, nature limits the frequency and duration of orgasm. But fortunately nature does not limit the duration or frequency of orgastic cruelty. You can torture someone for as long as you want. In hardly any time at all you can hurt or kill as many as you want.

If one does not want to say "pornographic books," for fear of using a censor's word, one says "sex-and-violence books." *And*, not *or*. Sade wrote a few books in that genre himself.

It need not be said here that "puritanism" is one of those slippery words. Normally we would call D. H. Lawrence a pagan, not a puritan. Dr. Leavis seems to see Lawrence as a puritan—because he is serious not frivolous, radical not graceful, intelligent not clever. Or we think puritanism hated sex. But historically puritanism is Protestant, and Protestantism had little use for celibacy: the monk Luther married a nun. (Queen Elizabeth was not so Protestant that she could quite get used to a married Archbishop of Canterbury.)

To disagree with the conventionally progressive Jewish view, I have been exaggerating the puritanism of the Jewish tradition. That point having been made, it remains to add that of course Judaism is not Calvinist—or, for that matter, Thomist or Augustinian. Calvin taught total depravity; and until recently—only a few hundred years ago—all the major Catholic and Protestant traditions agreed on the logically related doctrine of *paucitas salvandorum*. That is to say, the strong consensus of the Doctors of a religion that had come to replace Jewish law and vindictiveness by Christian freedom and love was that very few even of the faithful would be saved, the great mass being doomed to eternal punishment in hell. Judaism, so legal and vindictive, does not agree. It was not Isaiah Berlin's intention to speak as a Jew when he denied historical inevitability, a modern secularist counterpart of predestination; but he expressed the central Jewish doctrine, or rather, a central Jewish feeling: often, Berlin said, the irresistible is only the unresisted. The Torah lesson of the Sabbath before Rosh Ha-shanah ends this way (Deuteronomy 30:19–20):

I call heaven and earth to witness against you this day: I have put before you life and death, blessing and curse; therefore choose life, so that you may live, you and your progeny. Love the Lord your God, listen to His voice, and cleave to Him; for so you shall have life and length of days. . . .

Nothing predestined, inevitable, or irresistible about that.

So Judaism is not Calvinist. But it is puritan, in that it likes chastity and does not like celibacy. In the historian Jacob Katz's study of the East European Jewish family as it was three hundred years ago, he has shown us Jewish law and thought concretely at work. The Rabbis may have been naive about other things, but they were not naive about the sexual drive. They knew how strong it is. They did not try to deny it or suppress it or divert it—they just tried to hallow it, in marriage. (Their term for marriage is *qiddushin*, "hallowing.") In the time and place Professor Katz has examined, Jews married young. Like any law, Jewish law deals with obligations and rights. East European Jews knew that Jewish law obliges a husband to give his wife sexual gratification, and entitles her to it.

Hume, and later Nietzsche, thought ill of Christianity for teaching men humility. Nietzsche was wrong in thinking that the source of that doctrine was Judaism. To be sure, man's humility is Jewish; but it is coupled, kept in permanent tension, with an equally Jewish belief in man's grandeur. In my part of the congregation, these last Days of Awe, the visiting rabbi preached a sermon based on the aphorism of a hasidic master: "Everyone should have two pockets. In the first he should keep a slip on which is written, 'I am but dust and ashes' [Genesis 27:18]. In the second he should keep a slip on which is written, 'For my sake was the world created' [Mishnah Sanhedrin 4:5]."

Paganism

In that verse from Genesis, Abraham is abasing himself before the Lord, though the abasement is somewhat *pro forma*: he is questioning the Lord's justice in dooming Sodom. The Mishnah quotation comes toward the end of a long section about the warning that must be given to witnesses in a capital case: a man's life depends on what they say, together with the lives of all the descendants he could have:

. . . one man alone was created in the world, to teach you that if any destroys a single soul, Scripture regards him as if he has destroyed a whole world; but if any preserves a single soul, Scripture regards him as if he has preserved a whole world. . . . one man alone was created [from whom we are all descended], so that none should say to another, "My ancestor was greater than yours," . . . and in order to proclaim the greatness of the Holy One, blessed is He. For a man stamps many coins with one seal and they are all alike; but the King of the kings of kings, the Holy One, blessed is He, has stamped every man with the seal of the first man, yet none is like another. Therefore each must say, "For my sake was the world created." . . .

The major Torah lesson on Yom Kippur is the eighteenth chapter of Leviticus. Once I suggested why it had been chosen for reading on Yom Kippur. Mostly it is about unchastity—incest, adultery, sodomy, and bestiality. Unchastity is forbidden not only as wrong in itself but also as an expression of paganism. Unchastity is the piety of paganism: the things that are "abominations" for Israel are the "statutes" and "abominable customs" that "they do in the land of Egypt, where you dwelt, and . . . in the land of Canaan, to which I am bringing you." An equally abominable custom is the sacrifice of children: "You shall not give any of your children to be offered up to Molech. . . ." Bloodshed is likewise the piety of paganism.

Then I stopped just short of understanding that for the Rabbis this chapter must be a concentrated scriptural statement of the practical negative theology of Judaism. It is a negative theology, because in one rabbinical definition Judaism is that which is not pagan: "[Mordecai] is called 'the Jew' because he repudiated idolatry, since everyone who repudiates idolatry is called a Jew" (Megillah 13a). On "My statutes and my ordinances, by doing which a man shall live: I am the Lord" (Leviticus 18:5), the Midrash comments: "R. Jeremiah said: Why may one say that even a gentile, if he fulfills all the Torah, is like a High Priest? Because Scripture says, 'by doing which a man shall live.'"

It is practical, because it is not a theologumenon, it is binding law, about life and death. "Having voted, they passed this law . . .: Concerning all the transgressions prohibited in the Torah, if a man is told, 'Transgress and do not be killed,' let him transgress and not be killed; except for idolatry, unchastity, and bloodshed" (Sanhedrin 74a). Since this is law—the most important law—normal legal reasoning applies. Is it legally permissible for a Jew, out of supererogatory piety or devotion, to allow himself to be killed rather than violate any other prohibition? Maimonides limits a Jew's right to allow himself to be killed in such circumstances: by insisting on martyrdom rather than making the Muslim profession of faith, a Jew would be acting unlawfully, since Islam is completely monotheistic and aniconic. In this Maimonides agreed with the Midrash: "R. Ishmael says: Why may one say that if a man is told privately, 'Worship idols and do not be killed,' he should worship and not be killed? Because the Torah says, 'by doing which a man shall live,' not 'by doing which he shall die.' Should he also obey a public order to worship idols? The Torah says: 'You shall not profane My holy name, that I may be hallowed in the midst of the people of Israel; I am the Lord who hallow you' [Leviticus 22:32]. If you hallow My name, I too shall hallow My name in you." Halowing the Name is *qiddush ha-Shem*, which is also the term for martyrdom.

Paganism/idolatry, unchastity/licentiousness, and murder/bloodshed are for Judaism the unholy triad. (Respectively, they are [1] *'avodah zarah*, or *'avodat elilim*, or *'avodat gillulim*, or *'avodat kokhavim umazzalot*; [2] *gilluy 'arayot*, narrowly incest, literally "uncovering of nakednesses," as in Leviticus 18; and [3] *shefikhut/shefikhat damim*.) The three have an affinity for one another. In Genesis 6:13, "God said to Noah, 'I am determined to make an end to all flesh; for the earth is filled with violence [*hamas*; Jewish Publication Society, 1962: lawlessness]. . . .'" On this the Midrash says: "R. Levi says: *Hamas* is idolatry, *hamas* is unchastity, *hamas* is bloodshed. . . ." Yoma 9b gives a striking conglutination of the cardinal sins: "Why was the First Temple destroyed? Because of three things: the idolatry, unchastity, and bloodshed in it. . . ." Examples from rabbinical literature could be multiplied. Maimonides sums it up, in the Guide of the Perplexed, when he refers to "the mothers and roots of the commandments, namely [the prohibitions against] idolatry, unchastity, and bloodshed."

The Rabbis—founders of that in the Jewish tradition which is most distinctly and specifically Jewish, to this day—were not simply repeating what the Bible had told them, nor in their legislation were they carried away by some kind of exalted urge for martyrdom. They did not need to read Ovid or Petronius or Tacitus or Juvenal to know how the pagans were about sex and about blood. They were contemporaries of Roman paganism, sensible men with eyes to see and ears to hear. Besides the law about martyrdom, they also enacted more prosaic laws, like this one: "Cattle may not be left in the inns of the [pagan] gentiles, since they are suspected of bestiality; nor may a woman remain alone with them, since they are suspected of unchastity; nor may a man remain alone with them, since they are suspected of shedding blood" (Mishnah 'Avodah Zarah 2:1).

For the Rabbis paganism was idolatry, and they could not understand it. They knew, because the Bible told them, that in the olden times the Israelites had repeatedly backslid into idolatry, and they knew that the contemporary gentiles were idolators, but how people could take it seriously was a mystery to them. It seemed reasonable to the Rabbis that paganism must be a pretext for something else: "R. Judah said, quoting Rav: Israel [in the days of the First Temple] knew very well that idolatry has no substance to it. They were idolators only to permit themselves public licentiousness" (Sanhedrin 63b).

What about pluralism? I know it is anachronistic to read a modern sensibility back into the Rabbis' outlook. They insisted on a total Jewish repudiation of paganism, honored gentiles who abandoned paganism, and longed for the day when the Lord will be King over all the earth; but sometimes I like to think that maybe they also had a quiet weakness for pluralism. I cannot fault the Rabbis for being harsh to Esau and I am glad my descent is from Jacob. But the price Jacob paid for his qualities was that he could not at the same time have Esau's qualities. Is there no room in God's world for Jacob and Esau, both? I want to think there is, and to think the Rabbis thought so, too.

Certain virtues—if that word may be used here—primarily aesthetic, go with paganism: Balinese temple dances, for instance, and Polynesian graces. When in the 'Alenu I join the congregation in hoping for the time when the Lord has removed the idols from the earth and all flesh invokes His name, sometimes I become a little anxious. What will the world be like when everyone is a Jew? Then I calm myself. That is not likely to happen right away. Right now, Bali and Tahiti are rather more immediately vulnerable to jet airliners than to Judaism.

For a pluralist, that is too bad. As with liberty and equality, so with pluralism and the unity of mankind: In each set the two members do not get on easily with each other, but the intellectual difficulty of holding on to both is nothing compared with the moral difficulty of giving up either.

I suppose the Rabbis could have justified a measure of pluralism by appealing to some such verse as Micah 5:4, which—for varied, sometimes contradictory reasons—has been popular with the Jews of modernity: "For let all the peoples walk each in the name of its god, but we will walk in the name of the Lord our God for ever and ever." Not that Rabbis could have approved human sacrifice, then or now. For Jews and gentiles alike, the Rabbis wanted none of the practices of the bad old Israelite days, when, more or less like that Indian contractor, "Hiel the Bethelite [re]built Jericho. With Abiram his first-born he laid its foundations, and with his youngest son Segub he set up its gates" (I Kings 16:34). But maybe the Rabbis were not entirely unhappy that others were so foolish as to think paganism had some substance to it. Maybe they did not object to pagans preserving un-Jewish virtues or graces in the world. That could be one meaning of the famous answer in 'Avodah Zarah (54b):

> Philosophers asked the elders in Rome, "If your God dislikes paganism, why does He not abolish it?" They answered, "If the pagans worshipped something the world has no need of, He would abolish it; but they worship the sun and the moon and the stars and the planets. Shall He destroy the world because of fools? The world goes its wonted way, and the fools who have behaved unworthily will be held to account."

—November 1968

. 40 .

Hebraism and Hellenism Now

Matthew Arnold's *Culture and Anarchy* was published in 1869. In an inaugural lecture as Professor of Poetry at Oxford, Roy Fuller has reminded us that "Sweetness and Light," the first chapter of *Culture and Anarchy*, was Arnold's final lecture when *he* was Professor of Poetry. "Hebraism and Hellenism" is another chapter.

Hebraism and Hellenism Now

There is a difficulty in assessing great men, an irony that will out; but the irony may tell us more about ourselves than about its objects. Who has not written that Philosophy I term paper demolishing Hegel? The temptation is old, and the description of it is old. Not completely, but yet in some stubborn part of ourselves we would rather forget that if we are taller than our predecessors, maybe it is because we stand on their shoulders. And when a man's name is linked to "sweetness and light"—never mind what it actually meant for him, and for Swift before him—the temptation to patronize him becomes all the stronger. Arnold respected Goethe, and Goethe may have something to tell us: No man is a hero to his valet; true; but perhaps more because the valet is a valet than because no man is a hero.

Is Arnold relevant to us? He refused to be relevant even to his contemporaries, in the terms in which they understood relevance. Relevant or not, he can be useful.

We are solemnly approving of the individualist mob. Arnold says: "Thinking by batches of fifties is . . . as fatal as thinking by batches of thousands."

For us "nonconformity" is good and "establishment" bad. Arnold on nonconformity and establishment does not give us a final, full truth; but how many truths are final and full? He says:

The great works by which, not only in literature, art, and science generally, but in religion itself, the human spirit has manifested its approaches to totality, and to a full, harmonious perfection, and by which it stimulates and helps forward the world's general perfection, come, not from Nonconformists, but from men who either belong to Establishments or have been trained in them . . . Milton, Baxter, Wesley.

Another good word for us is "dissent." If I am not mistaken, the founders of *Dissent* had in mind, favorably, a phrase of Arnold's, "the Dissidence of Dissent." He did not coin that phrase. "The Dissidence of Dissent, and the Protestantism of the Protestant religion" was the slogan of a journal of the English Nonconformists, who had taken it from Burke. For Arnold the Nonconformists' "Dissidence of Dissent" expressed all that was cranky, Philistine, "hole-in-corner."

And last, for archeological interest:

I remember my father [Thomas, of Rugby], in one of his unpublished letters written more than forty years ago, when the political and social state of the country was gloomy and troubled, and there were riots in many places, goes on, after strongly insisting on the badness and foolish-ness of the government, and on the harm and dangerousness of our feudal and aristocratical constitution of society, and ends thus: "As for rioting, the old Roman way of dealing with *that* is always the right one; flog the rank and file, and fling the ringleaders from the Tarpeian Rock!"

(Arnold withdrew this crusty remembrance from later editions.).

. . . for the sake of the present, but far more for the sake of the future, the lovers of culture are . . . the opposers of anarchy.

Thus can Arnold be relevant by his very irrelevance, by the shock of his strangeness, by—a word he would not have welcomed—his non-conformity. And he did believe that "the men of culture are the true apostles of equality.'

Arnold defines culture, or rather enumerates its elements, astutely. Making culture pretty nearly the sum of all good things, he takes care that it will be if not impossible, then difficult to show that his idea of culture is defective, lacking in some essential. He is as clever as we; knowing we will look for exposed salients to attack, he strengthens them. He defines culture, or inventories it, positively. Yet his "culture" affects us not altogether differently from the Polish Marxist philosopher Kolakowski's "socialism." Kolakowski's "What is Socialism?" tells us what socialism is not. For instance, it is not a system

in which a person who has committed no crime sits at home waiting for the police. In which there are more spies than nurses and more people in prisons than in hospitals. In which one is forced to resort to lies and com-pelled to be a thief. . . . In which the philosophers and writers always say the same thing as the generals and ministers, but always after them. . . .

And so on. There are seventy-two things that socialism is not. "But now listen attentively, we will tell you what socialism is—well, then, socialism is a good thing." Kolakowski enumerates negatively and Arnold positively, but like Kolakowski's socialism, Arnold's culture is a Good Thing.

What G. K. Chesterton says of Christianity, many socialists say of *their* religion: it has not failed, it has never been tried. Matthew Arnold redivivus would say culture has not failed, it has never been tried. For culture is Arnold's real religion. To him it is more or less what before his revolutionary times, the nineteenth century, religion proper had been to the great mass of mankind. He sees the human spirit, and more particularly the Western spirit, as having not one but two parts, Hebraism as well as Hellenism—"the governing idea of Hellenism is *spontaneity of consciousness*; that of Hebraism, *strictness of conscience*"—but he gives the lion's share to Hellenism.

Hellenism is the specifically Greek tradition. Arnold was not one who mocked "*culture!* . . . a smattering of the two dead languages of Greek and Latin." How could you be a Hellenist, Hellenic, if you could not read the Greek authors in their own words? But more generally, Hellenism is mind, intellect—a free mind and a free intellect, resistant to cant and prejudice, connected with imagination and emotion, open to all excellence, past, present, and future. It is mind and intellect flexible and self-correcting, the enemy of fanaticism, rigidity, and one-sidedness. Therefore culture is largely Hellenic. Culture is the best that has been known and thought, the best that has been thought and said in the world, a stream of thought upon everything, the study of perfection, that power which enables us to see things as they really are. Or rather, Hellenism is that power. Those predicates can be assigned almost indifferently to either Hellenism or culture as their subject.

On the other hand, ". . . to Hebraise . . . is, to sacrifice all other sides of our being to the religious side. . . . it leads to a narrow and twisted growth of our religious side itself, and to a failure in perfection."

What has struck many Jews in Arnold's definitions or descriptions of Hebraism is that he was not talking about, was in fact not concerned to talk about, the Jews and the Jews' religion, character, ways of being. Since the Maccabees, the Jewish tradition itself has insisted on the distinctness of Hebraism from Hellenism; but Arnold was defining the spirit, as he understood it, of sectarian Protestantism in nineteenth-century England. His Hebraism keeps pointing to sectarian Protestant bibliolatry—the doctrine of the open Bible carried to a kind of democratic extreme. In that doctrine anyone can read his Bible as well as anyone else, and can understand it as well.

Bibliolatry is not Jewish. Classically, how a Jew read and understood the Bible was regulated by the learned, rabbinical tradition. No ignorant Jew, in Spain or Germany or Poland, could pretend, even to himself, that he understood the very Hebrew or Aramaic of the Bible or Talmud as well as a learned Jew. Why then did Jews never demand an open—i.e., vernacular—Bible with nearly the same vehemence as Christians? I think the answer is to be found in this: that many Christians were persuaded that the priests kept the Bible in Latin to keep it from the people, a priestly monopoly; while Jews knew that at least in principle, it was the ideal and the effort of Jewish society that every (male) Jew should be taught all the sacred literature he could master—and, along the way, the Hebrew and Aramaic in which it was written. When modern Jews began to rebel against Hebrew in favor of the vernacular, that was not because they resented a rabbinical monopoly. What modern Jews resented, in fact, was that the rabbis wanted Hebrew *not* to be a monopoly. The rebels thought that their time, and their children's time, was being wasted by rabbis who wanted everyone to be rabbinically learned, or almost. (Actually, the scholars tell us that the first full-length translation of any kind was Jewish: the Hebrew Bible into Greek. In traditional Jewish Bible editions, an Aramaic version has pride of place next to the Hebrew text. It alone shares with the text the distinction of being vocalized, and in square characters.)

Some years ago Isaiah Berlin revived Archilochus's saying: the fox knows many things, but the hedgehog knows One Big Thing. Hellenism is fox, Hebraism is hedgehog. Among the many things that the fox knows—that Arnold, *ondoyant et divers*, the foxy Hellenist, knows—is the necessity of hedgehog Hebraism. Looking about him, Arnold sees an excess of Hebraism and an insufficiency of Hellenism: heavy mid-Victorian England is too Hebraic and insufficiently Hellenic. He tries to right the imbalance. At other times in history, he says, there was too little Hebraism and too much Hellenism. If he had lived then, he would have tried to right *that* imbalance. But in England, with its Barbarian aristocracy, Philistine middle class, and unknown, half-frightening, half-appealing Populace, his duty is to recall his countrymen to more Hellenism and less Hebraism.

He is telling the truth. That is how he sees his England. But beneath his estimate of what his England needs, there is something more general. Arnold believes that while it is possible to have too much Hellenism, it is easy to have too much Hebraism.

Only three years after *Culture and Anarchy* the work of a young man, of a genius greater though darker than Arnold's, was published —the *Birth of Tragedy*. Arnold's Hellenism stands under the sign of Apollo, Nietzsche's under the sign of Dionysus. For Arnold the great figure of Hellenism, actual as well as symbolic, is Socrates: he invokes Socrates in what we may call the peroration of *Culture and Anarchy*. For Nietzsche, Socrates is a fake.

Arnold's Hellenism is like Freudian ego, his Hebraism like superego. He wants to lighten the burden of Hebraic superego, letting in

Hellenic ego. The ego is the guardian of the reality principle, and for Arnold it is Hellenism that enables us to see things as they really are. Nietzsche agrees that Hebraism is superego. Much more than Arnold, he wants us liberated from Hebraic superego. But for Nietzsche the liberation is not in the name of ego. It is in the name of id—passion, instinct, primal force.

The god of ego is Apollo, the god of id Dionysus. Apollo is *"ordre et beauté,/Luxe, calme, et volupté"* (especially if we are not vulgar about *luxe* and *volupté*). Dionysus is orgy, ecstasy—etymologically "ecstasy" is standing outside one's self—derangement of the senses, blood, lawlessness. Dionysus is the horse, Apollo the bit and bridle. It is quite clear which is primary and which secondary. Roy Campbell says:

> You praise the firm restraint with which they write—
> I'm with you there, of course.
> They use the snaffle and the curb all right,
> But where's the bloody horse?

That is, id-Dionysus first and ego-Apollo a long way second.

Is it to be guilty of an it-is-no-accident, Leninist kind of argument to recall that Campbell was a fascist—called himself a fascist—and fought in Spain for Franco? A spokesman for Dionysian theater (the producer, in fact, of *Dionysus in 69*), a man of the Left rather than the Right, has said: "Ecstasy doesn't come cheap. You pay for it in blood." He has written: "The hidden fear I have about the new expression is that its forms come perilously close to ecstatic fascism."

Who are, or should be, the chief custodians of Hellenism? Professors of Greek. When Arnold thought of professors of Greek, he was likely to think of his friend Jowett, priest of the Church of England, translator of Plato, Master of Balliol, Vice-Chancellor of Oxford. But so was Nietzsche a professor of Greek, and so is or was Norman O. Brown. From Jowett to Brown—that is the history of Hellenism since Arnold. If Arnold were our contemporary, he might say that the balance had tipped again and had to be redressed again, particularly since the preponderant Hellenism of our time is not at all what he had in mind.

As a cozy, even endearing specimen of our Hellenism, consider the Beatles' *Yellow Submarine*. The Blue Meanies are the enemy, cruel, destructive. For them "yes" is a dirty word. When an inferior clicks his heels and salutes his superior, he does not say, "Yes, sir." A Blue Meanie says, "No, sir."

The submarine, as a phallic symbol, is a symbol of life. The submarine's element is the ocean: the ocean is the womb; it is the mother of all living things, the origin of life. Yellow is life: the sun is yellow, it nurtures life.

Blue is coldness, gloom, death: laws that forbid pleasure are blue laws, blue Monday is suicide Monday. In the middle of the film a throw-away line, apparently unmotivated, is spoken: "That's funny, you don't look blueish." It makes no difference how this was intended: trust the tale, not the teller. Blueish, Jewish; blue is Hebraism.

Yellow is Hellenism. The end of the film is an insistent yellow flashing: Yes, love, yes, love, yes, love. It celebrates the victory of yellow and yes and love over their enemies, blue and no and—what is the enemy of love? Hate? Death?

Celebrating yes is rather more highbrow than this may suggest. Nietzsche praises the yea-sayers and dispraises the nay-sayers. Joyce's *Ulysses* ends much as *Yellow Submarine* does. In that famous soliloquy of Molly Bloom's, she says yes, yes, yes—to life, to love; to adultery.

And indeed, Hebraism has a way of saying no and not. The preeminent sequence of Hebraic noes and nots is in the twentieth chapter of Exodus (with a variant in the fifth chapter of Deuteronomy);

I am the Lord thy God, who brought thee out of the land of Egypt, out of the house of bondage. Thou shalt have no other gods before Me. Thou shalt not make unto thee a graven image, nor any manner of likeness, of anything that is in heaven above, or that is in the earth beneath, or that is in the water under the earth. Thou shalt not bow down to them nor serve them, for I the Lord thy God am a jealous God. . . . Thou shalt not take the name of the Lord thy God in vain; for the Lord will not hold him guiltless who takes His name in vain. Thou shalt not murder. Thou shalt not commit adultery. Thou shalt not steal. Thou shalt not bear false witness against thy neighbor. Thou shalt not covet thy neighbor's house; thou shalt not covet they neighbor's wife . . . nor anything that is thy neighbor's.

Is *Yellow Submarine* exoteric, public propaganda for Dionysian Hellenism? How could it be? It is pleasant, not ecstatic; calm, not violent; tranquil, not lawless. On the surface it is even sexless. At most, Dionysianism is hinted at—in its "yes," with its recollection of Molly Bloom, and its "love," which is ambiguous. The Hellenism that *Yellow Submarine* exemplifies for us and commends to us may well be Apollonian. Which leads to a supposition. There is a play about an extraordinary physician, Dr. Knock, who has discovered that *un homme bien portant est un malade qui s'ignore*—a well man is a sick man unaware. In like manner, and from one point of view, perhaps Apollonian Hellenism is sometimes Dionysian Hellenism unaware, or without the courage to be aware.

We come now to a difficult question, the question of woman, the womanly. Routinely, the neofeminists of our time condemn the Jewish tradition for subordinating women. Less is said about the Greek tradition—Sparta, even Periclean Athens; or Plato, or Aristotle.

Matthew Arnold considers himself to be a disciple of Spinoza, but it is with Nietzsche that Spinoza joins hands, in hostility to woman and the womanly. For Nietzsche, Hebraism—Judaism and Christianity—is the resentment and revenge of the weak: women and slaves. Spinoza, contemptuous of the moral and psychological state of the Jews, says that the foundations of their religion have effeminated their character. That is, Judaism has made the Jews womanish. For Spinoza, pity is *muliebris misericordia*, womanish pity—not in praise of woman but in dispraise of pity.

Though etymologies prove nothing, they can suggest something. Greek *hystera* means "womb," as in surgical words like "hysterectomy"; but its best-known derivative is "hysteria": Hellenically, the womb generates hysteria. From Hebrew *reḥem*, "womb," derives *raḥamim*, "pity": Hebraically, the womb generates pity. Hellenism has something antiwoman, antiwomanly, misogynist; and so has our culture, high or low, under Apollo's sign or Dionysus'. The eponymous Marquis de Sade, a hero for our time, was homosexual. The editor of an edition of Oscar Wilde's criticism recalls for us that André Gide, having read Wilde first, said he had found Nietzsche less exciting than he would have been otherwise; and that for Thomas Mann many of Nietzsche's aphorisms might have been expressed by Wilde, and vice versa. Wilde linked art with lawlessness and criminality, and independently of Nietzsche was moved to transvalue all values.

Surely Arnold never heard of his older, Italian Jewish contemporary Samuel David Luzzatto, but Luzzatto too had thought a great deal about Hellenism and Hebraism—which he called Atticism and Judaism/Abrahamism. Like Arnold, Luzzatto recognizes the necessity of both; but unlike Arnold, he gives priority to Hebraism. Luzzatto cannot forgive Spinoza that *muliebris misericordia*. Luzzatto prefers the Rabbis' "He who feels no pity is not of the seed of Abraham"; and quotes the nineteenth-century German classicist

Böckh, "Mercy is no Hellenic virtue." (What I know about Luzzatto I owe to Shalom Spiegel's *Hebrew Reborn*.)

The rabbi of my congregation once preached on the unpromising lesson in Leviticus (*Shemini*) about clean and unclean foods. Conceding the force of the jokes about stomach religion and of the arguments for a concern with higher things than hooves and cuds, fins and scales, he said only that Judaism—the Jewish tradition—is a unitary, a whole regimen. The Rabbis, serious about what is kosher and what is not, legislated, in what he insisted was the same spirit, about other things as well. He cited Tosefta 'Avodah Zarah:

Whoever sits in the stadium [where gladiators fight] is a murderer [sharing the guilt, with the others there, for encouraging gladiatorial combat]. But R. Nathan says it is permitted, for two reasons: because he [sc., a Jew in the stadium] can shout [for mercy, when the victorious gladiators ask whether to spare or to kill the defeated] and thereby save lives; and by testimony can help a woman to be remarried.

The last parts needs explanation: A Jew who has been in the stadium can testify that he has seen the woman's husband die—a Jewish captive of the Romans sent as a gladiator to the arenas. Then, known to be a widow, she is allowed to remarry.

So for those most Hebraic of Hebrews, the Rabbis, helping a woman to remarry was a motive not unworthy of mention with saving lives. Womanish. As Edmund Wilson has reminded us, Tacitus called the Jews enemies of the human race because, among other reasons, they were uncivilized—un-Hellenic—in that they refused to practice infanticide. (Infanticide means killing babies, usually girls—in the ancient world the popular means of keeping children few enough to prevent the parceling of estates.) The blues have been saying no for a long time, even to such sensible, pleasurable, useful, or civilized things as gladiatorial shows and infanticide.

Maybe *Yellow Submarine*, in indicting blueness and meanness, lacks the courage, the honesty, to admit to itself what the worship of Dionysus requires. Nietzsche did not lack courage or honesty. He was explicit about what follows once we say—as he says—that the God of Hebraism is dead. What follows is that we recognize Jewish (or Jewish and Christian) mercy, and kindred notions, to be nothing more than the restraints that the envious weak, women and slaves, try to impose on the strong; and the duty of the strong—aristocratic, heroically hard—to throw off those restraints. Nietzsche said he would believe only in a god who could dance. Like its original, the

Bacchae of Euripides, *Dionysus in 69* is about dancing; and the producer (a Jew), who knows about ecstatic fascism and about blood as the price of ecstasy, is described as rejecting Judeo-Christian culture. At least he is candid: "If you dance with Dionysus you kill Pentheus —that is the action of the play."

For her "Temptations of Cultural Fascism" (*Wiener Library Bulletin,* Winter 1968–1969), Renee Winegarten takes the title from Saul Bellow: Herzog's "cultural fascism." She is interested in writers who are liberals, or radicals, or Jews, yet are culturally Dionysian:

> The fact that a man really belongs with those who would be the first victims of the Dionysian urge does nothing to lessen the fascination, just as the fact that he is neither aristocratic nor heroic does little to prevent the exaltation of the reader's imagination at the idea of an élite of noble and remarkable souls to which he can fancy he belongs. . . .
> Until very recently, for the majority of students and lovers of literature (as Lionel Trilling pointed out), there was no accord between what stirred them in books and practical political life: aristocrats in fancy, they remained democrats or radicals in fact. Yet that disruptive and subversive element in literature which served many readers merely as a stimulant for the imagination has now descended into the streets, in the United States, in France and Germany, even in England. The aristocratic outlook of the exceptional individual or the rare élite has been adopted by those for whom it was never intended: the dissatisfied, half-educated mass of the young. . . . [There] are tokens of a new kind of cultural fascism (emanating from the Left instead of the Right).

An English poet and painter has described the "ambience of tenderness, intelligence, total licence and crackling undercurrents of a kind of sad cruelty" in the Dionysian milieu he used to frequent. From the visitors' graffiti at a Happening he staged, he learned that "what was hell to puritans was heaven to sadistic fetishists."

For *Yellow Submarine,* it is the puritan Blue Meanies who are sadistic; and in a Catholic and ecumenical journal of religious thought, a Protestant theologian publishes a "Manifesto for a Dionysian Theology," introduces it by citing Nietzsche's dancing god, and then is silent about killing Pentheus, and ecstatic fascism, and mercy as womanish, slave morality. Wholesome antiuptightness —that seems to be what he wants to suppose Dionysianism is, and wants us to suppose.

Why should we keep paying the homage of embarrassment or hypocrisy to traditional religion's virtue? For moderns the dominant religion, the religion that has superseded religion, is a cross between

Arnold's culture and Nietzsche's art. Obedient to Nietzsche, we faithfully assert the primacy of the aesthetic: let me, as the lawyers say, incorporate by reference Trilling's *Beyond Culture*. I would only mention a further resemblance between traditional and modern religion. When the God of religion was pronounced dead, the god of art was proclaimed. That god—or one of his persons—was beauty, but in no time at all "beauty" became just as quaint as "God," just as otiose and shy-making. Where the central principle of the new religion was, a void now is.

In the old religion, God created. In the new, man—especially the artist—creates. The characteristically modern, Nietzschean insistence is on art as the creative act and element above all others. May this not be in part, as some have suggested, masculine protest, womb-envy? (If so, it is probably truer of the appreciators, the Berensons, than of the artists themselves, who tend to be earthy, not given to mooning about Creativity.) Is "creative" to be taken seriously, has it to do with "create," is it more than just another O.K. word, interchangeable with our "relevant" and "meaningful" and with yesterday's "dynamic"? Then, since life is what it is, willy-nilly we have to recognize the womanly—the maternal—as most nearly creative, simply. When Judah Ha-levi said of Greek culture that it bore flowers but no fruit, he knew Greek culture (in Arabic). He meant that it was intellectual and aesthetic rather than moral; but he also knew about traditional Mediterranean forms of masculine protest.

Before we leave the theme of woman and the womanly, a final irony at Arnold's expense is unavoidable. A man so severe about bathos—he thought it characteristically Philistine—should himself stay clear of bathos. In the matter of marriage with a deceased wife's sister, he did not stay clear. That was not, as we may think, only comic stuff for W. S. Gilbert and Bernard Shaw. By Church of England law, marriage with a deceased wife's sister was forbidden. Against this, non-Anglican reformers adduced the licitness of such marriage in Leviticus, among other arguments. Knowing what Arnold knew about Sparta and Athens ("the race which invented the Muses") and Rome, scourge that he was of the bathetic, he yet allowed himself this:

. . . who, that is not manacled and hoodwinked by his Hebraism, can believe that, as to love and marriage, our reason and the necessities of our humanity have their true, sufficient, and divine law expressed for them by the voice of any Oriental and polygamous nation like the Hebrews? Who, I say, will believe, when he really considers the matter, that where the feminine nature, the feminine ideal, and our relations to them, are brought into question, the delicate and apprehensive genius of the Indo-European race, the race which invented the Muses, and chivalry, and the Madonna, is to find its last word on this question in the institutions of a Semitic people, whose wisest king had seven hundred wives and three hundred concubines?

("Indo-European race" was the science of his day.)

Naturally, Arnold's Hebraic-Hellenic dualism is not original with him. In the early Christian centuries Tertullian asked, *Quid Athenis cum Hierosolymis*, what has Athens to do with Jerusalem? In Arnold's time Ernest Renan, whom he thought well of, addressed a "Prayer at the Acropolis" to Apollo, god of clarity, reason, and harmony, begging forgiveness for having bothered so much with unclear, unreasonable, and discordant Semitic things. But, as Trilling suggests, it is Jews who are most conscious of the dualism. Not only Trilling's Heine and Börne; and not only Talmud, Judah Ha-levi, and Luzzatto; but also, in this century, Hermann Cohen and Leo Strauss.

Arnold cites Heine as a Jew who, because he is modern, prefers Hellenism to Hebraism. (In Heine's later years he was to say that being Greek is a young man's game; one matures into being a Jew.) There have also been the Jewish Nietzscheans. Chernikhovsky's "Before the Statue [= idol; *pesel*] of Apollo" is even more anti-Hebraic than the title suggests, because that Apollo looks remarkably Dionysian. Like the philosophical since Xenophanes, the poet takes for granted that man creates gods in his image. The passionate, warrior Israelites had the passionate, warrior god YHWH, Chernikhovsky says; but then alas! they became Jews, "and bound him in phylactery thongs." And so Babel, with his Cossacks. For a Jewish Nietzschean, the Jews were not so virtuously chaste (peace-loving, etc.) as they liked to believe. They were only eunuchs, self-made: womanish.

Arnold speaks of the miracles of the rise and spread of Christianity; but if only as an admirer of Spinoza he does not really believe in miracles. Neither do we, of course. It is less that we have disproved miracles than that we have defined them away. By definition, for us, there can be no such thing, especially since our very science is statistical and probabilistic. If a miracle is not fraud or delusion, or suggested by superstition and ignorance, it is merely statistically unusual: as if this table were to fly upward at my command; or a voice were to speak to Moses out of a bush that burned but was not consumed. For Arnold as for us, "miracle" is what it was at the beginning—

"marvel" is from the same root. One gapes, one stares at miracle and marvel.

A rereading of Arnold must make a Jew realize how the old Jewish sentiment of being (or of ancestors having been) caught up in miracle has come to life again. In spite of miracle's low standing, in spite of its nonexistence by definition, our renewed consciousness of miracle—of miraculous things done to and through Jews—has brought about a curious reversal. Arnold, who knows of the "cultivated and philosophical Jews," commends their Socinian-like estimate of Jesus to Christians. Jews of that sort have also been cultivated and philosophical about God, and miracle. Today they may find it less difficult than Christians, similarly cultivated and philosophical, to imagine the God of history (and of tradition) present and active.

Not that Arnold paid much attention to the Jews and Judaism of his time. Why should a Victorian Englishman in his position have noticed the Jews and their Judaism otherwise than incidentally? That is almost the best Jews can expect. Even incidentally, it would have been easy for him, natural, to say harsh things. Both in what he says and in what he does not say, Arnold is kind to us. By the standards of the eighteenth, nineteenth, and first half of the twentieth centuries, he is a friend.

Certainly he was more a friend than his father. Liking plural establishments rather than disestablishment, Matthew Arnold approved the establishment of the synagogue, as in France. Thomas Arnold, who insisted on the harm and dangerousness of a feudal and aristocratical constitution, clearly was not illiberal, but Trilling's *Matthew Arnold* has this to say of him:

> . . . with Jews he was intransigent, believing that they should be barred from the universities and from citizenship. He held that citizenship required an almost mystic homogeneity, which was supplied . . . in the modern world by religion. He denounced "that low Jacobinical notion of citizenship, that a man acquires a right to it by the accident of his being littered [human beings are born, animals are littered—MH] *inter quattuor maria* [on the nation's soil], or because he pays taxes." England, he said, was the land of Englishmen, not of Jews, and "lodgers" had no claims to more than an honorary citizenship. . . . he dreaded the possibility of examining a Jew in history at the University of London . . . and of having to avoid calling Jesus the Christ.

What is the lexicographical evidence, in the Oxford English Dictionary? (We will no doubt find worse if we consult OED's German or even French counterpart.) OED's first definition of "Jew" is: "A person of Hebrew race; an Israelite." So much for adherence to a faith, identification with a history, practice of a ritual, study of a culture; or Jonah: "I am a Hebrew, and I worship the Lord the God of heaven, who made the sea and the land." OED's second definition is more interesting still: "*transf.* As a name of opprobrium or reprobation; *spec.* applied to a grasping or extortionate moneylender or usurer, or a trader who drives hard bargains or deals craftily." Thus Coleridge: "Jacob is a regular Jew, and practices all sorts of tricks and wiles." Coleridge! "Jew-bail" is insufficient bail, and Captain Marryat's "Jew carts" carry stolen goods. As a verb ("colloq.") it means "To cheat or overreach, in the way attributed to Jewish traders or usurers," teste Dante Gabriel Rossetti: "But as to his doing and jawings and jewings, William brought me the news."

This sort of thing could have only one effect on Jews who wanted European culture to be theirs and took its standards as theirs. Rahel Varnhagen writes of "what was so long the greatest shame, the bitterest sorrow and suffering to me, my Jewish birth. . . ." In one of his moods Heine says that Judaism is not a religion, it is a misfortune; being a Jew is like being a hunchback.

In good Franz Josef's time, two Jews in a Viennese cafe are arguing about Dr. Herzl's idea. Neither can convince the other. A third Jew has been listening attentively, and they ask him to judge. He says he is not a proper, impartial judge: he regards himself as a follower of Dr. Herzl's—a Zionist, if you will—though, to be sure, with three reservations. Will he be kind enough to explain? Gladly.

First, why Hebrew? Everybody who is anybody speaks German. Besides, reviving Hebrew is a mad, utopian scheme. Patiently the great Semitist Renan has reminded the half-baked enthusiasts that Hebrew has long been dead, and that in all of human history not one dead language has ever been brought to life again, to be spoken by children and shopgirls as well as the learned.

Second, why Palestine? You would have to look hard to find another place so infertile, rocky, and eroded, with such desert and insalubrious marsh, such a lack of natural resources, harbors, and navigable waterways. Besides, people are already living there, the Arabs. Israel Zangwill is right: we should accept the British government's offer of Uganda. It is fertile, and the natives will give no trouble for hundreds and hundreds of years.

Third, Dr. Herzl's idea is a great idea. It needs a great people. And whom do you waste it on? Jews!

As an example of usage for a new edition of OED—the present one stops at the twentieth century—I submit an order of the day by Lieut.-General Sir Evelyn Barker, G.O.C. Palestine, after the explosion in the King David Hotel:

. . . you will put out of bounds to all ranks all Jewish establishments, cafes, restaurants, shops, and private dwellings. . . . the troops . . . will be punishing the Jews in a way the race dislikes as much as any, by striking at their pockets and showing our contempt for them.

That was in 1946, and by one British military authority. In 1967 the Institute for Strategic Studies, in London, had other things to say of "the race." Predicting that the 1967 war would be "studied in staff colleges for many years to come," the Institute for Strategic Studies said that "the performance of the Israeli Defense Force" was "like the campaigns of the younger Napoleon." (For Napoleon it was the English who were a nation of shopkeepers.)

When the *Saturday Review* asked Harold Macmillan whether Great Britain should try to be like Athens or like Sweden, he ruled out Athens—living on slavery, imperialist, and overtaken by decay and death. He continued:

It may well be that Britain will someday follow in the footsteps of Sweden, but if so I'm glad I won't be here to see it.

No, the future I hope for Britain is more like that of Israel. In the time of Elizabeth we were only two million people, in the time of Marlborough only five or six million, in the time of Napoleon only ten million. The other day, while the world debated, Israel's three millions imposed their will on their enemies. They had what any great people need—resolution, courage, determination, pride. These are what really count in men and nations.

The new OED may have to enter a new definition.

For a modern Jew this is miraculous. A modern Jew is a man whose outlook has been apt to be the one we find in OED—and Heine's equation, and the Viennese joke. Some of the most significant modern Jews, native neither to England nor to English culture, have looked upon England and English ways as models: Freud, Chaim Weizmann, even Ahad Ha'am. Now comes Macmillan—of the line of Churchill, Gladstone, Wellington—and says what he says. With our eyes we see and with our ears we hear the fulfillment of the promise repeated to Abraham, Isaac, and Jacob, that the nations of the earth would bless themselves by them and their descendants. How long we have been accustomed to the fulfillment of other prophecies, that the nations would curse themselves by us!

Here is unexpectedness, improbability, uniqueness. That so many are unimpressed does not mean it is unimpressive. Aesthetically almost, as a spectacle if as nothing else, it should impress. When Toynbee, who is supposed to have a historical imagination, applies to Israel a canting, shabby substitute for thought—"neo-colonialism"—he only shows us that Goethe's valets are numerous and diverse.

On the Sabbath of Passover the Torah lesson is read in which the Lord, complementing His redemption of the children of Israel, vouchsafes a revelation of Himself to Moses—or, rabbinically, reveals His "thirteen attributes": ". . . compassionate and gracious, slow to anger," etc. The Prophetical lesson, from Ezekiel, is also about redemption, but future rather than past—redemption that is at the same time revelation:

The hand of the Lord was upon me, and He . . . set me down in the midst of a valley, and it was full of bones . . . very many . . . and . . . very dry. And He said to me, Son of man, can these bones live? And I answered: O Lord God, Thou knowest. Again He said to me: Prophesy to these bones, and say to them, O dry bones, hear the word of the Lord. Thus says the Lord God to these bones: Behold, I will cause breath to enter you, and ye shall live . . . and ye shall know that I am the Lord. So I prophesied as I was commanded . . . and the breath came into them, and they lived, and stood upon their feet. . . . Then He said to me, Son of man, these bones are the whole house of Israel. Behold, they say, Our bones are dried up, and our hope is lost, we are clean cut off. Therefore prophesy and say to them, Thus says the Lord God: Behold, I will open your graves, and raise you from your graves, O my people; and I will bring you home into the land of Israel. . . . And I will put my Spirit within you, and ye shall live . . . then ye shall know that I, the Lord, have spoken, and I have done it, says the Lord.

Jewish triumphalism, some will say; chauvinism, or actually militarism (of megalomaniacal would-be Napoleons)—even some Jews will say that. Not so. Over all lies the shadow of 1939–1945. Unable to bear thinking of 1939–1945, I appeal to Wittgenstein: "Whereof one cannot speak, thereof one should not speak." Dissatisfaction with God's justice is as old with the Jews as Abraham; but after the crematoria, theodicy—arguing for God's justice—is more difficult than arguing for His existence, difficult as *that* is.

If there is any answer at all, if there is any answer for Jews, its elements must be in that chapter from Ezekiel. The dry bones are the bones of the dead. It is only figuratively that the dead live again; nothing can cancel out their deaths. Yet there has also been redemption. (*Hatikvah*—not a good poem but, as an anthem, informative— echoes Ezekiel. The despair Ezekiel quotes, "Our hope is lost," is *avedah tiqwatenu.* The refrain of *Hatikvah* is '*od lo' avedah tiqwatenu,* "our hope is not yet lost.") In Isaiah the Savior God of Israel, a God who conceals Himself, shapes light and creates darkness, makes weal and creates woe. It should be possible to mourn darkness and woe, and to rejoice over light and weal.

For the religion of culture and art, theodicy is an even more nearly impossible enterprise than for the older religion. The religion of culture and art is a religion of salvation. If salvation has any meaning, then it is the god of that religion who has failed most completely and who is, or should be, dead. Among an infinity of possible citations, this, mild, is from Ralf Dahrendorf's *Society and Democracy in Germany:*

> . . . thousands of alumni of German Gymnasia did not let the cultivated humanism of their intellectual formation prevent them from stamping out people like ants whom one may not notice because one is so busy looking up to the stars that one does not watch the streets.

"Cultivated humanism" is Apollonian Hellenism. And what might a Dahrendorf not have had cause to say if those Gymnasia had been largely Dionysian? Let this be said for Apollo, that of all the—it goes without saying, non-Hebraic—gods, he is the least given to drinking blood.

For modern Jews now, the status of Hellenism may be lower than at any time since we became modern; and if only for that reason— though I think not only—the status of Hebraism may be correspondingly higher. Ezekiel was Hebraic simply. He called Renan's and Chernikhovsky's statue-idols wood and stone; reproved our lust to worship wood and stone, as the nations do; and swore in the Lord's name that with mighty arm and outstretched hand (with which He had redeemed and led Israel forth from the Egyptian house of bondage) He would be King over us. For us, now, that Hebraism is still insufficient. Even Luzzatto would agree; and so testify even the miracles we have seen. But if by itself Hebraism is insufficient, and too simple, yet now, more than in many years, we can hold it to be essential, and its necessary proportion to be high.

—*July 1969*

.41.

Translating the Psalms

O sing to the Lord a new song. . . .
—Psalms 96:1 (98:1, 149:1)

Some of the fundamental texts of Chinese antiquity are so ambiguous, a scholar once told me, that not only what they mean is in dispute, but even what they are about. When I heard that, I felt sorry for the Chinese and the Sinologists. It is all very well to say that if ambiguity makes you uneasy you're an authoritarian personality, but such texts are too much of a good thing.

Of course, neither is ambiguity completely absent from the more occidental languages and literatures. A Latin teacher I knew used to amuse himself by giving his students a sentence of five short words to translate: *Mea mater sus est mala.* (Punctuation was unknown to the ancients.) It can mean: "My mother, O pig, is wicked." It can also mean: "Priestess, my sow is ugly"; or, "Come on, goddess, a boar is eating the apples" or peaches, or pomegranates, or bad things. And so on. But that sentence is exceptional. If a Latin text is hard, that is seldom because it is more than normally ambiguous.

Similarly with Hebrew. Spinoza did not doubt he knew what the Bible was saying, since he did not doubt he knew Hebrew. And that was not only because our printed Bibles are "vocalized" or "pointed," i.e., have vowel signs. Arthur Koestler has said he could never learn to read unpointed Hebrew, and has complained about the imprecision and ambiguity of words presenting themselves to a reader in the bare bones of their consonants. But we do not normally read isolated words, we read sentences, or words in a context. Without a sentence or a context, vowels do not always help: taken by itself, what exactly does *sound* mean? On the other hand, if you are in a car heading from New York to New Jersey and you pass a marker with the legend G WSHNGTN BRDG, you have no right to grumble about ambiguity. Spinoza understood not only the vocalized Bible, but also the unvocalized books of the Rabbis and Maimonides.

If he was confident he knew what his Hebrew (and Latin) au-

313

thors meant, we should be more confident. A century after him, Rousseau was still able to define etymology as a science in which vowels count for nothing and consonants for very little. Then Indo-European and Semitic historical linguistics hardly existed, now they are firmly established. With the help of the late E. A. Speiser's translation and notes, in the Anchor Bible, we can understand Genesis better than the men of an earlier day. Above all, Speiser was a linguist.

Reading the first fifty psalms with the help of Mitchell Dahood's translation and notes, also in the Anchor Bible, what do I understand? I am not sure. The only thing I am sure of is that Father Dahood's volume is different in kind from Speiser's. Someone who has no Hebrew can be given the Anchor Genesis with the assurance that it will bring him close to the original, and to the world of things and thoughts in which that came into being. You would be doing such a person a disservice if you gave him Dahood's Psalms. Even if he has Hebrew, the book may irritate him beyond bearing. I am myself an equable sort, but reading Dahood, though it pleased me sometimes, exasperated me often. That is less his fault than the editors'. His work simply does not belong in the Anchor Bible, with its implicit promise to the common reader. It is a kind of demonstration project.

Dahood, a Jesuit, teaches Ugaritic literature at the Pontifical Biblical Institute. (Ugaritic is a language uncovered in Syria between the two World Wars. Most scholars think it is a form of Canaanite, and therefore closely related to Hebrew. The Ugaritic texts are several hundred years older than the oldest parts of the Bible.) Together, Dahood's introduction, translation, and notes make up a sort of manifesto. He is saying, in effect: "The day of the Bible scholar not expert in Ugaritic is past, particularly if he specializes in such books as Psalms and Job. Only Ugaritic can help with those books, because even the Septuagint, the most ancient version, no longer understands their Canaanite archaisms—of vocabulary, grammar, style, imagery, and the rest. Of course the Masoretes do not understand either, since they are later still. Hence we may ignore what the Masoretes added to the text or imposed on it: vowels, punctuation, verse division, sometimes word division. The psalms were always in liturgical use, so that the consonantal text the Masoretes received and transmitted is trustworthy." In Dahood's words: "[In] the first fifty psalms . . . resort to emendation can be justified in fewer than a half a dozen instances."

When it suits Dahood's purpose, though, he is ready enough to follow the Septuagint's example, and even the Vulgate's. (Most unscientific, that. The Vulgate is late and has little independent value as a witness.) Between the lines Dahood seems to be saying: "Ugaritic gives me a bag of tricks. With Houdini's tricks, he could have himself shackled and immured, and yet escape. With mine, I can hold myself to the transmitted consonants and yet make of them pretty well what I choose, by adducing Ugaritic precedents. I do not really believe all the things I say here. I say them only to make you see the virtuoso performances that Ugaritic makes possible, and the stodginess you are condemned to without it."

At one point Dahood becomes aware that this is what he sounds like, and he hurries to deny it is what he means. He has told us things like these: that the suffix -*i*, first person in Hebrew, can be understood as third person, if convenient, in the light of "Phoenician and probably Ugaritic"; that similarly a troublesome *l*-, "to," can be taken as an Ugaritic vocative or emphatic particle ("O" or "indeed, surely"); and that a difficult *lō'* (*l'*) "not," can be read as **lē'* (since it, too, is *l'*) "Victor, Victorious One." He assures us that while "this . . . may sound much like 'you name it, we have it,' " it isn't. Really? I find it hard to believe that so many prepositions have to mean "from" quite so often—not only the one we always knew meant "from," but also those we thought meant "to" and "in" and "on." When there is not much perceptible difference between "in" and "from," why insist that thunder *bashshamayim* "in the sky" should be "from the sky"?

An example of the lengths Dahood will go to in order to avoid facing the need for emendation—or, alternatively, of the joy he has in showing off his bag of tricks: If only because in the bad old days Ps. 2:11–12 were a favorite proof-text for Christian theologians trying to convince Jews that the Hebrew Bible foretold Jesus the Christ, those two verses are well known for their difficulty. In the Masoretic Text the end of the first and the beginning of the second are *wegilu bire'adah. nashshequ-bhar.* King James: ". . . and rejoice with trembling. Kiss the Son . . ."; Jewish Publication Society: ". . . and rejoice with trembling. Do homage in purity . . ."; Revised Standard Version: ". . . with trembling kiss his feet . . ." (this last annotated as "conjectural. The Hebrew of 11b and 12a is uncertain"). RSV's conjecture follows the recommendation of the critical apparatus in the third edition of Biblia Hebraica. The consonants that have caused all that trouble are *wgylw br'dh nšqw br.* With a minimum of rearrangement and the loss of only one *w*, Biblia Hebraica tells us to add the first word to the fourth, reading *br'dh nšqw brglyw*, i.e., *bire'adah nashshequ beraglaw*—"with trembling kiss His feet": neat, economical, and satisfactory.

Dahood goes all around Robin Hood's barn: ". . . and live in trembling, O mortal men. . . ." He keeps the consonants, but divides the last two words in his own way—*nš qbr*. (He says this is "no consonantal change," but note that he has dropped the *w* after *q*. If challenged, he would probably say that the *w* was a mistaken semi-vowel introduced into the text by a scribe trying to make the spelling a little fuller. Canaanite texts are characterized by *scriptio defectiva*, skimpy spelling.) Either because he is constrained by the new meanings he has erected, or just for the fun of it, Dahood gives "live" for *gilu* instead of "rejoice." He has to twist and turn for that, and I do not think it comes off; but no matter. The real innovation is "O mortal men": *nš qbr*, vocalized *neshe qebher*, "men of the grave." *Neshe*, "men of"? It means "women of"; "men of" is *anshe*. Quite all right—". . . *nashim* 'men' [and therefore *neshe* 'men of'] is well-documented in Ugaritic. . . ." (He gives only one example.) Should not the consonants of *neshe* be *nšy*, not *nš*? Blame the skimpy spelling. The Bible has compounds in which the first element is *ish* "man of," or *bene* "sons of," and the second element is *mawet* or *temutah* "death." "Men of the grave," Dahood says, is of a piece with such constructions.

The fact remains that there is no straightforward instance of *neshe qebher*—or *ish/anshe qebher*, or *ben/bene qebher*. If RSV calls "kiss his feet" conjectural, what shall we call Dahood's "O mortal men"? He does not give us "O mortal men" in a discursive note, as a possible alternative to a standard translation. It *is* his translation. And then, demolishing his own elaborate structure, he notes: "The recent proposal of Henri Cazelles . . . in *Oriens Antiquus* 3 (1964), 43–45, who translates '*Saluez le Brillant*' [Pay your respects to the Shining One], on the basis of Ugar. *brr* 'to shine,' is possible though it requires further confirmation." Determined to immortalize his mortal men, Dahood will not change his translation. Yet in a note to Ps. 36, he can say of another scholar's emendation that it "is too clever by half."

It is unsettling that Dahood cannot even be relied upon *not* to be directly helpful. Every now and then one of his suggestions is so elegant that it compels admiring assent. Close by, another suggestion is complicated and ungainly.

Take denominative verbs. Dahood is fond of them. Ugaritic, he says, liked to form verbs from nouns, especially parts of the body, and from numerals; and such verbs, until now mostly unrecognized, abound in the text of Psalms. In 22:26 (25) he is fine. King James, JPS, and RSV all translate, more or less, 'From Thee comes my praise [i.e., the praise of me] in the great congregation," while Dahood says, "One hundred times will I repeat to you my song of praise [i.e., the song of praise by me] in the great congregation." Let us dispose of secondary matters first: *tehillati* is equally "my praise" and "my song of praise." (The Hebrew for "Psalms" is *tehillim*.) The problem is in the first part of the verse. KJV, JPS, and RSV straightforwardly render *me'ittekha* (*m'tk*), "from thee (is)," as "from Thee comes." For Dahood those consonants clothe a verb based on *me'ah* (*m'h*), "hundred." He reads *m'tk* as **mē'itīkā* = *mē'ītī*, a *pi'el* verb, + *-kā*, here dative: "I have repeated (repeat, shall repeat) to you a hundred times." Why is it spelled *m'tk* and not, as we should expect, *m'ytyk* (or *m'tyk*)? *Scriptio defectiva* again.

Here the denominative verb is a success, in 20:8 (7) a failure. KJV: "Some *trust* in chariots, and some in horses; but we will remember the name of the Lord our God." JPS: "Some trust in chariots, and some in horses; but we will make mention of the name of the Lord our God." RSV: "Some boast of chariots, and some of horses; but we boast of the name of the Lord our God." (I prefer "Some invoke chariots, and others horses; but we the name, etc.") There is only one verb in the Hebrew text—in the second clause, where "we" is its subject. In the first clause it is implied, with "some" and "others" as subjects. The verb is *nazkir*, from the root *zkr* "remember"—in this form, "cause to be remembered"; and all the translations cited so far understand it in that sense. Not so Dahood, who renders: "Some through chariots, and others through horses, but we through the Name of our God are strong." *Nazkir*, he thinks, is a denominative verb from the *zakhar* (*zkr*) that means "male." Just as elsewhere *nagbir* is from *gebher* or *gibbor* (*gbr*), and means "we shall be powerful," so here *nazkir* means "we shall be (are) male, i.e., masculine, i.e., strong."

Dahood is wrong. *Zakhar* means only "male." It refers to what is common to rams and infant boys, distinguishing them from ewes and infant girls. It is biological only—one might say, anatomical; whereas *gbr* is social. *Gbr* and its derivatives, in the sense of "man, manliness,

---

* His *mū'etīkā* must be a typographical error.

power," are frequent in Psalms, but *zakhar* "male" is not to be found there at all. In the whole Bible no form of *hizkir* suggests the meaning "to be male," let alone "to be strong"; and every locution similar to our *beshem . . . nazkir* (see especially Exodus 23:13, Joshua 23:7, and Isaiah 48:1) is related to "cause to be remembered, mention."

What led Dahood astray? The critical apparatus of Biblia Hebraica, noting the Septuagint's "we shall be made great," records that some would therefore emend *nazkir* to *nagbir*. Dahood wants to accomplish the same thing without emending, so he shows off—in a rather unfortunate way, because we have to ask ourselves whether he is so lacking in linguistic finesse as to confuse the different connotations of *gbr* and *zkr*. But it is as a linguist that he addresses us.

Generally, the verb in biblical poetry, always difficult, with Dahood enters the domain of total arbitrariness. Whatever he prefers, he can justify: perfect imperfects, precative perfects, *-ah* as Canaanite-influenced third-person perfect *masculine* singular, *-u* as Canaanite-influenced second-person imperfect masculine *singular*. That is true also of his infixed *-t-*'s, enclitic *-m*'s, intensive *b-*'s, and inserted *ki*'s. Not that such things may not exist, but that he makes entirely too free with them. My most common marginal note is the exclamation point, meaning "Everything can be anything!" On a higher turn of the spiral, the linguist Dahood seems to have put us back in the prelinguistic conditions Rousseau laughed at. .

A final comment on these matters. Of the Forty-first Psalm Dahood says: "The language of this lament is very archaic (probably Davidic era) and difficult, so that the translation of several clauses is doubtful." The Davidic era—that is, about 1000–950 B.C.E. Most of the psalms, therefore, are in his view later; but not so late as was thought two generations ago, when the critics spoke confidently of Maccabean psalms. From this and other things Dahood says, we may infer that he thinks most of the psalms to be no more than 400 years younger than this archaic one. That is to say, he perceives a marked difference in language arising in the course of four centuries. But he also says that the Ugaritic texts were composed or first written down about 1800 B.C.E., or earlier. They are at least eight centuries older than the oldest psalms. How, then, does he allow himself to understand the language of the psalms as if it were contemporary with his Ugaritic? Ugaritic has something to tell us, but what, precisely? Surely something a little less unequivocal than Dahood appears to believe.

An analogy. That German *Knabe* and *Knecht* are cognate with

English *knave* and *knight* is certain, but we would be making a mistake if we thought we could explain one set by the other. Again, *magistrate* is from *magis*, "more," and *minister* from *minus*, "less," but it does not follow that a police-court magistrate is greater than a minister of state. It is taking much for granted to assume that what a word probably meant in Ugaritic in 1800 B.C.E. it certainly meant in Hebrew in 800 B.C.E. Because *'pr* is "mud" in Ugaritic—so Dahood tells us—that is how he translates Hebrew *'aphar*. But the biblical evidence is for "dry earth, dust," as we have always supposed. It is good for us to know what the meaning was a thousand years earlier. It is always good for us to know things. Only, we then have the job of determining how to understand our knowledge, and what to do with it. Rarely will we be well-advised to perform tricks with it.

What Dahood thinks of the large questions about the psalms—types, functions, origins, theology—he does not tell us here, but promises us in his concluding volume. Or rather, here he neither considers them at the length they require nor refrains from considering them at all, but touches on them lightly, which is to say, unsatisfactorily. Some psalms he characterizes as an individual's laments or prayers for deliverance. Then he translates certain words, novelly, as "eternal life" and "resurrection." Why should a lament or a prayer for deliverance include pleas for such boons? What is being prayed for, right now, is surcease here below. And it will not do for Dahood to throw out a remark about Canaanite belief in an afterlife, like the Greeks' Hades and Elysian Fields, and deduce that the Israelites had such a belief, too. The subject needs more than a hit-and-run treatment. Anyway, if that really is an individual's prayer for deliverance, then the sickness or evil that has him in thrall can only be paranoia. All those foes, enemies, and evildoers who compass him about, digging pits and laying snares for him! The "I" of those prayers must be a special kind of individual—an exemplary one, probably a royal one, who in his person and life enacts conflicts of a national or even cosmic bearing.

I have said that Dahood is conservative about the (consonantal) text. But textual conservatism does not necessarily imply conservatism about the meaning of the text, or the theology of its authors. The Scandinavian myth-and-ritual school, for instance, is reluctant to emend, but ready to find paganism everywhere. A representative work, by a disciple of the masters of that school, is G. W. Ahlström's *Psalm 89: Eine Liturgie aus dem Ritual des leidenden Königs* (Lund,

1959). Conservative about the text, Ahlström nevertheless considers the possibility that he is dealing with a ritual of the suffering king, in the cult of a YHWH who is a dying and rising god like Tammuz-Adonis (*adon*, "Lord"). Ahlström is even suspicious of the name David. It means "beloved." Is it really a name? Perhaps it is the appellation of an officiant? Tammuz is called "beloved."

Dahood does not go so far—probably. Of the Twenty-ninth Psalm he says that it is a "Yahwistic adaptation of an older Canaanite hymn to the storm-god, Baal," reminding us that in the 1930s H. L. Ginsberg called it "a Phoenician hymn in the Psalter." That the Israelites took it over from the Canaanites seems hard to dispute. But if so, why does Dahood translate the first verse as ". . . Give Yahweh, O gods, give Yahweh glory and praise . . ."? RSV: ". . . Ascribe to the Lord, O heavenly beings, ascribe to the Lord glory and strength. . . ." (Note to "heavenly beings": "Heb *sons of gods*") JPS: "Ascribe unto the Lord, O ye sons of might, ascribe unto the Lord glory and strength." (Note in the Soncino Psalms: "*sons of might*. Hebrew 'sons of the mighty' or 'sons of God,' a double plural of *ben-el*. The same phrase occurs in 89:7, where the parallelism shows that the angelic hosts are intended. . . .") This is not quite the purest or most austere monotheism, but surely the Israelites would not have left the psalm out-and-out polytheistic? In a note Dahood says: "In Canaanite mythology the *bn ilm*, 'the sons of El,' . . . are the minor gods . . . of the pantheon. . . . In the Old Testament the term was demythologized and came to refer to the angels or spiritual beings who are members of Yahweh's court and do his bidding. . . ." Then why not translate, with RSV, "heavenly beings"? Why "gods"?

Above all, why "gods" in the Twenty-ninth Psalm? Father Dahood may not know, but that continues to hold a special place in the Jewish liturgy. It is a Sabbath psalm par excellence, sung Friday night and again Saturday morning, when the Torah scroll is returned to the Ark. (Rabbi Simeon J. Maslin has shown that to this day the Portuguese Marranos recite the same psalm—without knowing what the Hebrew means, of course, and therefore corrupting the text in their oral transmission of it.) In all these many centuries, our pious and learned have been invoking angels—celestial beings—not gods. It must have been so from the time when Jews (or Israelites) first began the liturgical use of this psalm.

Another point about liturgy is suggested by the last verse of the Twentieth Psalm, frequent in Jewish prayer: *YHWH hoshi'ah hammelekh ya'anenu bheyom qor'enu.* JPS follows the punctuation of the Masoretes: "Save, Lord; let the King answer us in the day that we call." RSV, like the ancient versions, divides the verse differently, and probably better: "Give victory to the king, O Lord; answer us when we call." (Again Dahood is ostentatiously fancy.) A Jew who tries to learn from the Bible scholars may agree that RSV is right, but when he leads the congregation in prayer it will not occur to him to shift the pause from *hoshi'ah* to *hammelekh*.

In short, what is the text that is being translated? Is it one or many? Fixed or labile? If you translate what the text was "originally," aren't you ignoring what it is "really"? Haven't we the right to say to Dahood that a hymn with an invocation to gods was not yet an Israelite psalm; and that since he is translating Israelite-Jewish psalms rather than Canaanite hymns, only "heavenly beings" will do? Going to the very origin, Dahood may mistranslate. Yet the ideal of translation, generally, is to render a text as nearly as possible as it was understood by the writer (or "writer") and his first hearers. Which is only another reason why the enterprise of translation, so necessary and useful, is doomed from the start. E. H. Gombrich says, in *Norm and Form*: ". . . a work of art carries with it the barnacles of its voyage through the centuries . . . anything we say or write about a painting may change it in a subtle way." The text won't sit still for you.

One moral of all this is utopian, but inescapable. It is a Jew's business to know Hebrew. Reading a psalm, or intoning one, he should have simultaneously present to his mind as many different meanings as possible. He cannot depend on a translation, or translations.

What is close to you, or should be close to you, you should know. If you know what is remote and not close, you are Levantine—like the upper class in the Egypt of the pashas and effendis, whose beaux-esprits, while knowing little of Arabic or the Arabs, might write delicate little essays about Proust. (So I have seen them described.) Greek is "objectively" a more important language to know than Latin, for literature, philosophy, history of science, rabbinics, or New Testament; but Latin is the language of the West, and when only one of the two is taught in the West, it will rightly be Latin. If we may trust T. S. Eliot and Edmund Wilson, Dante is greater than Shakespeare; yet an Englishman or American has to know Shakespeare, and only ought to know Dante. A German without Goethe is uncultured, an Englishman or American with Goethe is a curiosity. And so with Jews and Hebrew.

Maybe this is one meaning for us of the old Jewish sigh that it is hard—or, as someone said about something else, it is a complex fate —to be a Jew. You are that lady's son the nuclear geophysicist, and you should be able to weigh one translation of Psalms against another.

—*February 1968*

VII

ISRAEL

. 42 .

Scholars in Jerusalem

In 1961 a World Congress of Jewish Studies was held at the Hebrew University in Jerusalem. About fourteen sections, covering Archeology to Yiddish Language and Literature, met simultaneously, more than 150 papers were read, and the attendance sometimes went as high as 2,000. The patron of the congress was the President of Israel, and a large audience at the opening festive session heard the only two prime ministers Israel had ever had deliver speeches they had obviously written themselves. Besides the Israelis, lecturers and visitors came from all over Western Europe, the United States and Canada, South Africa, and one or two Latin American countries. Scholars from several countries behind the Iron Curtain had been expected, but the only one actually allowed out was a Christian from East Germany, a specialist in the Dead Sea literature. Among the many other Christians present were a large number of Catholic priests, mostly from Belgium, Italy, and especially Spain.

The congress was a success, with a high average level of presentation and discussion. Besides, people from all over the world had a chance to meet and assay each other. Friendships were formed and invitations given and accepted. When any scholarly conference does this, it has done well.

I was there to learn what I could about the state and direction of Jewish studies and, more particularly, about the effects of Israeli circumstances and outlooks on the practice of Jewish scholarship in Israel. As to state and direction, no generalization is possible. Mostly, the methods and approaches that have always characterized modern Jewish scholarship are still in use, and rarely was there evidence of a sensibility or an angle of vision that could only be contemporary. Perhaps the feeling one got of the Jewishness of early Christianity, from both Jewish and Christian scholars, might be considered as new; but the newness would then be less in the idea itself than in its being

325

more widely shared and perhaps more deeply felt, on both sides, than ever before.

The importance of Spain in Bible scholarship *was* strikingly new. Modern Bible scholarship has been largely German, Scandinavian, Dutch, Anglo-American, and French. It is easy to explain the eminence of those nations in this branch of learning—the Calvinist and Lutheran traditions of a learned clergy; scholarly interest in Near Eastern culture and civilization, whether ancient or modern, arising out of imperial conquest; a strong academic tradition in linguistics and the classics; application of saga and folklore research to the ancient Near East. Spanish circumstances have not encouraged scholarship of that kind. Yet a handful of Spaniards have been doing much work toward publishing an edition of the Hebrew Bible which may challenge the long monopoly of the German Kittel-Kahle Biblia Hebraica. For some reason, perhaps related to Franco's concern with the southern and eastern Mediterranean, the Spanish government decided to encourage Arabic and, by extension, Hebrew scholarship. A few scholars, mostly priests, set themselves to master the new subject matter, and they now rank among the outstanding students of the Bible text in the world.

As to how Israelis cultivate Jewish scholarship, I brought with me some information about what they had been doing and some expectations about life in Israel. I thought I understood that life, understood the attitudes it gave rise to, and understood the effect of those attitudes. What I saw and heard led me to change my mind, slightly on some points and considerably on others. I had arrived as a friend with certain apprehensions about parochialism and Israelism. I left less apprehensive.

The Israelis themselves keep worrying about parochialism. One reason for their having an international congress in Jerusalem was to relieve that worry, which arises from their smallness and their being hemmed in by hostile neighbors. In the same summer they were hosts to city managers and plastic surgeons from everywhere. They joke about their passion for international conferences.

They are right to be worried, because parochialism is a danger. I had supposed that it was something more as well, an actuality, but I think I was wrong. In that year fell the 2,500th anniversary of what has been called Cyrus the Great's Balfour Declaration, which authorized the Judean exiles in Babylonia to return to Palestine. Not only to celebrate the anniversary, but also to assert Israel's contemporary friendships in Asia and the non-Western world generally, the committee in charge invited an Iranian authority on Old Persian to open the first plenary session with a paper on Zoroastrian messianism. (He droned it, in French.) Obviously, this was as much a gesture by the government as a decision by the scholars, but whatever their motives, the Israelis were consciously doing what they could to ward off parochialism.

Then there was the very nature of the congress itself—its inclusive definition of Jewish studies and the participation in it of a large number of Christians. The agenda of the congress was what a composite agenda of four American societies might be like: the American Academy for Jewish Research, cultivating the *Wissenschaft des Judentums* as it has been understood for a century and a half, with a textual and philological emphasis and a preference for rabbinics, history of philosophy, and the Arabic age in Jewish history; YIVO Institute for Jewish Research, emphasizing Yiddish language and literature and East European Jewish folklore, economics, and politics; the Conference on Jewish Social Studies, for modern and contemporary history and sociology; and the American Society for Biblical Literature and Exegesis, with a predominantly Christian membership. In the United States, Bible and archeology appear infrequently on the programs of the Jewish scholarly societies. At the congress in Jerusalem too, if the sections on Bible, archeology, Dead Sea Scrolls, and the ancient Near East had been excluded, there would have been few Christian lecturers or auditors; but in Israel it would have been absurd to exclude those subjects. In the United States what we call Jewish studies has a relation to Bible and archeology something like the relation of Jewish education to general education: it is supplementary. In Israel, a Congress of Jewish Studies could attract men like André Dupont-Sommer of the Sorbonne.

In fact, the congress was not only less parochial, in this sense, than a Jewish scholarly society in the United States, it was also less parochial than the average learned society of any kind in the United States. At the sessions I sampled, the papers and discussion were in Hebrew, English, French, and German. In contrast, American scholarship is almost completely dependent on English. Durkheim and Weber are translated from French and German as much for our professors as for our undergraduates, and in an American social-science journal a footnote reference to a work in a foreign language is rare. We take this so much for granted that we do not see how scandalous it is, how offensive to the ideal of an international republic of learning. By the linguistic standard—though of course it would be wrong to judge by that alone—American scholarship is more parochial than Swedish, or Dutch, or Israeli, or even Spanish scholarship. At the sessions I attended there were papers by two Spanish scholars: one, by a layman, was in German and the other, by a priest, was in French.

The congress took place during a lull in the Eichmann trial and shortly after a crowd in Jerusalem had shown its displeasure with an American fundamentalist missionary's use of candy and other spiritual inducements of that sort to entice children from poor and devout families into his mission. In the American press there had been some talk of powerful anti-gentile sentiments in Israel. I saw nothing of the kind. The Israelis who made up the congress's audience were hardly a representative cross-section of the population, but I think it meant something that even the obviously Orthodox seemed to be hospitable, rather than merely correct, to the Christian clergymen among the visitors.

More generally, if parochialism implies sameness, Israeli society is as far from parochial as can be. Everywhere there was a great variety of human types. One morning I saw an old Jew from an Arab country on a donkey in a busy Jerusalem street, and an hour later I was speaking at the university with two men, a poet in his forties and a former revolutionist about sixty, who between them had spent thirty-five years in Soviet slave-labor camps. Nor were the newspapers and radio parochial. They had a sensible coverage of domestic and foreign news, and in foreign news a sensible distribution between what was of special importance to Israel and what was more general.

Not many languages of comparable historical and cultural importance are spoken by so few people as Hebrew, but that has not made Israel parochial, either. The first and obvious fact is that most educated Israelis are more proficient in foreign languages than most educated Frenchmen or Americans, who are tempted to believe that their tongues are universal rather than national. In Jerusalem the university and private bookstores are more polyglot than in New York or Paris.

The priest who wrote his paper in French being ill, a Spanish monk stationed in Jerusalem read it for him, rather haltingly. After a few minutes, annoyed by a draft, he called out in rapid-fire Hebrew, "Will someone please shut that damned window!" (An American murmured to a colleague, "It's frightening.") Again, of the papers read in Hebrew one of the most impressive, for language as much as for content, was by Professor Schubert, a Catholic scholar from Austria, on an aspect of the Dead Sea Scrolls. Hebrew was used less in the Bible, archeology, and related sections, with their many Christian participants and auditors, and in the section on contemporary Jewry, with many Jews from abroad, than in most others. Even the Israeli scholars in those sections tended to use English, out of courtesy to their guests. But the signs are unmistakable. Though Christian Hebraists have been the great lexicographers and grammarians of the Bible, only a few have been like Franz Delitzsch, who translated the New Testament into Hebrew, in mastering the whole range of the language. Now they will have to learn more than is found in the classical lexicons and grammars.

Impressed as I was by all this, I was not surprised. Lectures in Hebrew were an old story, and it is also an old story that for an elite even dead languages can be living. When Berlin classicists, honoring Gilbert Murray, praised him in Latin, he was so moved that he forgot himself and responded in Greek. To this day Latin is spoken in some Catholic seminaries, and in the first part of the nineteenth century it was still the language of the Hungarian parliament —though the Latinity was not Cicero's.

What shook me was to hear the chambermaids in my hotel chattering away in Hebrew. I told myself that I should not have been surprised, that I had known this was so, and that I was yielding to the sentimentality derided by the Israeli joke: "Jewish train engineers, for the first time in two thousand years!" But knowing-about and really knowing are not the same, and the chambermaids *were* gossiping in Hebrew for the first time in two thousand years. As long ago as in the age of R. Judah the Prince it was something to wonder at that his maidservants spoke Hebrew, and spoke it so well. Aramaic had long been the vernacular.

A young man attending the section on Hebrew language and literature was a Christian Ethiopian studying at the university. Just as other students from Africa and Asia were learning how to apply Israeli irrigation or cooperative or trade-union methods to their countries, so he was learning from the example of Hebrew how to help his people make an old language say new things. It is the scholars and writers, amateur as well as professional, who have accomplished this. At the congress my teacher Abraham S. Halkin lectured to a large audience on the attitude of medieval Jews toward Hebrew. In the Arab lands, especially Spain, they felt guilty about neglecting Hebrew, but wrote in Arabic. They thought that Hebrew could not express complex philosophical thought, while Arabic seemed to have been almost providentially appointed for that purpose. The thoughts Professor Halkin was expressing in Hebrew, like the thoughts of the historians, philosophers, mathematicians, and scientists at the university itself, were not lacking in complexity yet he, like the university teachers, found Hebrew quite adequate. Only a few months before, the Tunisian students' association had declared that French should continue to be their language of higher education because Arabic was not suited for it. The irony was almost too heavy—in the Middle Ages Jews thought Hebrew hopelessly clumsier than Arabic; today Hebrew meets the needs of a vigorous intellectual life, while Arabs regard Arabic as being out of place in a university.

I had feared that an excessive Israeli patriotism and feelings of superiority toward Jews and Jewish scholars in the diaspora might be distorting the Jewish scholarship of Israel. Some years ago, for instance, an Israeli historian indulged his Palestinocentric bias so extravagantly as to date the beginning of modern Jewish history from a time in the eighteenth century when some Hasidic rabbis and their followers went up to Palestine. The usual dating is from the French Revolution, with its transformation of European and Jewish society and thought. My own preference is for the mid-seventeenth century, with the Peace of Westphalia's secularization of politics, the victory of cash-nexus economics, the reversal of the Jews' west-to-east migration in Europe after Khmelnitzki, the settlement of Jews in New Amsterdam, and their resettlement in England. That was also when the mystical heretic and false messiah Shabbethai Zevi and the rationalist heretic Benedict Spinoza—Sephardim, and therefore with family memories of expulsion from Spain, or of expedient baptism—pointed the way to modernity for Jews. Shabbethai Zevi, as Gershom Scholem has shown, had some later followers active in the French Revolution, and others in the creation of Reform Judaism; and Spinoza was the first not only to advocate a secular, neutral society, but also to assert the possibility of a secular Zionism.

Other instances of Palestinocentric distortion are less clear-cut. When an Israeli historian of the period before the state described Rabban Johanan ben Zakkai as a collaborator with the Romans not essentially different from Josephus, rather than as the hero who assured the continuity of Judaism after the Temple was destroyed, he could make a good scholarly argument for that proposition. Still, his ideology was showing. Micah Joseph Berditchevsky, whose Zionism was a kind of Nietzschean protest against rabbinical and diaspora

330

Judaism as an unmanly, spiritualizing passivism, had said the same sort of thing. So had the poet Saul Chernikhovsky. And so, in an important sense, had their ideological enemies, the Yiddishist diaspora nationalists. All agreed that Western Jews, writing in gentile languages, were afraid to tell the full truth or could not even see the truth, because they wore the blinkers of accommodationist ideologies and of myths of Jewish nobility, if only in the form of noble suffering.

This could not be dismissed so easily as dating modern Jewish history from the *'aliyah* of some Hasidim. After all, it was Leopold Zunz, the founder of modern Jewish studies in the first decades of the nineteenth century, who had said: "If there are ranks in suffering, Israel takes precedence of all the nations; if the duration of sorrows and the patience with which they are borne ennoble, the Jews can challenge the aristocracy of every land," etc.; and the requirements of emancipation had always been present to his mind. So the Israelis, and the Zionists, and the autonomists had a point.

But might they not be making too much of a good thing? It is a diaspora historian in the great tradition of Zunz, Salo Baron, who has shown the roots of the "lachrymose interpretation" of Jewish history in religious ideology and the needs of communal discipline and control. At the congress I was amused that it was a French Jew, not an Israeli, who in an aside accomplished a neat bit of Baronian debunking. In medieval Latin documents relating to Jews, the abbreviation *dus* sometimes appears before the name. *Dus* can represent either *dominus* (Master or Sir) or *dictus* (the aforesaid or aforementioned). Scholars used to assume that for a Jew the abbreviation must have the second meaning, because if a Jew was a sufferer by definition, how could Christians give him a title of respect? Dr. Blumenkranz showed that whatever we may have supposed, the *dus* before a Jew's name is often to be read *dominus*.

The Israelis are using some of the real advantages of their experience for understanding the past more perspicuously. After the Iranian had read his paper on Zoroastrian messianism, two Israelis lectured, Dr. Tadmor on the political background of Cyrus's edict to the Jews and Professor Urbach on the Rabbis' attitudes to him. Dr. Tadmor observed that Cyrus, a foreign monarch, was encouraged by the priesthood of Marduk to overthrow their own king, who had demoted their god from his primacy in the Babylonian pantheon, and that Cyrus's restoration of the Jews was a kind of incidental by-product of his general policy of restoring the cultic *status quo ante* throughout the empire. By being an Israeli, by having personally experienced the Balfour Declaration and having learned how a great power can arrive at decisions fateful for Jews, this scholar was helped to understand the earlier Balfour Declaration in a new and convincing way.

Professor Urbach's paper almost demonstratively refused to apply such labels as collaborationism to the Rabbis' political philosophy. It pointedly asserted that while attitudes toward the present can affect attitudes toward the past, sometimes it is the other way around. His problem was the Rabbis' equivocal feelings about Cyrus, centuries before them. On the one hand, Cyrus was the Lord's shepherd (Isaiah 44:28)and anointed (*meshiho*, His *mashiah!*—45:1), who brought the exile to an end; but on the other hand, he did not abolish idolatry or himself acknowledge the true God. When another would-be Cyrus appeared, Julian the Apostate (sc., from Christianity to paganism), the Rabbis' coolness to the past Persian emperor made them ignore the contemporary Roman's offer to restore the Temple destroyed by his predecessors. It was just as well. Julian died within the year.

As striking as the new Spanish eminence in the study of the Bible text is the Israeli lead in the study of Jewish mysticism. One can understand why that is a more respectable field of research now than it was in the last century, when nearly every Jewish scholar treated it with revulsion. The victory of the Jewish rationalists in their struggle with the obscurantist enemy; the Freudian revolution; the repeated demonstrations since, say, the Dreyfus case, that myth and nonrational belief affect the destinies of men and nations—all have had their effect. Even the classicists, who used to hold up the Greeks as a model of rationality, have long since had to come to terms with the Greeks and the Irrational. But why, in the Jewish field, should mysticism—including Hasidism—be so predominantly an Israeli subject of inquiry? Hasidism is treated extensively and sympathetically in Yiddish literature—Peretz, Bashevis Singer, etc.—while Hebrew writers like Bialik, though not strangers to it, tend to ignore it. It may be that Yiddish writers had a linguistic and a social fondness for a movement that expressed itself largely in Yiddish and was plebeian, while the more elitist Hebrew writers disliked it for those reasons. But even if this conjecture is sound, there must be other reasons as well.

It is not enough to say that the Israeli domination in the study of Jewish mysticism is due to one man. To be sure, the great explorer and cartographer of this dark continent, Gershom Scholem, has been at the Hebrew University since the 1920s, and the influence of an outstanding man is not to be underestimated. He could have done his work and probably raised up disciples anywhere. But Scholem himself implies that there is a relationship between his being a Zionist (and an Israeli) and his specialization. He has written that after beginning his university studies in mathematics and physics, he turned to Semitic languages, and then to Jewish mysticism. After publishing his first book, he met the ranking German authority, who was exceptional in bothering with mysticism at all—an old, alert rabbi, a nineteenth-century liberal and disciple of the great Heinrich Graetz (who hated mysticism). Impressed by that scholar's manuscripts and rare books, Scholem congratulated him on being able to study such documents. To which the old man answered: *"Was? Den Quatsch soll ich auch noch lesen?"* ("You don't really expect me to *read* that drivel, too?") Then, says Scholem, he understood much that he had not understood before. He is emphatic about "our readiness to know and acknowledge *all* the forces that have sustained the Jewish people *as a living body* in all the vicissitudes of its history"— presumably in contrast to the unreadiness of the German (French, etc.) citizens of the Mosaic persuasion, who had to deny, to themselves and others, that the disreputable Kabbalah had been so powerful for so long.

There is in Israel, then, a willingness, or rather an eagerness, to recognize and make public Jewish realities that non-Israeli Jews are squeamish about. (For me some of the citations in Scholem's *Jewish Gnosticism . . . and Talmudic Tradition* are strong meat, grossly anthropomorphic.) But beyond that, and beyond Scholem's ability to attract and inspire, I think there is something about Israeli life which helps to explain why so many young people—not absolutely, perhaps, but at least relatively—specialize in his field. It may even explain why so many of his students, relatively, are women. (The equality of the sexes in Israel does not seem to have produced many women Talmudists or, as far as I could make out, Bible scholars.) In Israel Jewish mysticism, or more precisely messianism, or pseudo-messianism, is felt to be relevant. Scholem has demonstrated, for the Kabbalah, its close link to the yearning for national redemption; and for pseudo-messianism, especially of the various wings of Shabbethai Zevi's movement, the ambiguous relation of its antinomianism to normative Judaism and its capacity to be channeled from a kind of proto-Zionism into aspirations of a universally messianic character.

For Israeli intellectuals, whether Zionists or the heirs of Zionism, that complex of affirmations and negations, visions and discontents, is not merely something out there, in the past. If we set aside the theosophy of Shabbethai Ẓevi and his descendants, much remains of their doctrine which has a contemporary flavor—the attempt to affirm while transcending or actually negating traditional Judaism, the blending of Jewish and universal longings, activism in the pursuit of the impossible. Above all, Israelis know, by the lives they have lived, how an obsessive vision can overcome reality.

So much for the ideology of Jewish scholarship in Israel. As for its sociology, Israeli Jewish scholars stand in a favorable relation to their subject, to their public, and to their colleagues in other fields of learning. Ever since the beginning of the *Wissenschaft des Judentums*, its practitioners in Europe and America have been in a situation resembling the one that modern poets complain about: isolated, talking to each other, without a public, without a recognized and respected place in the community. (The annual *Proceedings* of the American Academy for Jewish Research are distributed in a few hundred copies.) Those committed to Jewish learning of the old-fashioned kind have had little use for the new scholarship, suspecting it—often correctly—of heterodoxy. This leaves the emancipated as a potential public. But few emancipated Jews in Europe or America have the equipment or the interest to follow what the scholars are doing. Even emancipated former students of the old-fashioned *yeshivot* usually turn their backs on Jewish studies. If they are scholars or retain scholarly interests, their fields are the sciences, or the social sciences, or the general humanities. The loneliness of Zunz and Steinschneider in the nineteenth century was not much more intense than their successors' in the twentieth.

Instead of being likened to poets in the United States, the Israeli scholars may be likened to historians of the Civil War in the United States. They do not talk to themselves. They have a public and a standing. What they do and say is reported in the newspapers. The President and the Prime Minister take them seriously. President Ben Zvi, who had a reception for the guests of the congress, has done important things in Jewish ethnology, and Prime Minister Ben Gurion is an eager consumer of Jewish scholarship. In his opening address to the congress Mr. Ben Gurion urged the scholars to do more research into Jewish messianism and messianic ideals. Afterward I heard someone, not an Israeli, grumble about a would-be

Zhdanov telling scholars what they should do. The critic had it all wrong. If I were an Israeli scholar I would not resent the interest or even the advice. It is lack of interest I would resent. English classical scholars must envy their predecessors, who lived when the classics counted and when every other Mr. Bennet was trying his hand at translating Horace, the Government and Opposition benches capped each other's quotations from the elegiac poets, and Gladstone wrote a fine book on the Homer question.

About the same time as the congress, a yeshivah in Bene Beraq, an Orthodox stronghold near Tel Aviv, was conducting an annual week-long session of Talmud study. This too was covered in the press, which reported an attendance of several hundred workers, farmers, businessmen, men in the professions, and government officials. One interview I remember was with a lieutenant colonel, who had fallen away somewhat from Orthodox practice but looked forward every year to his week in the yeshivah as a chance to refresh mind and spirit. People like that can be an informed, enthusiastic public for Jewish scholarship, and despite secularization, Israel is likely to continue producing them over the years. At the congress I was impressed by the number of Israeli lecturers and auditors with heads covered, and by the easy relations between them and the bareheaded. There are many, whom we may describe as liberal Orthodox, who are entirely at home in the Hebrew University, whether as historians or physicists or physicians. And for all the talk of a *Kulturkampf* between the Orthodox and the rest of the Israelis, no one is stared at because he wears a *kippah* on the street or at work. (A man who wears the skimpy, varicolored *kippah* one sees in Israel is likely to encounter unpleasantness only among the stand-pat Orthodox, who seem more offended by headgear that is not black and ample than by none at all.)

In the academic community itself, Israeli practitioners of Jewish scholarship are in the thick of things and not, as they would probably be somewhere else, off in a corner, having merely personal relations with scholars in other fields. In Israel there is contact between those in Jewish scholarship and classicists, general historians, orientalists, sociologists. Many of the learned are themselves part of the public for Jewish scholarship. In short, the difficulties of people pursuing Jewish scholarship in Israel are the difficulties of all scholars—income, jobs—rather than the disabilities of people in a specialty regarded as eccentric and irrelevant.

This does more than keep the Jewish scholars from being too

actively unhappy. Knowledge that their public has fairly high standards offsets temptations to court celebrity by hasty popularization and vulgar modernization of the past. They are also aware that they are, after all, men of here and now. That awareness, which comes harder to scholars when their field is remote from general interest, is a safeguard against unconscious bias. (To be free of bias altogether is not given to us.)

Still, the Israeli scholars would be better served if there were an informed non-Israeli public for them as well, to balance the Palestinocentrism of both scholars and public in Israel.

After the congress a two-day tour in Galilee was arranged for the visitors. As a handsome gesture of hospitality, two distinguished archeologists talked about their digs, each at the site for which he was responsible—Professor Mazar at Bet She'arim and Professor Yadin at Hazor.

At Bet She'arim, R. Judah the Prince's seat, parts of a large necropolis had been uncovered, where members of the Jewish upper classes from Palestine and neighboring countries were buried in the early Christian centuries. Their coffins were stone sarcophagi, carved in what appeared to my inexpert eyes to be a somewhat clumsy, provincial Roman style. But what were Jews doing with stone sarcophagi —especially since the inscriptions commemorate not only *archisynagogoi* (presidents of congregations) but also rabbis? Perhaps naively retrojecting into the past the unadorned wooden coffin, with wooden pegs, of our more immediate ancestors, I had always thought that law-biding Jews were buried in great simplicity. The Mishnah records that when the poor began to abandon their dead without burial, because of the crushing expense of a funeral à la mode, Rabban Gamaliel decreed the simple shroud for all. Apparently he did not decree the simple coffin. Or if he did—or if a simple coffin is to be inferred from the reason for a simple shroud—his contemporaries and the immediately following generations may have regarded the decree as a counsel of perfection rather than as unbreachable law. If, then, later generations took as obligatory what earlier generations had taken as pious advice, that would not be exceptional in Jewish history, which has consistently shown successors extending and legislating what was personal and supererogatory for their predecessors. That which the learned more or less contemporary with Gamaliel disregarded, even the masses of a later age observed with all meticulousness.

An epitaph at Bet She'arim commemorates a certain Julianus,

employed in the Roman administration, who was Judah among Jews. The Greek-translation name of a relative of his, R. Nehemiah, was Paregorios (Comforter). Earlier, the Hellenizing Jews against whom the Maccabees made their revolution used to adopt Greek names that sounded something like the Hebrew, e. g., Jason for Joshua, and in the modern period this has been so common that many believe it to be a kind of religious custom, e. g., Arthur for Aaron. Similarly, in modern times Baruch is often translated as Benedict (the same initials helping) and Arieh as Leon, while in the Middle Ages Shem Ṭov (Good Name) became the Greek Kalonymos. I should have known from the books and journals, but I had to be physically in Bet She'arim to realize that even in Palestine, and even when rabbinical Judaism ruled almost unchallenged among the Jews, they were doing the same thing.

Much has been said about the archeological passion of the Israelis. It has been linked to their feeling, often expressed by Ben Gurion, of being closer to the Israelites of antiquity than to the diaspora Jews of much more recent times. The archeology of Palestine, after all, is about Palestine. Yet Bet She'arim shows that Palestinian archeology has an ineradicably Jewish quality about it. The comedy of names is Jewish, and if contemporary Israelis are writing a new act—all those thumping, bisyllabic, pristinely Hebraic surnames, and all those long-unused biblical given names ("names from the *haftarah*," the lesson from the Prophets, as they are called in Yiddish)—the Israelis are not breaking with a Jewish habit, but merely adding another variant to it.

At Hazor, "the head of all those kingdoms" (Joshua 11:10), Professor Yadin showed us two strata, a Canaanite city built a few centuries before Joshua and immediately above it the Israelite city built by King Ahab centuries later. It was not hard to follow the demonstration that Ahab's city was less impressive than the Canaanite one on whose ruins it had stood. One of our party found it hard to accept that the Israelite city, though much later than the Canaanite, was yet inferior to it. He must have forgotten that the Bible takes for granted the inferiority of Israelite material culture: it is Phoenicians (Canaanites) who build Solomon's Temple in I Kings. W. F. Albright's Penguin *Archaeology of Palestine*, which no one at the congress had the right not to have read, shows how much more advanced than the Israelites their Canaanite predecessors and contemporaries were, and says that only in the realm of the spirit did the Israelite excel. Yadin, a former chief of staff of the Israeli army, is less given than Albright

337

to saying things that can be regarded as homiletical, yet he too had to give Albright's answer. The facts exclude any other. It is, again, a Jewish rather than a Palestinian set of facts.

Everything else about Israeli archeology seems to teach the same lesson. There is the brute reminder of conquest and domination in the Hellenistic, Roman, Byzantine, Crusader, and Arab-Turkish remains. There is the provincialness of the local imitations of metropolitan styles. There is, in contrast to the weight and size of all those foreign monuments, the smallness of, say, R. Isaac Luria's (rebuilt) synagogue in Safed. It is small, but from it radiated the Lurianic Kabbalah, which so profoundly affected not only Shabbethai Zevi, and not only Hasidism, but even that arch-*mitnagged* R. Elijah, Gaon of Vilna.

It was my first visit, and I had not expected Israel to be quite that Jewish. For a few months before the congress I had been participating from time to time in an informal colloquy between some Israeli and some American Jews. One of the things the Americans would tell the Israelis was that from what we knew of Israel, it was not Jewish enough. We were thinking, I suppose, of a moral-emotional tradition associated with minoritiness, including a certain irony about power. We gave examples. We had heard that some young Israelis observe the Fast of the Ninth of Av with parties, on the ground that the exile it was supposed to lament has come to an end in Israel, which is the opposite of exile. For the Americans, that was coarse, literal, and insensitive to the traditional Jewish distinction between the Jerusalem below and the Jerusalem above, as well as to the doctrine that all men, everywhere, are still in exile. (Luria taught a relation between Jewish exile and cosmic alienation. It was Shabbethai Zevi who turned fasts into feasts.) Or we had read that some Israelis actually call their children Nimrod, who in the Jewish tradition is the anti-Abraham, the symbol of all that is un-Jewish.

Perhaps I changed my mind in Israel more than the facts themselves, in the absence of my expectations, would have warranted. But I do not think so. Mr. Ben Gurion, a contemner of the diaspora's past, scoffer at its present, and skeptic about its future, celebrates rootedness, normalization, sovereign independence; but he is also a visionary believer in the power of the spirit and in a prophetic, messianic future which will be simultaneously Jewish and universal. Indeed, he regards Israeli strength and normality as means, and Jewish spirituality as end. One can say that Ben Gurion is an exception, or that he is old. Then one discovers that younger men, even among his opponents, seem to believe as he does.

Whether or not Israel's most useful course might be to strive for a normality uncomplicated by such visions, the most unexpected people in Israel cannot forget the old Jewish dream. The very archeology of their country will not let them.

—August 1962

. 43 .

The Israelis' Religion

Surprisingly little was known about Jewish religion in Israel until the publication of a study by the sociologist Aaron Antonovsky, "Political and Social Attitudes in Israel," jointly undertaken by the Israeli Institute for Applied Social Research and the Institute for International Social Research in Princeton. While it examines a wide range of questions—party preference, attitudes toward the United States and the Soviet Union, and the like—the most interesting and curious part of it has to do with religion.

Many Israelis, and many American Jews too, have been skeptical of the synagogue affiliation and religious self-identification of American Jews. They see this as being not truly religious but primarily a cover for Jewish ethnic feeling. In Israel, they say, evasiveness and self-deception of that kind are unnecessary. There no Jew need pretend to be religious in order to feel that he is a Jew or to make sure that his children will be Jews. There people are religious or irreligious, with no ambiguous middle ground.

That is the assertion. It is not, as we now discover, the fact. Dr. Antonovsky's interviewers asked each respondent to choose one of four answers to a question about his religious conduct: (1) completely observant; (2) mostly observant; (3) partly observant; (4) not observant at all, irreligious. By far the largest group of respondents, 46 percent, described themselves as partly observant! (Thirty percent chose one or the other of the first two, strongly religious answers, and 24 percent chose the fourth, irreligious one.) The Israelis

339

are recognizably like us, with our vacillations and inconsistencies and our compromises that drive the philosophers mad. Perhaps their resemblance to us means that our own religious behavior is not merely what our critics say it is.

Reading the study, one becomes interested in Antonovsky. He has not succeeded in concealing himself. He is clearly disappointed in those 46 percent, perhaps having hoped that he had seen the last of them in America. Whenever he can, he links them with the irreligious 24 percent, including them among those he says hold "an exclusively secularist [*hilloni*] position" or calling them near-secularist, though he could just as well link them with the religious 30 percent. They belong by themselves, of course, although continuous at one end with the 30 percent and at the other end with the 24 percent.

Antonovsky's attitude toward religion becomes even clearer when he discusses the answers to this question: "Should the Israeli government see to it that public life is in accordance with the Jewish religious tradition?" Those who answered yes he calls clericals, and those who answered no anticlericals. His clericals came to 41 percent and his anticlericals to 55 percent; 4 percent did not answer. His discussion of what he considers to be inconsistency—people who are personally religious saying that the government should not be concerned, and secularists and "near-secularists" saying that it should be concerned—need not occupy us here. He does not try to get at what his respondents thought they were saying when they answered his question with yes or no, although nothing can be more certain than that they did not understand the question alike and that many understood it differently from him. If you asked his secularists or near-secularists who nevertheless say they approve a governmental concern with the religious tradition whether they are for permitting civil marriage, most would probably say yes; but they are also probably for kosher food in the army and for closing government offices on holy days. Some might even mean that the government ought to do something about high interest rates. Of his anticlericals, who say they are opposed to a governmental concern with religion, doubtless more would like to see civil marriage permitted than feel that mail should be delivered on Yom Kippur. Besides yes or no, Antonovsky should have allowed his respondents to say yes-and-no.

A minor but intriguing point has to do with the first two possible answers to Antonovsky's question about personal religiousness. (The first was, "Yes, decidedly, I observe all the details [*diqduqim*] of the

Jewish tradition," and the second was, "I observe it in large part, in most of its details.") Almost by definition—by definition from within the religion, that is—a religious Jew cannot say he does everything the tradition requires of him. He should be modest, like our teacher Moses. Anyway, he knows what Solomon knew, that there is no man who does not sin. Why, then, did about 15 percent of the respondents choose the first answer (with another 15 percent choosing the second)? Perhaps they were just pulling the interviewer's leg, telling him what they would not dare tell their fellows, in derision of his ignorance. Or perhaps they were making an accommodation to the mind of the heathen, using his language to say something they themselves would use quite different language for. Almost certainly, some who said they were mostly observant are more pious than some who said they were completely observant, and there may even have been pious Jews among the 46 percent who said they were only partly observant. This social scientist apparently did not think it necessary to get a sense of what religion means to the religious before he framed his question about it.

Those brothers of mine, the 46 percent, find it hard to move out of the muddled middle. One reason may be that while some of the religious 30 percent are impossible, some of the secularist 24 percent are not very attractive either.

—January 1964

. 44 .

Our Cloistered Virtue

A debate in the Keneset over relaxing security restrictions on the Israeli Arabs did not evoke much feeling among the Jews of the United States. Israeli parties and distinguished personalities, like Martin Buber, were for the removal of all restrictions, while Ben Gurion wanted to retain as many as possible. In the United States most Jews were prepared to go along with whatever the Israeli government decided. In the end, a partial liberalization was enacted.

How are we to understand this indifference in a community more passionate about civil liberties and civil rights than any other in the

American population? There are two possible explanations. The first is that for American Jews, Israel is a kind of surrogate old country, and Americans with an old country often tend to be more royalist than the king. When Mussolini's Italy conquered Ethiopia in the 1930s, probably a higher proportion of Italians in America supported him than in Italy. The Irish Republican Army probably has had greater proportionate support among the consciously Irish of the Irish Americans than in Ireland. Ben Gurion is less controversial here than in Israel.

The second explanation is that while American Jews are often unrealistic about Israel, in one sense we are more realistic and less ideological about Israel than about America. It has often been observed that here we are distinctively ideological in our politics—given to regarding compromise as betrayal and to seeing the final conflict of Good and Evil in the daily push and pull of interests. Our peace of mind needs a liberalism that is explicit about itself.

Being a minority, Jews cannot avoid we/they thinking. We, as a group, have no political power. We have watched, sometimes with approval but more often with anxiety, how *they* exercise power. Having no experience of power, we have been unable to acquire anything but an intellectual understanding, if that, of power's moral ambiguities. The powerlessness that has kept us relatively free from sin has encouraged in us a self-righteous moralism. Our unexpressed feeling has been that if only *we* were in power, we would show *them* how to govern morally and by principle.

Israel is a small country, but in that country Jews rule and must take the responsibility for their rule. If political power may be likened to sexual potency, then it may be said that in Israel the Jews have became potent again for the first time in many centuries. Any political virtue of theirs will no longer be the cloistered, unexercised, and unbreathed kind that Milton could not praise.

It is the vicarious experience of political power which Israel provides for American Jews that largely accounts for our failure to react as ideologically to the imperfect civil liberties of the Israeli Arabs as we would to similar imperfections in the United States—that, and the tendency of all groups to forgive or actually deny in themselves, or in those with whom they identify, what they would not forgive in others. For similar reasons, most American Jews are less critical than many Israelis of the state-religion link in Israel, while sounding the alarm over religion in the civic life of the United States.

It will do us good to realize that when we have power, actually or vicariously, we too are subject to temptation. Our voice may stop being so soprano.

In an *Eranos Jahrbuch* there is a great essay on Jewish messianism by Gershom Scholem. At the end, after showing the majestic tension and pathos of the messianic tradition, he contrasts it to the flawed reality of the State of Israel, the fruition of so much longing. But he is not ironical at the expense of the state. Quietly he says that reality, for all its lack of visionary grandeur, is more wholesome than feverish daydreaming.

It may be that Israel will help to reinstate reality not only for its own citizens but also for Jews in other lands. One test would be whether American Jews can come to understand how resistant to unambiguous solution is the problem of relations among religion, culture, society, and state.

—*May 1962*

. 45 .

The 1967 War

It is easy to forget. The news from Israel is of headache and annoyance, trouble and difficulty. We have almost forgotten the joy of unbelievable victory, and all the more our fear and depression in those weeks before the actual fighting broke out, when Nasser was tightening his noose. Political metaphors from the thirties kept running through our minds and conversations. We said, Munich; we said, Czechoslovakia; we said, salami tactics. As the days drew on we asked ourselves, "What are they waiting for? Why didn't they jump on Sharm el-Sheikh right away? The longer they wait, the worse it will be."

Some of us surprised ourselves and each other by our concern. Thirty and forty years ago we would not have felt that way. Then, not to be parochial was our pride. Now, there is less of that kind of antiparochialism—not none at all, only less.

In the same way, there is less self-hate than there used to be. The surprise is that some Jews still had to find a reassurance about themselves in the valor of the Israelis. One would have thought that that had been taken care of in 1948, with the Israeli war of independence. Israel, it then became clear, provided for the Jews of the United States and other countries like it a kind of contemporary pioneer or cowboy ancestry, reassuring us by showing us what we wanted and needed to have shown—that while Jews can be pretty good with a fountain pen and briefcase, they can also, if necessary, be pretty good with a rifle or tank.

An unreconstructed antiparochialist Jewish scholar was sarcastic. The Jews talk a great game of internationalism, he said, but when the chips are down they are nationalist. The answer to this is: not always; only now. Those of his age and mine are not happy about where our internationalism led us a generation ago. That the Nazis wanted to murder every Jew they could get their hands on was the last thing about Nazism that interested us. For us the big question, the question that called forth all our dialectical virtuosity, was, Is Nazism the final stage of capitalism? The middle-aged do not want to incur *that* guilt again.

As for the young, I think that what happened to them was a sudden realization that genocide, antisemitism, a desire to murder Jews —all those things were not merely what one had been taught about a bad, stupid past, not merely the fault of elders who are almost a different species. Those things were real and present. Internationalist, antiparochial young Jews had taken it for granted that the Jews are the fat cats of this world and that no concern need be wasted on them. Concern should go to the wretched of the earth. Suddenly the Jews of Israel were seen to be potentially as wretched as anyone can be.

Each generation finds its own good reason for not being concerned about the Jews. Now it is that we are fat cats. Maybe so—though not all are—but earlier in the century most Jews were undeniably skinny. That made no difference. From prison Rosa Luxemburg once wrote a friend: "Why do you pester me with your Jewish sorrow? There is no room in my heart for the Jewish troubles." The sorrow and troubles of others had filled all the room in her heart. On this J. L. Talmon has commented: "Twenty-five years later, after the Germans had occupied it, there was not a single Jew left alive in Rosa's native Zamosc, which was also the home-town of I. L. Peretz."

Today internationalism is less automatically an O.K. word or idea than it used to be. What is internationalism today, who is internationalist? Nasser? Nasser called for genocide. Old-fashioned pro-

Sovietism? The Soviets were disgusting in the UN, cynical, even antisemitic. At best they were coarsely philistine, unable to understand that the things they said were repulsive—especially the repeated equation of the Israelis with the Nazis.

In fact, the Soviets' calling the Israelis Nazis was itself Nazi-like. The Nazis told their lies for more than the usual reason. They told lies because they were sadists. Lying, and above all their kind of lying, is a sadistic gratification: it twists, it tortures, it murders the truth. And this sadistic gratification can have an added, utilitarian advantage. By appalling and terrifying opponents, it can paralyze them. It can scare them into submission, or into the kind of weakness that makes their defeat probable. The Soviet authorities harp on Nazism and call Israel Nazi, but in their own country they have consistently repressed the truth about what Nazism did to the Jews.

Arabs, Castroites, and some of the New Left have been saying that Israel is an artificial state. When intellectuals were the leaders of the Algerian independence movement, before the toughs had banished or imprisoned them, they admitted that Algerian consciousness was new: like the demarcation of the territory itself, it owed its being to the French rulers and oppressors. Yet today no leftist would argue that Algeria is artificial. Israel is called artificial—a country whose people have a consciousness of historical distinctiveness thousands of years old, affirmed in a literature that is ancient and living; a country, moreover, whose citizens identify their fate with its fate, and who were more determined than their government itself to pay the price of war for continued independence.

In 1967 Jews of all kinds, from the most parochial to the most internationalist, were resolved that there should be no more genocide against the Jews—particularly against the Israelis, whose Jewish weight, so to speak, is greater than that of other Jews. We thought of the Syrians in Haifa or Tel Aviv and felt sick. Compared with the Syrians, the Egyptians are calm and reasonable.

The change was best seen in France, and precisely among the French Jews of old stock. One of these people has said about himself and the others like him, "We aren't assimilationist, we're just assimilated." In 1917 they (or their parents) were dismayed by the Balfour Declaration. They were zealous, spirit-of-'89 Frenchmen. What was supposed to be in the French interest they held to be in theirs, and they would never oppose their government out of mere Jewish interest. In 1967 they opposed their government. The French government was neutral against Israel and the French Jews were for Israel. Experienced in what genocide against Jews is, they would have no more of it.

Once Maurice Samuel debated a Reform rabbi of the old school. The rabbi: "Mr. Samuel, how would you feel if you were an Arab?" Mr. Samuel: "Rabbi, how would you feel if you were a Jew?" Which does not mean that we are anti-Arab or do not want to be friends with the Arabs. We would like to help them and be friends with them. But how? They will not even talk to us. We feel for them in their humiliation, but what can we do? Our charity would only compound their humiliation.

In short, the Jews seem to be changing a little; but not as it may have been thought we would. For example, if by Zionism is meant agreement with Zionist ideology, we are no more Zionist than we used to be. Two or three days before the shots were fired, a Midwestern professor told me about a plan he had for airlifting Israeli children to the United States, so that they would be out of danger when war broke out. He was sure that he could place five hundred children in his city. That was a personal undertaking. In France it was the official Jewish community that got ready to receive Israeli children. According to Zionist ideology, Israel is supposed to be the refuge.

How then shall we describe the change that seems to be taking place among us? What has been happening is a slow bringing into consciousness of a disillusionment that has been going on for a long time now with the characteristic outlook of modern, Enlightened Jews. It is a shift from the general to the particular, from the abstract to the concrete.

The disillusionment is greatest with our old idea that all our enemies are on the Right. For most practical purposes, that is where our enemies were, in the nineteenth century. The French Revolution had equality for the Jews as a corollary. We were for the Revolution and its extension, and the Right was against. Now the location of our enemies is not quite so simple. We have enemies on the Right, but also on the Left; and sometimes it is hard to distinguish between Right and Left. Sometimes our enemies on the Right and Left are happy to cooperate with each other against us.

Among all the Arab countries the one least our enemy is Tunisia, in the moderate center. Bourguiba jailed the ringleaders of a mob that wanted some fun with a pogrom. In Morocco the right-wing Istiqlal called for a purge of Jews from the civil service. So did the head of the left-wing labor movement, until the king jailed him.

Nasser is supposed to be of the Left. After the war his newspapers went back to publishing the *Protocols of the Elders of Zion.*

Actually, there was a more than negligible amount of antisemitism on the Left in the nineteenth century, as the historian and economist Edmund Silberner has shown. August Bebel had to warn the German workers that antisemitism is the socialism of fools, and a reasonably firm anti-antisemitism does not date from much before the time when Jean Jaurès was able to persuade the French Socialists, against important opposition, that the Dreyfus case was more than just an internal squabble of the bourgeoisie. As for the *Protocols,* their Stalinist version was the scenario of the Jewish Doctors' Plot, which only Stalin's death kept from being staged. In Stalinist Czechoslovakia the scenario was staged in court, and Slansky and others were hanged.

In the summer of 1967 the Soviet authorities started another propaganda campaign that made you wonder whether Stalin was not alive and in hiding, in the Soviet office of Jewish affairs. An article in the pro-Soviet *Nouvel Observateur* represents "a high Soviet official" as saying:

. . . some of our leaders began thinking of taking the risk of limited military action on behalf of Egypt within the framework of a "prudent challenge" to the United States. However, this solution was finally rejected. (As elsewhere, the pressure of Jewish opinion made its weight felt in the USSR right up to the leading circles.)

There speaks the antisemite, who knows that the inmost secret of things is the Jewish conspiracy. This high Soviet official and Marxist can imagine no other reason for his leaders' avoiding an insanely rash adventure than "the pressure of Jewish opinion." In the Soviet Union, the pressure of Jewish opinion—a melancholy joke.

India is generally held to be of the Left. In the United Nations India came up with a remarkable theory of international relations. India said to Israel: "If someone is strangling you, you have no right to shoot in self-defense. You have a right to shoot only if shooting is the method your killer has chosen." What India did not say, because it hardly needed to be said, was that this applied to Israel alone. Certainly India would not adopt it for herself, as in her relations with Pakistan. Whoever supposed that hypocritical, self-righteous moralism was essentially Western, because a by-product of biblical monotheism—"the Judeo-Christian tradition"—must have been wrong. Look at India.

In the United States, later, the Student Nonviolent Coordinating Committee brought this forth: "Zionists lined up Arab victims and shot them in the back in cold blood. This [a blurred photograph] is the Gaza Strip, Palestine, not Dachau, Germany." Then followed a few kind words about the Rothschilds. (The fascist National States Rights party's *Thunderbolt* said the same things, at the same time.) SNCC antisemitic? Of course not. In answer to questions, it explained that it does not oppose all Jews, "only Jewish oppressors"—including, besides Israel, "those Jews in the little Jew shops in the [Negro] ghetto." Say what you will about Marxism-Leninism-Maoism-Fidelism-Fanonism, what other mode of analysis would have been able to trace the causes of Negro oppression so unerringly to the real centers of economic and political power in international colonialism-imperialism and American capitalism—Israel and the little Jew shops? The New Left hasn't much use for such old monuments as Bebel. Of what pertinence can it be to the young that the middle-aged remember a Nazi Left—the Strassers and their gang —which was anticapitalist and anti-(British)imperialist? Mostly, the New Left is back on the pro-Nasser and anti-Israel track.

If we are becoming disillusioned with the Left, that could mean we are becoming more conservative. Hence, perhaps, some of our gentile neighbors and friends' irony at our expense during the excitement. The irony was not necessarily malicious. In general, it was a way of saying: "Welcome back to common humanity. Your old enthusiasms always seemed strange to us, but your present enthusiasm we can understand very well. Naturally, a Jew would be worried about Israel's danger and rejoice over its victory. That is the point. You Jews are becoming more natural."

More natural, yes; conservative, not quite. In England the Conservatives were said to be the stupid party. (But if the Liberals were so clever, why are they dead?) In the United States the conservatives are the stingy party. The Jews still belong to the generous party, as is proved by the uproar in Wayne, New Jersey, where we were accused of being liberals, always voting for more liberal school budgets. The Jews of Wayne did not attempt to deny it. They said that the purpose and effect of the statement were antisemitic, not that its substance was false.

What then are we becoming? To use symbols from the English political tradition, let us say that having been Radicals, we are slowly moving toward the Whigs (left-wing Whigs, of course). Or, to use an American symbolism of persons, we may say that having been partisans of Jefferson, we are growing more friendly to Lincoln.

Maybe it is as Whigs that we are learning new respect for old wisdom—such as that admonition of Oxenstierna's: "My son, if you only knew with how little wisdom the world is ruled." To the degree that we are not incapacitated for living in a practical world, we have always known that to be true, and we have made allowances for it in our own affairs and the affairs of government. We have done what engineers do. We have assigned to future events a Murphy factor—a margin of safety to guard against the accident and error and silliness that are bound to befall any human enterprise. (Engineers, told that a bridge should be able to bear a load of N tons, design it to bear 3N tons.) But here was a case where even an extravagant Murphy factor was not enough to guard against the surprise of human stupidity. Nasser deliberately goads the Israelis into acting militarily. He knows that a shooting war is about to break out, that it must break out. He is not quite sure whether his men or the Israelis will pull the trigger first, but he knows that someone is about to pull it. Then he is caught with all his planes on the ground.

There is the folk wisdom: too smart is dumb. General de Gaulle was too smart. A machiavellian, he overlooked Machiavelli's caution against being caught practicing machiavellianism in broad daylight. "Put not your trust in princes": everyone knows that governments will break their word when it suits them. But de Gaulle went too far. Who will now be prepared to give him even the small amount of confidence that earlier might have been given to him? Having so publicly betrayed Israel, how can he expect anyone else to believe him?

An old illusion was that war is good, to which moderns and liberals responded with the illusion that any peace is better than any war. It has been a long time now, at least since Rupert Brooke, that anybody has been able to hear that line of Horace's, *dulce et decorum est pro patria mori*—sweet and fitting it is to die for your country—without gagging or giggling. The proper stance has been black humor: *Catch-22*. But rather less so for the Israelis. Theirs was no artificial state, no absurd Molech. Its citizens were willing to die for it because they knew that if it died, so would they and their families and their hopes. Not much alienation there. One almost envies them.

It is an old, sad truth: a state acquires its legitimacy—the opposite of artificiality—by the blood that its citizens shed in its defense; as

349

the early Christians said, the blood of the martyrs is the seed of the church. An elite acquires its legitimacy by being prepared to die in a higher proportion than others. Israel's elite died disproportionately. The war dead included many colonels and majors.

Modern, enlightened people, and especially Jews, have generally had a certain amount of contempt for the military enterprise. Our two great culture-heroes, Einstein and Freud, were notably contemptuous. What business is war for an intelligent man? (Note that this is bourgeois. Engels's friends called him The General, because of his interest in military theory; Lenin annotated Clausewitz; Trotsky commanded the Red Army; Mao made the Long March and says that power grows from the barrel of a gun.) Now, for people like us, the Israeli generals are redeeming the military reputation. It is not easy to belittle what they did, or to upstage them.

One reads that the Israelis are a major military power in the Middle East. One reads that they have the best tactical air force in the world. Unbelievable. How could they have become such good soldiers? They had no living martial tradition. Peaceable men can become warriors because of love of country, and the roots of the Israeli army today lie in the more or less underground Haganah; but while the Haganah could train company commanders, it could not train a general staff. Where does the skill of the Israeli generals come from?

It remains true that the military temptation is a certain kind of stupidity. Fortunately the Israelis have not lost the old Jewish suspicion of *goyim-nakhes*—roughly, "Gentile fun." This expression is to be found in *Ulysses*, Joyce having learned it from his friend Svevo, a modern Jew of the Hapsburg empire who remembered some scraps of moribund German Yiddish. (The East European phrasing would be *goyish nakhes*.) The first time I actually heard it used in speech was when an Israeli official, of German birth and early education, told me about a visit he had made at the Pentagon's invitation to a crack unit of the United States army. Mostly he was impressed, but the spit and polish, snappy saluting, marching to the words and tune of a special song—all these struck him as *goyim-nakhes*.

When he said that, I remembered when the idea behind the words had become clear to me—at, of all things, a not very good movie of Walter Scott's *Ivanhoe*. To defend Rebecca against an accusation of witchcraft, Ivanhoe fights the Templar Front de Boeuf. So that was what it was like when knighthood was in flower, I thought—grown men in iron, mounted on horses in iron, hitting each other with axes and huge swords, the iron clanging on iron making the whole thing sound like a machine shop. Isaac of York in the stands, looking scared and disgusted, seemed to me the only adult there. Maybe it is to avoid *goyim-nakhes* that the Israeli army affects sloppiness and informal manners.

If our respect for fighting and military men has gone up, for talking and diplomats it has gone down. Those were weeks when we could not tear ourselves away from the proceedings at the UN. At home we compulsively watched television, in our cars we kept the radio on, to work we brought portables. We had no mind for anything else, and it was not edifying. You asked yourself how grown men could sit there and pretend to take it seriously. Business was transacted somewhere, off in a corner, but the diplomats had to be physically present at the open sessions, pretending to listen to words—countless words, words innumerable—that were mostly meaningless and often malignant. It appeared to me then that the career of diplomat might not be much superior to the career of king. What can a diplomat learn from that sort of thing that is better than what the Duke of Windsor says he learned from his experience as Prince of Wales and King Edward VIII? The Duke of Windsor says that he learned never to pass up a chance to sit down, or to go to the toilet.

In America the UN has had few friends more devoted than the Jews. Now we know not only that the UN can be no better than the states of which it is composed—including the so-called non-aligned nations, scurrying about on their little Soviet errands—but also that the organization itself, quite apart from the members, is a little lower than the angels. "U Thant's war" is unfair—about the most that can be said for him. Ralph Bunche was loyal to Thant—about the most that can be said for *him*.

We relearned the old truth that you can depend only on yourself: Israel had promises and friends, but even if it had not wanted to fight on its own, it would have had to. We relearned the old, hard truth that only you can feel your own pain. Who cares about the Christian Assyrians? Does anyone even know whether any Christian Assyrians are left alive? More Christian clergymen worry about the whooping crane than about the Christian Assyrians. When the last speaker of Old Prussian died, and the last speaker of Cornish, did anyone care? Did any Roman care when the last speaker of Etruscan died?

Jews who maintain relationships with the Christian clergy were taken aback by the generally reserved attitude of official Christendom toward Israel in its hour of greatest peril. Why the surprise? Christian ecclesiastics have an interest in the Arabs, whether institutional or theological. Through the Christians' eyes they could really not see what through our eyes we saw as most urgently obvious. We saw the incommensurability of Israeli and Arab war aims. We saw that the Arabs wanted to destroy Israel—which is to say, to destroy the Israelis. They saw Israeli prowess and Arab refugees.

When Jews talk with each other about Arab refugees, we should not defend ourselves against charges of heartlessness. We should leave that to our friends. Among ourselves we should remind each other how often we are commanded to love the stranger, not to wrong him or oppress him, to have one law for him and for the homeborn, because having been strangers in the land of Egypt, we know the heart of the stranger. Having been refugees, we should know what it is to be a refugee.

But our friends are not saying it and it needs to be said. Those who had to flee Bolshevik Russia or Nazi Germany were refugees, because there was no other Russian or German country to receive them. The Arabs are, or should be, more like the Greeks from Turkey after World War I. If the Greeks in Greece had not received the Turkish Greeks, there would have been a Greek refugee problem, but the Grecian Greeks could not bring themselves to deny refuge to the Turkish Greeks. After the partition of India there were Moslem and Hindu refugee problems, until Pakistan absorbed the Moslems and India absorbed the Hindus. Neither the Moslems nor the Hindus could bring themselves to deny refuge to their fellows from across the border. The West Germans could not bring themselves to deny refuge to their fellows from across several borders. Only the Arabs have been able to do it, for twenty years. Therefore they have had a triumph. The Arabs turn their backs on other Arabs, and the opinion of the world agrees that the Israelis are at fault. Israel, which receives Jews from the Arab lands, in a *de facto* exchange of populations, is condemned for the Arab refugees.

A distinguished Protestant theologian wrote a letter to the editor of the New York *Times* condemning "Israel's assault on her Arab neighbors." All, he said, "stand aghast at Israel's onslaught, the most violent, ruthless (and successful) aggression since Hitler's Blitzkrieg . . . aiming not at victory but at annihilation." Using Nazi analogies and direct references ("Hitler's Blitzkrieg"), this man implies that the Israelis are Nazis. He actually says that the Israelis wanted to annihilate the Arabs. A learned man, he knows what "annihilation"

means. It means making nothing (*nihil*) out of something, destroying utterly. His emotions make him condemn the Israelis for a war
aim that was not theirs but, as he concedes, the Arabs'. (He was
answered by another Protestant theologian, a former student of his,
who was not so much pro-Israel or anti-Arab as anti-antisemitic.)

The letter was a reaction to a stimulus—a rabbi's persistence, after
the Israeli victory, in blaming the Christian churches for their indifference to the probable fate of Israel's Jews. Now, in our more Whiggish mood, we can see that it was not reasonable to expect ecclesiastics to take our peril as seriously as we did.

These are only innocent Americans. For them, what Hitler did is
true but not real. Having failed to understand what Hitler did in
fact, they could hardly be expected to understand what the Arabs
only wanted to do. Europeans understood better—clergymen and
leftists together. To be sure, Bertrand Russell and Ralph Schoenman
were indignant about Israeli aggression; but they are not European,
never having experienced a Nazi occupation. Jean-Paul Sartre was not
anti-Israel. In the Communist countries, and even in the Communist
parties in other European countries, the official anti-Israel line was
unpopular.

The fluttery censoriousness of certain Christian clergymen comes
through nicely in a satire by Michael Frayn, a letter to "My dear
Israel" from "Your affectionate Great-aunt Britain," in the *Observer*,
London—though Frayn had others in mind, as well:

> . . . I have . . . felt obliged to condemn your *unseemly haste* in opening
> hostilities [and] your insistence on *winning* the war—particularly in such a
> brash and violent fashion. . . . To insist upon defeating your opponents is
> a discourtesy which they may find *very hard to forgive*. . . . What makes
> your behavior all the more perplexing is that when the war commenced
> you enjoyed the approval and sympathy of polite society as a whole.
> There you stood, surrounded on all sides by greatly superior hostile forces,
> whose proclaimed intention was to destroy you utterly. Everybody was
> *deeply touched!* . . . We shouldn't have have let you down! If things had
> gone badly, we had ships standing by which could have evacuated *several
> thousand* Israeli survivors—who would have had the *unreserved sympathy*
> of the entire world! . . .

Now we can be tolerant of that sort of thing. As the poker players
say, winners crack jokes and losers snarl, "Deal the cards." We can
admit to ourselves that this behavior is normal. Are we much better?
Think of the Armenians. What did I ever know about the Armenians, or what sorrow did I ever feel for them? I do not suppose I had

thought about them for ten minutes at a time until in a hospital I met an Armenian who had escaped massacre by the Turks fifty years earlier. Jews and Armenians ought to feel that they have a good deal in common—a favorite expression of his was, "We Armenians are a tiny people." Yet when I was a boy what I knew of them came from an incidental remark in one of those Mr. Tutt stories I was fond of— where, of a do-gooding New England maiden lady, it was said with affectionate exasperation that "the starving Armenians" were her favorite cause. The Armenians had been massacred and their survivors starved, but the only impression all that left upon me was of something faintly comical. Granted, *Forty Days of Musa Dagh* was written by a Jew, of sorts; but I have never read it. Why?

Another Whiggish outlook we have now, or have in a more pronounced way, is a respect for statehood. The enlightened, modern way of looking at things is to scoff at states and governments, but Israel has shown us they are nothing to scoff at. It has even begun to occur to some of us that if there had been an Israeli state in World War II, Hitler would not have been able to murder quite so many Jews—and not only because they would have had a place to escape to. If Israel had been a state, and an ally in the war against Hitler, the murder camps would have been bombed. In the absence of a Jewish state the grand strategy of Allied victory gave such a low priority to disrupting Hitler's machine for murdering Jews that the camps were never bombed. Israel would have effected a higher priority—not that the strategists and planners would have been persuaded, but simply that otherwise Israel could have made too much trouble, as by threatening to send its planes on independent bombing missions. (The Israelis could have taken de Gaulle as their model.) With the bombing of camps and railroads, the gassed and cremated would have been fewer.

We may even be readier than before to appreciate the cultural importance of a state. Modern Hebrew would not be what it is if it were not the language of a state. As Max Weinreich has said, a language is a dialect that has an army and a navy. Before Hebrew was recognized as one of the three official languages of Palestine, with the Mandate, it had long had a literary, religious, and philosophical vocabulary, but no real vocabulary for tariffs and sanitary regulations. It was legal status and responsibility that compelled Hebrew to develop.

Something else we have learned—again—is to appreciate bourgeois democracy. After all, in the United States, in Great Britain, and in

France, Jews can go counter to government when they feel that vital Jewish interests are at stake. In Great Britain the Jews could be pro-Israel even when the Irgun was hanging British sergeants. Contrast a Communist state. In Poland Gomulka was horrified. He had heard that some Polish Jews were celebrating the Israeli victory with drinking parties. How shocking, in that abstemious country! He warned the Polish Jews about dual allegiance and being a fifth column. What a threat they must represent! In the thirties the ratio of Jew to Gentile in the Polish population was 1 to 9 or 1 to 10; in 1967 it was 1 to 1,250.

In a bourgeois democracy Jews may decide for themselves how Jewish they want to be, and when; and that is why they respond with gratitude and devotion. Some time ago a radical sociologist, critical of America and American Jews, said that self-respecting people have no obligation of gratitude for the elementary decencies, which should be taken for granted. As in the Soviet Union and Poland? In our circumstances it is ingratitude that would be problematic, not gratitude.

Finally, religion. Religion is complicated. It is both conservative and revolutionary.

In the past century or two religion has been criticized for being a conservative force, for helping to avert needed revolution by giving opiates to the oppressed, or promises of pie in the sky. This criticism would have surprised Thomas Hobbes. In his experience and doctrine, the trouble with religion was the ease with which it could become revolutionary. Any jumped-up prentice, having learned to read, might open his Bible and conclude that the established religion was not in accordance with the Lord's will; and then, incited by dreamers and visionaries, he might band together with other presumptuous enthusiasts and overthrow a king, who knew better than they what religion would insure domestic tranquillity.

The Jewish religious situation may be changing. Israeli Jews have generally been the kind of people who are bashful about using the word God, but after the victory many lost that bashfulness for a while. Speaking or writing, Israelis of whom it was not to be expected thanked God quite seriously.

It would be easy to dismiss that as chauvinistic religion. The Kaiser used to say, *Gott mit uns,* and one cause of the revulsion from religion after World War I was that the churches of all the belligerents had prayed for victory and had assured the faithful that God wanted their country to win. But most of the Israelis who spoke of God

355

spoke of Him only after the war. (A minority had intensified their prayers and Talmud study.) It was the Arabs who invoked God constantly. A Jew must assume that He did not want the Arabs to do what they wanted to do—for, like Haman, they purposed "to destroy, to slay, and to annihilate all Jews, young and old, women and children, in one day." And we shall be misled if we confuse the diminished Israeli (and Jewish) bashfulness about God with foxhole religion. The Israelis did not so much petition God for victory as thank Him for it.

I hope I shall not be thought fetishistic about religious objects. I have already mentioned *tefillin* in Israel. After the victory it was hard to find *tefillin* to buy in Jerusalem. There was a run on them. Men who had never had them before, or had lost them years ago, wanted to wear their own while thanking God at the Western Wall.

In an Orthodox synagogue in New York soon after the war, a friend of mine has told me, the rabbi called upon a young member of the congregation to speak—a student at the Hebrew University who had been one of the foreigners substituting for the Israeli teachers and social workers called into service. Of what he said my friend remembers this best: "We Orthodox usually distinguish between religious and irreligious Jews, especially in Israel. My experience during the war showed me that this is wrong. Some Jews are more religious and some are less." Now of course this is not altogether true. It exaggerates our religiousness. But if not altogether true, then at any rate it is less untrue than in a long time. With the Israeli war there was a reassertion of an old Jewish feeling about God and Providence, of a kind that we have not seen in many years—in the United States as well as in Israel.

The newspapers here reported that in those days of strain before the shooting broke out, a great scholar who teaches at the Jewish Theological Seminary gave to the United Jewish Appeal a sum of money large in its own right and immensely large for a professor, a member of a class not usually noted for its philanthropic capacity. The letter he sent to the alumni of the Seminary was not reported. This was no time, he said in the letter, for any effort short of the maximum; everything depended on exertion and sacrifice. Then, having put the greatest possible emphasis on human effort, he concluded with a verse from the Twentieth Psalm: "Some invoke chariots, and others horses; but we the name of the Lord our God." That was enough for the rabbis. Naturally, they completed the psalm in their minds: "They will totter and fall down, but we shall rise and stand upright. O Lord, save; may the King answer us when we call." Rabbis can be expected to know this psalm particularly well because it is read on most weekdays, toward the end of the morning prayer. And because psalms, especially the liturgical ones, recall each other even when they contradict each other, in the end emerging into a harmonized tension with each other, this weekday-morning psalm, about not invoking chariots and horses, must inevitably have recalled the 144th Psalm, which introduces the evening prayer after the Sabbath. It begins: "Blessed be the Lord my Rock, who trains my hands for war, my fingers for battle."

Not long before this, the Reform rabbinate had said it was going to revise the Union Prayer Book. The last revision, made in the days of Franklin D. Roosevelt, is considered to be no longer relevant to contemporary needs. Especially does the prayer then inserted for the welfare of coal miners seem a little irrelevant now.

Well, if you make revisions every twenty or thirty years, you run the risk of being irrelevant much of the time. If this year you compose a prayer for the welfare of computer operators, in twenty or thirty years computer operators may be technologically obsolete. In our desire for relevant texts we can produce something like a daily newspaper, and there is nothing so dead as a newspaper from the day before yesterday. The Twentieth Psalm speaks of chariots and horses, which no army has used for some time now. Would it be more relevant if it spoke of tanks and planes? Chariots and horses make the point quite well.

The Twenty-third Psalm says, "The Lord is my shepherd." *There* is an obsolete occupation for you. We have few shepherds in the United States, and them we call sheepherders; yet somehow, to say that the Lord is my shepherd seems to have meaning. Or the 107th Psalm: "They that go down to the sea in ships, that do business in great waters—they see the works of the Lord, and His wonders in the deep." Not only a sailor but also a flyer, or even an astronaut, might find this psalm relevant, though it speaks of ships rather than planes or spacecraft.

In fact, the Jewish liturgy of the entire period in May and June, from the beginning of the crisis to the end of the war, suddenly seemed to have the most immediate relevance to our anxieties and hopes—above all, the specifically scriptural parts of the liturgy, both the fixed passages and the Pentateuchal and Prophetical lessons of the annual cycle. (Not to mention the very names of the Israeli captains: Abraham, Isaac, and Jacob; Moses and Aaron; Amos and Isaiah.)

Every morning a Jew who prays recites the Song of the Sea, from Exodus: ". . . when Israel saw the wondrous power which the Lord had wielded against the Egyptians . . . they had faith in the Lord and in His servant Moses. . . . The Lord is my strength and might; He has become my salvation. . . . The enemy said, 'I will pursue, I will overtake, I will divide the spoil. My desire shall have its fill of them. I will bare my sword, my hand shall subdue them.' . . . The Lord will reign for ever and ever!"

On the last Sabbath of May we read the final two chapters of Leviticus, which hold out the blessing and the curse. The blessing: ". . . I will give peace in the land, and you shall lie down, and none shall make you afraid. . . . I am the Lord your God, who brought you forth out of the land of Egypt, that you should not be their slaves. . . ." But the curse: ". . . you shall be smitten before your enemies; those who hate you shall rule over you, and you shall flee when none pursues you. . . ."—and worse. On the first Sabbath in June, two days before the shooting, the Prophetical lesson was from Hosea, with the verses we recite when we bind the *tefillin* as a sign on our hand: ". . . I will betroth you to me for ever; I will betroth you to me in right-eousness and in justice, in steadfast love and in mercy. I will betroth you to me in faithfulness; and you shall know the Lord."

On the next Sabbath, the war over, the second group of chapters from Numbers was read as the Pentateuchal lesson, including the Priestly Blessing: "Thus shall you bless the children of Israel. . . . 'The Lord bless you and keep you; the Lord make His face to shine upon you, and be gracious to you; the Lord lift up His countenance upon you, and give you peace.'" The Prophetical lesson was the annunciation to Samson's mother, in Judges: ". . . the angel of the Lord appeared to the woman and said to her, Behold, you are barren . . . but you shall conceive and bear a son . . . and he shall begin to deliver Israel from the hand of the Philistines."

Then came Shavu'ot, with the Ten Commandments of Exodus as the Pentateuchal lesson: "I am the Lord your God, who brought you out of the land of Egypt, the house of bondage. You shall have no other gods beside Me." . . . And, as if to warn us and our brothers in Israel, a seemingly legalistic and priestly passage follows: "Make for Me an altar of earth. . . . But if you make for Me an altar of stones, do not build it of hewn stones; for by wielding your tool upon them you have profaned them." Here "your tool" is the right translation, but what the Hebrew actually says is *ḥarbekha*, "your sword." The sword profanes. (A horror of impious iron inherited from the Bronze Age?) It was given not to David the warrior but to Solomon the man of peace to build the Temple.

On Shavu'ot we recited the Hallel. Not much irrelevant about the 118th Psalm: "It is better to take refuge in the Lord than to trust in princes. . . . Hark, glad songs of victory . . . the right hand of the Lord does valiantly. . . . The stone which the builders rejected has become the chief cornerstone. This is the Lord's doing; it is marvelous in our eyes." And the verse that the fierce Huguenots liked to intone, in Clément Marot's version, as they spurred their horses into battle: "This is the day which the Lord has made; let us rejoice and be glad in it."

This little religious thing we now have is not much of a creed, but for many of us it is rather more than we have ever had before. And it is ours. We can recognize it.

Each Jew knows how thoroughly ordinary he is; yet taken together, we seem caught up in things great and inexplicable. It is almost as if we were not acting but were being acted through. In the 1961 *Commentary* symposium one man said we had been a big thing in antiquity and were now only a little thing. That is not so. In Deuteronomy we are told that even then we were "the smallest of peoples." How many are we? The number of Jews in the world is smaller than a small statistical error in the Chinese census. Yet we remain bigger than our numbers. Big things seem to happen around us and to us.

If one may say at all that the Bible argues for the existence of God, it has two kinds of argument. The first is the argument from nature, as in the Nineteenth Psalm: "The heavens declare the glory of God." The second is the argument from history, or from Israel, as in Deuteronomy:

For ask now of the days that are past, which were before you, since the day that God created man upon the earth, and ask from one end of heaven to the other, whether such a great thing as this has ever happened or was ever heard of. . . . has any god ever attempted to go and take a nation for himself from the midst of another nation . . . with a mighty hand and an outstretched arm . . . as the Lord your God did for you in Egypt before your eyes? To you it was shown, that you might know that the Lord is

God; there is no other besides Him . . . know therefore this day, and lay it to your heart, that the Lord is God in heaven above and on the earth beneath; there is no other.

Those big things that happen to us, those things that are bigger than we, are not always good things. We have not been promised that they will always be good. We have been told about the curse as well as the blessing. In I Samuel the Psalm of Hannah says, "The Lord deadens and quickens"; and Jews continue to declare that, several times a day, in the Standing Prayer.

In this last third of the twentieth century we may be beginning to believe again that the history of the Jews points to some kind of providential order, which—for reasons having to do not with our merits, but at most with the merits of the Fathers—has a special place for it.

On Shavu'ot the first chapter of Ezekiel was read—a Prophetical account of revelation to accompany the Pentateuchal revelation of the Ten Commandments. I suspect I was not alone then to be reminded of another passage in Ezekiel (ordinarily not my favorite prophet): "What comes to your mind shall never happen—your thinking, 'Let us be like the nations, like the tribes of the countries, worshipping wood and stone.' As I live, says the Lord God, surely with a mighty hand and an outstretched arm, and with wrath poured out, will I be king over you."

When the Psalmist says, "I," the pronoun is singular and plural, individual and collective, personal and communal—as in that other verse from the last of the Hallel psalms: "I thank Thee, for Thou hast answered me, and art become my salvation."

—*October 1967*

Index

Index

Index

Index

Index